Politics and Economic Policy in the United States

POLITICS AND ECONOMIC POLICY IN THE UNITED STATES

Second Edition

Jeffrey E. Cohen

FORDHAM UNIVERSITY

HOUGHTON MIFFLIN COMPANY   Boston   New York

Editor-in-Chief: *Jean L. Woy*
Sponsoring Editor: *Melissa Mashburn*
Associate Editor: *Katherine Meisenheimer*
Project Editor: *Aileen Mason*
Editorial Assistant: *Jane Lee*
Associate Production/Design Coordinator: *Jodi O'Rourke*
Manufacturing Coordinator: *Andrea Wagner*
Senior Marketing Manager: *Sandra McGuire*

Cover design: *Deborah Azerrad Savona*
Cover image: *Gary Randall/FPG International*

Printed in the U.S.A.

Library of Congress Catalog Number: 99-71990

ISBN: 0-395-96110-6

456789-FFG-09 08 07 06 05

Contents

Preface

In the 1930s and 1940s, economic policy was a major interest of political scientists. The economic problems of the Great Depression served as the stimulus for that interest. With the economic rebound of the post–World War II years, however, interest shifted to other policy areas. The economic ills of the 1970s and 1980s rekindled interest among political scientists in economic policy, as it also re-emerged as a major concern of citizens and students alike. Interest in the economy, and government policies that affect the economy, has remained high despite the strong economy as we near the end of the twentieth century. Several cable networks are dedicated to coverage of economic news, especially the ups and downs of the stock market. Almost anywhere, casual conversation turns to such topics. Students now seem well aware of the implications of the economy on their futures, but they often lack the knowledge to understand how government policy decisions may affect them. And although economic policy and its implications have remained fertile topics for political scientists doing research, few books exist for students and average citizens who want to know more about the topic. The lack of text material led me to write this book for use in my own course.

Politics and Economic Policy in the United States aims to introduce students to important terms, ideas, and concepts associated with economic policy-making in the United States. Some of these terms, like *fiscal policy, monetary policy, economic efficiency,* and *equity,* are quite technical and complex, but they are discussed in important public and political forums, and voters are asked to decide among the competing economic policy proposals of political candidates. Economic policy often stands center stage in election campaigns and other policy discussions. I introduce and present these ideas and controversies to help students in their role as citizens, but avoid overwhelming them with excessively technical discussions. The basic logic behind the ideas and debates, rather than formal mathematical proofs, is the focus of the material presented in this book. *Politics and Economic Policy in the United States* is written for the student with no economics or mathematics background and with only minimal background in political science, and thus can be used in undergraduate courses at any level.

FEATURES OF THE BOOK

There is a logical structure to the book. The early chapters (1 and 2) set the framework, introduce important vocabulary for understanding economic policymaking, and provide a historical overview. The next four chapters (3–6) discuss the important participants in economic policymaking: the public, interest groups such as business and labor, and government officials. The remainder of the book details specific types of economic policies, beginning with macroeconomic policies—that is, taxation, fiscal, budgetary, and monetary policy (Chapters 7–9). This section ends with a treatment of the interconnections between economics and elections. The last part of the book focuses on sectoral economic policies, including regulation (Chapters 10 and 11), distributive economic policy (12), and international economic policy (13). The final chapter (14) summarizes the discussion of the previous chapters into a framework of concepts, interests, ideas, and institutions.

Although the book focuses on the United States, comparisons with other countries are offered when instructive. Similarly, the book focuses on the post–World War II era, but important matters are followed back to the early days of the nation when such a historical perspective is important. Thus, the book is broad in both geographic and historical scope. Moreover, I make extensive use of cases to help illustrate the issues and add concrete details to what might otherwise be a highly abstract discussion. For example, the budget issues that plagued the nation across the 1980s and 1990s, NAFTA, and the military-industrial complex as a distributive economic policy subsystem are all discussed extensively.

NEW TO THIS EDITION

Although the basic framework of the first edition is retained, a large number of changes and improvements are incorporated in this second edition based on the input of reviewers, friends and colleagues, students, and my own thoughts and experiences with the first edition. Thus, I have added and clarified the discussion of important terms from economics, which is very important in Chapter 1, and also peppered throughout the text. I have also updated the data, examples, and discussions throughout the book. This is especially evident in Chapter 3, which relies heavily on public opinion polls. Thanks to the Roper Center at the University of Connecticut and Fordham University's subscription to Lexis-Nexis, which allowed me access to that archive, I was able to track down poll questions that otherwise would have required a major commitment of time and surely would have delayed publication of this edition.

Many of the other chapters have also witnessed heavy revision. The material in Chapter 2, which focuses on changes in the nature of the economy and the historical development of U.S. economic policies, has been integrated into a more coherent framework. Chapter 8, which deals in part with budget making and the deficit, has been heavily modified because of the budget surplus that now exists. Also, a rather significant change was that I brought on board my colleague, Jonathon Crystal of Fordham University, a specialist in international political economy, to redraft Chapter 13 on that topic.

In addition to the revisions, I have also incorporated some new pedagogical aids that were absent from the first edition. Because a large number of new terms, many of them technical, are used in the text, I have bolded key terms the first time that each one appears, provided a definition at that location, and collected them at the end of each chapter in a new section called "Key Terms." Thus, after reading each chapter, a student can turn to that list and ask, "Do I know what the term means and where I encountered it in the text?" Also, at the end of each chapter I have included a list of related web sites so that students can explore chapter topics in more depth and see the connections between what is discussed in the text and what happens in the real world.

ACKNOWLEDGMENTS

I owe thanks to many people who assisted in the preparation of this second edition. The staff at Houghton Mifflin, especially Katherine Meisenheimer, my editor, deserve my deepest thanks. Without them, their encouragement, hard work, and understanding, this second edition would not have seen light. I also thank my department chair, Richard Fleisher, for making a working environment that encouraged and supported this project. Conversations with four other colleagues at Fordham, Bruce Berg, Jonathon Crystal, Paul Kantor, and David Lawrence, also helped tighten up my ideas and exposition. My friends and colleagues John Hamman, Southern Illinois University; David Nice, Washington State University; Ray Tatalovich, Loyola University; and Dan Wood, Texas A & M University, all conveyed at one time or another comments about the book's content and use in class, issues of presentation, room for improvement, and the like. I thank them all. Also, the reviewers of the manuscript merit special gratitude for the time and care that they put into reviewing the book for the second edition, offering innumerable suggestions. These include Gerard S. Gryski, Auburn University; William J. Hughes, Southern Oregon University; Kristina Kauffman, Riverside Community College; and Gerald A. McBeath, University of Alaska-Fairbanks. Phyllis also deserves a hearty thank you, but she'll blush if I tell why.

Last, I dedicate this book to my students. I'm better for knowing them and trying to teach them about this topic.

J.C.

Politics and Economic Policy in the United States

1

Politics and the Economy: Basic Themes

ON FRIDAY, February 12, 1999, the U.S. Senate voted to acquit President Bill Clinton of the perjury and obstruction of justice impeachment charges that the House of Representatives had presented against him. Despite the personal failings that the public saw in Clinton, a direct result of the sexual scandal that ignited the impeachment process against him, Clinton's job approval ratings remained high throughout the impeachment process, and even seemed to grow as the process progressed. For instance, a *Washington Post* poll issued on February 12 gave Clinton a 68 percent approval rating. Other polling organizations showed similarly high approval ratings. Why would the public want to retain a president of such obviously flawed character?

One explanation that some have suggested is that the economy was in good shape and that the public applauded Clinton's handling of the economy. A January 1999 Gallup poll gave Clinton an 81 percent approval rating for his handling of the economy. There seemed to be good reason for the public to approve of Clinton's economic policies. Unemployment stood at a record low and inflation seemed under control. With little or no inflation, the modest wage gains that workers earned translated into more money to spend. Moreover, the healthy economy seemed to have helped the budget deficit problem, which had plagued the nation since the early 1980s. In fact, the Clinton administration showed a budget surplus for 1998 and the next half-decade. Consequently, consumer confidence was high, the economy was growing, and despite expected ups and downs, the stock market stood at near record levels. Moreover, the U.S. economy seemed somewhat impervious to the economic ills that were plaguing much of the world, especially Southeast Asia, Latin America, Russia, and Japan. With such strong public backing for Clinton, it is little wonder that the Senate failed to convict him of the impeachment charges.

However, the tale here is not only of presidential scandal but of the political implications of the economy and economic perceptions, the impact of economic policies on economic well-being, and the importance of economic policies on the careers of politicians. As the Clinton impeachment case illustrates, the economy may even affect aspects of government not directly tied to the economy or economic policymaking. The economy has large and profound effects on the quality of people's lives and on their government. Also, government can have large and profound effects on the economy and on the quality of people's lives. These interrelationships between the economy and the political system are the subject of this book.

THE POLITICAL SYSTEM AND THE ECONOMY

The two most important problem-solving institutions in modern society are the economy and the government.[1] In earlier times, religion and the family were also major social problem solvers. Both are still important, but they play a smaller role today than they did generations ago. Our focus will be on the economy and the government, both of which have grown in importance and affect almost all aspects of modern life.

The **economy** is a production and distribution system: producers make goods and provide services, which they sell to consumers. We will be concerned primarily with market economies in this book. In **market economies,** the means of production and distribution are privately held. Furthermore, in market economies economic transactions between producers and consumers are voluntary, and prices for goods and services help to regulate the market. In contrast to market economies are **command economies,** in which the means of production and distribution are publicly owned, such as by the government.

In market economies, prices for goods and services are regulated by the laws of supply and demand. At its most elemental, the **law of demand** says that the lower the price of a good, the larger quantity of the good will be demanded by consumers. Similarly, the **law of supply** says that the higher the price of a good, the larger quantity of that good will be supplied or produced. Both the laws of supply and of demand refer to the price of a good. The price of a good regulates supply and demand. As price increases, so does supply, but demand drops off. In mirror image, when price falls, demand picks up, but supply declines. A market economy that is built on the notions of demand, supply, and price aims toward **equilibrium.** More formally, equilibrium is the point at which the demand for a good equals the supply of the good. Markets rarely settle or stay at such equilibriums. Rather, the tendency is to head toward such a state. Many factors, such as changes in tastes for goods; new technologies, inventions, and products; population growth and/or decline; and political events, such as wars, new policies, and the like, may disrupt a market at equilibrium.

In command economies, economic transactions between producers and consumers are conducted quite differently. Instead of allowing demand and supply to set prices, government authorities set prices, often by determining supply. For example, in the former Soviet Union, when it was ruled by the Communist Party, five-year plans were instituted and used by the government. Basically, these plans were policies that determined how much of a good or service would be produced over the course of the next five years. At the same time, prices for these goods were set. Consumers in the Soviet Union would purchase all goods, from clothing to food to housing, on the basis of these prices.

The inefficiency of such a system is obvious. If the five-year plan produced goods in quantities greater than those desired by the population, excess goods would remain on store shelves, while desired goods would not be available. Furthermore, the relatively long time horizon, five years, made it difficult to take into account unanticipated factors, such as bad weather, which might affect demand, and production levels. Readjusting production schedules was difficult in such a system because each factory's production quota was set in relationship to all other factory production quotas in an intricate balancing among all of the nation's production facilities. Production shortfalls were traditionally handled by purchasing necessary goods, especially food, from foreign providers.

Scarcity is an essential element of economic systems. Goods attain their value in part because of their scarcity, or limited supply. The **law of scarcity** means that not enough resources exist to meet the demands of all consumers.[2] Thus, there is ever-present competition for scarce economic goods. Determining how this limited supply of goods is to be distributed is one of the major issues of both economics and politics. In general, the economic system deals with distribution through market mechanisms, such as price adjustments and supply and demand adjustments. Another way to distribute scarce resources is through the political system—the government. As you will see throughout, political solutions to the distribution of limited resources may at times differ from economic solutions.

Although the term *government* refers explicitly to those authoritative institutions that make policy decisions, such as Congress, the presidency, and the courts, other groups, such as voters and lobbyists, can also influence policy decisions. Dissemination of knowledge about government actions through the mass media and other channels is also important in the policy-making process.

Modern governments and economies have had an increasing impact on people's lives. Governments now have at their command more impressive means of control, such as police, military forces, and other bureaucracies, and a greater ability to communicate swiftly and clearly across large distances.[3] Modern governments have also been bolstered by the rise of nationalism, which has helped to link the aspirations of people to a set of governing institutions. Nationalism, plus the rise of democratic forms of political participation, has legitimized the actions and policies of modern government. Though modern governments, even democratic ones, may have to resort to force and coercion at times, most of their policies are built on a foundation of voluntary compliance and consent. People obey the laws because the government is viewed as a legitimate authority.

The economic sphere has also grown in importance, primarily because of the ability of modern economies to provide material goods to people. The economic quality of life in the more well developed regions of the world is quite high by historical standards. People are, for the most part, well fed and well housed and have come to rely on the economy for economic security and the comforts of life. An economic optimism pervades much of modern life in the developed economic regions. For the first time in history, residents of these regions have come to expect a good standard of living. Grinding poverty, premature death, and limited hopes are memories of the past or experiences of peoples not residing in these advantaged places.

GOVERNMENT DECISION MAKING VERSUS ECONOMIC DECISION MAKING

Government and the economy rely on different decision-making processes. Ideally, decision making in market economies is voluntary and highly decentralized. It is voluntary because no one is forced into a particular economic transaction. People may shop around until they find the transaction terms they like best, the ones that are most favorable to them. Thus, they may look for lower prices or higher quality or a seller with a reputation for service and integrity.

Decision making in the economy is also highly decentralized. No one setting exists where all buyers and sellers come together. Rather, buyers and sellers act as individuals, engaging in economic transactions only when it is profitable or desirable to do so. No centralized authority structures the market. The voluntary behaviors of myriads of people provide the market economy with its structure, which is very fluid.

In contrast to the voluntarism and decentralization of decision making in market economies, decision making by democratic governments is collective, centralized, and binding. Unlike the separable and individual decisions of actors in the market economy, democratic decision making is a collective process. People come together in decision-making settings to act as a united, or collective, decision-making unit.

Generally, voting processes—both those that involve citizens electing government officials and those that involve the votes of government officials themselves, like congressional floor voting—are the primary decision-making mechanisms in democratic political systems. Although voting is often associated with freedom and the personal liberties that liberal democracies guarantee their citizens, it is actually a highly centralized decision-making process whereby voters make one collective decision. The institutions of voting, such as the secret ballot, eligibility requirements, and rules for winning (for example, majority rule), structure the decisions of voters. Although mass participative voting gives the public some control over its government institutions and policies, it is, ironically, a less free and voluntary process than decision making in the market economy.

Moreover, democratic decision making is binding, especially on the losers. Decisions that are made in democratic settings apply to the collectivity—to all persons considered citizens of the governmental unit. In the economy, a loser may refuse to enter an economic transaction. In the democratic political setting, even if one assumes that one will lose the voting contest, one must abide by the result of the election. Again, ironically, democratic governments are less free than the economy.

In a sense, the economy aims to satisfy individual wants and needs through personal choices. In contrast, government tries to deal with the collective needs of its citizens. Not only do the processes of decision making between the economy and government differ, but the values that the two decision processes maximize may differ as well.

THE EFFICIENCY-EQUALITY TRADEOFF

The economic and political spheres solve social problems in different ways, each of which emphasizes different values. They also offer different views of what society should look like and how society should arrive at those desired ends. Basically, the economy solves social problems through market mechanisms, while the political system solves social problems through government. And where the economy generally strives toward *efficiency,* the political system sometimes aims for greater *equity.*

Economic efficiency can be defined as the absence of waste. The economy is at its most efficient state when it cannot produce any more of one good without decreasing the production of another.[4] A market-based economy is often thought to be more capable of achieving efficiency than government. Deborah Stone summarizes the efficiency argument this way:

> First, people do not engage in exchanges unless someone expects to be made better off by the exchange and no one expects to be harmed. Thus, barring incorrect information and unpredictable disasters (such as weather destroying a commodity after a deal has been struck), exchanges must necessarily lead to improvements in the welfare of individuals. Second, every exchange is, besides a physical exchange of resources, a conversion of market values into higher subjective values. Every exchange, in other words, should lead to a situation in which the new holders get more value out of the resources than the old holders. And finally, if exchanges

make people better off as individuals, they necessarily make society better off as a whole. Since welfare (and the "best" use of resources) can be judged only subjectively by individuals, the only concept of social welfare that makes any sense is one that identifies societal welfare with the aggregate welfare of individuals.[5]

The lure of the market is based, then, on its voluntary nature and its supposed ability to be more efficient than government. The logic of the market is that no one will voluntarily enter into a trade or exchange if he or she will be harmed. That is, everyone is assumed to be rational in the sense that no one will intentionally seek to harm himself or herself.

Efficiency is not the only economic value or condition that is deemed desirable, however. Some seek **equity.** The equity argument comes in many guises, such as fairness, equality, and so on. At bottom, however, it states that the distribution of wealth the market produces is sometimes inequitable, less than satisfactory, or unfair. Some critics even say that the market is biased, especially against those without economic resources.

This is a good time to discuss the concept of class, before we discuss government efforts to promote equality. Class is a complex concept, with many different meanings. Most commonly, class refers to economic status. In its Marxist formation, two classes, owners of business and capital (money), and workers, are identified. While their economic wealth divides these two classes, the control of owners over the means of production is the underlying tension that Marxists emphasize. Others who emphasize wealth differences across classes sometimes distinguish among three classes: upper, middle, and lower. The middle class often comprises middle management in corporations, as well as professionals and small business people, and is distinguished from the lower class: factory and hourly workers, the unemployed, and the poor. Not everyone subscribes to using economic indicators to distinguish among classes. Some point to subjective indicators, focusing on the class that a person feels he or she belongs to. Again, distinctions among upper, middle, and lower are often identified. However, in some countries, like the United States, almost all people will identify themselves as middle class. Even the economically wealthy might call themselves "upper middle," and low-wage workers might call themselves "lower middle." All of these definitions of class point to economic wealth in some fashion as the critical criterion, but other, broader criteria are also used in some other definitions of class, what we may term *social class*. Thus, education level, birth, and occupation may be added to economics in defining wealth. The policies dealing with economic equality, which we discuss later, all aim to reduce the spread between those who have a lot of money and other economic resources from those who have less.[6]

Equity advocates argue that markets may produce great disparities, or gaps, in income or wealth. Most societies that rely on markets to distribute economic benefits display ranges of wealth. Often a small segment of society commands a large proportion of its wealth. This means that some people command proportionately small amounts of wealth.

Even if markets reach a highly efficient state, the gap between rich and poor may grow, as the rich are able to make themselves better off in the bulk of exchanges but the poor are not. Although the poor are not harmed by such market exchanges, they are not necessarily helped or helped as much as the rich. Thus, the gap between rich and poor may widen without the living standard of the poor eroding. Social jealousy may arise as one group sees others' lots improving but not its own.

Marxist, socialist, and communist critics of capitalism often jumped on this characteristic of capitalist market-based economies and pointed to the generally more equal distribution of wealth in their economies in the competition to win adherents during the cold war.[7] The inequality of wealth in capitalist economies has been an embarrassment to those systems, also, something that less radical critics point to as well.

Democratic societies are based, in part, on some conception of equality. Equality of treatment before the law, equality in political participation, and the like are hallmarks of a democratic society. Sometimes the quest for political equality spills over into a quest for economic equality.[8]

Large gaps in wealth may create political tensions. Democracies, especially conservative ones like the United States, which value the market so highly, can tolerate some level of economic inequality, but when it becomes too severe and obvious, political attempts to **redistribute** wealth—to narrow the gap between rich and poor—may follow. Redistribution can be thought of as political efforts to balance economic inequalities and reduce the income gap between those at the top and the rest of society. There may exist a threshold level that determines when the political system will take action to narrow the income gap. That threshold may vary from country to country depending on their history, current economic state, and the values of their citizens. When the gap in income is below that threshold, the inequality gap is tolerated. When it goes above that threshold level, the political system may be compelled to do something, such as redistribute wealth.

Moreover, within political systems, different people may hold different threshold levels. In the United States, Democrats tend to have a lower threshold for income inequality than Republicans. Democrats and Republicans may compete for votes by trying to convince voters that they are right and their opponents wrong about the allowable level of economic inequality. In this fashion, economic inequality gets transformed into a political issue.

The gap between rich and poor increased during the Reagan-Bush years.[9] Although the economy grew during much of that time, most of the wealth was concentrated in the hands of the upper classes. It is not clear that much wealth improvement flowed down the economic ladder. Consequently, Democratic politicians attacked the Republicans on the fairness issue, which proved useful to Bill Clinton in his 1992 campaign for the presidency. He criticized Bush and Reagan for failing to promote policies that would enable everyone to share in the economic expansion of the 1980s. He especially attacked Bush for doing little to deal with the recession of 1991, which seemed to hurt the lower and working classes more than the middle and upper classes. And he attacked Bush for failing to promote policies that would improve the performance of the economy, so that the living standards of the working class would improve. After his election in 1992, Clinton partially delivered on the fairness theme by increasing taxes on the upper income brackets.[10]

Many of the profound political debates in modern societies revolve around the question of efficiency versus equity. Generally, parties of the right, like the Republicans, prefer the efficiency argument, saying that everyone will be better off if the economy is allowed to operate at its maximum potential. Conditions like poverty are best alleviated by a growing economy. Parties of the left, like the Democrats, are more suspicious of markets, feeling that some people are not as able to take advantage of market exchanges as others. They may need government help to make the market fairer.

Efficiency and equity are important social values. Promoting one, however, may undermine the other.[11] It is difficult, if not impossible, to frame a policy that is both efficient and equitable. In other words, there is often a tradeoff between equity and efficiency; improving one of these values may harm the other.

There are several reasons for this tradeoff.[12] First, there is the argument that equity policies that redistribute from the rich to the poor will reduce the incentives and rewards for productivity. If people feel that each successive gain in wealth will result in some large chunk of their earnings being taken away, or taxed, they may decide to work less, to substitute leisure for work. Thus, the economy may be less efficient than it could be. Second, government policies may restrict individual choices and thus interfere with the voluntary nature of the market. Exchanges that might take place may not, with consequent reductions in economic efficiency and growth. Third, government consumes resources that may otherwise be applied to economic activity. Government has costs—for example, the salaries of administrators and bureaucrats, offices and buildings, pensions and fringe benefits. These costs of government represent a drag on the economy, a **dead weight loss,** as government activities are usually not economically productive, though some government activities and programs may help the operation of the economy. We will say more about this later.

In general, it is fair to say that markets promote efficiency, sometimes to the neglect of equity. Politics and government, however, do not always promote equity over efficiency. Whether they do depends heavily on who is in power and the political conditions that influence the decisions of those in power. In the United States, Democrats have been faster to promote equity policies and to try to implement policies that push for greater levels of equity than Republicans. Often equity policies require some degree of government intervention in the economy. Policies aimed at maximizing efficiency in the economy tend to restrict government intervention in the economy. As you will see, partisan debate in the United States frequently raises the issue of the desirable level of government intervention in the economy.

COMPATIBILITY AND TENSION BETWEEN CAPITALISM AND DEMOCRACY

As the debate between efficiency and equity demonstrates, the relationship between government and the economy is sometimes tense. However, the governmental system of democracy and the economic system of capitalism have a long, entwined history. Both have similar roots, are based on some similar values, and often are found together, because most democratic political systems have basically a capitalist economy.

The Compatibility Between Capitalism and Democracy

Capitalism and democracy both evolved in the seventeenth and eighteenth centuries, offering similar criticisms of monarchy, absolutism, mercantilism, and feudalism. Monarchy often took an absolutist form, in which the monarch's actions were unconstrained. Thus, taxes were high and climbed higher in many countries to support the lifestyle and policies of the monarch and the state. Both capitalists and democrats objected to the absolute monarchy. (Here the term *democrats* does not refer to members of the Democratic party but to supporters of democratic forms of government. Also, strictly speaking, capitalists did not exist in the eighteenth century. They grew out of a group, which we call **economic liberals,** who, like capitalists to follow, believed in relative freedom in economic relations among people, but they did not have a solid theoretical understanding of the operation of the economy.) Economic liberals objected to the expropriation of private holdings by the state, as well as to high and climbing taxes and limitations on economic activity. Democrats objected to the lack of legal safeguards and the often capricious use of state power.

Both economic liberals and democrats also objected to the reigning political-economic doctrine of the era, **mercantilism.** Mercantilism was a system under which "wealth was conceived as a stockpile of treasure gathered from neighbors and colonies. Government, under this policy, should control all aspects of economic activity in order to increase the wealth, unity, and power of the state."[13] In other words, the economy was subservient to the state, and the state directed economic activity toward its ends and interests, not the ends and interests of business. Economic liberals were vehement opponents of mercantilism because it curtailed their activity. For instance, to operate a business, one had to purchase a government charter. Although government charters allowed and protected much economic activity, these charters usually granted monopolies. Those who did not hold charters but wanted to enter markets were prohibited from doing so. Furthermore, profits had to be shared with the state, though the state's participation in the daily operation of the business's affairs was usually minimal.

Similarly, economic liberals and democrats criticized **feudalism.** Under the feudal system, human relationships were hierarchically structured and built on notions of tradition and mutual obligation. Many people, called serfs, were tied to the land, under obligation to the owners of the estate. Serfs had few rights and protections. Some democrats compared serfdom to slavery, whereas capitalists saw serfs as an untapped pool of labor and markets for their goods and wares.

Economic liberals and democrats both called for a society built on individualism, freedom and liberty, limited government, equality before the law, and rational decision making.[14] Together, these values would protect individuals, their property, and actions from undue interference and harm by government. Plus, they would allow greater latitude of action in both the political and the economic spheres.

Capitalism Versus Democracy: Egalitarianism

Whereas modern capitalism accepts the individualistic assumptions and values of democracy, democracy is built on majoritarian and egalitarian values. Democratic egalitarianism is seen in such ways as equality before the law and, more important, in voting. Through the doctrine of one person, one vote, majority-rule institutions are created and legitimated, and through these majoritarian institutions, the will of the majority may be expressed.

Some of the tension that arises between capitalism and democracy is a function of the egalitarian and majoritarian side of democracy. Herbert McClosky and John Zaller describe this tension well:

> Capitalism is primarily concerned with maximizing private profit, while democracy aims at maximizing freedom, equality, and the public good. From this difference, others follow. Capitalism tends to value each individual according to the scarcity of his talents and his contribution to production; democracy attributes unique but roughly equivalent value to *all* people. Capitalism stresses the need for a reward system that encourages the most talented and industrious individuals to earn and amass as much wealth as possible; democracy tries to ensure that all people, even those who lack outstanding talents and initiative, can at least gain a decent livelihood. Capitalism holds that the free market is not only the most efficient but also the fairest mechanism for distributing goods and services; democracy upholds the rights of popular majorities to override market mechanisms when necessary to alleviate social and economic distress.[15]

Thus, the democratic emphasis on individual rights and liberties and minority rights sets the basis of democratic compatibility with capitalism; capitalism and democracy come into conflict over democracy's majoritarian and egalitarian values. This brings us back to the efficiency-equity tradeoff. As long as democracy values equity, it will be in tension with capitalism, but capitalism's and democracy's shared respect for individualism help mute their conflict and tie the two systems together.

Capitalism Versus Democracy: Wealth Concentration

The huge accumulation of wealth amassed by modern corporations and the personally rich adds to the tensions between democracy and capitalism. This wealth concentration accentuates economic inequalities and disparities, while also posing questions of how much political influence and control huge enterprises and wealthy individuals should hold.[16]

For instance, critics charge that large corporations and other moneyed interests can buy legislators and elections and otherwise exert undue influence on the political system.[17] In the late nineteenth century, the U.S. Senate was criticized for being filled with numerous millionaires, who, it was charged, bought their post by paying off or giving money and campaign contributions to state legislators.[18] (Prior to the adoption of the Seventeenth Amendment to the Constitution in 1913, the state legislatures selected those who were to serve in the U.S. Senate, so they became prime targets for the wealthy who wanted a Senate seat.) Although the direct election of senators has ended that specific abuse, money is still a vital ingredient of campaigns for public office, and the wealthy are still overrepresented in the national legislature.

Perhaps more important is the influence of money on election campaigns. Money, whether private or corporate, is needed to pay the campaign workers, buy the advertising time, and fund the other aspects of running a campaign. Supposedly, an election is a democratic arena where equality and the one-person, one-vote rule should determine the outcome. But when candidates rely so heavily on money to get elected, and that money comes from well-heeled sources such as corporate political action committees (PACs), those moneyed interests may have a louder voice in the election process than the average voter. Thus, economic inequality spills over into the democratic system, creating political inequality along the way. Protests against this inequality were important in stimulating campaign finance reforms in the 1970s, which set limits on contributions to presidential election campaigns, and campaign finance is still an issue on the nation's agenda.[19] (We discuss PACs and campaign finance in more detail in Chapter 4.)

Capitalism and Democracy: Values in Conflict

The tensions between capitalism and democracy are not merely textbook abstractions without any real-world implications. They resonate in the political attitudes and opinions of ordinary citizens and political leaders alike. One study looked at the attitudes of both the general public and opinion leaders toward capitalism and democracy.[20] Opinion leaders are defined as members of "twenty organizations and groups widely known for their ideological commitment and activity" plus members of five nonpartisan organizations. In this study, a national sample of ordinary citizens, plus the opinion leaders, were asked a range of questions about their attitudes toward capitalism and democracy. The capitalism questions focused on attitudes toward private ownership, profit, the fairness of private enterprise, regulation, and sources of poverty. The democracy questions asked about attitudes toward individual rights and liberties and majority rule systems. From these questions, a scale of support for capitalism and another scale of support for democracy were constructed. The scales were used to classify people as being high, medium, or low in support for capitalism and democracy.

The study found that the more strongly one accepts capitalist values, the less strongly one accepts democratic values, and vice versa, and this is true for both average citizens and the opinion leaders. In particular, only 21 percent of strong supporters of democracy in the general public are strong supporters of capitalism, while 53 percent of strong supporters of democracy are weak supporters of capitalism. Of the opinion leaders, only 22 percent of strong supporters of democracy are strong supporters of capitalism, while 53 percent of strong supporters of democracy are weak supporters of capitalism. Weak supporters of democracy are stronger supporters of capitalism in both samples.[21]

But the authors of the study are careful to point out that strong democrats do not reject capitalism, and strong capitalists do not reject democracy.[22] Rather, strong democrats are critical of aspects and outcomes of capitalism. They exhibit no tendency to replace capitalism with a command, or government-driven, economy. More likely, strong democrats aim to smooth the rough edges of capitalism. In this way, capitalism and democracy can coexist, though that coexistence is sometimes fraught with tension (see Table 1.1).

TABLE 1.1 Capitalism and Democracy in Conflict (in percents)

Index of Support for Capitalist Values	Index of Support for Democratic Values					
	General Public			Opinion Leaders		
	Low	Middle	High	Low	Middle	High
Low	20	32	53	8	20	53
Middle	33	32	26	8	24	25
High	47	36	21	84	57	22

THE ECONOMIC FOUNDATIONS OF DEMOCRACY

The preceding discussion has focused on the tension between democracy and capitalism. Another way to view the relationship between politics and economics is to look at the impact of economic affluence on the political system and the impact of the political system on the performance of the economy.

Study after study has found a correlation between economic development and the presence of democracy.[23] Wealthy societies are more likely to be democracies and to remain democratic over longer periods of time than poorer societies. Thus, we find that the more economically advanced nations of Western Europe, North America, and Japan are democratic, while dictatorships are more common in the poorer regions of the world.

There are several possible explanations. Perhaps the presence of democratic institutions paves the way for economic development: democracy may thus promote wealth. Or, perhaps affluence comes first: economic development may be a precondition for democracy. A third possibility is that the association between democracy and economic affluence may be mere coincidence. They may develop independently of each other, or perhaps some other factor may promote both democracy and economic wealth.

The idea that democracy helps promote wealth is based on several assumptions. First, this model assumes that a capitalist market system is better at producing wealth over the long haul than any other type of economic system. Second, this model assumes that democracies, with their high regard for individualism and limited government, are more likely to allow market economies than other political systems. Nondemocratic systems are more likely to interfere with market decisions and mechanisms to control the population or for other state purposes, such as to develop the military. Although democracies might regulate the economy, regulation is often a policy of last resort. More of the economy is kept in private hands in democracies than in any other type of government. Third, this model also assumes that voters reward and punish political leaders for the state of the economy. When the economy falters, incumbent governments are turned out of office, to be replaced by their competitors. Thus, politicians in democracies have a strong incentive to promote policies that will generate wealth and prosperity.[24]

Proponents of the idea that democracy leads to wealth often point to the Western democracies to make their case. They also compare the economic performance of these Western democracies with that of the nations of Eastern Europe and the former Soviet Union when those nations were communist. For the most part, the communist economies could not compete with the Western democratic ones, and some attribute the decline of communism in those nations to the feeling among its citizens that communism was failing economically. Those citizens saw that life was better in the West, and they toppled communism to gain those two icons of Western life, democracy and capitalism.

The second theory, in contrast, suggests that affluence precedes democracy. This argument states that wealthier societies are better able to forge strong democratic institutions and that these institutions are able to withstand challenges. First, rich societies are better able to provide for the poor through modest redistributions from the wealthy and middle class. With the harshness of poverty somewhat alleviated, the poor are less likely to be attracted to radical and demagogic movements that hold out the promise of economic redistribution. Moreover, rich societies possess the resources to redistribute, thereby improving the lot of the downtrodden without wholly undoing the position of the wealthy. Some argue that it is actually in the best interests of the wealthy to support modest redistributions that would undermine the appeal of radical redistributors.

Rich societies also contain large middle classes. Middle classes are, like upper classes, conservative. They have a stake in the preservation of the society because of their relatively comfortable lives. Moreover, the middle classes are protected by democratic regimes. Participation in government and civil liberties are especially attractive values to the middle classes. They aim to preserve and safeguard these democratic benefits and conditions, providing the democracy with a wellspring of support to draw from during crises and challenges. The middle classes, thus, tend to support redistributive programs to help the poor. Again, rich societies are likely to promote democratic stability.

The history of the Western democracies may be used to support this theory, but some wealthy societies have not weathered antidemocratic storms successfully. The prime example is Germany, which was one of the wealthiest of nations in the world in the late nineteenth and early twentieth centuries. However, the country's economy succumbed to a deep recession after its defeat in World War I. The discontent caused by this recession became fertile ground for the Nazi movement to thrive in. In several of these cases where democratic institutions failed, they later reemerged, most notably in Germany.

Other examples of wealthy, nondemocratic societies exist, including Singapore, Malaysia, and until recently South Africa. However, in South Africa, democratic institutions have begun to take root, and democratic stirrings are evident in those other nations.

The third alternative we are exploring is that the coexistence of democracy and economic affluence is coincidental. Proponents of this idea look at the cultural foundations of both democracy and capitalism, finding their roots in England. The dominant role England played on the world stage from the late 1700s until the mid-1900s allowed that nation to export its culture of democracy and capitalism throughout the world. Among the oldest capitalist democracies in the world are English-speaking nations that were once British colonies, the United States included. This may help explain why one of the world's poorest nations, India, has had a democratic form of government for most of the years since it gained independence from Great Britain in 1948. When England's world position declined, the United States stepped in as a replacement. This became critical in the aftermath of World War II, when U.S. occupation of Japan and Germany forced democratic regimes on those nations. The spread of democracy and capitalism in Eastern Europe and the old Soviet Union after the fall of communism can also be viewed from this cultural perspective.

Recent research suggests that economic affluence causes democracy.[25] Yet it is possible that each of the theories just discussed is correct to some degree, depending on the country and the times. What seems beyond dispute is that affluence and democracy usually occur together.

TYPES OF RELATIONSHIPS BETWEEN THE GOVERNMENT AND THE ECONOMY

In the late nineteenth century, a doctrine called **laissez faire** became popular in Great Britain and the United States. That doctrine held that the economy and the political system should be kept as separate as possible. Most important, the political system should not interfere with the operation of the marketplace. The market, according to the advocates of laissez faire, was both a fair and an efficient system and, if left unfettered, would lead to the highest levels of national and personal wealth. This idea of maintaining a wall between the economy and the political system dates to the mid-1700s in the work of such English economists as Adam Smith.

Another doctrine concerning the relationship between the economy and the political system, **Marxism,** was also popular in the nineteenth century. Marxism and its variants, communism and socialism, held that the economy and the political system are and should be closely enmeshed but that the political system, operating in the name of workers toward the goal of economic equality, should dominate the economy. Thus, the government should maintain control over the economy, owning and operating it. Unlike the laissez faire advocates, these advocates of government command over the economy viewed the market as inherently unfair because it was inequitable.[26]

These two doctrines became the foundation for much economic policy debate around the world in the twentieth century, as well as the global competition between the West and the Soviet bloc during the cold war. For present purposes, they are a good starting point to talk about the relationship between the economy and the political system, and the *variety* of economic policies that the political system can pursue. The concept of variety is important: the world is more complex than the simple laissez faire–Marxist debate would indicate.

In this section, we will look at several varieties of government policies toward the economy. In describing these policies, we will examine how much interaction there is between the government and the economy, and what the degree of conflict or cooperation is between government and the economy of each type. Plus, we will relate these types of relationships to the tradeoff between equity and efficiency, mentioned earlier.

Economic Policy Regimes: Styles of Economic Government Policies

The overall style of government policies toward the economy can be called an **economic policy regime.**[27] One kind of regime may impose regulations on the economy and assume that conflict between the economy and the political system is ever present. Another type of regime may seek to create a wall between the economy and the political system, assuming little inherent conflict between the two. A regime is composed of the many policies that are aimed at the economy. The more alike the policies—the greater the similarity of their guiding assumptions—the more coherent the regime. As you review these types, ask yourself where you think the United States fits. As you will see, U.S. economic policies tend not to be very coherent, but still we can characterize different periods of time as different economic policy regimes. Each historical era seemed to implement policies that resembled each other, emphasizing an aspect or characteristic of the relationship between the economy and the political system.

Economic policy regimes range along a continuum of the degree of government intervention in the economy, from little or no intervention to complete government control. These opposites, from no intervention to complete control, reflect ideal types more than reality, and most nations have policy regimes that fall somewhere in between. Some have policy regimes that span several of these categories; that is, they have mixed policy regimes. Rarely is the wall of separation between the economy and the political system so high that there is no contact between the two, and rarely are the two so intermeshed that government controls all economic activity and decisions.

There are basically five varieties of economic policy regimes. Arrayed from the least contact between the government and the economy to the most, we have (1) laissez faire, (2) antitrust, (3) regulatory, (4) mixed, and (5) command.[28]

Viewing the degree of government involvement in the economy as a series of steps along a continuum emphasizes once again the conflicting goals of economic efficiency versus equity. Laissez faire advocates, who argue for limited government intervention, emphasize efficiency over equity. In contrast, command advocates, who seek to maximize government intervention, emphasize equity over efficiency. Pushed to their extremes, laissez faire will concern itself only with the efficiency of the market, and command only with equity. In between the two approaches are styles of interaction that mix the two values in differing proportions.

Laissez Faire

Economic policy regimes that aim to limit, or restrict, government intervention in the economy are termed *laissez faire,* as we have already mentioned.

Laissez faire approaches are based on the premise that markets and the self-interest of individuals are better able to solve economic problems than governments. Economic efficiency, rather than equity, is the direct goal of laissez faire advocates, but all citizens will benefit due to the overall increase in wealth that laissez faire style regimes may produce. Thus, with economic expansion, economic benefit will "trickle down" from the top of the economic hierarchy to the bottom, allowing "all boats to rise." "Trickle down" and "rising boats" are two common metaphors associated with this style of economic regime.

The term *laissez faire* dates to eighteenth-century France and is also associated with the early British capitalist economists of the same era, like John Locke, Thomas Robert Malthus, and, most important, Adam Smith. John Locke (1632–1704) was an important British philosopher. His contributions emphasized the linkage between personal liberty and private property, and the U.S. founders who wrote the Constitution were heavily influenced by his writings. Thomas Robert Malthus (1766–1834) was an economist, whose most famous writings deal with the impact of population growth. In essence, Malthus argued that economic growth is additive. In contrast, population growth is geometric. In other words, population growth will outstrip economic growth, leading to mass poverty and starvation. His work has become important in understanding economic development, but his doomsday predictions, at least for the Western developed world, have not come to pass because he overestimated long-term population growth and underestimated economic growth and the impact of technology on food production. Adam Smith (1723–1790) is perhaps the most important of these early British economists. Smith discovered the laws of supply and demand, and their relationship to prices. In a famous metaphor, he saw the market economy as controlled by an *invisible hand,* where supply and demand would readjust, or tend toward equilibrium, if left alone. His theory became the foundation for much of modern economics, as well as the major justification for laissez faire advocates.

The use of laissez faire concepts as arguments against government involvement in the economy was not systematized until the late nineteenth century.[29] Laissez faire doctrine developed then in part because of the governmental and societal attacks on the corporation, which was a comparatively new form of economic enterprise but one that was gaining considerable economic and political power. Laissez faire held sway in Britain until the early 1900s and served as the foundation of most economic thought and policy in the United States until the Great Depression of the 1930s. In other guises, the basic tenets of laissez faire are still popular among Americans, and one can see similarities between laissez faire and the deregulatory movement of the 1970s and 1980s and the Republican Contract with America of the 1990s.

Extreme laissez faire, the complete absence of government from the economy, is probably impossible. Even under laissez faire, government provides the economy with important services. First, government usually provides a currency or regulates currency and money in the marketplace. This helps to ensure a uniformity of value across the land, facilitating economic transactions. Although private money, such as banknotes, stock holdings, and the like, may be used in the place of money, having a common currency on which to peg the value of a good, service, or asset is extremely useful.

Second, government helps ensure contracts by enforcing their provisions. Market transactions require a certain level of trust. At a minimum, the parties of a contract or transaction must believe that their counterpart in the transaction will carry out the bargain. Government enforcement of contracts is one way to ensure that contracts and transactions will be carried out as negotiated. In this way, government helps to build trust in the marketplace.

Third, government provides for civil order. Lack of civil order—the wanton disregard for private property, the wholesale destruction of private assets, crime and the fear it produces, all forms of social disruption—inhibits economic transactions. The economy needs an orderly society. People must not be afraid to go out in public, where most economic transactions take place. Investors need some sense of predictability before they will invest their money into new or existing ventures. Government provides the social order necessary for economic transactions to take place. Thus, in several senses, even under laissez faire regimes, there is some government intervention in the economy, however minimal it may be.

Antitrust

Antitrust is a style of economic policy regime that, like laissez faire, values efficiency, but it also recognizes inherent limitations in the market. Antitrust advocates, as well as the other advocates whom we will discuss, see real markets falling short of the idealized market of the laissez faire advocates, which operates perfectly. They do not see the market as always operating perfectly; in fact, they see that markets may sometimes fail, though they suggest that failed markets may, with government assistance, more closely approximate the ideal than totally free market.

Market failure is also a justification for regulation, discussed in the next section. Market failure occurs when supply and demand do not adjust to each other because of the presence of monopolies, poor information, deceitful practices, and the like. But the antitrust advocates focus on a different type of market failure from that focused on by the regulatory advocates.

To antitrust advocates, market failure occurs when not enough competition exists. Without competition, the laws of supply and demand cannot operate. This type of failure often leads to one firm dominating a market, known as **monopolization**. Competition may also be squeezed out when several firms act together, or collude. This is termed a **cartel**. In the 1970s, a number of oil-producing nations formed the most famous cartel in history, the Organization of Petroleum Exporting Countries (OPEC). Cartels may be formed to restrict competition among themselves, to restrict the flow of goods into the market, or to undermine other competitors. When they act to restrict the flow of a good into the market, they may create a shortage of that good; this results in its price's increasing. This was the strategy that OPEC used on world oil markets. Such actions work only if demand stays stable or does not erode much and if no substitute good can be found.

Free transactions cannot take place under monopoly conditions because the buyer has only one seller from which to purchase a product. Under monopoly conditions, the monopolist may charge higher-than-market prices for his product, thereby directing a larger portion of the economy in his direction. In this sense the market is not operating efficiently.[30]

Antitrust advocates try to build policies that correct these types of market failures. Since the late 1800s, the United States has enacted several antitrust policies and laws that deal with the size and concentration of firms in a market and their behaviors. Most of these policies aim at breaking up monopolies and prohibiting cartels from forming. In the early 1900s, for instance, the great oil combine, Standard Oil, was broken up into several smaller companies to reintroduce a measure of competition into that industry. In the 1980s, the mammoth telephone company, AT&T, which provided most of the nation's local telephone service and almost all of its long-distance service, was similarly broken up into several regional telephone companies and a separate long-distance provider. Recently, the federal government has held that the Ivy League colleges have been engaged in price fixing, a form of cartel collusion. And in perhaps the most important case as we enter this decade, the federal government is challenging the business practices of two putative monopolies in the computer sector, Microsoft, the distributor of Windows, and Intel, the microchip manufacturing giant. Using government to ensure the operation of the market and thus promote greater economic efficiency is the goal of antitrust advocates.

Regulatory

Regulatory advocates seek to redress a different type of market failure. Antitrust deals with market failures that stem from lack of competition. Regulatory advocates seek to address the problems that result from too much competition. Moreover, some regulatory policies seek to increase equity within markets. Regulation of the prices that public utilities charge is one classic example.

Regulation in the United States began in the 1870s when state governments in the Midwest attempted to curb abuses of railroads. One of the most notable abuses involved discrimination in fees: farmers in the Midwest were charged more to move their goods to cities on the East Coast than were eastern manufacturers who sent their goods to those living in the nation's interior. Also, railroads offered secret rebates to special customers, especially oil and coal companies. The energy companies would force railroads into offering the rebates, which would allow the energy companies to sell their products in a region at prices below their competition. Many competitors, especially small and regional companies, were bankrupted because of this practice.

Unlike antitrust advocates, who are confident that government help can restore the market, regulatory advocates are less sanguine about market restoration. In the place of markets, regulators use government to produce outcomes that they feel would look like, or might even be superior to, market outcomes. Most regulations in the United States allow private ownership of regulated firms. These regulations also guarantee a "reasonable" profit. *Reasonable* is often defined as the average of what similar companies in nonregulated activities earn.

Regulations may also try to ensure equal access to the product or service, something that markets may not guarantee. Equity concerns may be critical here. For example, telephone policy in the United States has been built on a **universal service** model. Universal service aims to provide telephone access to consumers, as well as business, and to people living in rural, as well as urban, areas. Businesses usually command the resources to pay for telephone service; not all consumers do. Plus, provision of service to rural areas is more costly than to urban areas because of the combination of lower traffic levels and the longer telephones lines that are required in rural environs. To establish the universal service policy, the government has used **cross-subsidies,** whereby some users pay more than others or more than the cost of providing the service to them. Thus, businesses and urban users are assessed more than consumers and rural residents. These higher assessments are used to offset the higher costs of providing telephone service to these targeted recipients. The universal service model has been broadly applied to all types of utility regulation, such as gas and electric power and water service. The cross-subsidy system is one type of redistribution, or equity, system that is used to establish the universal service goal.[31]

Mixed Economies

In some nations, the government owns an entire industry or is a shareholder in parts of an industry, while most of the economy is still privately held. Thus, until the Thatcher government in Britain in the late 1970s and 1980s, the British government owned much British industry, like the coal mines and steel industry. Under Margaret Thatcher, many British government industrial holdings were **privatized.** The French government is a major shareholder in Renault, the French automobile manufacturer, and Sweden is famous for government ownership or partnership in its major industries.

By comparison, the U.S. government is not as heavily invested in private firms. But several exceptions do exist. For instance, on the bankruptcy of the major railroads in the Northeast in the 1960s, the U.S. government began to operate two rail systems, Conrail and Amtrak. On the subsequent financial success of both rail systems, they were privatized in the 1980s.

Government has several goals when it intervenes in the economy in this way. It may, for instance, try to ensure that the company or industry stays in local or domestic hands, or it may try to protect a company, industry, or economic sector from competition, especially foreign competition. Although there may be important private-sector beneficiaries of such government intervention in the economy, government actions are usually justified by invoking the public interest: the defense and economic health of the nation are at stake, and government intervention is thus required. However, even with such major intrusions into the private economy, in most cases of government–private sector partnerships of this sort, the economy remains essentially market driven.

Command Economies

At the far end of the continuum of possible economic policy regimes are command policies. Command policies invest economic direction or ownership in government. Command economies, all of which emphasize equity over efficiency, vary in the type of political system that they espouse and the degree to which the central government controls the economy. The two major governing styles found in command economies are **socialism** and **communism.** Socialism believes in democratic political institutions. Thus, socialists will create political parties to compete in free elections, feeling that they can attract enough voter support to gain electoral success. Furthermore, socialists feel that their economic policies will be popular among voters, and thus, the electorate will keep the socialist party in power.

Communists differ in that they have little faith in electoral and democratic institutions. They believe that only through violent revolution will they be able to take over government. Furthermore, communists dispense with free elections and party competition, instead granting the Communist Party a monopoly of political power in the government, its bureaucracy, and the economy. Communist government existed in the Soviet Union from 1917 until the late 1980s and throughout much of eastern Europe from the end of World War II until 1989. Communist regimes still exist in Cuba, North Korea, and mainland China, although the Chinese case exhibits several deviations from the model of communism found in the former Soviet Union.

Command economies also vary in terms of how much of the economy the central government controls. While complete command over the economy is probably impossible, extensive control was generally the case during communist rule of the old Soviet Union. In contrast, two important command systems allowed for some free market enterprise. The first of the communist countries to break from the Soviet model was Yugoslavia under the direction of Marshall Tito. Later, in the mid-1970s, after the death of its leader Mao Zedong, Communist China, under Mao's successor, Deng Xiaoping, opened up the Chinese economy to allow for more private property, business enterprise, and foreign investment.

Most of the command economies that existed under the Soviet mantle no longer exist. After old-style Soviet leader Leonid Brezhnev died in 1982 and after a brief period of leadership chaos, reformer Mikhail Gorbachev became the Soviet leader in 1985. Gorbachev instituted two types of reforms, **perestroika** and **glasnost.** Perestroika involved restructuring all Soviet institutions of the Soviet Union, while glasnost involved opening up the political system to free discussion by its citizens. Further reforms followed, including the outlawing of the Communist Party in 1990. In 1989, three Baltic nations that were part of the Soviet Union, Estonia, Latvia, and Lithuania, declared their independence. When it was apparent that the Soviet Union under Gorbachev's leadership would not stop their move, the entire Soviet Union disintegrated, as other people desired their political independence also. From the old Soviet Union, the Commonwealth of Independent States was created, composed of fifteen states, including Russia and Ukraine, the largest. In Russia, free elections were held in 1991, when Boris Yeltsin was elected president. By 1989, the Communist Parties that ruled East Germany, Poland, Czechoslovakia, Hungary, Romania, and Bulgaria also lost power, and East Germany was absorbed into West Germany.

The transformation in eastern Europe and the former Soviet Union was sweeping, and included two elements, political and economic. Politically, Communist Party rule was replaced with democratic institutions, free elections, and civil liberties. Economically, the command economies were partially or wholly replaced with market economies.

In many of the nations, this transformation has been painful. Some nations, like Hungary and the new Czech Republic (Czechoslovakia split into two nations, the Czech and Slovak Republics) have displayed relatively strong economies, with considerable economic growth and prosperity. Others, especially Russia, have had a harder time transforming from a command to a market economy. The countries that seem to have made the most economic progress are those that already had some markets in place, those that produced goods that could be sold easily in foreign nations, and those that were able to attract investment from other nations. Russia has also suffered from high inflation and unstable currency values, a bankrupt government, and an economy that was heavily geared toward the production of military goods rather than goods that could be exported or that consumers or industry at home would want. Widespread corruption has also slowed Russia's economic progress.

Unlike the European nations, Communist China, while experimenting with market economics long before the Soviets, has not allowed political reforms. The communist political system has stayed intact; political freedom and competitive elections are still alien to the Chinese. Chinese Communist Party resistance to political change became strongly evident in May 1989, when the Chinese military violently put down the student demonstration in Beijing's Tiananmen Square. Subsequently, many Chinese dissidents and students were arrested and jailed.

The story of the transformation of command economies in the 1980s and 1990s is long, complex, covers many nations, and is not yet complete. It also illustrates the interrelationships between the political and economic systems.[32]

The United States and the Varieties of Economic Policy Regimes

Where does the United States fit into this classification of economic policy regimes? Recall that examples of U.S. policies were mentioned in the antitrust, regulatory, and mixed categories and that laissez faire was a popular notion historically in the United States. Thus, we cannot easily place the United States under any one of the types mentioned. Rather, U.S. economic policy is inconsistent, that is, simultaneously includes several different types of economic policy regimes. How did this come about? The answer to this question will be addressed in more detail in the next chapter, but fundamentally, during different historical periods, one type of economic policy regime would predominate. When the United States entered the next historical period and a new economic policy regime became popular, the old policies from the former policy regime were not discarded. Thus, new economic policies were often layered on top of existing policies, which were maintained; this produced an inconsistency and complexity in the economic policies of the United States.

Conflict and Cooperation Between the Economy and the Political System

Given all of the heated antigovernment rhetoric and the generally high regard in which business is held in the United States, one would suppose that the relationship between government and the economy is mostly conflictual. But this is not the case. Cooperation is common, and many government policies aim at promoting or helping business, rather than restraining it.

It is easy to comprehend cooperative business-government relations in a laissez faire policy regime, but such cooperation is also possible under other regimes. For instance, many regulatory policies that were implemented during Franklin Roosevelt's New Deal in the 1930s aimed at promoting particular industries, such as the airline and telecommunications industries. And mixed systems may promote business when government becomes a financial base for selected businesses to operate from.

Conflict between government and business may be muted and cooperation enhanced because both at times need the other. For instance, business may receive important benefits from government, such as financial support. This may come in many forms, including subsidies, tax breaks, low-interest and/or guaranteed loans, contracts, and restrictions on competitors. Government may restrict competition in a number of ways, for instance, by requiring licenses and other permits to operate, establishing quality standards, limiting entry into markets, and, in the international context, imposing tariffs on imports. The number of ways in which government can aid business in this fashion is limited only by the imagination and the creativity of policy-makers.

Business, however, may also ask government to absorb some of the cost and risk of doing business. To operate efficiently and effectively, business needs the support of a well-established and well-developed **infrastructure.** Infrastructure itself is not a production sector of the economy, but infrastructure enables the economy to operate. The more well developed and efficient the infrastructure, the more efficient and productive the economy. Examples of infrastructure include the transportation, communication, and financial systems. Goods and services flow from seller to buyer through the transportation system, and money is the medium of exchange. Early on in U.S. history, the government aided in the development of the transportation system, building roads, canals, and railroads and, in more modern times, airports and highway systems. The government also helped develop the financial system. One of the important changes from the Articles of Confederation to the Constitution was that the Constitution specified the federal government would provide for a uniform currency to allow greater cross-state economic activity. Government tends to be especially important in the development of the infrastructure.

Similarly, government in the United States has played a major role in educating the population, in developing the economy's human capital, much like infrastructure development enhances the economy's physical capital. Part of the rationale for this role is that a more educated workforce supposedly will be more productive.[33] Government support for education comes in many varieties and has a long history, from granting federal lands to localities for the local provision of public education to loans to attend college. Government also helps business with product development, some of which comes about through government-sponsored scientific activity. In agriculture, government helps farmers by developing new crop strains and lending assistance on agriculture technology. Last, as mentioned earlier, government provides for civil order, which is necessary for the economy to function. Overall, business and the economy derive important benefits from government.

But the U.S. government also needs the economy; this makes the condition of the economy a crucial factor in most government policymaking that is economic in nature. First, a healthy and growing economy provides financial resources that the government can tap into. Government needs revenue to operate and to respond to demands for services. Most of these revenue sources come from the private sector, that is, the economy. The stronger and bigger the economy, the faster it is growing, the larger the resource pool that government has from which it can extract resources.

Third World regimes are weak, not only because their political institutions are fragile but also because their national economies are not rich enough to provide their governments with necessary resources. Public demands may not be met satisfactorily, especially in areas of health and safety, and these countries may not be able to defend themselves effectively against neighbors or former colonial powers. Much of the political turmoil of the Third World is a function of economies that are too weak to support basic and necessary government services. Nations with economies that are relatively strong may provide government with resources to deal with social problems, societal disruptions, public demands, and external threats.

But political leaders also need a vibrant economy for more selfish reasons. The public tends to reward or punish governing leaders on the basis of the state of the economy. If the economy is growing and healthy, public support for political leaders tends to increase. If the economy is weak and/or faltering, the public will often withdraw its support. Political leaders may find their reelection chances plummeting due to economic distress, and between elections, the popularity of leaders may drop.

Charles Lindblom suggests that this need of government for a strong economy makes government a "prisoner" to the economy and private-sector leaders.[34] In fact, government may be blamed when the economy dives because of decisions made in the private sector, decisions that government leaders were not a party to. For example, the U.S. automobile industry was slow to respond to the Japanese challenge to its dominance in the mid-1970s, losing a considerable part of the domestic market to foreign competitors. Government was partly blamed for this occurrence, though it is arguable whether government policies or decisions had anything to do with it.

The reliance on government for a healthy economy makes government especially sensitive to the needs and demands of the business community when making public policy.[35] We will talk about this issue more in later chapters, but for now we can say that economic concerns are a constant presence in government policymaking.

There is another way government relies on business and the economy: for information about the state of the economy and expertise about its functioning. Government clearly has economic experts, but it still cannot compete with the expertise of businesses about production techniques or even the reaction of business decision makers to pending policies. Moreover, government requires the assistance and compliance of the private sector in the collection of information about the state of the economy. Thus, the government needs business for information that is used in the policymaking process.

CONCLUSION

In this chapter we have presented several major ideas that will be explored in more detail throughout this book, including the debate between efficiency and equity, economic versus governmental problem solving, and the relationship between the government and the economy. We also discussed the intertwined development of capitalism and democracy and the tension between the two. That tension, which has its roots in the competing values of efficiency and equity, provides the basis from which to understand much economic policy debate. Moreover, we have introduced the concept of economic policy regime, an idea that will be referred to at different points later in the text. These lay the foundation for what is to follow.

This book is structured into three parts. The first part includes only Chapter 2, which looks at change and development of the U.S. economy and of U.S. economic policy. The ideas of the tradeoff between equity and efficiency and the incoherence of U.S. economic policies are picked up again in that chapter. The second part concerns the people who influence economic policymaking in the United States. This part includes Chapters 3 through 6 and moves from those farthest from the actual making of economic policy to those nearest to the actual decision point. Thus, we move from the general public (Chapter 3), to organized interests (business, Chapter 4, and labor, Chapter 5), and finally to the government personnel who have the responsibility and authority to make economic policies (Chapter 6). The third part deals with the economic policies themselves. Chapters 7 to 9 focus on macroeconomic and financial policies, such as taxes, budgets, and fiscal and monetary policies. Chapters 10 and 11 look at regulatory policy, Chapter 12 at distributive policies, and Chapter 13 at international economic policy. Thus, across this book we move from the foundations of economic policy to those who influence economic policy to the policies themselves. Along the way we reencounter the equity-efficiency tradeoff and the inconsistency of U.S. economic policy.

Key Terms

antitrust	glasnost	redistribute
cartel	infrastructure	regulation
command	laissez faire	socialism
economies	law of demand	universal service
communism	law of scarcity	
cross-subsidies	law of supply	
dead weight loss	market economies	
economic efficiency	market failure	
economic liberals	Marxism	
economic policy	mercantilism	
regime	monopoly,	
economy	monopolization	
equilibrium	perestroika	
equity	privatize,	
feudalism	privatization	

Explore the Web

For a very good glossary of major economic concepts see http://www
.auburn.edu/~johnspm/glossind.html. Good discussions of major economic
terms and events are located at http://www.utexas.edu/world/lecture/eco/.

Notes

1. Charles E. Lindblom, *Politics and Markets: The World's Political-Economic Systems* (New York: Basic Books, 1977), 11.

2. The term *law of scarcity* appears in Paul A. Samuelson and William D. Nordhaus, *Economics,* 14th ed. (New York: McGraw-Hill, 1992), 8.

3. See, for instance, Benjamin Ginsberg, *The Consequences of Consent: Elections, Citizen Control and Popular Acquiescence* (Reading, MA: Addison-Wesley, 1982), for a discussion of how the development of popular participation systems not only increased citizen input in government decision making but also increased government control over its citizenry.

4. This definition comes from Samuelson and Nordhaus, *Economics,* 23.

5. Deborah Stone, *Policy Paradox and Political Reason* (New York: HarperCollins, 1988), 57.

6. A study that discusses the many meanings of class in the United States is Harry M. Hodges, *Social Stratification: Class in America* (Cambridge, MA: Schenkman, 1968).

7. Lindblom, *Politics and Markets,* 43–44, 269–272, reviews some of these points. A good review of economic inequality in the United States is found in William E. Hudson, *American Democracy in Peril: Seven Challenges to America's Future* (Chatham, NJ: Chatham House, 1995), 221–260.

8. Hudson, *American Democracy in Peril.* Robert Dahl raises this issue in *Democracy and Its Critics* (New Haven, CT: Yale University Press, 1989), 130–131, 323–328.

9. Douglas A. Hibbs, Jr., *The American Political Economy* (Cambridge, MA: Harvard University Press, 1987), 280–328; and Kevin Phillips, *The Politics of Rich and Poor: Wealth and the American Electorate in the Reagan Aftermath* (New York: Random House, 1990).

10. We should also note that the faltering state of the economy had much to do with Clinton's victory and Bush's defeat, yet the fairness theme was an important element of Clinton's campaign.

11. Arthur Okun, *Equality and Efficiency: The Big Tradeoff* (Washington, DC: Brookings Institution, 1975).

12. Stone, *Policy Paradox,* 65–68; also, Okun, *Equality and Efficiency.*

13. Richard Lehne, *Industry and Politics: United States in Comparative Perspective* (Englewood Cliffs, NJ: Prentice-Hall, 1993), 7.

14. Herbert McClosky and John Zaller, *The American Ethos: Public Attitudes Toward Capitalism and Democracy* (Cambridge, MA: Harvard University Press, 1984), 2–3.

15. Ibid., 7.

16. Thomas R. Dye, *Who's Running America? The Clinton Years* (Englewood Cliffs, NJ: Prentice-Hall, 1995).

17. One example of this thinking is found in Philip M. Stern, *Still the Best Congress Money Can Buy* (Washington, DC: Regency Gateway, 1992).

18. A good historical review of money and politics in the United States is found in Larry L. Berg, Harlan Hahn, and John R. Schmidhauser, *Corruption in the American Political System* (Morristown, NJ: General Learning Press, 1976).

19. On the campaign finance reforms and their impact, as well as a good analysis of the impact of money on elections, see Frank J. Sorauf, *Inside Campaign Finance: Myths and Realities* (New Haven, CT: Yale University Press, 1992).

20. McClosky and Zaller, *The American Ethos.*

21. The correlation between the two scales for the general public is −.44, and for the opinion leaders −.52. McClosky and Zaller, *The American Ethos,* 174.

22. Ibid., 176.

23. Seymour Martin Lipset, "Some Social Requisites of Democracy," *American Political Science Review* 53 (1959): 69–105. For a good review of this literature, see Ross E. Burkhart and Michael Lewis-Beck, "Comparative Democracy: The Economic Development Thesis," *American Political Science Review* 88 (1994): 903–910; and Dahl, *Democracy and Its Critics,* especially chaps. 17, 18.

24. The literature on the effect of economic conditions on elections is huge. We will discuss this in more detail in Chapter 9.

25. Burkhart and Lewis-Beck, "Comparative Democracy."

26. A good description of these alternative economic theories and their assumptions is found in Robert Gilpin, "The Political Economy of the Multinational Corporation: Three Contrasting Perspectives," *American Political Science Review* 70 (1976): 184–191.

27. This notion of an economic policy regime is inspired by Eisner's concept of regulatory regimes. See Marc Allen Eisner, *Regulatory Politics in Transition* (Baltimore, MD: Johns Hopkins University Press, 1993).

28. Jeffrey E. Cohen, "The Telephone Problem and the Road to Telephone Regulation in the United States, 1876–1933," *Journal of Policy History* 3 (1991): 42–69.

29. Seymour Martin Lipset, *The First New Nation* (New York: Anchor, 1967), 54–59.

30. There are limits to monopoly power, however. Monopolization may force people to seek substitute goods. Moreover, monopolists are somewhat restricted in the prices that they can charge. Prices cannot be so high that they keep people from purchasing the good or service.

31. Jeffrey E. Cohen, *The Politics of Telecommunications: The States and the Divestiture of AT&T* (Armonk, NY: Sharpe, 1992).

32. The literature on the transformation in eastern Europe and the Soviet Union is immense. Some good studies that review political as well as economic aspects include James F. Brown, *Hopes and Shadows: Eastern Europe after Communism* (Durham, NC: Duke University Press, 1994); Roger East, *Revolutions in Eastern Europe* (New

York: Pinter, 1992); M. Steven Fish, *Democracy from Scratch: Opposition and Regime in the New Russian Revolution* (Princeton, NJ: Princeton University Press, 1995); Jeffrey C. Goldfarb, *After the Fall: The Pursuit of Democracy in Central Europe* (New York: Basic Books, 1992); Reneo Lukic, *Europe from the Balkans to the Urals: The Disintegration of Yugoslavia and the Soviet Union* (New York: Oxford University Press, 1996). A study that focuses on economic changes of the new economies in several eastern European nations and Russia is *Economies in Transition: Comparing Asia and Eastern Europe,* eds. Wing Thye Woo, Stephen Parker, and Jeffrey D. Sachs (Cambridge, MA: MIT Press, 1997).

33. Another purpose of broad-based public education is to create a citizenry capable of engaging its democratic rights and responsibilities.

34. Charles E. Lindblom, "The Market as Prison," *Journal of Politics* 44 (1982): 324–336.

35. See on this point Charles E. Lindblom, *Politics and Markets;* and Cathie J. Martin, *Shifting the Burden: The Struggle over Growth and Corporate Taxation* (Chicago: University of Chicago Press, 1991).

2

Patterns of Change in the U.S. Economy and U.S. Economic Policy

TWO CENTURIES ago, most Americans worked on the land as farmers, without the aid of mechanical devices. Cities were small, and no corporations existed. Today life is much different. Most Americans live in cities, many work for large corporations, and few are employed in agriculture. Government is now a pervasive fact of life, something that was not the case in the late eighteenth century. Yet government did have economic policies in the country's early years. In this chapter we will look at patterns of change in the U.S. economy and in government policies that affect that economy.

We shall look at how the U.S. economy developed over time from an agrarian to an industrial to a postindustrial economy. Because the U.S. economy also shows cyclical changes, we must distinguish those cyclical changes from the economy's historical development. Two types of cyclical changes are most important to our discussion, the **business cycle** and the **cycle of equality-inequality**. The business cycle refers to changes from good to bad times, from periods of economic growth to periods of economic contraction, which sometimes become recessions. The equality-inequality cycle refers to increases and decreases in the distribution of wealth and income in the United States.

Policy changes will also be dealt with in a historical fashion. As you will see, different mixes of economic policies—different economic policy regimes—occurred at different times in the nation's history. Subsequent eras did not discard the old as much as add their own style of economic policy. This layering accounts for the complexity, multiplicity, and inconsistency across U.S. economic policy and may help us understand the pressures that have led to the deregulatory movement of the past twenty years.

The discussion of economic and policy change contained in this chapter will set the stage for understanding the current state of U.S. economy and economic policy by showing how we got to this point.

CHANGES IN THE U.S. ECONOMY

In this section we discuss changes in the U.S. economy that are relevant to economic policymaking and that have been concerns of government.[1] Economic change often places stress on people, who then may seek government redress. The status quo is threatened by change, and the status quo may seek ways to stop change from happening and/or to reverse the tide back to the status quo. Political action is one method used to both impede and impel change. Thus, economic change finds its way into the political and governmental arenas. Economic change becomes one stimulus for government economic policymaking.

First, we will look at change in the structure of the economy. From its beginning as a predominantly agricultural economy, the U.S. economy industrialized, becoming the most important manufacturing economy on earth. In recent years that manufacturing base has declined, and service and information industries have become more important. Some say that we have entered a **postindustrial era.** In postindustrial economies, manufacturing becomes less important as an economic activity and is replaced by services such as banking, finance, telecommunication, and information management.

Second, we will review the business cycle. The economy cycles from boom to bust. At times it is overheated, with high levels of inflation and low unemployment. At other times it grows slowly, if at all, and exhibits higher levels of unemployment and comparatively low levels of inflation. Changes in the structure of the economy are measured in decades, but changes in the business cycle are measured in months. From a historic perspective, then, these cyclical changes are very rapid. Smoothing the business cycle, to produce growth and high levels of employment with low inflation, has been a major preoccupation of the U.S. government since the Great Depression of the 1930s.

A third type of change in the economy we will look at relates to the distribution of income and the concentration of wealth. During some periods the gap between rich and poor narrows; during other periods it widens. During the 1960s and 1970s, for instance, the gap narrowed, but it widened again during the 1980s. Changes in the structure of the economy and the business cycle may affect the distribution of wealth, but so do government policies, such as taxes and income support. Changes in the distribution of wealth may lead to political action. When the gap widens, the poor may place demands on government for assistance. When the gap narrows, the rich may feel that too much of their wealth is being redistributed to the poor. They may seek changes in government policies to keep more of their wealth and income. The cycle of increasing or decreasing economic equality relates to the equity-efficiency tradeoff discussion in Chapter 1.

Changing Economic Structures

We can roughly divide the U.S. economy into three eras: agrarian, industrial, and postindustrial. The agrarian period lasted for about the first century of the nation, from the late 1700s until the post–Civil War era. In the latter part of the nineteenth century, industrialization became the keynote of the U.S. economy. There is no clear marker for the end of the industrial era, but some time during the period from the 1960s to the 1980s, the economy began its transformation into the postindustrial age. Although industrial sectors are still important to the economy, as is the agrarian sector, the postindustrial sector of services and communications has steadily occupied an increasing proportion of the economy.[2]

During the nation's first century, agriculture provided the bulk of the jobs. We do not have good statistics on farm populations prior to the middle of the nineteenth century, but we do know who lived where. Most of the population was rural (defined as communities of less than 2,500). About 90 percent or more of the population lived in rural communities until the mid-1840s. As late as 1900, 60 percent of the population lived in rural communities, meaning that the rural percentage of the population had declined by over 30 percent in about fifty years. After the turn of the century, the rural population continued to slide, dipping to 30 percent by 1960. From the late 1800s, we have good numbers on actual farm populations. In 1880, about 44 percent of the population lived on farms. That number declined steadily across time, dipping to under 10 percent by 1960 and to under 5 percent by 1970.[3]

Several factors led to the transformation of the economy from agrarian to industrial.[4] First were the inventions associated with the industrial revolution, especially the harnessing of steam power and later electricity, which allowed machines and engines of greater strength to be built and operated. Among the most important of these was the locomotive engine. Similarly, mass assembly processes that used interchangeable parts were developed in the United States. These were critical in the development of the early U.S. arms industry.

There was also demand for industrial goods. Some of the demand came from the growth of the nation and the push to settle the West. But a growth spurt also occurred because of the Civil War. Huge armies had to be armed, clothed, fed, and moved from one theater of operations to another. Vast fortunes were made from government contracts to supply the army, especially in the North. The South had a smaller industrial base and was more dependent on imports to prosecute its war effort.

Among the most important outcomes of the industrialization process was the invention of the **corporation.** Corporations differed from earlier business organizations. They tended to be much larger than existing business enterprises, and their internal structure was more rationalized, specialized, and bureaucratic. Also, unlike previous business organizations, which competed in small, local markets, corporations competed in large, sometimes national markets. Finally, unlike most previous businesses, corporations required a charter, granted by a government entity, like a state, to operate. The charter defined the financial obligations and responsibilities of those involved, especially investors, and allowed the corporation to sell shares of itself on the open market in order to raise investment capital. The charter also protected the private wealth of the owners and investors. The corporation, not its owners, became responsible for the corporation's financial liabilities. In this sense, the chartering of corporations makes them "public" enterprises.

The development of the corporation had several important consequences. One was that the offices and operations that were spread around the nation or a region had to communicate with each other and coordinate their activities. Specialized managers arose to perform these tasks.

Another consequence was that the economy began to become national in scope. Corporations in several industries became national. Small, local business enterprises began to be pushed out by these new firms. Corporations arose in many industries besides rail: in manufacturing, especially steel; in mineral extraction, such as coal and oil; in food production and distribution, especially meatpacking; in consumer goods, like tobacco; and in retailing, with the development of the catalog giants Sears Roebuck and Montgomery Ward. Advertising began in the late part of the nineteenth century, and brand names began to be common. Instead of buying bulk flour, people bought Gold Medal flour or Pillsbury flour, and they could do this across the wide expanse of the nation.[5] Just as the Civil War helped to create a national identity, an association with nation over state, the industrialization of the economy helped to forge a national economy. Each of these forms of national organization, governmental and economic, was dependent on the other.

Industrialization had other effects, too. People moved from the farms to the cities, and rather than work for a food crop to be sold on the market, people sold their labor for money wages. As people moved to the cities, the close contacts among people that defined rural life gave way to a more anonymous style of life, where people lived and worked surrounded by strangers. To fill the void this new atomized life created, associations and groups sprang up throughout the nation.

The transformation of the economy to industrialized had several important political consequences. Farmers mobilized to try to stop the trend. Workers organized, often into labor unions, to try to adapt to the new industrial work environment. Corporations became politically active, and the issue of corporate power was placed on the political agenda. The large, educated middle class that filled the ranks of corporate middle management became the foundation for the **Progressive movement,** which offered major political reforms during the late 1800s and early 1900s.

The agenda of the Progressives was quite broad, covering political, as well as economic, issues. On the political front, the Progressives attacked the political parties and the bosses who controlled those parties. Thus, they advocated the use of the secret ballot and primary elections to nominate candidates for office in place of the bosses, who had traditionally decided who would run. Moreover, the Progressives believed in good government and brought with them the notion that government could be run efficiently and scientifically if government modeled itself on business, especially the corporation, as an organizational form. Progressives, too, had faith in the positive uses of government and were quite willing to use government to regulate aspects of the economy and society. Large corporations, especially those that verged on monopoly power, were constant targets of the Progressives. To this end, Progressives believed in a professional bureaucracy, one in which people would attain employment through merit and civil service examinations, not through patronage, that is, appointment by political party bosses. Again, we see here the Progressive attack on traditional party leaders of the era. Lastly, Progressives had a darker side, often opposing easy immigration into the United States by people from eastern and southern Europe. During the late 1800s and early 1900s, there was a massive wave of immigration from those European regions.[6] The period of transformation from agrarianism to industrialization was a politically turbulent one; the economic transformation was one source of that turbulence.

The new corporate style of the economy had further effects. The most important of these were the concentration of economic power in relatively few hands and the management style of corporate capitalism. Unlike the preindustrial age, in the industrial age, economic power became concentrated in the hands of corporate decision makers. The decisions they made not only affected their companies but had major economic implications. Whether a corporation decided to build new factories affected the supply of jobs, and decisions to raise prices affected the inflation rate. And this power to affect the larger economy was being exercised by relatively few people, the managers of the nation's largest corporations.

A related issue concerned the decision-making style of corporations. A style of decision making that we can call **managed capitalism** emerged in which corporate leaders not only tried to respond to market changes but also tried to manage the direction that markets would take.[7] In a sense, managed capitalism is about businesses' creating and developing markets for their goods, not just responding to demands. Corporate managers tried to minimize the instability and unpredictability of markets because huge sums of money were required to invest in new products, and long lead times were required to develop products, equip and build factories, and get new products onto the market. The combination of huge investment sums and long lead times in production increased the degree of risk that corporations faced.

Thus, corporate managers were vitally interested in ensuring that a demand for their good existed when they finally got it onto the market. To aid in this quest, demand was created, nursed, and maintained, in part through advertising, planned obsolescence of goods, and control of the supply of goods manufactured. It is important to note that this style of capitalism deviated from the pure supply and demand market model developed by Adam Smith and other capitalist theorists. Those capitalist thinkers and theories emphasized the power of supply and demand to regulate and change economic behavior, but with managed capitalism we see business enterprises trying to control the forces of supply and demand rather than be totally at the mercy of those market forces.

In the third quarter of the twentieth century, the economy began a transformation into a new era, the postindustrial age. In the postindustrial age, a major aspect of the economy is the movement of information from one place to another. Technological developments, especially electronic communications media and the computer, made this possible.[8]

Although corporations remain the important organizing element of the economy in the postindustrial age, the nature of work and of worker-management relations has changed. Factory and physical work has given way to intellectual work. The ability to use and manipulate information has become a major aspect of work. Consequently, education, especially college education, is important in developing labor market advantages for those seeking employment. No longer do people enter the job market directly from high school. More schooling is needed.

But these educational skills also instill a sense of independence and individual competence in people; postindustrial workers are thus less inclined to join unions and other collective work associations than the blue-collar factory workers of the industrial age. The union presence in society has markedly declined. A new fault line has emerged dividing those with education from those without.

New kinds of demands are being placed on the government as the economy shifts toward the information age. The status quo, industrial manufacturing concerns and workers, seeks to block postindustrial changes and has sought to insulate the United States from international competition to protect their industries and jobs. Those ready and willing to take advantage of the information economy have placed pressure on government to cease regulation of industries that can use these new technologies. These two factions are often at odds over the direction of public policy and may find allies in both political parties. New interest groups and movements, and third-party candidates like Ross Perot, often speak to audiences on either side of this divide, with the political parties in the crossfire, as the political system tries to come to grips with the stresses that this new economic transformation is creating. Ross Perot, the billionaire Texas businessman, ran for the presidency in 1992 and again in 1996. He gained notoriety for, among other things, bankrolling his campaign from his private fortune, starting up a new political party (which to date has not achieved much electoral success), and his flamboyant personality and speaking style.

Changes in the Business Cycle

In addition to the long-term evolution discussed in the previous section, the economy is also characterized by short-term changes. One kind of short-term change—the economy's ups and downs as it cycles through different levels of inflation and unemployment—is associated with the economy's growth rate. Figure 2.1 plots a hypothetical business cycle. In reality, the business cycle is not so smooth or uniform, but the concept helps us visualize the changes in the economy over short periods of time.

The business cycle has four phases. The highest level of economic performance is called an **economic peak.** As the economy slows down, it enters a period of **economic contraction.** The lowest level of economic performance is called an **economic trough. Recessions,** when the total output of the economy declines for two or more quarters, start with the beginning of the contraction period and end with the trough. Before the term *recession* came into use, declines in the economy were called **panics. Economic expansion** begins once the economy starts to grow again, and the cycle begins anew.

The U.S. economy, like any capitalist economy, has periods of high growth and periods of low growth. Recessions are a normal part of the business cycle.

Several consequences flow from recessions. Among the most politically important is that unemployment grows. Governments are often under great

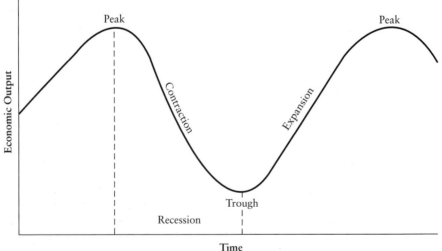

FIGURE 2.1 The Phases of the Business Cycle

pressure to promote policies to stimulate growth and thus get people back to work. But when the economy grows too fast, when demand outstrips the ability of the economy to meet that demand with supply, inflation may set in. Inflation is another part of the business cycle. Government's task since the Depression has been to promote growth and resist recession, but also to avoid inflation—a difficult, if not mutually contradictory, set of goals.

Before the Depression, the economy was often plagued by recessionary periods, or periods of economic contraction. In fact, the economy of the late nineteenth and early twentieth centuries seemed very volatile. It grew tremendously during this period but in great fits and starts. From the Civil War to 1930, nearly 45 percent of all months exhibited contraction in growth. Since the government has become active in directing the economy, fewer and shorter recessions have been the norm. From 1945 to 1990, only about 20 percent of the months exhibited contractions in the economy.[9]

Since 1945, however, there have been some deep recessions and some high inflations, some with important political implications. For instance, in 1957–1958, the economy took a severe dive. The conservative Eisenhower administration refused to take strong action, and the Democrats won a sweeping victory in Congress. Many of these Democratic legislators became important social reformers and policy innovators in the following decade. President Richard Nixon so feared the inflation of the early 1970s that he imposed wage and price controls. The combination of high inflation and slow growth plagued both the Ford and Carter administrations, contributing to their one-term tenures. Even George Bush, who scored very high in popularity polls during the first two years of his term, was blamed for a recession that hit the second half of his tenure and was not returned to office by the voters. Elections and public moods may be influenced by the business cycle.[10]

It is important to distinguish change that comes from structural transformation of the economy from change associated with the business cycle. Both, however, may place demands on government for action, as those buffeted by these changes seek government assistance.

Changes in Wealth Concentration

In mid-April 1995, newspapers throughout the nation ran stories on the growing economic inequality in the United States Those stories discussed the trend toward the greater concentration of wealth and the decline of the middle class. In comparison to the rest of the developed world, the United States looked extremely economically unequal. For instance, in Britain, generally regarded as a society divided by class, the wealthiest 1 percent owned about 18 percent of the wealth. In the United States, the top 1 percent held 40 percent.[11]

A few conservative analysts have even taken note of the increasing economic inequality in the United States in the 1980s and 1990s. Kevin Phillips made this the theme of his book on the politics and policies of the Reagan years, *The Politics of Rich and Poor.*[12] Phillips cautioned that the gap had grown too wide and policies were needed to address the problem, lest the fabric of the nation pull apart. He worried about the destabilizing impact of too much economic inequality.

In his first economic report to the nation, President Clinton made a similar point. "[I]nequality had been rising for more than a decade, leaving the American economy with the most unequal distribution of income in its post-war history. . . . Starting some time in the late 1970s, income inequalities widened alarmingly in America. [T]he share of the Nation's income received by the richest 5 percent of American families rose from 18.6 percent in 1977 to 24.5 percent in 1990, while the share of the poorest 20 percent fell from 5.7 percent to 4.3 percent."[13] Clinton cited two major reasons for this widening gap. First were the policies of his Republican predecessors, which included tax cuts for the upper income brackets along with reductions in social welfare supports. Second were changes in the wage distribution, where those at the top saw large gains in wages, while middle- and lower-income workers saw their wages stagnate.

Whatever the causes of the growing inequality gap, the fact that it is reported in newspapers, commented on by conservative analysts like Phillips, and addressed by the president in his economic report indicate that it is a political issue of some importance. Over the course of U.S. history, there have been periods of growing equality, and like the 1980s, periods of increasing inequality. It is also important to note that both structural change and business cycle change can affect the concentration of wealth.

Phillips argues that when Republicans control government, increasing concentration of wealth among the upper class results. He cites three examples: the Gilded Age, from the end of the Civil War until the turn of the century; the 1920s; and the 1980s. During the Gilded Age the number of millionaires increased, and it is estimated that from 3 to 5 percent of national income redistributed toward the top 1 percent.[14]

Prior to the early 1900s, data on income and the distribution of wealth either do not exist or are unreliable, but since then, we can trace more definitively the ups and downs in wealth concentration. During the 1920s the very wealthy got wealthier, holding ever-increasing percentages of the national income. In part this was tolerated because of the overall growth of the economy. Although the wealthy gained wealth at a faster rate than everyone else, the standard of living of most other Americans also improved.[15]

The Great Depression burst this bubble. The income of the average person plummeted, and standards of living declined precipitously. When Franklin Roosevelt took office, he increased taxes on the wealthy and the corporations, while providing increased assistance to those most in need. These redistributive policies caused the amount of wealth held by the wealthiest to fall. Another ratchet of **redistribution** occurred with the onset of World War II. Redistribution is when assets, like income, are taken from one group and given to another. To finance the war, taxes were increased dramatically and an income tax was instituted. These tax increases were borne most heavily by the upper classes, though it should be noted that standards of living surged during the 1940s at all income levels, and corporations profited handsomely from war contracts. Still, incomes evened out somewhat during the war as workers made wage gains, primarily due to increased employment opportunities, and heavy taxes were levied on all, especially the rich.

With the cessation of the war, the United States entered a twenty-five-year period of enormous economic growth. Productivity registered great gains, and the standard of living improved as a result. Primarily because of this economic base, wealth further redistributed from the upper classes downward, especially to the middle classes. The institution of more generous welfare programs in the 1960s also promoted economic equality. Table 2.1 details these movements.[16] It is important to note here that income is only one source of wealth. Many wealthy people have other sources of wealth, such as property and stocks, that if we could add their values to the figures reported in Table 2.1, would give an even wider gap or concentration of wealth in the upper-income tiers.

By the mid-1970s, the economic engine that had been pushing these equity gains began to slow down. In the 1980s, wealth again became concentrated in the hands of the upper classes. There are many reasons for this redistribution, including the tax cuts implemented during the Reagan years,[17] less generous social welfare spending, the decline of high-paying industrial jobs, and generous pay policies of corporations for their top-line managers. By the 1990s, the degree of economic inequality resembled that of the late 1940s.[18] Although this is a major shift back in economic equalization, income and wealth is more evenly distributed than it was in the 1920s, though the lack of good comparable data does not allow us to assess this very precisely.

TABLE 2.1 Percentage of Families in Select Income Levels, 1947–1994

Year	Poorest Fifth	2nd Fifth	3rd Fifth	4th Fifth	Richest Fifth	Richest 5 Percent
1947	5.0	11.9	17.0	23.1	43.0	17.5
1959	4.9	12.3	17.9	23.8	41.1	15.9
1969	5.6	12.4	17.7	23.7	40.6	15.6
1974	5.5	12.0	17.5	24.0	41.0	15.5
1979	5.2	11.6	17.5	24.1	41.7	15.8
1984	4.7	11.0	17.0	24.4	42.9	16.0
1988	4.6	10.7	16.7	24.0	44.0	17.2
1992	4.4	10.5	16.5	24.0	44.6	17.6
1994	4.2	10.0	15.7	23.3	46.9	20.1

Source: U.S. Census Bureau, *Current Population Reports,* series P-60, no. 146, April 1985, Tables 17 and 184, and September 1993, Table B-7; and no. 191, May 1998, Tables 1 and 2.

When income distribution goes too far in either direction—too concentrated in the hands of the wealthy or too equally distributed—the losers seek government help while the winners aim to protect their gains. Income distribution thus becomes a political issue. Unlike change in economic structure or the business cycle, whose effects often cut across political parties, change in wealth concentration is a highly partisan issue. Although we cannot say that most Republicans are wealthy or upper income, it is the case that more people from the upper economic strata consider themselves to be Republicans than Democrats. Similarly, more from the lower economic strata consider themselves to be Democrats than Republicans. For instance, in 1996, 41 percent of those in the highest income class ($50,000 and over) called themselves Republicans compared with only 19 percent in the lowest income category ($20,000 and under). Further, 47 percent in the lowest income category identified themselves as Democrats compared with only 29 percent in the highest income category.[19] This party standoff has been a constant in U.S. politics since the Depression.

Changes in economic structures, in the business cycle, and in wealth concentration affect people's lives, sometimes for better and sometimes for worse. Each of these kinds of economic changes may become a political issue, as people seek public policies to address them. Making matters more complicated is that all three kinds of change may happen at the same time. When this occurs, it is possible for people to mistake the cause of the economic stress. Consequently, government may not produce policies that deal with the issue most affecting people's lives. How government makes policy in such a complex economic environment is one of the topics we will deal with throughout this book.

THE DEVELOPMENT OF U.S. ECONOMIC POLICY

Over time, the amount of interaction between government and the economy in the United States has generally increased, though there have been important efforts to decouple the two across the past two decades. The increasing interaction between these two sectors is a function, in part, of the growth of government. But it is also a function of increasing attempts by the private sector to influence government policies and secure benefits from government. It is not accurate, however, to depict the interaction between government and the economy as steadily increasing from some mythical, near-zero starting point. Even in the early days of the country, the government did not follow a laissez faire policy. Early American government had important economic policies and tried to steer the development, growth, and direction of the economy, especially with regard to infrastructure and the financial system. Still, it is true that early governments were not as involved with the economy as government is today.

This section briefly traces the history of U.S. economic policy, which can roughly be divided into five eras[20]: building the infrastructure, the era of economic regulation, the rise of the welfare state and macroeconomic regulation, the military-industrial economy, and the social regulatory state. There are no distinct beginnings and endings to these eras; rather, each adds a new dimension of economic policies to the already existing inventory of government economic policies.

We start this history of U.S. economic policy by discussing the British heritage and the Constitution. These serve as the foundation for our nation's economic policies.

The Foundation

The British heritage provided our young country with something to oppose. Primarily, this opposition focused on what was considered excessive state intervention in the economy under the system of mercantilism (see Chapter 1). Mercantilism inhibited the development of capitalist economic institutions, which were striving to emerge in the late eighteenth century. For instance, as already discussed, to operate a business required a government charter, which in many circumstances constituted a monopoly. Moreover, high taxes were imposed on American colonials, the Stamp Act Tax of 1776 being the most infamous. Also, the British Navigation Acts, which required that all imported or exported goods pass through Britain before getting to their final destination, choked economic development in the colonies. As a result, the American colonials not only threw off British rule but also created a culture that was suspicious of government intervention in the economy.

This antipathy toward government intervention expressed itself in the Articles of Confederation, the country's first attempt at a written constitution. To pass commercial, that is, economic, legislation required the support of nine of the thirteen states. Getting nine states to agree on anything was nearly impossible when the divisions between the slaveholding and nonslaveholding states were so severe. Essentially, this clause, requiring such a large majority, blocked the passage of national legislation. The dominant governmental force of the time was the states, not the federal government. Trade wars and barriers between states existed, and currency that was legal tender in one state was unusable in another. Moreover, many states, under pressure of farmers and other debtors, printed money, often without specie, such as gold or silver, to back up the value of the printed paper money. States that printed paper money essentially flooded the economy with currency that was nearly valueless, inciting inflation in many regions and creating disincentives for money centers, like banks and other lending institutions, to lend or invest. The economy was in chaos.

In part to deal with this economic problem, the Constitutional Convention was held. The Constitution that emerged had important consequences for economic policymaking. First, only Congress could impose import duties and tariffs. Further, the states could not restrict the flow of goods across state borders. In effect, the states became the first free trade zone in the world. Second, Congress was responsible for coin money and the national currency. States no longer could print or coin their own local currency. Third, only simple majorities were required to pass commercial legislation, and Congress was granted such legislative power under the commerce clause. Taken together, these provisions gave economic policymaking power to the federal government, though states still possessed local powers, such as the regulation of labor and occupations.[21] The federal government immediately put its policymaking power to use.

Early Years: Building the Infrastructure

It is a common misconception that laissez faire characterized government economic policy in the eighteenth and nineteenth centuries. According to Seymour Martin Lipset, "The doctrine of 'laissez-faire' became dominant only after the growth of large corporations and private investment funds reduced the pressures for public funds"[22] to finance large-scale ventures. Recall from our earlier discussion that the economy was primarily agrarian during the 1700s and early 1800s. This had two consequences for economic policymaking. It was small in scope compared with current policymaking. And it focused on the construction of the infrastructure and the creation of a financial and monetary system to spur economic development. In general, the states led the way in physical infrastructure construction, with the national government's playing a leading role in the development of a monetary and financial system, the financial infrastructure.

Financial Policy

Alexander Hamilton, the first secretary of the Treasury, was architect of the nation's financial system. Three elements made up Hamilton's initial economic policy.[23] First, the national government assumed the debts associated with the Revolutionary War, including those that the states had accrued. This was intended to help bind the states to the new national government and to ensure that the debts were repaid, something that was necessary if the national government was to secure credit in the future.

The second part of the policy developed a method to repay the debts. Hamilton decided not to tax land or property. This would provide an incentive for westward expansion. Instead, he relied on **excise taxes,** especially on whiskey and distilled spirits, and a tariff. The **tariff** passed in 1789 was one of the first acts of Congress. Its aim was twofold. Not only was it used to generate government revenue, but it was discriminatory. Tariffs were held high on goods, especially manufactured items, that could be produced in the

United States but were lower on other goods. This protective tariff helped to expand the manufacturing base of the U.S. economy. Even agrarian sentimentalists, like Thomas Jefferson, supported the expansion of the manufacturing sector to ensure U.S. independence from Europe, especially England, and to provide for the nation's defense. The development of the postal system, roads, and especially harbors were also important elements of Hamilton's economic program to develop the U.S. economy and its manufacturing capabilities.

The third part of the policy was more controversial, the establishment of the U.S. Bank. The bank served two purposes, to lend money to the national government and to serve as a place to deposit government revenues. Most agreed that the second purpose was necessary, although some felt that private banks could discharge that duty. Hamilton, however, saw other purposes for the lending aspects of the bank. Through lending, the government could regulate the value and size of the nation's money supply and thus help divert panics, inflations, and deflations in the currency. It could provide a measure of stability to the nation's currency and attract foreign investment.

The bank was controversial because it helped parts of the economy more than others. In particular, it aided manufacturing over agriculture and creditors over debtors. Manufacturing was aided because stable money with solid interest rates attracted foreign capital, which could be invested in manufacturing concerns or used to purchase bonds, from which manufacturers could also borrow. Long-term, stable sources of money and return on investment were the requirements of the industrializing sector of the economy. Agrarian interests preferred looser money, easier credit, and inflation, which tended to moderate old debts.

Farmers borrowed money each yearly cycle, usually to purchase seed. After their crops were sold, they would repay their loans, the profit being used to secure new loans. Inflation would lower the value of preexisting debts and also increase the price of their crops relative to prices when the loans were taken out. Thus, manufacturing and credit sectors of the economy were often opposed to agricultural and debtor sectors of the economy. This divide was to define much economic policy debate for most of the nineteenth century.

The first bank was chartered for twenty years; however, financial emergencies associated with the War of 1812 led President James Madison, an original opponent of the first bank, to support a charter for the second bank in 1816, again for a twenty-year term. By the 1830s, the second bank, and its manager, Nicholas Biddle, ran afoul of President Andrew Jackson.

Speculation led to inflation, which Biddle dealt with by contracting the money supply. This tight money policy hurt farmers, debtors, and those wanting to move West, the key elements of Jackson's political support base. Creditors supported tight money during inflationary periods to ensure the value of their loans. Debtors, small landowners, farmers, and others who operated under credit favored looser money and easier credit. Jackson vetoed the bank and deposited federal money in state banks, which became the banking mainstay until the reforms that created the Federal Reserve system just prior to World War I.

Physical Infrastructure

The ups and downs of the first and second national banks display a pattern of centralization and decentralization that mirrors the ongoing political debate over whether monetary policy should be under federal control or reserved to the states. In contrast, the country's physical infrastructure development was left almost wholly to the states.

Why is the development of physical infrastructure a government responsibility at all? Consider the case of building a road. A road linking factories to their marketplace would reduce the cost of transportation and the time involved, and increase the ability to deliver wares predictably and timely. Thus, businesses need a good transportation system. However, it is not economical for a business to offer to build a road unless it can keep it exclusive, or private. A private road, though, restricts the market and would be costly to police. A nonexclusive, or public, road, however, raises the problem of the **free rider.** The free-rider problem is that no one wants to pay for something that benefits everyone. The result is that no one will pay for the road and it will not be built. Government often steps in in such circumstances, taxes people, and uses the revenue to build the road.

In effect, the road we are talking about is a **public good.** Public goods are those goods that cannot be divided among people, and people are given the public good whether or not they want to consume it. Defense is a classic public good. **Private goods,** in contrast, are those that, if consumed by one person, cannot be consumed by another. A meal is an example. The free-rider problem affects the provision of public goods, as the road example illustrates. The need to provide public goods is one major justification for government.

Much political debate centers on whether a good is or should be public or private. Confusion exists because some members of society reap extra benefits from the provision of public goods. For instance, defense contractors and their employees reap profits and jobs, private goods. It is often in their interest to convince society to consume more of the public good, defense, than most people might want, in order to increase the profits and job security.

A major activity of state governments during the nineteenth century was the provision of support for physical infrastructure development. States invested heavily in the canal and turnpike systems in the early part of the century. Later in the century they were indispensable to the development of the railroads.

State governments had several ways of dispensing benefits to induce economic activity and infrastructure construction. They granted charters to operate, which were in effect monopolies. Large tracts of land were given to railroads, as well as rights of way. Other subsidies, and even direct investment, were used to stimulate activity. Lipset reports that state governments were often larger investors than private concerns.[24] Foreign investors sometimes preferred not to invest directly in U.S. business concerns, but they would buy government-issued bonds. Government would direct the revenue from these bond sales into these ventures, thereby acting as a venture capitalist but also as an agent for private investors who were concerned about the security of their investment.

State governments also invested heavily in banks, especially after the demise of the second national bank. They used the banks to deposit revenue but also to stimulate lending activity within the state. At times, state governments even owned shares in these state banks.

Early policy also focused on education, developing what we might call the human or labor infrastructure. One action taken by the Congress before passage of the Constitution was the Northwest Ordinance Act. That act, which established procedures for incorporating political bodies in the nation's territories, set aside land in each district for a public school. Although not purely economic in objective, the act established a federal presence in education and institutionalized an early feeling that an educated populace was necessary for the stability and proper functioning of the new democracy.

The Morrill Land Grant College Act, passed in 1863, during the height of the Civil War, built on the earlier act. Each state was given federal land to open a state university, especially one devoted to the agricultural and mechanical arts. Here government policy had a clear economic aim—to provide a skilled work force for the emerging industrial economy.

These early government economic policies were aimed at developing the institutions to allow the economy to prosper and expand. Thus, they were mostly a type of **distributive policy,** a distribution of government resources into the economy to direct, stimulate, and help defray the cost and risk of certain desirable economic behaviors. Here we need to distinguish distributive from redistributive policy, which we discussed on page 7. Whereas redistribution is taking assets, like income, from one group and giving them to another to promote economic equity, distribution is government's giving its assets or financially helping someone or some group to promote economic growth and efficiency. Distribution comes in many forms, from tax breaks to subsidies to guaranteed or low-interest loans.

Government is still involved in promoting the development of the aspects of infrastructure mentioned in this section. Many important current policy issues involve debate over the government's role in education and in the financial and transportation sectors. This gives us a sense of the layering of policies over time, as government has added new policies and functions on top of policies already in place.

The Economic Regulatory State

The distributive policies of the first hundred years had an impact: the nation grew. Labor was in short enough supply that workers had to be imported from other countries. Thus commenced a huge immigration from central, southern, and eastern Europe in the late decades of the 1800s. The manufacturing policies also paid off. By 1900, industrial workers were as numerous as agricultural ones, and by 1920 more people lived in urban than nonurban areas.[25]

Industrial firms grew hugely. The modern corporation was invented after the Civil War, with profound effects for the economy and the polity. Corporations, compared to earlier businesses, were enormous, employing thousands of workers across the entire expanse of the nation. More important, massive concentrations of wealth accumulated in corporate coffers, and economic decisions with broad-ranging effects were made by a relatively small number of corporate managers. Rather than being composed of many small firms, the new industrial economy was more greatly affected by a small number of large firms. In some industries, monopolies existed. In others, large firms banded together and agreed to set prices, supply, and levels of competition. In still others, firms secretly combined into trusts and pools. For example, the Standard Oil trust effectively controlled the oil industry until it was broken up in 1911, and Alcoa held a complete monopoly of the aluminum industry until the dawn of World War II in 1940.[26] Alcoa was unable to meet the military's demand for aluminum, so government officials worked with Reynolds Metal Company to process aluminum, thus increasing aluminum supply and eroding Alcoa's monopoly.

The railroads were the first of the new massive corporate enterprises; they were also the first to feel government regulation. The political impetus for government regulation of business came from small farmers, shippers, and other consumers. The economic rationale for regulation came from the theory of market failure. Market failure occurs when the market does not operate efficiently, according to the laws of supply and demand. Goods, in essence, may be over- or underproduced. There are many sources of market failure, including limited competition.

Railroads engaged in a number of practices that hurt small farmers, shippers, and consumers, especially those living in the midwestern and western regions of the nation. Railroads discriminated against these customers in favor of large industrial concerns, like the oil and steel companies. Secret rebates were offered to large shippers, as were preferences in loading and delivery. Shippers in urban areas or areas served by multiple railways were offered lower rates. Those in small towns and rural areas served by one rail line often faced monopolistically high rates, as the railroads lowered rates to unprofitable levels on competitive lines to meet or beat their competition, while making up the loss on noncompetitive routes.

As a consequence of these practices, many of the midwestern states passed Granger laws in the 1870s.[27] The Granger laws regulated the railroads, including their rates, but the Supreme Court struck them down, arguing that states could not regulate interstate commerce.[28] In 1887, the federal government began the regulation of the railroads with the passage of the Interstate

Commerce Act. That act established the Interstate Commerce Commission (ICC) and created a new type of governmental body, the independent regulatory commission. Independent regulatory commissions were given fairly wide discretion to implement the laws under their jurisdiction. Moreover, they were designed to limit partisan political interference and control.

Three years later, in 1890, Congress passed another landmark piece of regulatory legislation, the Sherman Antitrust Act. This act gave the newly created Antitrust Division of the Justice Department power to dismantle monopolies and trusts. The Standard Oil trust was perhaps the most famous, but other trusts existed in the aluminum, meatpacking, and tobacco industries, among others. Trusts were often able to engage in monopolistic behavior and thereby control their markets.

The Interstate Commerce and Sherman Acts had several features in common. First, both displayed a belief in the market.[29] Their goal was to correct for market failures, basically the tendency toward monopoly and anticompetitive behaviors. Second, both statutes were founded on confidence in government. In both cases, regulatory bureaucrats were granted immense discretion to fulfill their mandates. There was a belief at this time that government could act in a nonpartisan manner to further the public good and that it could do this by employing scientific and business management techniques. Those who held this belief were called Progressives, discussed earlier in this chapter. During the Progressive era, roughly 1880–1920, government not only took on regulatory activities but also increased its capacity to govern, administer, and regulate behavior.[30]

Early regulatory efforts at the ICC and Antitrust Division were hampered by vague statutes and a narrow reading of regulatory powers by the Supreme Court. The Court, for instance, forbade the ICC to set rates. In response, Congress passed reform legislation in both areas, expanding and tightening the regulatory powers of these agencies and creating new ones. By the 1920s, the ICC not only had the power to set rail rates and routes but also regulated water commerce, telegraphs and telephones, and trucks. Antitrust laws were bolstered in 1914 with the passage of the Clayton Antitrust and Federal Trade acts. Congress created the Federal Trade Commission, which could regulate deceptive and uncompetitive behaviors, as well as attack monopolies and trusts. Regulation of other areas also ensued. In 1906, the Food and Drug Act was passed, and hydroelectric power and radio came under regulation in 1920 with the passage of the Federal Power Act and Federal Radio Act. Regulation is still an important issue today and provides another example of the layering of government economic policy over time.

One of the most important actions of this period established the Federal Reserve System and Federal Reserve Board in 1913. One of the aims of the Federal Reserve System was to enable government to respond to the financial panics that had plagued the monetary and financial systems of the nation periodically ever since Andrew Jackson destroyed the second national bank in the 1830s.

Financial panics occur when major bank creditors, such as depositors, call in their assets from banks. This forces banks to call in the money that they loaned out long before the loans' due dates. Panic ensues when other depositors follow suit, withdrawing money from their banks in fear that the bank will not be able to cover its financial obligations to its creditors and depositors. The panic of 1907 had just such calamitous effects when British depositors began withdrawing money from U.S. banks. The panic was so widespread that a consortium of bankers led by J. P. Morgan had to pool resources to stabilize the financial markets. This show of immense power by Morgan led government reformers to propose a governmental system to deal with this issue, rather than leaving it in the hands of private-sector bankers.[31]

During this era the doctrine of laissez faire became the rationale for business opposition to government regulation.[32] Accompanying this development was a belief in **Social Darwinism,** which also was used to justify laissez faire economic policies. Social Darwinism borrowed from Charles Darwin's ideas about evolution and the conception of survival of the fittest to justify nonintervention of the government in the economy, as well as the existence of monopolies. Social Darwinists argued that the market and competition among firms and industries produced an economic effect much like the one Darwin suggested takes place in the natural world. Only those species (companies and people) that can adapt to competition and changing conditions will survive. If government comes to the aid of those who cannot adapt and compete, economic and social welfare will be sacrificed.

The regulatory era did not mean the death knell of distributive policies or of programs to stimulate and subsidize economic activities. Cabinet status was given to business with the establishment of the Commerce and Labor Department in 1904; ten years later Commerce and Labor were split into two departments. Agricultural assistance programs were expanded, and government still relied on tariffs to generate revenue and protect industry. During the regulatory era, distributive-subsidization policy continued, but a layer of regulation was added to government economic intervention in the economy.

The Welfare State and Regulation of the Business Cycle

The laissez faire mentality reached its height in the 1920s, a period of economic expansion, rising standards of living, and increasing concentration of wealth. The last was tolerated because most Americans saw an improvement in their economic life. Accumulation of wealth among the rich and corporations was justified because in general they invested their resources wisely, generating even more wealth, which "trickled down" the economy, improving everyone's economic circumstances.

The laissez faire bubble burst with the stock market crash of October 1929 and the depression that followed. The **Great Depression** was severe and long lasting, with profound effects. Probably only the Civil War was more socially destructive and disruptive to the United States than the Depression. For instance, the gross national product (GNP), a measure of the size of the economy, stood at $827 billion in 1929 (in constant dollars). In 1933, the depth of the Depression, the GNP stood at $590 billion, a decline in the size of the economy of 29 percent. As late as 1939, the economy had recovered only to the level reached in 1929, with the 1939 economy's totaling $844 billion. Unemployment figures also reveal the depth and longevity of the Depression. In 1929, unemployment was a modest 3.2 percent. In 1933, it reached almost 25 percent, and in 1939, it still stood at about 17 percent.[33] Unemployment had devastating effects on families during the Depression because the norm then was one wage earner per family. When unemployment hit, there were no wages to fall back on, nor were government aid programs very extensive.

As a consequence of the depth and longevity of the Depression, public confidence in the ability of the market to restore economic growth crumbled. The public, although reluctant to accept a high degree of government control over the economy, began to look to government as an institution that could help the economy and soften the harshness of the Depression. Still, the public was not supportive of radical redistribution efforts or the nationalization of industry by government.[34]

Into this atmosphere stepped Franklin D. Roosevelt. On soundly defeating incumbent Herbert Hoover in the 1932 election, Roosevelt began a program termed the **New Deal,** which had three basic goals: to get the economy moving again, to provide assistance to those most in need, and to redistribute economic wealth and power. Despite these goals, the New Deal was not a fully articulated or integrated program. Rather, it was a set of experiments, and thus was often full of contradictions, failures, and unnoted successes.

The New Deal came in two waves, the first associated with Roosevelt's first term in office, the second coming with his reelection in 1936. The first New Deal was very much a patchwork of ideas, many responsive to immediate emergencies, such as calling for a bank holiday to calm the banking panic sweeping the nation. The second New Deal was a somewhat more coherent package of policies, which focused more on using "fiscal policy to stimulate growth" than the patchwork approach that was used in the first New Deal.[35]

The turn to fiscal approaches, that is, increasing government spending, to stimulate the economy was a solution that British economist John Maynard Keynes also promoted. Although Roosevelt's New Deal was not avowedly Keynesian, in the sense of explicitly implementing Keynes's economic ideas, it marked the beginning of government use of Keynesian ideas to manage the economy.[36] We will discuss this in more detail in Chapter 8.

To stimulate the economy, Roosevelt insisted on a broad regulatory and reform framework. First and foremost, he wanted to restore confidence in the basic economic institutions. Banks had failed by the thousands, and millions of people saw their life savings wiped out. To restore confidence, the Federal Deposit Insurance Program (FDIC) was begun, whereby the federal government insures deposits. The stock market, where insider trading and panic exacerbated the crisis and the Depression, was reformed, and a new agency, the Securities and Exchange Commission, was created to oversee it. **Insider trading** was prohibited (insider trading occurs when people who know about a corporate decision prior to its being made public act on that information by buying or selling stocks; thus, before the stock market crash that incited the Depression, many market insiders sold their stocks before their prices tumbled, knowing that the prices would drop on the next day). In addition, stock trading was regulated, and lending to purchase stock was separated from selling stocks. New Deal programs added another layer of regulation in specific industries, like telecommunications and air transport, regulated by the Federal Communications Commission and the Civil Aeronautics Board. The goal was to protect newly emerging industries and technologies that, it was hoped, would provide economic growth and jobs.

The New Deal expanded the scope and scale of regulation beyond that of the Progressive era at the turn of the century. Regulation traditionally sought to restrict the behavior of economic agents. For instance, the ICC set railroad rates. But many New Deal regulatory bodies were created with the aim of stimulating new economic enterprises and industries. Valuable rights to transmit over the airwaves were given to telecommunications firms to expand that industry, and air routes with limited competition were given to air carriers to help stabilize and expand the transportation industry. Many New Deal regulations were, thus, similar to the distributive and subsidization programs of earlier eras.

One New Deal innovation was federal acceptance of a social welfare role. Prior to the New Deal, welfare had been a function of charities and of a few states, like New York. With the New Deal, a broad social welfare establishment was initiated. Thus began the social security program. That program included two parts, social insurance and public assistance. Understanding the ethic of self-reliance in the United States, Roosevelt figured it would be more politically and socially palatable to build the system around the insurance model. In this model, workers and employers would contribute through payroll deductions into an insurance pool. Workers would feel a property right to social security benefits on retirement, and the system would not be stigmatized as charity or relief. A smaller public assistance, or welfare, program was also initiated, packaged in the Social Security Act and geared to the blind and to children. The Social Security Act was passed in 1935.

Equally important were the New Deal employment and public works policies. Vast numbers of unemployed persons were hired by the government, mostly for public works, like road and bridge construction and conservation. The two most famous of these programs were the Civilian Conservation

Corps (CCC) and the Work Projects Administration (WPA). The objective was to stimulate demand by putting money directly into people's pockets. Also, by requiring them to contribute to the nation through their labor, these programs would enable them to retain their dignity in a society that still sneered at charity. Rather than rely on traditional trickle-down policies, which focused on investment and supply, this New Deal effort proposed to stimulate the economy by creating demand.

The third goal of the New Deal involved redistribution of economic wealth and power. The public works programs and stimulation of consumer demand illustrate one aspect of the power shift away from the scions of capital and toward consumers. Increased tax rates on those with the highest incomes were also employed for such ends, as well as to generate revenue.

There has been much controversy over the nature and effect of the New Deal. Some point to the increases in government intervention in the economy to suggest that during the New Deal the federal government came to exercise too much control over the economy. Others argue that the New Deal was fundamentally conservative in that it aimed to shore up existing capitalist institutions. The private economy was never undermined. Roosevelt wanted to save capitalism, not replace it.[37]

Another controversy focuses on the impact of the New Deal. Michael Lewis-Beck and Peverill Squire argue that the New Deal was not really very innovative.[38] Many of the policy directions in regulation and the scope of government began in the 1920s under Herbert Hoover. Moreover, despite the attention and energy put into the New Deal, it may not have been very effective. The economy did not regain its 1928 level until 1939, and it took World War II to bring it into full recovery. Further, although Roosevelt proposed several budget deficits in the 1930s, he still believed in a balanced budget. In 1938, when he tried to reduce the deficit, the nation actually fell into recession. Adoption of Keynesian policies to stimulate the economy was slow to come. Roosevelt never fully accepted them, though his policies often moved in directions that Keynes approved of. It was not until John F. Kennedy became president, twenty years later, that Keynesianism fully arrived as an articulated economic policy.[39]

Still, it is clear that many of the policies first articulated during the Great Depression had a profound and lasting impact on the U.S. government and economic policy. For instance, social security still exists and is one of the largest items in the U.S. government budget. How to ensure its financial solvency into the future is a current major issue. Ideas that government should be involved in the economic welfare of its citizens and should regulate the business cycle, ideas that began during the era of the Great Depression, are also still with us today. It may be the case that the ideas and policies of the Great Depression era had a greater effect on how we think about the role of government in the economy than those of any other era in U.S. history. This underscores the importance of that era to our lives today and illustrates again the layering of policy that characterizes U.S. economic policymaking.

In 1946 the federal government took formal responsibility for the state of the economy with the passage of the Full Employment Act. This institution-alized economic intervention policies designed to smooth the business cycle, adding another layer of economic policies to those already present. This act can be considered the final piece of New Deal legislation, settling until the late 1970s the issue of whether government should intervene in the economy. For the next thirty years, government intervention would be an accepted and common approach to dealing with economic problems and issues.

The Military-Industrial Economy

Historically, the United States has demobilized its military to rather low lev-els with the cessation of wars. At the conclusion of World War II, however, a large military establishment remained in place for the first time in U.S. his-tory. The cold war, the rivalry between the United States and the Soviet Union, led policymakers, for the first time in U.S. history, to keep a large standing army during peacetime. Keeping as many as two million personnel in uniform and another one million as civilian support staff had huge impli-cations, not only for U.S. foreign relations but for the economy as well.

One important implication was that a large segment of the economy be-came tied to government military spending. Whole communities became, in effect, government company towns, with either military bases or defense contracting firms providing the bulk of local employment. Ups and downs in local economies were affected by changes in government military and defense spending policies. Local economic implications became one driving factor in defense spending issues, in addition to expected defense needs. The size of military spending became so important to the economy that business cycles could be influenced by expansions or contractions in such spending. A sort of "military Keynesianism" seemed to operate, where military spending was used for its economic effects.

In addition, a new concentration of corporate wealth resulted from mili-tary spending policies. The military, beginning in World War II, felt that small firms could not deliver on the huge orders that it was placing for equipment, supplies, and arms. To ensure an uninterrupted supply to U.S. fighting forces, military decision makers funneled the bulk of their orders to large firms with the capacity to meet their requests.[40] This practice continued during the cold war. A new set of extremely large corporations emerged, some of which were almost entirely dependent on military contracts for their existence.

From this, a tight relationship developed between the defense establish-ment and military contractors, a relationship described by President Dwight D. Eisenhower as the **military-industrial complex.** The military saw the con-tinued existence of these companies as necessary to ensure the nation's de-fense, and the companies saw military contracts as their economic lifeline. Both parties saw mutual advantage in helping each other.

Into this web, smaller contractors and members of Congress were recruited. The large contractors thought they could increase their influence in Congress by subcontracting to smaller firms spread around the nation. This would create an economic presence for the military across many congressional districts. As a result, many members of Congress became supporters of military spending projects. Again, local economic concerns became an element of military spending and procurement policy.

Finally, national security became an important rationale for nondefense programs. Everyone could rally behind defense needs; politics stopped at the water's edge. Coalitions of conservatives, who supported defense, and liberals, who wanted to expand social programs, could be brought together if the social program was given a defense rationale. Thus, in the 1950s, the highway construction program was labeled the Highway Defense Act, and federal aid to higher education was called the National Defense Education Act.

The Social Regulatory State

In the 1960s and 1970s, government intervention in the economy expanded greatly. The size of social welfare and entitlement programs increased, and the government began to experiment with a new type of regulation, social regulation. The stimulating factor in this expansion was Lyndon Johnson's landslide election in 1964. Johnson put together a program, called the **Great Society,** that had profound effects on the relationship between the government and the economy. The country seemed ready for such a trend. Public opinion was at its most liberal,[41] and the public philosophy about the role of government was greatly revised.[42] Reducing risk—protecting people—became the foundation for new government excursions into the economy.

The size and number of social welfare programs increased during the 1960s and 1970s. Social security, the largest program, saw its benefits liberalized with the institution of the **cost-of-living adjustment (COLA)** in 1976. Before that, Congress determined payment levels. Often, payment increases came after a need was demonstrated, meaning that the many senior citizens who lived primarily on their social security retirement checks were living near the edge of poverty. The COLA adjustment was set quarterly and was pegged to the increase in the cost of living (the consumer inflation rate).

Other social welfare programs were added during these years, such as food stamps and worker training. Among the most important and fastest growing were the federal medical insurance programs, Medicare and Medicaid. Medicare was a companion to social security in that it was geared toward senior citizens. Like social security, Medicare was paid for through employee payroll deductions. Medicaid was directed to the impoverished. Funding for that program was a state responsibility, though the program was standardized at the federal level with the federal government's setting payment levels to doctors and determining which medical procedures would be covered. Both social security and the medical insurance programs are **entitlements;** that is, all who qualify for these benefits receive them.

Part of the rationale for these programs can be found in the postwar economic expansion. After World War II, the U.S. economy sustained one of its longest and steadiest growth periods. The standard of living of most Americans improved, fear of depression was extinguished, and the United States came to be thought of as the richest nation in the world with the most economically privileged citizens. In such a climate of affluence and abundance, many felt that the country could afford to redistribute some of its wealth to help the impoverished and the elderly. Others held an even more extreme position—that it was immoral for poverty to exist alongside such wealth.

The second major aspect of government expansion into the economy in the 1960s and 1970s was through regulation. Numerous regulatory statutes were enacted into law, new types of problems were regulated, and the pace of government regulatory rule writing increased. These regulations differed from those of the Progressive and New Deal eras in their emphasis on such social issues as pollution, health, and consumer protection.

The Progressive and New Deal regulations were mainly economic in orientation. Thus, they regulated the business and competitive practices of industries and firms in those industries. The new social regulations cast a wider net. Rather than focusing on any one industry, they often spanned the whole economy, affecting everyone and every firm. Moreover, they focused on the **spillovers** of economic activity, rather than on actual business behaviors.

Spillovers, which are also called **externalities,** are those effects of an economic activity that are felt by those not directly involved in the economic activity. Externalities can have negative or positive consequences. **Negative externalities** hurt those who are not part of the economic transaction. Pollution is a prime example. Industrial activity and manufacturing may lead to air pollution. People who do not purchase a particular product may breathe the polluted air. In some cases their health will be affected. Three types of regulations from the 1960s and 1970s stand out—regulations on environmental pollution, worker safety and health, and consumer protection.

These regulatory policies differ from past government economic policies also in terms of the public ethic behind them. Until the New Deal, self-reliance was the ethic that ruled the economy. People were expected to take care of themselves, and the economy was believed to be self-correcting. With the New Deal, the public ethic changed. People were still held responsible for themselves—the ethic of individualism remained—but government was expected to play a role, to ensure that the conditions for economic prosperity prevailed and to help the economy when it veered from that course. According to Samuel Beer, the new public ethic emphasized government's responsibility to ensure and protect people before harm could even come to them, but without a corresponding citizen responsibility or duty to the state.[43] Government should now regulate through command, often usurping private decision making. Its role was now to eliminate many of the risks of life in a modern industrial society.

The Deregulatory Impulse

The size and scope of government in the United States, as well as the ethic of reliance on government, came under attack from many quarters in the late 1970s, an attack that has continued into the 1990s. This was not the first time that government intervention in the economy had come under attack. Andrew Jackson railed against federal government involvement in banking with the second national bank in the mid-1830s, and the Supreme Court stymied much government regulation from the late 1880s through the mid-1930s, declaring many programs, agencies, and activities unconstitutional.

This latest attack, however, was widespread and had a strong popular base. It also had an ideological character, as many wanted to replace the ethic of reliance on government with the more traditional ethic of self-reliance, substitute market decision making for government decision making, and curb equity in favor of efficiency.

The attack on government began in the mid-1970s with criticism from liberals about many government regulations.[44] Liberals, in modern U.S. politics, tend to support government intervention in the economy, promote economic equality, and call for a smaller military establishment. Conservatives tend to take the opposite positions on these issues. In particular, liberals attacked many of the economic regulations of the Progressive and New Deal eras. They argued that these regulations had been perverted from their original intent, which was to protect consumers. They also argued that regulations in many industries were no longer needed, as the fledgling, vulnerable industries were now quite secure and profitable. These critics made the case that government economic regulation of such industries as transportation (railroads, trucking, airlines), banking, and telecommunications in fact subsidized these businesses, which were able, because of regulatory protection, to extract higher prices than would exist if competitive markets were in place. Furthermore, government economic regulation hindered innovation in those industries, limited consumer choice, and left unmet much consumer demand for products and services.

Shortly thereafter, conservatives joined in, attacking regulation more broadly. They criticized economic regulation for many of the same reasons as liberals but also argued that government regulation imposed a drag, or cost, on the economy, lowered productivity, fueled inflation, and lessened the international competitiveness of U.S. goods. This economywide assessment allowed conservatives to attack social regulations, such as environmental, worker safety, and consumer product protection, as well. During the 1970s, the transportation, banking, and telecommunications industries saw major deregulatory acts, and under President Reagan, social regulatory agencies suffered major budget cuts, though their regulatory mandates remained intact.

On the state level, a taxpayer revolt materialized in the late 1970s.[45] It began in California, where voters put on the ballot a rollback in property taxes in 1978. The success of the California revolt was repeated in other states. That revolt also came to the national government with the election of Ronald Reagan in 1980. With Reagan's election, many of these antigovernment feelings came together into a program called **Reaganomics.** Reaganomics represented a shift in policy from the equity approaches that had dominated government policy since the New Deal to a more market oriented, efficiency approach. Taxes and program cuts redistributed wealth away from government and its beneficiaries to the private sector, and business was allowed to make decisions with less government interference. Social welfare programs were also scaled back, though public outcry limited that effort and forced the Reagan administration to argue that the **social safety net** would not be cut; only inefficient, overly generous, or unnecessary benefits would be eliminated. The social safety net is the complex of government policies to provide aid to the poor, elderly, and disabled to prevent them from falling into poverty and/or from suffering too gravely because of impoverishment.

The taxpayer revolt seemed so popular and powerful that politicians were afraid to increase taxes very much to offset the rising deficits of the 1980s and 1990s. In 1988, George Bush's pledge not to raise taxes played a large role in his successful bid for the presidency.

Economic Policymaking in the 1990s

Some of the trends evident in the 1980s continued into the 1990s. But with a Democratic administration in power, shifts in policy direction are also notable. Further, the state of the economy altered in the 1990s. Our three themes of changes in economic structure, changes in wealth distribution, and changes in the business cycle will help us organize our observations about economics and economic policy in the 1990s.

First, in the 1990s, the United States was clearly on the road to transforming into a postindustrial economy, if it was not already one. However, economic inequality is still much wider than it was twenty years ago, and there are only small hints at a possible redirection toward greater income and wealth equality. Last, the economy was still in the expansion phase of the business cycle in the late 1990s, with the last recession's occurring in 1991–1992. The speed with which the business cycle moves may alter this condition rapidly, however.

The relatively long period of sustained economic growth and expansion across the decade, along with low unemployment and low inflation, has created a sense of economic optimism within the U.S. populace, at least in the short run. Despite some ups and downs in the stock markets in 1997 and

1998, due in part to the financial crisis in East Asia, Americans continue to pour money into the stock markets and similar investments.

The other side of the popular mood with regard to the government and the economy is a general preference for smaller government with less regulation and government intervention in the economy. President Clinton gave voice to this mood in his second Inaugural Address (January 20, 1997), when he uttered these word: "As times change, so government must change. We need a new government for a new century—humble enough not to try to solve all our problems for us, but strong enough to give us the tools to solve our problems for ourselves; a government that is smaller, lives within its means, and does more with less. . . . The preeminent mission of our new government is to give all Americans an opportunity—not a guarantee, but a real opportunity—to build better lives."

However much the era of big government may be over, there is much government activity on the economic front. In late July 1998, congressional Republicans threatened the cable television industry with rate regulation if the industry did not slow the pace of rate increases. As mentioned in Chapter 1, antitrust actions against Microsoft and Intel were initiated in 1998. Also the budget situation turned around. Deficits, resulting from the government's spending more money than it collects in taxes and other revenue forms, gave way to surpluses, resulting from the government's spending less than it collects, beginning with the budget of 1998. This seemed to have stemmed the call to roll back on many distributive programs. Instead, funding increases were granted to some distributive programs, like the large transportation funding bill, which Congress passed in 1998. On the other hand, the military-industrial side of the political economy has been scaled back considerably ever since the fall of the former Soviet Union.

Before we can understand economic policy, we need to know something about how such policies are made. The logical place to begin is with those who influence and make economic policies. In the next chapters, we look at those people who influence economic policy decisions, beginning with the general public in Chapter 3.

CONCLUSION

Economic change causes stress. As people try to adapt, slow down, or take advantage of the changes, economic issues may become politicized, and in some instances economic policies may be implemented. Three major kinds of economic change are changes in structure, in business cycles, and in wealth distribution. Each type of change has stimulated government policy action at some time in American history. Table 2.2 summarizes the economic and policy changes and developments discussed in this chapter.

TABLE 2.2 Summary of Economic and Policy Changes and Developments over U.S. History

| Decade | Economic State | | | Policy Regime‡ |
	Economic Structure	Business Cycle (major downturns)*	Economic Equality†	
1790s	Agrarian			Distributive policy
1800s				
1810s				
1820s		1818–1820		
1830s		1836–1837		
1840s		1839–1843		
1850s		1857		
1860s				
1870s		1873–1879	Increasing inequality	
1880s		1884–1885		Plus regulation and antitrust
1890s	Industrial	1893–1897		
1900s				
1910s		1913–1914	Increasing equality	
1920s		1920–1921	Increasing inequality	
1930s		1929–1940	Increasing equality	Plus welfare state
1940s		1946–1949		Plus military-industrial state
1950s		1958		
1960s			Increasing equality	Plus Great Society
1970s		1973–74, 1979–80		
1980s	Postindustrial	1981–1982	Increasing inequality	Plus deregulation
1990s		1990–1991		

*From Gary W. Copeland, "When Congress and the President Collide: Why Presidents Veto Legislation," *Journal of Politics* 45 (November): 704; and John P. Frendreis and Raymond Tatalovich, *The Modern Presidency and Economic Policy* (Itasca, IL: Peacock, 1994), 171–172.

†From Kevin Phillips, *The Politics of Rich and Poor* (New York: Random House, 1990).

‡Terms indicate new types of policies added to the types of policies already in existence.

Policy responses across U.S. history have ranged from laissez faire to regulation. In different historical periods, different economic policy styles or regimes have been more popular than others, although the government rarely discards preexisting economic policies. Instead, a new set of economic policies is offered, and some old policies may be updated. Only within the last twenty years has there been a widespread attempt to dismantle previous economic policies. This has met with some success, but much of the past still exists.

To summarize, the several types of economic change, the varying policy responses to them, the different styles of different historical eras, and the reluctance to do away with the old has led to an incoherence in U.S. economic policymaking. There is a bewildering array of government economic policies, some of which work at cross-purposes. But there is also a stability to our economic policy because so many policies are continued for long periods of time. This stability prevents wild swings from one kind of economic policy to another, with all the disruption and confusion such sharp changes in direction would cause.

Key Terms

business cycle
corporation
cost-of-living
  adjustment
  (COLA)
cycle of
  equality-
  inequality
distributive policy
economic
  contraction
economic
  expansion
economic peak
economic trough

entitlements
excise taxes
externalities
free rider
Great Depression
Great Society
insider trading
managed capitalism
military-industrial
  complex
negative externalities
New Deal
panics
postindustrial era
private goods

Progressive movement
public good
Reaganomics
recession
redistribution
Social Darwinism
social safety net
spillovers
tariff

Explore the Web

There are several good places to find historical statistics on the economy and how it has developed. The Census Bureau keeps a good record on its easily useable page at http://www.census.gov/. A major government publication, the *Statistical Abstract of the United States,* also published by the Census Bureau, is online at http://www.census.gov/statab/www/. A central site where one can find economic and other statistics and information for a large number of federal government agencies is FEDSTATS at http://www.fedstats.gov/.

Notes

1. There are many good histories of the U.S. economy. I have found Mansel G. Blackford and K. Austin Kerr, *Business Enterprise in American History*, 3d ed. (Boston: Houghton Mifflin, 1994), very informative.

2. James R. Beniger, *The Control Revolution: Technological and Economic Origins of the Information Society* (Cambridge, MA: Harvard University Press, 1986), 23.

3. The figures come from the U.S. Department of Commerce, Bureau of the Census, *Historical Statistics of the United States: Colonial Times to 1970* (Washington, DC: U.S. Government Printing Office, 1975), series K2, A69, A6. Also see Douglas North, *The Economic Growth of the United States, 1790–1860* (Englewood Cliffs, NJ: Prentice-Hall, 1961).

4. There are a number of good histories of this transformation. The most famous is Alfred D. Chandler, Jr., *The Visible Hand: The Managerial Revolution in American Business* (Cambridge, MA: Harvard University Press, 1977). On the importance of the railroads to the industrial development of the United States, see Alfred D. Chandler, Jr., ed., *The Railroads: The Nation's First Big Business* (New York: Harcourt, Brace, & World, 1965). Also see Blackford and Kerr, *Business Enterprise in American History*.

5. Richard S. Tedlow, *New and Improved: The Story of Mass Marketing in America* (New York: Basic Books, 1990), gives a good overview of the history of advertising and the importance of brand-name loyalty.

6. The literature on the Progressive movement is voluminous. The classic treatment is Richard Hofstadter, *The Age of Reform: From Bryan to F.D.R.* (New York: Knopf, 1955). On the Progressives and the uses of government, see another classic study, Gabriel Kolko, *Railroads and Regulation, 1877–1916* (Princeton, NJ: Princeton University Press, 1965). On the anti-immigrant attitudes of Progressives, see Leslie W. Koepplin, *A Relationship of Reform: Immigrants and Progressives in the Far West* (New York: Garland, 1990).

7. See Blackford and Kerr, *Business Enterprise in American History*, 229–237.

8. I have found Beniger, *The Control Revolution*, to be the best discussion of the development and consequences of this change in the economy and society. He offers a comprehensive bibliography of related material, and on pp. 4–5, he identifies scores of related works. Wilson P. Dizard, Jr., *The Coming Information Age: An Overview of Technology, Economics, and Politics*, 3d ed. (New York: Longman, 1989), gives a good overview. Political changes are chronicled and analyzed in the work of Ronald Inglehart, *Culture Shift in Advanced Industrial Society* (Princeton, NJ: Princeton University Press, 1990).

9. These figures are estimated from John P. Frendreis and Raymond Tatalovich, *The Modern Presidency and Economic Policy* (Itasca, IL: Peacock, 1994), 171–172.

10. On the impact of business cycles on the public mood, see Robert Durr, "What Moves Policy Sentiment?" *American Political Science Review* 87 (1993): 158–170.

11. Keith Bradsher, "Nation's Economic Equality Erodes," *Topeka Capital-Journal,* April 17, 1995, 1A, 6A. This story originally ran in the *New York Times* and was syndicated across the nation.

12. Kevin Phillips, *The Politics of Rich and Poor: Wealth and the American Electorate in the Reagan Aftermath* (New York: Random House, 1990).

13. The quotes are taken from his 1994 economic report.

14. Phillips, *The Politics of Rich and Poor,* 57.

15. *Historical Statistics of the United States,* series G338.

16. The table is partially adapted from William E. Hudson, *American Democracy in Peril: Seven Challenges to America's Future* (Chatham, NJ: Chatham House, 1995), 235, and updated with more recent Census Bureau reports.

17. This case is made in Douglas A. Hibbs, *The American Political Economy: Macroeconomics and Electoral Politics* (Cambridge, MA: Harvard University Press, 1987).

18. Many researchers have tried to document and understand the sources of the growing income gap over the past twenty years. See, for instance, Sheldon Danziger and Peter Gottschalk, *America Unequal* (Cambridge, MA: Harvard University Press, 1995); Nan L. Maxwell, *Income Inequality in the United States, 1947–1985* (New York: Greenwood, 1990); and Joel Slemrod, ed., *Tax Progressivity and Income Inequality* (New York: Cambridge University Press, 1994).

19. Harold W. Stanley and Richard G. Niemi, *Vital Statistics on American Politics, 1997–1998* (Washington, DC: CQ Press, 1998), 111.

20. Marc Allen Eisner, *The State in the American Political Economy* (Englewood Cliffs, NJ: Prentice-Hall, 1995), was extremely valuable in helping me prepare the following sections.

21. On early regulation of occupations and labor by the states, see Jonathan R. T. Hughes, *The Governmental Habit Redux: Economic Controls from Colonial Times to the Present* (Princeton, NJ: Princeton University Press, 1991).

22. Seymour Martin Lipset, *The First New Nation: The United States in Historical and Comparative Perspective* (New York: Basic Books, 1963), 59.

23. Forrest McDonald, *The Presidency of George Washington* (Lawrence: University Press of Kansas, 1974), 47–64.

24. Lipset, *The First New Nation,* 58–60.

25. David B. Robertson and Dennis R. Judd, *The Development of American Public Policy: The Structure of Policy Restraint* (Glenview, IL: Scott, Foresman, 1989), 36.

26. On the Standard Oil trust, see Daniel Yergin, *The Prize: The Epic Quest for Oil, Money, and Power* (New York: Simon & Schuster, 1991). The Alcoa monopoly is discussed in Doris Kearns Goodwin, *No Ordinary Time: Franklin and Eleanor Roosevelt: The Home Front in World War II* (New York: Simon & Schuster, 1994), 259–261.

27. On the Granger movement and the laws that it spawned, see Gabriel Kolko, *Railroads and Regulation, 1877–1916* (Princeton, NJ: Princeton University Press, 1965).

28. That case was *Wabash, St. Louis and Pacific Railway Co.* v. *Illinois* (U.S., 1886).

29. Marc Allen Eisner, *Regulatory Politics in Transition* (Baltimore, MD: Johns Hopkins University Press, 1993).

30. Stephen Skowronek, *Building a New American State: The Expansion of National Administrative Capacities, 1877–1920* (New York: Cambridge University Press, 1982).

31. The panic of 1907 is discussed in Blackford and Kerr, *Business Enterprise in American History,* 212; and Edwin Palmer Hoyt, *The House of Morgan* (New York: Dodd, Mead, 1966).

32. Lipset, *The First New Nation.*

33. These figures come from Harold W. Stanley and Richard G. Niemi, *Vital Statistics on American Politics,* 3d ed. (Washington, DC: CQ Press, 1992), 410, 425.

34. Details on public attitudes toward economic policies in the 1930s are found in Benjamin I. Page and Robert Y. Shapiro, *The Rational Public: Fifty Years of Trends in Americans' Policy Preferences* (Chicago: University of Chicago Press, 1992), 127–129.

35. Frendreis and Tatalovich, *The Modern Presidency and Economic Policy,* 27–30.

36. Herbert Stein, *The Fiscal Revolution in America* (Chicago: University of Chicago Press, 1969).

37. The literature on the New Deal is vast. Studies that argue that the New Deal was not very radical and aimed more to shore up capitalism than control it include Kenneth Finegold and Theda Skocpol, *State and Party in America's New Deal* (Madison: University of Wisconsin Press, 1995); Ellis Wayne Hawley, *The New Deal and the Problem of Monopoly: A Study in Economic Ambivalence* (New York: Fordham University Press, 1995); Mark Hugh Leff, *The Limits of Symbolic Reform: The New Deal and Taxation, 1933–1939* (New York: Cambridge University Press, 1984); and James Stuart Olson, *Saving Capitalism: The Reconstruction Finance Corporation and the New Deal, 1933–1940* (Princeton, NJ: Princeton University Press, 1988). More positive assessments of the New Deal that view it as a period of major social change include William E. Leuchtenberg, *Franklin D. Roosevelt and the New Deal* (New York: Harper & Row, 1963); William Ranulf Brock, *Welfare, Democracy, and the New Deal* (New York: Cambridge University Press, 1988); and George Wolfskill and John A. Hudson, *All but the People: Franklin D. Roosevelt and His Critics, 1933–1939* (New York: Macmillan, 1969). Two collections present many differing views of the New Deal: Melvyn Dubofsky, ed., *The New Deal: Conflicting Interpretations and Shifting Perspectives* (New York: Garland, 1992); and Robert Eden, ed., *The New Deal and Its Legacy: Critique and Reappraisal* (New York: Greenwood, 1989).

38. Michael Lewis-Beck and Peverill Squire, "The Transformation of the American State: The New Era-New Deal Test," *Journal of Politics* 53 (1991): 106–121.

39. Stein, *The Fiscal Revolution in America.*

40. Blackford and Kerr, *Business Enterprise in American History,* 285–288.

41. James A. Stimson, *Public Opinion in America: Moods, Cycles, and Swings* (Boulder, CO: Westview, 1991).

42. Samuel H. Beer, "In Search of a New Public Philosophy," in *The New American Political System,* ed. Anthony King (Washington, DC: American Enterprise Institute, 1978), 5–44.

43. Ibid.

44. A concise history of the deregulatory movement can be found in Larry N. Gerston, Cynthia Fraleigh, and Robert Schwab, *The Deregulated Society* (Pacific Grove, CA: Brooks/Cole, 1988), 40–62.

45. On the tax revolt, see Susan B. Hansen, *The Politics of Taxation: Revenue Without Representation* (New York: Praeger, 1983), esp. 212–251.

3

The Political-Economic Culture of the United States

THE TERM **political-economic culture** refers to the set of values and institutions that governs the economy as well as the relationship between the political system and the economy. Americans tend to value capitalism, competition, and individualism very strongly, while relegating economic equality to second place. The Constitution, the structure of government, and the U.S. historical experience reinforce these economic values. Generally, Americans are conservative; they prefer to keep government out of the economy, but they still desire that the harshness of capitalism be muted, that no one be a permanent or extreme loser in the economy.

In this chapter we look at the attitudes of the public toward the economy in general and toward two specific problems, inflation and unemployment. We also discuss the role of public opinion in economic policymaking.

PUBLIC OPINION AND ECONOMIC STRUCTURES

The economic attitudes and values of Americans are conservative. This conservatism is shown in Americans' support for capitalism, their constrained economic egalitarianism, and their rejection of economic redistribution. Yet American conservatism is moderated by a desire to soften the harshness of capitalism. Thus, under specific circumstances, Americans will support regulation and welfare.

Support for Capitalism

Americans are highly supportive of capitalism. A 1981 survey found 90 percent of respondents agreeing with the statement "The private business system works better than any other system yet designed for industrial countries."[1] Support for the private enterprise system is still strongly evident in the 1990s. In 1993 and 1994, respectively, 59 and 53 percent of the public agreed or strongly agreed with the statement, "Private enterprise is the best way to solve America's economic problems." In contrast, only 13 and 12 percent disagreed or strongly disagreed—about 4½ to 1.[2] The McClosky-Zaller study mentioned in Chapter 1 provides further evidence of U.S. support for the capitalist system.[3] They found that about 35 percent of the general public are strong supporters of capitalism, 30 percent are moderate supporters, and 35 percent weak supporters.[4] They did not detect a wholesale rejection of capitalism, although less support for capitalism is found among those with strong democratic ideals.

We can see support for capitalism from another vantage point, attitudes toward business, business people, and their practices. The Gallup poll has been tracing public attitudes toward business, labor, and government since the 1960s. In one question, the poll asks, "In your opinion, which of the following do you think will be the *biggest* threat to the country in the future— big business, big labor, or big government?" Results of this question from 1965 to 1995 are presented in Table 3.1.

TABLE 3.1 Attitudes Toward Business, Labor, and Government (in percents)

Survey Date	Business The Biggest Threat	Labor The Biggest Threat	Government The Biggest Threat	Don't Know
Feb. 1965	16	29	36	19
Dec. 1966	14	21	48	16
July 1968	12	26	46	16
Nov. 1969	19	28	33	20
Jan. 1977	23	26	38	13
Sept. 1978	19	19	47	15
May 1979	28	17	43	12
Sept. 1981	22	22	46	10
May 1983	19	18	51	12
June 1985	21	20	50	9
Aug. 1995	25	9	64	3

Sources: American Institute of Public Opinion (Gallup poll), as reported in William G. Mayer, *The Changing American Mind: How and Why American Public Opinion Changed Between 1960 and 1988* (Ann Arbor: University of Michigan Press, 1993), 443; and unpublished report from Gallup (1995).

In one sense, this question is stacked against business by using the modifier *big*. Americans seem to dislike bigness, and much antibusiness activity, feeling, and policy is aimed more at the bigness of business than at business in general. For instance, small business has rarely been attacked in American politics. Rather, like the Thomas Jefferson model of the small farmer, the small business person is held up as a social icon in the United States, as a fundamental part of the capitalist system, the major generator of new jobs, and the key source of innovation, new products, and new businesses.

With this in mind, it is striking that big business is never as feared as big government, and on only one of the eleven polls does fear of big business outstrip fear of labor by a significant margin (1979). Across these eleven polls, the average fear of big business is 20 percent, compared with 21 percent for labor and 46 percent for government. Generally, it is fear of government, not business, that characterizes U.S. attitudes. This greater suspicion of government further secures business's place in U.S. society.

Consistent with this is the fact that Americans dislike socialist or communist alternatives and generally disapprove of government ownership of private enterprise. In the late 1930s, while the Depression was still raging, there was some mild sentiment for public ownership of electric utilities and banks, but polls from the 1930s through 1961 indicate that generally 70 percent or more of the public opposed government ownership of any industry, no matter how disliked the industry in question was.[5]

The ethic of self-reliance, with its emphasis on individualism, taking care of oneself, and hard work, is also plainly evident in the opinions of Americans. When asked about what it takes to get ahead, consistently over 60 percent of those polled point to hard work, while only about 10 to 15 percent say that luck or help was necessary to get ahead, with the remaining 20 to 30 percent feeling that equal amounts of hard work, luck, and help are required.[6] This attitude gives capitalism a firm foundation and creates barriers against too much state interference in the economy.[7]

To Americans, freedom and capitalism are strongly intertwined. The Mc-Closky-Zaller study found that 80 percent believed that "the free enterprise system is necessary for free government to survive," and 82 percent felt that "freedom depends on the free enterprise system."[8] Moreover, Americans believe that capitalism is fundamentally fair and just. Again, the McClosky-Zaller study provides clear evidence. Over three-fourths of respondents felt that "on the whole, our economic system is just and wise," 63 percent felt that the private enterprise system is "generally a fair and efficient system," and 65 percent felt that it "gives everyone a fair chance."[9]

Rejection of Economic Equality

When discussing U.S. attitudes toward economic equality, it is important to distinguish equality of *outcomes* from equality of *opportunity*. **Equality of**

outcomes is the idea that government policy should strive to equalize the wealth and/or living conditions of people. For example, taxes may be levied more heavily on the rich than the poor to reduce the wealth gap between them. **Equality of opportunity** is the idea that people should be provided with the same access to society's major institutions, such as those that provide education and jobs. How high a person rises in these institutions is up to the person and his or her performance level. Disparities in status, wealth, and success—that is, inequality of outcome—may still result from using equality of opportunity policies. Americans seem to loathe equal outcomes but are more supportive of policies that promote equality of opportunity. For instance, a 1993 *General Social Survey* found that 84 percent of respondents felt that the United States should promote equality of opportunity, compared with only 12 percent that chose equality of outcomes. As you will see, Americans at times support regulatory and redistributive efforts, which are probably best interpreted in light of the equality of opportunity perspective. In contrast to this limited support for economic equality, Americans are highly supportive of political equality. However, they tend not to transfer their political egalitarian attitudes into the economic sphere.

Robert Lane puts the matter of Americans' attitudes toward economic equality quite starkly, suggesting that Americans, especially the working class, "fear equality."[10] Fear of economic equality has many sources, according to Lane. The most important seems to be the feeling that equality deprives the meritorious of their rewards,[11] that it undermines the work ethic, leading to societal collapse. Too much equality of income destroys individual incentives, according to this view, and even those of modest means who work hard feel cheated if they see "less-deserving" people having the same economic resources. To most Americans, economic differentials are justified in that money and wealth are viewed as rewards for effort, educational attainment, sacrifice, hard work, and responsibility. Wealth is something to be earned. Thus, Americans tolerate larger disparities in wealth than most other societies.

Americans do seem quite tolerant of large disparities in income. As Benjamin Page and Robert Shapiro report, "Seldom have more than half of Americans backed the principle of reducing economic differences between the rich and poor."[12] In comparison to other nations, Americans seem more tolerant of inequality. Table 3.2 compares U.S. and European attitudes toward equality. It is important to note that the survey items on which the data are based are not perfectly comparable. The U.S. survey item does not refer to economic inequality, as the European question does. If U.S. respondents interpreted the question to refer to political rather than economic equality, the U.S. figures would be inflated. Still, the numbers show that U.S. citizens are 14 percent less egalitarian than the most inegalitarian Europeans (Danes) and 26 percent less egalitarian than the average European citizen.

Table 3.3 makes about the same point. In 1973, nearly half of U.S. citizens felt that the government should do more to reduce income inequality. These

TABLE 3.2 Attitudes Toward Inequality in the United States and Eleven European Nations

Country	Percent in Favor of Reducing Inequality
Greece	95
Ireland	90
Italy	88
Northern Ireland	76
Belgium	87
Great Britain	73
Luxembourg	82
Netherlands	78
France	93
West Germany	80
Denmark	71
European Average	83
United States	57

Survey item for Europeans: "Greater efforts should be made to reduce income inequality." (Numbers in the table are those who agree or agree strongly.)

Source: Ronald Inglehart, *Cultural Shift in Advanced Industrial Society* (Princeton, NJ: Princeton University Press, 1990), 255.

Survey item for Americans: "Efforts to make everyone as equal as possible should be increased or decreased." (Numbers in the table are for those who agree and those who agree strongly.)

Source: Herbert McClosky and John Zaller, *The American Ethos: Public Attitudes Toward Capitalism and Democracy* (Cambridge, MA: Harvard University Press, 1984), 91.

TABLE 3.3 Should the Government Reduce Income Differences?

Date	Percent Agreeing or Strongly Agreeing
1973	48
1978	30
1980	26
1983	31
1984	33
1986	32
1987	28
1988	29
1993	29
1994	23
1996	28

Sources: Data for 1973–1988 adapted from Richard G. Niemi, John Mueller, and Tom W. Smith, *Trends in Public Opinion: A Compendium of Survey Data* (New York: Greenwood, 1989), 35; and for 1993–1996 from *General Social Survey.*

numbers fell sharply in the later 1970s and throughout the 1980s. Even at the high point of U.S. economic egalitarianism, only half of the public was supportive of such policies, compared to about five-sixths of the public in the European nations. Even noting the differences in question wording, which make comparison difficult, the difference between the United States and the European nations is striking. Americans are generally more tolerant of economic inequality and less supportive of attempts to reduce inequality than people living in other advanced industrial nations.

Rejection of Efforts to Redistribute Income

Paralleling the rejection of economic equality is the rejection of government efforts to redistribute income, a common way to promote equality of outcomes. Most Americans most of the time are not supportive of government policies that would limit business profits. They also wholly reject the most radical policy proposals, such as confiscating wealth. This was even apparent during the Depression, a period when we might expect public sentiment in favor of redistribution to be at its highest. In 1939, a Roper poll found 83 percent of people surveyed opposed to confiscating wealth and 61 percent opposed to government redistribution,[13] even though unemployment levels surpassed the 20 percent mark at the most severe point of the Depression.

Generally, only about 30 to 40 percent support reduction of income differences between rich and poor, though in the early to mid-1970s, a majority of 50 to 60 percent supported that option.[14] Similarly, there is no widespread support for progressive income taxes, which would tax higher incomes at higher rates.[15] In fact, the federal income tax, arguably the most progressive tax in the nation, is also among the most disliked (see Table 3.4); only local property taxes are as disliked.[16]

Attitudes Toward Welfare and Regulation

Although Americans hold essentially conservative economic values, they are not strict adherents to a laissez faire doctrine. Americans feel that competitive markets are not always fair and that government should, under special circumstances, come to the aid of the disadvantaged and those who cannot compete effectively. Thus, Americans feel that capitalism should be tempered with a dose of welfare. Similarly, Americans are fearful of unbridled big business and consequently support limited regulation. Also, Americans seem to understand that the private sector cannot and will not take care of important social problems. In some circumstances, business activity adds to the problem, like environmental pollution. In such circumstances, Americans are supportive of government regulatory efforts. Thus, Americans deviate from strict loyalty to laissez faire ideals and are willing to use the agencies of government to help alleviate and/or correct these social ills.

TABLE 3.4 Attitudes Toward Taxes (in percents)

Date	Federal Income	State Income	State Sales	Local Property	Social Security	Don't Know
March 1972	19	13	13	45	*	11
May 1973	30	10	20	31	*	11
April 1974	30	10	20	28	*	14
May 1975	28	11	23	29	*	10
May 1977	28	11	17	33	*	11
May 1978	30	11	18	32	*	10
May 1979	37	8	15	27	*	13
May 1980	36	10	19	25	*	10
Sept. 1981	36	9	14	33	*	9
May 1982	36	11	14	30	*	9
May 1983	35	11	13	26	*	15
May 1984	36	10	15	29	*	10
May 1985	38	10	16	24	*	12
May 1986	37	8	17	28	*	10
June 1987	30	12	21	24	*	13
July 1988	33	10	18	28	*	11
June 1989	27	10	18	32	*	13
May 1990	26	10	12	28	15	9
July 1991	26	12	19	30	*	14
June 1992	25	9	16	25	10	15
June 1993	36	10	16	24	*	14
June 1994	27	7	14	28	12	11

*Not mentioned or provided as an option to respondents.

Question: "Which do you think is the worst tax, that is, the least fair?"

Sources: For 1972–1982, Advisory Commission on Intergovernmental Relations; and for 1983–1994, American Institute of Public Opinion. See Mayer, *The Changing American Mind*, 449.

Support for Welfare

There is fairly widespread support among Americans for programs to help the needy. Surveys from 1984 through 1988 also found that between 61 and 68 percent of the public felt that too little was being spent on "assistance to help the poor," whereas only 7 to 11 percent felt that too much was being spent.[17]

In the mid-1990s, a modest liberalizing trend is noticeable in the public, as the percentage claiming too much was being spent declined to 52 percent in 1996. At the same time, the percentage saying that too little was being spent on assistance to the poor increased to 17 percent in 1996.[18] It appears that as the economy improved into the 1990s, the public, perhaps feeling more economically secure, also became more generous to the poor. The irony in all of this is the public becomes more willing to help the poor as the problem of poverty becomes less severe, due to improvements in the economy.

Programs designed to alleviate specific conditions of poverty receive strong support from the public. McClosky and Zaller found that 53 percent felt it would be a good idea to spend some tax money "to provide a college education for those who can't afford it." Only 16 percent felt this to be a bad idea (31 percent had no opinion).[19] Programs aimed at hunger are even more popular. In the 1970s, over 90 percent felt that it was "not right to let people who need welfare go hungry," and food stamps generally received strong public support in surveys from the 1930s until the 1970s. In the 1980s, support for food stamps declined but rebounded by the end of the decade.[20]

Still, support for welfare and income maintenance programs is restrained because Americans are more likely to view the individual as the cause of poverty, rather than the economy or government policies. In both 1974 and 1977, surveys found that 47 percent held the individual responsible for his or her economic failure, while only about 30 percent agreed that "some . . . have so much more money than others shows there is an unjust condition in this country that ought to be changed."[21] In the 1970s, over half of the Americans polled felt that there is more concern paid to the "welfare bum" than the "hard worker."[22] Still, this view is somewhat moderated, as only 30 percent believed the poor are lazy and only 24 percent believed that the poor don't try hard enough; majorities had no opinion on the matter.[23]

When assistance to the poor is labeled "welfare," support for it dramatically drops. *Welfare,* like *charity* in the early part of this century and *relief* in the 1930s, is a politically charged term. All of the negative feelings about the poor are aroused when it is used. Consequently, public support declines, but the decline seems more a response to an emotionally and politically charged word than to a program. Thus, in every National Opinion Research Corporation (NORC) survey from 1973 through 1996 that asked if too much, too little, or about the right amount of money was being spent on welfare, the "too much" category was larger than the "too little" one (see Table 3.5).[24]

Similarly, people want to attach strings to welfare support. "Workfare," that is, requiring those who receive welfare support to work, has had very strong support since the 1970s, when the idea gained popularity. In the 1970s, over 90 percent agreed with such a notion, and similar consensual majorities have been found on surveys into the 1980s.[25]

However, as Table 3.5 also shows, the percentage of people feeling that too much was being spent on welfare climbed from 40 to 45 percent in the 1980s to about 55 percent in the 1990s. Thus, despite some greater generosity to the poor, welfare had become an even hotter political hot potato in the 1990s and perhaps helped stimulate the reform of welfare in 1996. ·

In 1996, after several decades of attacking welfare programs and their recipients, Congress passed a law that drastically overhauled the federal welfare program. The original program, which dated to 1935, was federally controlled,

TABLE 3.5 Attitudes Toward Welfare Spending (in percents)

Date	Too Much	Too Little	About Right	Don't Know
1973	51	20	24	4
1974	42	22	32	4
1975	43	23	28	5
1976	60	13	22	4
1977	60	12	23	5
1978	58	13	25	4
1980	56	13	26	4
1982	48	20	28	4
1983	47	21	28	4
1984	40	24	34	3
1985	45	19	33	4
1986	40	22	34	4
1987	44	21	31	4
1988	42	23	32	3
1993	54	16	25	5
1994	60	13	24	3
1996	56	15	26	3

Survey item: "I'm going to name some of these problems, and for each one I'd like you to tell me whether you think we are spending too much money on it, too little money, or about the right amount."

Sources: For 1973–1988, Mayer, *The Changing American Mind*, 454–455; and for 1993–1996, *General Social Survey*.

although states helped in its administration. Moreover, it was an entitlement program. Everyone who was eligible was entitled to welfare benefits. Plus, eligibility was potentially unending, and no work requirement was placed on recipients.

The new law changed most major provisions of the existing program. States were given broad authority to design their welfare programs, and while funding was still federal, it was dispensed as a block grant to the states, not as an entitlement. Block grants effectively limit the amount of welfare money available. Some specific welfare programs had their funding levels cut, in particular food stamps, and welfare benefits were denied to legal immigrants. Last and perhaps most important in the climate of public opinion were the requirements that current welfare recipients would have to secure work within two years of the bill's passage and that adults could receive only five years of welfare support across their lifetime.

The public climate, Republican control of Congress, President Clinton's previous record on welfare reform, and the pressures of the 1996 presidential election campaign all help explain why welfare reform came when it did. As the public opinion data just considered show, there was little public support for those on welfare and much support for a workfare program. Second, the

Republicans, who took control of both houses of Congress after the 1994 midterm elections, made welfare reform part of their program, which they called the Contract with America.

Equally important was President Clinton. As early as 1988, when he was governor of Arkansas, he pushed for welfare reform that included a workfare provision. It was this position that identified Clinton as a moderate Democrat, who was not captured by the liberal wing of that party. Moreover, in 1992, his presidential election campaign included a plank to "end welfare as we know it," although other than the workfare provision, he was quite vague on exactly how he would reform welfare. Once elected, Clinton did submit a proposal to Congress but did not work hard for it, focusing more energy on his health-care reforms.

Republican control of Congress in 1995 upped the ante, as twice congressional Republicans sent welfare bills to Clinton, who vetoed them. With the 1996 election nearing, Clinton needed a bill that he could sign, so that he could ward off Republican attacks in the presidential campaign, point out that he kept his campaign pledge, and speak of his administration's accomplishments and why it should be kept in office. Thus, despite some reservations, especially with regard to cuts in food stamps and legal immigrant eligibility, Clinton signed the bill, indicating that he would seek future legislation to amend these provisions. However, continued Republican control of Congress made such a prospect unlikely.

The consequences of such drastic welfare reform are not yet clearly evident. On the one hand, as intended, the welfare rolls have decreased in size. By June 1997, there were 10.5 million people on the welfare rolls, a drop of 26 percent since 1994. As the decline started two years before implementation of the law, not all of the drop can be attributed to it. Instead, a strong economy with a low unemployment rate has offered a large pool of jobs for welfare recipients to move into. When the economy sputters and unemployment rises, pressures will undoubtedly be put on those who administer the law.

Another intended hope of many reformers was to change the culture of those in poverty from one of dependence on welfare to self-reliance and having a work ethic. Whether such a program can affect people as such and whether it is true that people on welfare lack a work ethic are open to much scholarly and political dispute. A more tangible effect, though, focuses on the condition of people's lives. Whether the poor will be more economically stressed is not yet clear. Those who remain on welfare, with its less generous provisions than in the past, and those whose eligibility runs out will definitely suffer. And it is uncertain whether those who secure jobs will find jobs that pay enough to live on. We need several more years and research before we can address these issues more satisfactorily.[26]

Thus, to Americans the individual, not the government, is the more accepted solution to poverty. McClosky and Zaller report that 53 percent think that the poor should help themselves "to improve their conditions."[27] Only 22 percent feel that the poor "should receive special government help."

There is rather strong opposition to a guaranteed minimum income; on the other hand, there is mixed support for the idea that government should provide people with jobs and a good standard of living.[28]

Similarly, the public is very supportive of unemployment insurance programs, which provide individuals with economic assistance during the gap between jobs. Support for unemployment insurance and increasing unemployment benefits tends to rise when unemployment rates go up.[29]

Perhaps the most popular social welfare program is social security. Surveys have often found huge majorities of 90 percent or so opposed to cutbacks in social security benefits, with smaller yet still large (70-plus percent) majorities in support of increased benefits.[30] Social security, unlike welfare, is popular, according to Page and Shapiro, because "benefits are targeted to people in circumstances under which they have little or no control and which particularly evoke a sense of societal obligation . . . [it] is seen, primarily, as a compulsory insurance program in which wage earners are forced to put aside some current income to provide for future disability or retirement."[31] The contributory-insurance aspect of social security makes it popular and prevents it from being looked on as welfare.

We can sum up this attitude as **welfare capitalism**.[32] Here we need to distinguish welfare capitalism from **corporate welfare**. Welfare capitalism is a capitalist democracy whose government has welfare policies and programs that aim at helping the poor, mostly by providing them with some type of income assistance, such as direct cash payments, housing subsidies, food stamps, and the like. *Corporate welfare* refers to government programs from which business, especially big business, receives benefits. These may include tax breaks, grants, and subsidies. Critics use the term *corporate welfare* to attack these programs, as well as to moderate the stigma associated with the term *welfare*.

As Page and Shapiro describe U.S. attitudes toward welfare, "Americans want people to help themselves when they can but want government to help those who cannot."[33] Thus, Americans make a distinction between the deserving and the undeserving poor. The **deserving poor** are those caught in circumstances beyond their control—the sick and disabled, for instance. The **undeserving poor** have only themselves to blame for their economic plight.

Support for Regulation

Although, as we have noted, Americans are generally economically conservative, preferring the private sector to the government one, at times they are supportive of government regulatory efforts. Their support for regulation stems from a basic fear of the power of big business and its ability to disrupt the market. Big business may have undue power over consumers and small businesses, and the vast resources of big business may allow it disproportionate power and influence in the halls of government. The experience of the late 1800s with monopolies and trusts made Americans fearful of the ability of large firms to circumvent the market, destroy competition, and monopolize economic life. The Great Depression reinforced attitudes that the economy could not always be counted on to correct its problems. Further, the public was concerned about the concentration of economic power in the hands of the managers of the nation's largest enterprises. The decisions of this small group could have repercussions beyond their own corporations, potentially affecting the nation's economy.[34]

The size of big business, its ability to monopolize, and the power that Americans associate with bigness have been favored targets for regulation. Consistently, majorities feel that in "many industries, one or two companies have too much control" and that "there's too much power concentrated in the hands of a few large companies for the good of the nation."[35]

This suspicion of big business leads to public support for controlling its size. Thus, from the 1960s through the 1980s, not always a period of antipathy toward business, 36 to 57 percent of the public thought that it would be good for the country to break up the largest companies.[36] Strikingly, this antibigness sentiment increased, reaching its peak in the 1970s and 1980s, when the public was presumably more conservative economically than during the 1960s.

Moreover, in surveys conducted in 1966, 1970, and 1977, people generally felt better off rather than worse off due to "government control and regulation of the business practices of large corporations."[37] Only in 1981 did the scales tip in the other direction, which may be due to the antiregulatory rhetoric of Ronald Reagan. And in surveys conducted from 1973 to 1988, majorities usually felt that government regulation was effective in making "business responsive to people's needs." Again, positive assessments of regulation dropped off in the later surveys.[38]

Overall, Americans hold ambivalent attitudes toward big companies. On average, 80 percent or more feel that big companies are essential for the nation's growth and economic expansion, but almost as many feel that big companies are cold and impersonal in their relations with people.[39]

The American public is more inclined to support specific regulatory actions than regulation in general. Across the 1940s, 1950s, and 1960s, majorities felt that less regulation of business was better than more, and during the late 1970s and 1980s, more people felt that there was too much regulation rather than not enough.[40]

This contrasts with the willingness to impose specific regulations for specific purposes. Environmental protection regulation is one topic that receives consistent and strong public support. For example, from 1973 to 1983, only 13 to 21 percent felt that environmental protection laws and regulation had gone too far. In contrast, from 25 to 48 percent felt that such laws and regulation had not gone far enough.[41] Table 3.6 makes the same point about opinion during the 1980s and 1990s, an era that began with major efforts to scale back government regulation. These figures show that

TABLE 3.6 Attitudes Toward Environmental Protection and Regulation, 1982–1997 (in percents)

Date	Too Much	About Right	Too Little	Don't Know
July 1982	11	41	35	12
July 1983	9	34	44	14
July 1984	8	27	56	9
July 1985	10	28	54	8
July 1986	7	26	59	9
July 1987	12	30	49	9
July 1988	13	25	53	10
July 1989	9	24	58	9
December 1990	16	15	62	7
September 1991	16	16	60	7
September 1992	22	16	52	7
September 1993	25	21	49	5
September 1994	31	22	40	7
September 1996	24	30	41	5
August 1997	21	28	49	1

Survey item: "In general, do you think there is too much, too little, or about the right amount of government regulation and involvement in the area of environmental protection?"

Sources: For 1982–1988, Cambridge Research Inc., reported in Mayer, *The Changing American Mind*, 490; for 1989–1994, *Cambridge Reports*, Research International; and for 1996–1997, *Wirthlin Quorum Survey.*

those favoring environmental regulation ("Too Little" category) outnumbered those opposing it ("Too Much" category) for each year that the survey question was asked. As an aside, it is interesting to see in these numbers a weakening of public support for environmental regulation from its highs in the late 1980s. From 1990 to 1997, support dropped 13 points, from 62 to 49 percent, while opposition ticked up somewhat. Even given this trend, support for environmental regulation in the 1990s clearly outstripped opposition by about two to one.

ATTITUDES TOWARD THE CONDITION OF THE ECONOMY

The **macroeconomy** refers to the entire national economy and not particular economic sectors, like agriculture. There are several important aspects of the macroeconomy—for instance, inflation, unemployment, the money supply, interest rates, productivity, economic growth, and trade. All of the major macroeconomic characteristics of the economy affect the standard of living of the average person. Thus, productivity, growth, and trade balances influence how well people live. People, however, do not focus strongly on these macroeconomic conditions because they are not always able to trace the impact of these conditions on their lives. Thus, low productivity keeps people's incomes below what they could be, but most people are not aware of the direct impact of productivity on their incomes. Surveys find that although the United States has had one of the slowest economic and income growth rates of the industrialized nations in the post–World War II era, people rarely mention slow income or economic growth as a problem.[42] Rather, public attention turns to the twin problems of inflation and unemployment.

People tend to focus on **inflation** and **unemployment** because they can directly feel the effects of both on their daily lives. Inflation is the rate of increase in prices. If a good or service cost $100 in 1997 but cost $105 in 1998, the inflation rate is 5 percent.[43] Inflation leads to higher costs for goods and, thus, less overall purchasing power, which people encounter whenever they make a purchase.

Unemployment is when a person is actively looking for a job but does not have one. The government provides unemployment insurance benefits for thirteen weeks, and sometimes extends it to twenty-six or even thirty-nine weeks. Once people have exhausted their unemployment benefits, they can go onto the welfare rolls. Unemployment statistics that the government reports only include those who are receiving unemployment insurance benefits and those who are new entrants into the job market, like recently graduated students who are looking for their first job. Thus, one can be without a job but still not be counted in the unemployment statistics.

Unemployment has direct and severe effects on the unemployed and others seeking jobs. The public wants low inflation and low unemployment, making these two economic conditions among the most important for policymakers to deal with.

Policymakers, thus, have incentives to implement policies that restrain inflation and promote job growth. However, it is not always possible to do both. The conditions conducive to low inflation may limit job growth and increase unemployment. Similarly, policies designed to create jobs may fuel inflation. This is a classic dilemma, known as the **Phillips curve tradeoff.**[44] Figure 3.1 illustrates the concept. The degree of inflation and unemployment is defined by the line *AB*. Let us say that inflation is at point *A,* an undesirably high level, and policymakers desire to do something about this problem. Government implements a policy that lowers inflation to point *C.* Note that by traveling from point *A* to point *C,* unemployment increases. The problem for policymakers is to settle at a point on line *AB* with acceptable levels of both inflation and unemployment.

Another problem policymakers must contend with is the timing of policies that fight inflation or unemployment. Because the U.S. economy is so big, large lead times are required for most major economic decisions, so the economy

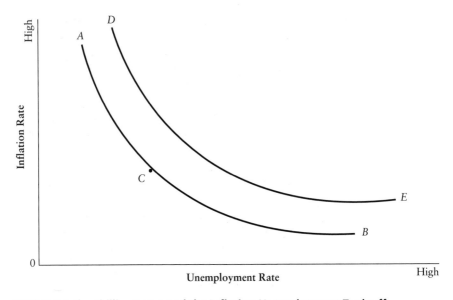

FIGURE 3.1 The Phillips Curve and the Inflation-Unemployment Tradeoff

is slow to change. The public may demand the continuation of policies long after they are needed because of the lag between the introduction of stimulus policies and their effect. The public may pressure policymakers to stimulate the economy long after unemployment stimulus is needed or to continue to fight inflation even though continued anti-inflation policies may raise unemployment to unacceptable levels.

Here we will simply look at public opinion toward inflation and unemployment and consider what people think the sources of these problems are, what the most preferable solutions to those problems are, and whether different types of people hold different opinions about inflation and unemployment. We will also consider whether the public is aware of the Phillips tradeoff problem and whether higher inflation or higher unemployment is better tolerated. We begin by looking at the placement of economic concerns on the public's agenda.

THE MOST IMPORTANT PROBLEM

Even in a political-economic culture like the United States's, with its biases for the market over government involvement in the economy, people recognize that economic problems are not merely personal. The accumulation of many personal economic problems results in a national problem, though the public does not always consider government the best agency to solve nation-wide economic problems.

Since the 1940s, the Gallup poll has been asking people what they think is the most important problem facing the nation. From the myriad of responses, the Gallup organization has classified these problems into three sets—foreign and international problems, domestic economic problems, and domestic social problems. Over the course of the last forty years, international and economic problems have predominated in the public's mind. This is illustrated in Figure 3.2, which plots the annual average percentage of responses in the three broad areas.

In the 1950s and 1960s, foreign affairs clearly dominated as a public concern. The Korean and Vietnam wars, plus the tensions associated with the cold war, fueled that concern. In the early 1960s, social problems catapulted onto the nation's problem agenda, at times rivaling foreign affairs for dominance. The civil rights movement of the late 1950s and early 1960s, urban disorder and crime of the late 1960s, and the energy crisis later in the 1970s were the main foci of attention.

The economy has also been important to the public, but it did not become an overriding concern until the mid-1970s. Several factors at that time seemed to focus public attention on the economy. First, détente with the Soviets during the Nixon, Ford, and Carter years helped reduce tensions

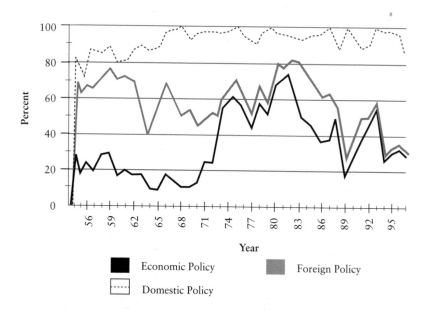

FIGURE 3.2 The Public's Most Important Problem, 1954–1997

Source: Gallup Polls, 1954–1997.

between the two superpowers and, consequently, reduced public anxiety over foreign affairs.

More important, the economy took a nosedive in the 1970s. Inflation heated up, in part a consequence of Vietnam War spending but also from the overall increase in government spending. Unemployment also rose, and during the mid-1970s, **stagflation** characterized the economy. Instead of the expected tradeoff between unemployment and inflation—the Phillips curve tradeoff—both escalated. Figure 3.1 traces out another line, *DE*. Note that by moving from the line *AB* to *DE*, both the inflation and the unemployment levels increase.

The impact of economic performance on public concern is shown in Figure 3.3, which charts public concern and the **misery index.** The misery index first came to political prominence in Ronald Reagan's 1980 campaign for the presidency. The index is the addition of the inflation and unemployment rates and, given the stagflation of the 1970s, seems a relevant indicator of economic distress. The misery index and public concern move in tandem. The index was quite low in the period from 1950 to 1970, hovering in the 2 to 6 range. In the mid-1970s it climbed, and across the 1970s and 1980s it

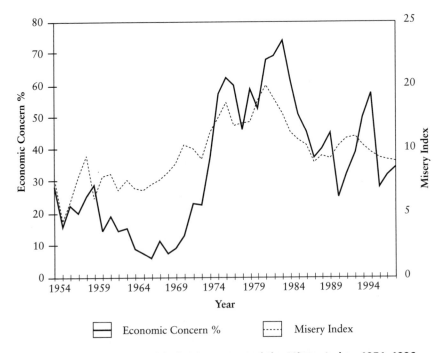

FIGURE 3.3 Public Concern with the Economy and the Misery Index, 1951–1996

Sources: Data adapted from the Gallup Polls, 1950–1996; and Harold W. Stanley and Richard G. Niemi, *Vital Statistics on American Politics 1997–1998* (Washington, DC: CQ Press, 1998), 388–389, 401–402.

ranged from 6 to 14. The fact that the economy performed well throughout most of the 1990s, coupled with the end of the cold war, helps account for why public attention turned to domestic problems in the 1990s. However, the bigger point is that if either the economy sours or international tensions flare up, it will push domestic concern downward in importance.

PUBLIC OPINION AND INFLATION

Americans fear inflation more than any other problem. Thus, they place great demands on politicians to quell inflationary pressures. These demands get articulated both as opinions and as votes. But the public has little understanding of the costs, causes, and remedies for inflation. This presents a problem for politicians, who may not be able to fashion effective policies because such policies are not palatable to voters. We begin this discussion with an assessment of the costs of inflation. From this foundation, we look at public opinions toward inflation, the extent of fear of inflation, public assessments of the causes and sources of inflation, and public preferences for policies to deal with inflation.

The Costs and Effects of Inflation

The impact of inflation—its effects and costs—can be classed into four categories, running along two dimensions. The first dimension refers to short-term versus long-term effects. The second dimension looks at the impact of inflation on economic performance and wealth versus its redistributive effects. Who gains and who loses because of inflation?[45]

Inflation has short-term wealth effects. Inflation is a continuous process, but wages are readjusted only occasionally, so there may be a lag between the timing of inflationary effects and when people's incomes are readjusted to meet the inflationary pressures. In effect, wages are "sticky." They do not adjust as fast as inflation rises, and, as a result, people lose money in the short run. This may also account for anti-inflation sentiment in the mass public. In time, however, income tends to catch up with inflation, thus diminishing any long-term income loss other than that associated with the effects just discussed. This short-term wealth loss is the most important factor conditioning the public to dislike inflation.[46]

Economists feel that inflation may also affect economic growth in the long run because it distorts economic behavior. Inflation creates incentives to consume because it erodes the value of money assets. Holding on to money makes little sense because inflation diminishes its worth. People and firms are thus likely to take on debt for fear that their current assets will not retain their value and the cost of future goods will go up. This effect results in less savings in the future for investors to draw on. As investment decreases, so does the future potential for economic growth.

Inflation also distorts economic behavior by injecting an element of unpredictability into economic decision making. Inflation leads many to think that prices will be unstable. People feel that they cannot predict accurately how much prices will rise. Inflation can induce inflationary expectations, which may cause inflationary spirals, making it even harder to predict future inflation levels. Thus, economic activity will not be efficient. People will over- or underconsume because they cannot predict future price levels accurately. Consequently, the economy will not perform as well as it could with stable prices. People will make more mistakes in their economic choices, leading to inefficiencies and wasted economic resources.

Inflation also affects stock market and production decisions. Stock market investors dislike inflation, fearing it will erode the value of their investments. Often inflation fears lead investors to move their money out of the market and into what they consider to be inflation-resistant investments, like gold. Businesses that were the focus of investments consequently have less money from investment to use. Also, production decisions are affected by inflation and inflationary fears. Corporate managers may feel that the costs of production will rise if inflation persists and thus may be reluctant to expand production or enter into new production ventures. Both of these impacts, on the market and on production decisions, may lessen the productive behavior and capability of the economy.

The redistributional effects of inflation are also politically important, but like the effects of short-term income loss, there may not be as much to inflation's redistributional effects as commonly believed. Inflation is thought to affect adversely three groups in the short run: those on fixed incomes, creditors, and the private sector.

People on fixed incomes are losers relative to those not on fixed incomes. Those not on fixed incomes find their incomes readjusted to compensate for inflationary effects. Fixed-income people cannot get this readjustment. Thus, their incomes erode with inflation, while incomes that are readjusted do not.

Similarly, creditors lose out to debtors. Again, creditors often hold money assets, like loans, and thus see inflation erode the value of those assets. Debtors, in contrast, see the value of the money that they borrow diminish; that is, the relative size of their loans decreases. Banks are notoriously inflation-averse because they are the prime holders of others' debts. Some contend that the Federal Reserve Board, which is closely associated and staffed with bankers, is more anti-inflationary than other economic decision-making institutions in the United States because of this "banker's bias."[47] Similarly, governments may adopt inflationary policies to help them minimize the effect of running deficits.

Last, the private sector often loses to the governmental sector. This is most apparent when taxes are progressive. **Progressive taxes** mean that each additional dollar earned is taxed at a higher rate. Thus, government can take a proportionately larger share of income and profit through taxation. In the

1970s, this type of **bracket creep,** where people were pushed in higher tax brackets through inflation, stimulated strong outcry against progressive income taxes. In response, the Reagan administration indexed income tax brackets to inflation, eliminating the bracket-creep problem. Indexing means that tax brackets are readjusted with the rate of inflation. Calls for a flat-rate income tax and the tax reforms of 1986 may also have been partially stimulated by this problem.

Although there are short-term redistributions as a consequence of inflation, the most detailed study to date, by Douglas Hibbs, has not found any major long-term economic redistribution associated with inflation.[48] That study found that the share of income received by each income quintile (fifth) has remained stable across the 1947 to 1980 period. The bottom fifth has received from 4.9 to 5.5 percent of income despite huge fluctuations in the inflation rate. The highest-income quintile showed somewhat greater variability, with incomes' ranging from 40.4 to 43.0 percent, but more detailed analysis shows that these fluctuations are not a function of changing inflation rates. Similarly, in an extensive review, Paul Peretz found few long-term redistributional effects, although he cites several studies that suggest that there is redistribution from the top and bottom of the income scale to those in the middle. However, the effect is small and other studies (such as Hibbs) question that the effect even exists.[49]

Public Aversion to Inflation

Public aversion to inflation seems stronger than inflation's effects.[50] Inflation has minimal effects on income distribution, and even short-term income losses are made up as income is readjusted to inflationary pressures. Moreover, those who might stand to benefit from inflation still fear it (the lowest and highest income classes).

Most people consider inflation harmful. Surveys indicate that 60 to 80 percent or more consider inflation to have negative effects.[51] Few consider inflation to be good for them. This holds among those who are harmed by inflation as well as those who might benefit from it. For instance, those who hold mortgages may find inflation a benefit to them, as mortgages should reduce the impact of that debt payment on their total income, yet mortgage holders seem no less averse to inflation than renters.[52]

Fear of inflation exists in the public mind even when the economy displays little inflationary pressures. Surveys in the 1960s found that inflation was considered one of the nation's most important problems, even though the economy showed little inflation during that period.[53] One study that compared inflation rates with people's attitudes about inflation estimated that in a zero inflation environment, 59 percent of the public would view inflation negatively, with 7 percent added to the total for each 1 percent increase in the rate of inflation.[54] At very low levels of inflation, then, negative views of inflation become nearly universal. This indicates that the public is very sensitive to inflation and that a reservoir of inflation fear exists that is easily spread once even small amounts of inflation are detected.

People in the lower income groups are more inflation-averse than those with higher income levels,[55] even though some studies suggest that the lowest-income group may stand to benefit from inflation. It is not clear why people may fear something that may be good for them. Part of the answer may reside in low levels of information about inflation or a misunderstanding of the causes and consequences of inflation. The public may even be manipulated into unduly fearing inflation because of the power of some anti-inflation elements of the economy (for example, banks, mass media). One study has found that media reporting about inflation, which is mostly negative, may be partially responsible for people's negative evaluations of inflation. As people recalled negative news stories about inflation, their fear of inflation increased.[56] Still these group differences pale in comparison to the strong anti-inflation attitudes across the entire population.

Other studies indicate that the public is not well informed about inflation. Most indicate that in the face of inflation, people will curtail their spending and increase their saving, though economic theory suggests that it may be wiser to spend more and save less under such conditions.[57] This "irrational" response may indicate that people tend to react to the uncertainty that inflation interjects into the economic environment and/or that they do not feel that their incomes will catch up with inflation. This latter reaction may make sense because most employees have little control over their incomes. Nonetheless, evidence indicates that most employee wages do go up with inflation. And the fact that spending on durable goods goes up with inflation, shows there is some rational adaption to it.[58]

A last reason for the widespread fear of inflation is that many people do not feel that it can be controlled, and an even larger group feel that inflation will not be controlled, even if it could be.[59] As inflation heated up in the 1970s, and government seemed unable to control it, public cynicism grew even further.[60]

Attitudes Toward the Sources of Inflation

There is little public consensus about the sources of inflation. Large segments of the public point to government, business, and labor as sources of inflationary pressures. However, when pointing to government, the public does not seem to attribute inflationary increases to the government policies that most economists feel contribute to the problem, such as high government spending, low taxes, and loose monetary policies, which allow a large supply of money in the economy.

In open-ended questions, where people are allowed to choose their own response, two sources of inflation stand out in the public's consciousness, a wage-price spiral and government. The **wage-price spiral**, where higher wages are sought to offset inflation, and business responds with price increases to offset wage concessions to workers, is the most commonly cited cause of inflation from surveys in the 1970s, accounting for about one-fourth of all responses. Government, through either its poor planning or its excessive spending, accounts for nearly the same proportion. About 20 percent of the respondents could not offer a source for inflation, underscoring the low information levels of many in the general public.[61]

Closed-ended questions, which force people to choose a response from a predetermined set of options, tell a related but different story. Government spending, wage-price spirals, and business pricing behavior again emerge as perceived sources of inflation. However, low taxation rates do not.[62] The public also seems to overlook government policy actions with clear inflationary consequences, such as the tax rise that Lyndon Johnson proposed in 1966, which aimed at curbing inflation, or the easy monetary policies of the same era. The public, then, seems to lack a clear understanding of the sources of inflation and is often incorrect, for instance, blaming high taxes for inflation when in fact they have the opposite effect.

Attitudes Toward Policies to Control Inflation

People seem willing in the abstract to pay to control inflation, though their policy choices belie this. Thus, surveys find that people would prefer to lose real income to control inflation rather than see their real incomes rise without controlling inflation.[63] Other evidence indicates that people are not willing to sacrifice to control inflation, as their most-preferred anti-inflation policies are the ones with the least cost to them. Nor do people seem to opt for policies that would most effectively treat the inflation problem. This reinforces the interpretation that people's understanding of inflation is plagued by low levels of information, if not misinformation.

According to economic theory, the most effective ways of curbing inflation are for government to raise both taxes and interest rates. These options, with considerable short-term consequences to voters, are soundly rejected in polls. Peretz reports that a survey in 1969 found that over 80 percent disagreed with such policies, while only about 10 percent agreed.[64] Other surveys show similar results. However, there is public support to cut government spending, perhaps indicating that the public understands that too much demand from government can stimulate inflation. The survey does not, however, ask people where the cuts should be made. Had such a question been posed, public consensus on spending cuts would surely decline. Cutting government seems to be a general response to all government actions and problems, not a reasoned response to specific ills. Polls on dealing with the deficit find broad agreement to cut spending, though when asked about specific programs, the public often supports spending increases.

Polls also indicate modest support for wage-price policies, that is, government policies that control wages and prices, with generally higher support for such policies than opposition to them.[65] As inflation heats up, public support for wage-price policies also seems to build.

In summarizing the public's preferences for policies to deal with inflation, Peretz argues that there is "resistance on the part of the public to solutions to inflation that involve real sacrifice. . . . [There is] an unwillingness by the public to see inflation as being in a trade-off relationship to unemployment and recession."[66] Thus, in 1970, 74 percent opposed higher taxes, and 89 percent higher interest rates even if these would halt inflation, but 80 percent supported spending cuts and 60 percent supported wage-price controls.[67] However, people were not willing to sacrifice future pay increases if it meant that any future income growth would be limited to the increase in the cost of living.[68] People seem to think that individually they can beat inflation.

Again, we find a great deal of misinformation about inflation, and a public that seems unwilling to sacrifice to curb inflation but that remains antagonistic and fearful of it. The policy choices open to politicians are mightily constrained under such circumstances, and this may contribute to the inability of governments to withstand inflation or do anything about it once it has appeared. Ironically, over time, the public has come to see government as more and more responsible for doing something about inflation, which only increases the pressures on government and may have contributed to the erosion of public confidence in government witnessed across the 1970s and 1980s.[69]

PUBLIC OPINION AND UNEMPLOYMENT

The Incidence and Costs of Unemployment

Unlike inflation, which seems to fall relatively evenly across the whole economic spectrum, the effects of unemployment concentrate unevenly. The most obvious personal costs of unemployment are economic, but its effects also spill over into other aspects of life, like the mental and physical health of those directly touched. Moreover, unemployment has general economic effects. Unemployment means that plant and other economic resources are left idle and unused. Thus, business is hurt by unemployment because it is unable to use all of its productive capacity.

Some types of people are more likely to find themselves unemployed than others. Unemployment is higher among blue-collar workers and lower-wage earners than among white-collar workers and higher-wage earners, women than men, teenagers than adults, and African Americans and other minorities than whites. Table 3.7 presents a typical demographic breakdown comparing the employed and unemployed.

African American unemployment rates in the 1980s often surpassed those of whites by 7 to 8 percent, lying in the 11 to 15 percent range across the decade. African Americans were about twice as likely to be unemployed as

TABLE 3.7 Unemployment Rates for Selected Demographic Groups, 1980–1996 (in percents)

Group	1980	1985	1990	1992	1996
Total	7.1	7.2	5.5	7.4	6.4
Men	6.9	7.0	5.6	7.8	5.4
Women	7.4	7.4	5.4	6.9	5.4
Whites	6.3	6.2	4.7	6.5	4.7
African Americans	14.3	15.1	11.3	14.1	10.5
Hispanics	10.1	10.5	8.0	11.4	8.9
Age					
16–19	17.8	18.6	15.5	20.0	16.7
20–24	11.5	11.1	8.8	11.3	9.3
25–44	6.0	6.2	4.8	6.7	4.6
45–64	3.7	4.5	3.5	5.1	3.3

Source: Data adapted from *Statistical Abstract of the United States*, 1997, Table 652.

the average worker. Hispanics also displayed higher unemployment rates than whites but not quite as high as those of African Americans. Similarly, young workers were much more likely to be unemployed than older workers. The unemployment rate for the youngest workers (16–19) ranged from 15 to 20 percent. Older workers are less often out of work, with the 45–64 age group seeing unemployment of about 3 to 5 percent, often only one-half of the national average. The gap in unemployment between men and women has narrowed, and by the 1990s women had unemployment rates similar to those of men.

All of these gaps in unemployment across workers narrow as the overall rate falls but widen as unemployment increases. Unemployment, thus, falls disproportionately on those with the fewest resources and those in the least affluent sectors of the economy and society, and it falls on them even more heavily relative to the rest of society as the economy sours. Inasmuch as governments fight inflation with policies that slow the economy, which increases unemployment, anti-inflationary policies are borne most heavily by the poorest sectors of the economy.[70]

Although unemployment falls hardest on the most-disadvantaged segments of society, it does not spare others. Table 3.8 reports results of fourteen national surveys across twenty-four years estimating the percentage of people who were unemployed for at least a month at some time during the preceding ten years. The results are striking; on average, about 30 percent of the population has been unemployed for a significant duration.

There are three major types or sources of unemployment, natural, cyclical, and structural. **Natural unemployment** refers to some percentage of people who will be out of work no matter what the extent of job possibilities in the

TABLE 3.8 Personal Experience with Unemployment During the Last Ten Years, 1973–1996 (in percents)

Date	Yes	No
1973	28	72
1974	26	74
1975	28	72
1976	28	72
1977	28	72
1978	29	71
1980	28	72
1983	34	66
1984	33	67
1986	30	70
1988	31	68
1993	32	68
1994	32	68
1996	33	67

Question: "At any time during the last ten years, have you been unemployed and looking for work for as long as a month?"

Sources: For 1973–1988, NORC, Niemi, Mueller, and Smith, *Trends in Public Opinion*, 245; and for 1993–1996, *General Social Survey.*

economy. Some people are in transition between jobs, others who can get jobs are searching for more desirable ones, and still others may be in school to improve their job skills. Each of these unemployed individuals may be said to be voluntarily unemployed. Thus, full employment will never reach 100 percent because of natural unemployment.[71]

Cyclical unemployment is associated with the swings of the business cycle. Thus, when the economy drops into recession, workers are laid off. Usually such layoffs, a function of a slower economy with less demand, are temporary, and cyclically unemployed workers can expect to return to their old jobs when the economy picks up. **Structural unemployment** differs. It refers to the chronically unemployed, those who are unable to get or retain jobs. Many factors lead to structural unemployment, including the lack of job skills, economic change such that skills once in demand are no longer needed, and overall economic decline.

Unlike inflation, which shows few or weak redistributional effects across classes, unemployment has a redistributional effect. Since unemployment tends to fall hardest on the less well off, it redistributes income upward. When unemployment is high, which is usually the case during recessions, income concentrates in the hands of the upper-income classes.[72]

The most direct effect of unemployment is on people's incomes. People try to cope with the financial burden by cutting back on expenditures, selling assets to raise cash, borrowing from friends and family, and dipping into savings. Savings are often low to start with because the unemployed are on the average less well paid as workers. In some cases, other family members are forced to seek work.[73]

The length and duration of the Great Depression of the 1930s led the federal government to institute an unemployment insurance program, which pays benefits to laid-off workers. The funds for unemployment claims come from workers and their employers, while the states administer the program. This program softens the financial blow of unemployment and spreads the burden of unemployment beyond the unemployed. Depending on the state and level of prior income, an unemployed worker can receive 50 to 60 percent of posttax income. Still, unemployment usually brings loss of medical benefits, and despite unemployment insurance benefits, the unemployed receiving those benefits still feel financially constrained.[74]

The effects of unemployment spill over into other aspects of life. Family tensions rise, general satisfaction with life declines, and for many used to working, the long hours without work result in boredom. The unemployed are often socially isolated, losing contact with former coworkers and sometimes shutting themselves off from others out of social embarrassment. One study has linked unemployment to increases in a whole host of social problems, including higher mortality rates, suicides, homicides, mental hospital admissions, and imprisonment rates.[75] Thus, the personal effects of unemployment not only impinge on private life but invade society as a whole.

Last, government itself feels the effects of unemployment. As workers are idled, tax revenues decline because wages are lost, sales decline, and overall economic activity slows. At the same time, however, demands on government resources mount, as some unemployed workers claim benefits, medical service needs are shifted to government, crime increases, and the like.

Attitudes Toward the Sources of Unemployment

There are very few data on Americans' attitudes toward the unemployed. What evidence exists presents a sketchy and muddled picture. There is strong support for unemployment benefits programs, like unemployment insurance, but little support for government-guaranteed jobs—government hiring of the unemployed just to put them to work.[76]

On the whole, studies find strong public sentiment for the government to do more about unemployment,[77] and public support for such actions increases when the economy declines into recession. This contrasts with public support for welfare, where support is less strong and not as sensitive to economic cycles.

In contrast, there is less support for using the government to hire the unemployed, and job-creation programs, often surrounded in political controversy, have found only intermittent support in Congress.[78] Some government jobs programs have at times found public support, but these tend to be focused on young people; such support came from about 80 percent of the population in the 1930s, 1960s, and 1970s, when polls queried people about such programs.[79] Public support for programs that increase jobs in the private sector is greater than public support for public-sector job creation.

In part this muddle results from the different images of cyclical and structural unemployment. (Natural unemployment does not enter the picture here.) The public is more predisposed to aid the cyclically unemployed, because these workers were displaced through no fault of their own. In contrast, many images of the structurally or chronically unemployed are fused with public attitudes toward welfare, the value of work, and the sources of poverty. Here Americans' general individualist and self-reliant ethic leads them to view the chronically unemployed in negative terms.

We can see the effect of this ethic in the results of studies on how the unemployed come to terms with their own job loss. There are three major sources of blame for unemployment: the individual, the work context, and government policies.[80]

In the 1930s, self-blame was widespread and seemed a natural outgrowth of the U.S. culture of individualism that may have been at its height during the Roaring Twenties. However, a study in the 1970s indicates that fewer workers now blame themselves for their job loss. The experience of the Depression may have altered Americans' thinking about job loss, providing a painful real-life case of a system gone awry. But modern workers have not generalized unemployment to government policies, nor do they seem to blame the economic system in general.

Instead, circumstances related to the work context account for their plight. Thus, they matter-of-factly point to plant closings, loss of contracts, business slowdowns, conflict with the boss, or desire for a change as the most common reasons for their job loss.[81] These reasons are often individualized and are not tied to overall political conditions. Although government is held responsible for the state of the economy, the individual's own circumstances are not seen as being directly affected by government policies. The ethic of individualism reigns here as well. Not only do idled workers view their unemployment as an individual, not a social, experience, but they feel individually responsible for doing something about it.[82]

PUBLIC OPINION AND THE INFLATION-UNEMPLOYMENT TRADEOFF

People almost always consider inflation a more important problem than unemployment.[83] Since the 1970s, the Survey of Consumer Sentiment of the University of Michigan's Survey Research Center has asked people about their relative concern about inflation versus unemployment. This is the question they pose to respondents: "Which of these two problems—inflation or unemployment—do you think will cause the more serious economic hardship for people during the next year or so?"[84]

On almost all surveys across the two decades, inflation outpaced unemployment as the more serious threat. Only for short spells in 1971, 1975, and 1982 to 1985 did unemployment surpass inflation in public concern. Notably, these were periods of high unemployment; the unemployment rates of the Reagan-induced recession of 1982–1983 approached double-digit levels, the highest since the Great Depression of the 1930s.

The data cited in this chapter would lead us to expect the general public to weigh inflation more heavily than unemployment. There is greater trepidation about inflation than unemployment, with most feeling that inflation is costly to everyone and holds no benefits. Unemployment is often caused by the unemployed themselves, especially in the case of structural unemployment, and the ethic of individualism and self-reliance prescribes that individuals have primary responsibility to take care of that problem. Inflation is less tractable; people are caught in its currents and can do little about it. Self-reliance can do little to combat inflation. The consumer is at the mercy of little-understood and hard-to-control forces. Thus, public demands on government emphasize inflation over unemployment.

Still, all of this must be put into context. The level of concern over both inflation and unemployment has varied over time, and as noted, in some instances unemployment surpasses inflation as a concern. The relative levels of both seem important in understanding the direction of public emphasis. Hibbs demonstrates that as inflation heats up, the public becomes more concerned with it as a problem than with unemployment.[85] As unemployment increases, the public turns its attention more to the unemployment side of the tradeoff.

But unemployment must rise to very high levels before a majority of the population focuses on it over inflation.[86] At unemployment rates of 5 to 6 percent, the majority of the public will always focus more on inflation than unemployment. Unemployment must rise to 7 to 8 percent to command majority concern, but inflation has to remain at modest to low levels (4 percent or less). Only when unemployment rests at the 10 percent mark or above will a majority focus on it over inflation even at high inflation rates (say 10 percent). Thus, we can see one reason why U.S. governments take stronger anti-inflation than anti-unemployment stands; there is stronger public demand to combat inflation than unemployment. Unemployment has to become a massive problem for it to divert public concern away from inflation. This is consistent with all we have learned about the economic preferences and values of the general public.

CONCLUSION

Public opinion in the United States leans in the conservative direction, strongly supporting capitalism, generally rejecting forceful government intervention in the economy, and willing to trade off higher rates of unemployment for lower inflation levels. This provides the context in which government leaders make economic policy.

Public opinion does not lead policymakers as much as provide a set of constraints under which policy is made. Thus, in the United States, not all economic policies are acceptable to the general public, and policymakers, as a result, will not offer unacceptable policy solutions. Specifically, the conservative nature of public opinion rules out any type of command regime and usually negates government ownership approaches. Even regulation is viewed suspiciously at times. Similarly, in building policy to moderate the business cycle, public preferences weigh inflation as a higher priority than unemployment.

Within these boundaries, policymakers are given wide latitude. Once policy is formulated, the task of policymakers is to lead the public, to mobilize support for the specific policy alternative. As long as formulated policy is safely within the acceptability zone, generating public support is a possibility. Policymakers also respond to the general contours of public opinion when making economic policy because economic concerns can gain easy access to the public's agenda. Furthermore, the public may act on its concern about economics by withdrawing electoral support from politicians. Thus, politicians have another incentive to pay attention to public opinion when making policy. The details of policymaking, however, are left up to political leaders.

Key Terms

bracket creep
corporate welfare
cyclical
  unemployment
deserving poor
equality of
  opportunity
equality of
  outcomes
inflation
macroeconomy

misery index
natural
  unemployment
Phillips curve
  tradeoff
political-economic
  culture
progressive taxes
stagflation
structural
  unemployment

undeserving poor
unemployment
wage-price spiral
welfare capitalism

Explore the Web

Much of the material in this chapter relies on surveys of the general public. A very good site that allows one to conduct direct analysis of the *General Social Survey* (GSS) of the National Opinion Research Center at the University of Chicago is http://gort.ucsd.edu/gss/, an address administered by the University of California at San Diego. The University of Michigan site, http://www.icpsr.umich.edu/GSS/, provides similar support and search engines for the GSS. The archive of the Interuniversity Consortium for Political and Social Research (ICPSR) houses an extraordinary number of surveys and other data sources at http://www.icpsr.umich.edu/. The Roper Center at the University of Connecticut has an archive of over 250,000 survey questions for the United States and the rest of the world. Its homepage is http:// www.ropercenter.uconn.edu/.

Aside from these academic establishments, there are several important commercial polling organizations that maintain Internet sites. These include the Gallup poll (American Institute of Public Opinion) http://www.gallup .com/, which produces the famous "Most Important Problem" series, as well as the longest series of presidential approval polls. The Harris organization http://www.louisharris.com/ and the Yankelovich organization http://www .yankelovich.com/ are among the best known. Most of the networks and major national papers and news magazines also run polls, most of which are archived either at the ICPSR or Connecticut's Roper Center. A nice page that provides links to many other public opinion organizations, categorized by type, is http://www.ropercenter.uconn.edu/links.htm, which is also administered by the Roper Center at the University of Connecticut.

Notes

1. Cited in Benjamin I. Page and Robert Y. Shapiro, *The Rational Public: Fifty Years of Trends in Americans' Policy Preferences* (Chicago: University of Chicago Press, 1992), 142.

2. From analysis of the *General Social Survey,* 1993, 1994.

3. Herbert McClosky and John Zaller, *The American Ethos: Public Attitudes Toward Capitalism and Democracy* (Cambridge, MA: Harvard University Press, 1984).

4. Ibid. These figures are recalculated from those presented by McClosky and Zaller, *The American Ethos,* 163.

5. See the polls reported in Richard G. Niemi, John Mueller, and Tom W. Smith, *Trends in Public Opinion: A Compendium of Survey Data* (New York: Greenwood, 1989), 29–32; and *The Political Culture of the United States: The Influence of Member Values on Regime Maintenance,* Donald J. Devine (Boston: Little, Brown, 1972), 211–214.

6. William G. Mayer, *The Changing American Mind: How and Why American Public Opinion Changed Between 1960 and 1988* (Ann Arbor: University of Michigan

Press, 1993), 463; and Paul M. Sniderman and Richard A. Brody, "Coping: The Ethic of Self-Reliance," *American Journal of Political Science* 21 (1977): 501–521.

7. McClosky and Zaller, *The American Ethos.*

8. Ibid., 133.

9. Ibid.

10. Robert E. Lane, *Political Ideology: Why the American Common Man Believes What He Does* (New York: Free Press, 1962), 57–81. Also see Jennifer L. Hochschild, *What's Fair?: American Beliefs About Distributive Justice* (Cambridge, MA: Harvard University Press, 1981).

11. Lane, *Political Ideology,* 73–74.

12. Page and Shapiro, *The Rational Public,* 127.

13. Ibid., 128; also Devine, *The Political Culture of the United States,* 218.

14. Page and Shapiro, *The Rational Public,* 127–128.

15. Ibid., 128.

16. Ibid., 163–166.

17. Mayer, *The Changing American Mind,* 453.

18. From analysis of the *General Social Survey,* 1993, 1994, 1996.

19. McClosky and Zaller, *The American Ethos,* 91.

20. Page and Shapiro, *The Rational Public,* 124.

21. McClosky and Zaller, *The American Ethos,* 126.

22. Page and Shapiro, *The Rational Public,* 125.

23. McClosky and Zaller, *The American Ethos,* 124–125.

24. Mayer, *The Changing American Mind,* 455. Also Niemi, Mueller, and Smith, *Trends in Public Opinion,* 89.

25. Page and Shapiro, *The Rational Public,* 125; and McClosky and Zaller, *The American Ethos,* 275–276.

26. On the 1996 welfare reform law and its early aftermath, see Jeffrey L. Katz, "Clinton's Changing Welfare Views," *Congressional Quarterly Weekly Report,* July 27, 1996, 2116, "After 60 Years, Most Control Is Passing to the States," *Congressional Quarterly Weekly Report,* August 3, 1996, 2190, and "Long-Term Challenges Temper Cheers for Welfare Successes, *Congressional Quarterly Weekly Report,* October 25, 1997, 2603.

27. Mayer, *The Changing American Mind,* 92.

28. Page and Shapiro, *The Rational Public,* 124–125; and Mayer, *The Changing American Mind,* 458–459.

29. Page and Shapiro, *The Rational Public,* 121.

30. Ibid., 118–121; and Paul C. Light, *Artful Work: The Politics of Social Security Reform* (New York: Random House, 1985), 58–73.

31. Ibid., 120–121.

32. McClosky and Zaller, *The American Ethos,* 237 passim.

33. Page and Shapiro, *The Rational Public,* 126.

34. Ibid., 144.

35. Mayer, *The Changing American Mind,* 479.

36. Ibid.

37. Ibid., 483.

38. Ibid., 485.

39. Ibid., 479.

40. Ibid., 482, 484.

41. Ibid., 490.

42. Paul Peretz, *The Political Economy of Inflation in the United States* (Chicago: University of Chicago Press, 1983), 87.

43. To compute the rate of inflation, subtract the current price from the previous price and divide by the previous price. In our example this is (1998 price − 1997 price)/1997 price, or (105 − 100)/100. This reduces to $\frac{5}{100}$, or 5 percent.

44. There is considerable debate among economists currently over whether the Phillips tradeoff actually exists.

45. A good, nontechnical review of inflation and its effects is found in Robert Eisner, *The Misunderstood Economy: What Counts and How to Count It* (Boston: Harvard Business School Press, 1994), 145–168.

46. Peretz, *The Political Economy of Inflation in the United States,* 104.

47. On policymaking at the Fed, with hints that there may be such a bias, see William Greider, *Secrets of the Temple: How the Federal Reserve Runs the Country* (New York: Simon & Schuster, 1987); Donald F. Kettl, *Leadership at the Fed* (New Haven, CT: Yale University Press, 1986); and John T. Woolley, *Monetary Politics: The Federal Reserve and the Politics of Monetary Policy* (New York: Cambridge University Press, 1984).

48. Douglas A. Hibbs, Jr., *The American Political Economy: Macroeconomics and Electoral Politics* (Cambridge, MA: Harvard University Press, 1987), 87.

49. Peretz, *The Political Economy of Inflation in the United States,* 52–58.

50. There exists only a small literature on public attitudes toward inflation. The most important and thorough analysis is Peretz, *The Political Economy of Inflation in the United States,* which is relied on heavily in the following pages. Also useful are Pamela Johnston Conover, Stanley Feldman, and Kathleen Knight, "Judging Inflation and Unemployment: The Origins of Retrospective Evaluations," *Journal of Politics* 48 (1986): 541–564; Pamela Johnston Conover, Stanley Feldman, and Kathleen Knight, "The Personal and Political Underpinnings of Economic Forecasts," *American Journal of Political Science* 31 (1987): 559–583; and M. Stephen Weatherford, "Economic Voting and the 'Symbolic Politics' Argument: A Reinterpretation and Synthesis," *American Political Science Review* 77 (1983): 158–174.

51. Peretz, *The Political Economy of Inflation in the United States,* 81.

52. Ibid., 98.

53. Ibid., 85–86.

54. Ibid., 82.

55. Ibid., 83–84.

56. Ibid., 101.

57. Ibid., 107–110.

58. Ibid., 110–111.

59. Ibid., 111.

60. Ibid., 112–113.

61. Ibid., 113–114.

62. Ibid., 114–115.

63. Ibid., 99.

64. Ibid., 117. Unfortunately, since 1969 no poll has directly addressed this issue. Thus we cannot be certain that the public is still resistant to tax increases and higher interest rates to curb inflation. But it is quite clear that well into the 1990s the public remained in a general antitax mood. Presumably, this mood would limit public support to fight inflation with tax increases at the present time.

65. Ibid., 118–119.

66. Ibid., 118.

67. Ibid., 121.

68. Ibid., 122.

69. Seymour Martin Lipset and William Schneider, *The Confidence Gap: Business, Labor, and Government in the Public Mind*, rev. ed. (Baltimore, MD: Johns Hopkins University Press, 1987).

70. Hibbs, *The American Political Economy*, 43–61.

71. On natural unemployment, again Eisner, *The Misunderstood Economy*, 169–194, is very good.

72. Hibbs, *The American Political Economy*, 43–61.

73. Kay Lehman Schlozman and Sidney Verba, *Injury to Insult: Unemployment, Class, and Political Response* (Cambridge, MA: Harvard University Press, 1979), 86–89.

74. Ibid., 93–97.

75. M. Harvey Brenner, *Mental Illness and the Economy* (Cambridge, MA: Harvard University Press, 1973).

76. There is also a small literature that deals with the origins of attitudes to unemployment, as opposed to the unemployed. See Conover et al., "Judging Inflation and Unemployment" and "The Personal and Political Underpinnings of Economic Forecasts"; and Weatherford, "Economic Voting and the 'Symbolic Politics' Argument."

77. Page and Shapiro, *The Rational Public*, 121–122.

78. Donald C. Baumer and Carl E. Van Horn, *The Politics of Unemployment* (Washington, DC: CQ Press, 1985).

79. Page and Shapiro, *The Rational Public*, 122–123.

80. Schlozman and Verba, *Injury to Insult*, 193–196.

81. Ibid., 193.

82. Ibid., 193–194.

83. Peretz, *The Political Economy of Inflation in the United States,* 87–88; and Hibbs, *The American Political Economy,* 129–138.

84. On some surveys the phrase "will cause the more serious economic hardship for people" is replaced with "may have the more serious consequences for the country."

85. Hibbs, *The American Political Economy,* 134–137.

86. Ibid., 137.

4

Extragovernmental
Actors and Economic
Policy I:
The Business Sector

ECONOMIC POLICY is formalized by those in government, such as the president, members of Congress, and bureaucrats. However, these policymakers do not craft economic policy in isolation from the rest of society, especially those who take an active interest in the course of government economic policy. In this and the next chapter we will discuss those people outside government who influence economic policymaking in the United States. We focus on business in this chapter, and in Chapter 5 we consider the two major challengers to business who also affect economic policy, labor and postmaterialists.

Lobbyists have long been political targets. They are viewed as corrupting influences in government, plying legislators with food, liquor, and holiday trips, and since those who work for big business have the most money to spread around, they are seen as the worst offenders. Similarly, the arms of interest groups that contribute money to election campaigns, **political action committees (PACs)**, are also viewed with suspicion. PACs came into existence as a consequence of campaign finance reform laws in the mid-1970s. Corporations are prohibited from contributing to election campaigns, but they may create and channel money into organizations that can contribute to candidates for election. We will discuss PACs in more detail later in this chapter.

Politicians of both parties have targeted lobbyists and PACS. In 1989, President Bush offered a set of reforms that focused on campaign finance. He sought the abolition of most PACs, allowing only those that are not connected with business or labor groups. He also sought to limit how much money congressional campaigns could accept from PACs.[1] President Clinton, too, submitted campaign finance and lobbying reform legislation to Congress. This legislation called for a tightening of the rules concerning who can be a lobbyist and what are permissible lobbyist activities. It also required disclosure of lobbying gifts to public officials. In addition, Clinton asked for limitations on campaign expenditures and greater federal subsidization of congressional campaigns.[2]

After the 1996 presidential elections, campaign finance reform moved to the top of the congressional agenda, again. The Clinton reelection campaign stimulated the reform discussion and proposals. His campaign was suspected of illegally accepting contributions from representatives of foreign nations, as well as improperly using government offices to solicit contributions. Republicans held hearings on the campaign finance alleged violations and reform proposals during the summer of 1997, but little came of those hearings. Other reform proposals were also floated throughout 1997 and 1998, several of which aimed at ending the use of **soft money** and of campaign advocacy advertisements. Soft money is money that corporations, unions, and wealthy individuals donate directly to the political parties. Soft money is one way to circumvent contribution restrictions to candidates. Advocacy advertisements, which do not explicitly support or oppose particular candidates, also are not regulated by existing campaign laws. Most of these efforts had a hard time gaining congressional support because the Republican leadership opposed them, plus incumbents, who won election under the old system, were unlikely to change a system that seemed beneficial to them in getting reelected. The main point, however, is the recurrent status of campaign finance on the political and policy agenda of Congress and the nation.[3]

The impact of money, especially that coming from the well-heeled business sector, is of special concern to the political world. Money is viewed suspiciously. Moreover, the money of business interests is feared even more because business is assumed to wield immense political influence. Some feel that influence derives from the sheer size of the business sector and its financial resources.[4]

In fact, some suggest that business occupies a privileged position in the political system, not because of the money and other resources that business can mobilize but because of the role of business in the economy and the reliance of politicians on the economy. As Charles Lindblom, the leading advocate of this position argues, "In the eyes of the government officials, businessmen do not appear simply as representatives of a special interest, as representatives of interest groups do, they appear as functionaries performing functions that government officials regard as indispensable."[5] These functions revolve around providing a healthy economy. In a sense, Lindblom argues that political systems that rely on market economies are somewhat captured by the needs of the market.[6]

Thus, business and business interests are a pervasive element of economic policymaking in the United States. But the privileged position argument is not without its critics. Many policies benefit business, but some do not. Some economic policy regimes are favorable to business, while others are less so,

and business impact on economic policy has varied over U.S. history. Moreover, as David Vogel demonstrates, although during some periods business
seems quite politically potent and gets the policies it wants, as was the case in
the post–World War II period up to the mid-1960s, during the later 1960s
and through much of the 1970s, business was successfully challenged from
many quarters and lost many important political and policy fights.[7]

Thus, the issue of business impact on economic policymaking is not as
simple as the story of money, although money is an important element in
business-sector influence. In this chapter, we look at the role of business in
the development of economic policy in the United States.

THE LEGAL POSITION OF BUSINESS IN THE UNITED STATES

Corporations are essentially multiple partnerships.[8] But they are also legally
created organizations, because they must be chartered by the state or sover-
eign to exist. Prior to the industrial revolution, the Crown chartered corporations in England, granting them special privileges and powers to operate.
Early corporate charters, even in the United States, were granted for specific
and well-defined activities.

After the American Revolution, the power to grant charters was lodged
mainly with the state governments. Although the Constitution granted the
federal government the power to charter corporations, before the Civil War
it did so only twice—the two banks of the United States. Until then, states issued thousands of special action charters. Such charters were very specific
and detailed and were issued one at a time by legislative action. Corporate
activity was bound by the limits of the charter; any changes required more
legislative action.

By the 1870s, general provision charters were allowed. These types of corporate charters no longer required legislative action, nor were they limited to
specific purposes. Corporate activity could be determined by business people
themselves and could change with changing business conditions.

Because incorporation required state sanction, the state could regulate corporate activities. Initial regulation came from the special action charters, with
their specified limitations on activities. As corporations were founded on general action charters, more general regulations were developed to provide the
government with control over their creatures. Thus, at the federal level, the Interstate Commerce Act of 1887 and the Sherman Antitrust Act of 1890 created
regulatory power vested in federal bureaucracies to control the behavior of the
large corporations that were becoming so important to the industrial economy.

Although incorporation may protect partners from each other, and their
private property from creditors, those protections come at a price: potential

government regulation. In this sense, corporations are legal entities with rights and protections, but subject to government control. Corporations are not purely private associations. They have an important public character.

BASES OF BUSINESS POLITICAL INFLUENCE

The U.S. business sector possesses a wide variety of resources that it can convert into political action and influence. These resources range from the tangible, such as the financial resources of the nation's corporations, to the intangible, such as the regard that the public and politicians hold for business leaders and the economy. We begin with the two underlying resources, business-sector legitimacy and money, and see how they underpin the many other resources at business's disposal.[9]

Usually, the first step for any interest group or social movement trying to gain access to the political system is to prove that it has a key role to play, that it is a legitimate part of U.S. society, and that the issues it promotes deserve a hearing. The business sector does not have to jump this hurdle, however. Business already holds a special legitimacy in U.S. society and politics. It does not have to prove its position or value to society.

There are several reasons for this special legitimacy. First, there is a cultural ideology that espouses the virtues of capitalism and the free market. Business, as a consequence, is often looked on as a good and productive part of society. The long-term success of the U.S. economy builds more respect for business leaders. Throughout U.S. history, business leaders have been looked on as heroes, as people to emulate.[10]

Although it is true that at certain times in our history, some business leaders have been seen as unscrupulous, such as the "robber barons" of the late 1800s,[11] the more common view is that business leaders are pragmatic, bold, and savvy. This cultural norm is so strong that during the Progressive era at the turn of the century, Progressive reformers wanted to clean up government corruption in part by bringing "scientific business practices" to government.[12]

From another vantage point this respect for business affects the kinds of policy solutions that get onto the nation's agenda. Those who propose government solutions, that is, using the government to solve problems, are often at a disadvantage, because they have to convince the country to try the government versus the market solution. "Governmentalists" are usually on the defensive. Market advocates are not in such a defensive posture.

A second source of business influence resides in its control over the economy and the political system's need for an expanding and healthy economy.[13] The limitations on government intervention in the economy mean that many economic decisions with national implications are made not in the councils of government but at corporate headquarters. Decisions that the nation's major firms make about their own operations have economic consequences beyond their corporate boundaries because of their large size. Thus, decisions to build a new factory, stop a product line, or lay people off may have national economic implications. In the United States, despite the amount of government intervention in the economy, most important economic decisions are made in the private sector. This means that there is a great degree of private control over the economy.

This private economic control gives those who lead the nation's largest firms a significant resource to influence government. Politicians in the United States need business people because they need an economy that is growing.[14] They need this growth for several reasons. First, politicians are more likely to retain their offices, and thus their political power, if the nation's economy is sound. Economic distress is a major cause of politicians' being defeated for reelection. Second, politicians need a growing economy to pay for the government programs that their constituents demand. When the economy is not in good shape, the government has less money for these purposes.

Business can also wield influence over government by threatening to leave one jurisdiction for another. Even if a threat is never voiced, there often exists the possibility that a business might relocate. Relocation naturally undermines growth, as jobs are lost (or transferred to other geographic locations). Political authorities, understanding the risk of a potentially "footloose" company, may refrain from promulgating laws that business opposes. Similarly, some jurisdictions may try to induce businesses to leave their current location and resettle in their locality. Many states in the United States now have "foreign trade" offices, where state officials will tour other nations in hopes of luring companies. They may carry inducements, such as tax reductions, infrastructure and other types of construction, worker training programs, government loan financing and underwriting, and so on. Without business even making use of the relocation threat, it may receive benefits as localities compete to attract and maintain business operations.

The control that corporate executives have over decisions with broad economic implications means that politicians must seek the cooperation of these private-sector decision makers. When business balks at a policy proposal, suggesting that it will harm the economy by costing jobs or fueling inflation, for instance, politicians are apt to listen. The merest suggestion from business leaders that an economic slowdown could occur if the government pursues a policy course is often enough to derail that option. No one else in the private sector has this kind of influence. Few in government can rival it either.

In addition to this control over the economy, the business sector has tremendous cash reserves. The largest one hundred firms in the United States account for about one-fifth of the entire economy. For example, in 1998, five corporations, General Motors (GM), Ford, Wal-Mart, Exxon, and General Electric (GE) had revenues of over $100 billion. The nation's four largest banks, Citigroup, Bank of America, Chase Manhattan, and Bank One, had assets that ranged from \$261 billion to \$668 billion. These figures are comparable to, if not larger than, the budgets of many nations.[15]

There is probably no resource as politically convertible as money. Money can buy the services of others, like lobbyists, lawyers, and public relations specialists. It can buy information. It can be donated to political campaigns. There seems to be no part of the political system that is immune to the power of money. Money need not be an insidious and corrupting force. It can buy many legitimate and useful resources for the business community, some of which may help improve policy debate.

For instance, money can purchase quality information and expertise. Corporations can use their financial resources to hire experts to study the effects of a policy option on the economy. They can hire scientists to study the health effects of a product. They can hire pollsters to study what is on the public's mind. The types of information coming from these experts can help inform public debate.

But corporate assets can also be used more selfishly. Lobbyists can be hired to press a corporation's case in the committee rooms of Congress and the chambers of regulatory commissions. Lawyers can be hired to help rewrite pending legislation and regulations, to plead a corporation's case in judicial proceedings, or to find loopholes that will enable a corporation to skirt or take advantage of a law. Public relations people can be hired to manage a publicity campaign to change the public's mind about an issue or policy approach.

The business organization itself is a vital resource. The organization provides business with a base for political mobilization. Having an organization already in place means that businesses do not have to pay the organizing costs that other interests must incur. Those organizing costs are already paid as a function of trying to sell goods and services. In addition, the organization provides firms with a cache of people, many of whom have the expertise to aid business in its political activities. These may include lawyers and policy experts, but also political activists who may have contacts among politicians.

Also, its organization gives a business a sense of history or memory of what happened in the past. This memory may concern strategies and tactics—which ones worked, which did not—and whom to contact in the political arena and whom to stay away from. This memory may also be about policies—what worked, what didn't, and why. Having an organization in place with a memory of past events allows business to learn and to retain learned lessons so that past mistakes will not be repeated. This may increase the efficiency of the business's political activity.

Further, business has some measure of control over its workers. It hires and fires people, and to retain their jobs, as well as sometimes help out their employer, workers may be mobilized in support of policies that their employer supports. Autoworkers, feeling the effects of competition from Japanese manufacturers as much as their corporate bosses, have supported many of the policies that the major U.S. car manufacturers have advocated, and the airline unions cooperated with many of the airline companies that opposed deregulation in the 1970s.[16]

Businesses are well situated to mobilize their workers on their behalf. Communicating with workers is relatively easy because most come to the job site to work. Business can facilitate worker activism on its behalf by offering release time from work to engage in policy-relevant activities, providing transportation, and otherwise subsidizing some of the costs of organizing collective action on the part of workers. For instance, in the 1970s the Atlantic Richfield company organized its employees, along with its stockholders and retired employees, into forty-five regional committees, which were encouraged to speak out on policies of concern to the corporation. As another example, the Fluor Corporation, which was to share in the 1978 arms deal with Saudi Arabia, helped organize a letter-writing campaign by its twenty thousand employees to members of Congress.[17]

Moreover, the credibility of the business message may be enhanced if workers actively support it. This broad base may lead politicians to worry about election day reprisals if they produce policies at variance with businesses' wishes. Thus, the work force becomes a resource that business can exploit to its policy ends.

The business sector, then, possesses a multitude of resources that it can apply politically. These resources derive from the prominence of business in the economic order, the money at its disposal, and its organizational presence and continuity. For the most part, this discussion of business resources has focused on those that may be applied in formal governmental settings, like the halls of the legislature and the offices within the bureaucracy. But business resources may extend into more public forums, like elections. It is to this issue that we now turn as we look at the role of business political action committees.

THE SPECIAL CASE OF BUSINESS PACs

Political action committees (PACs) are the formal arms of interest groups and associations that contribute money to political election campaigns. PAC money may be important in influencing the policymaking decisions of legislators. Those that receive contributions may feel obligated to make policies that their contributors like, if only to keep the money flowing for the next election. However, legislators may also be of a like mind with their contributors on policy, and PACs may give money to those who already agree with them. There is little direct evidence that PAC contributions affect the policymaking decisions of legislators, but the possibility is ever present.[18]

The money that business PACs receive must be kept separate from the corporation's finances, and soliciting money from corporate employees is heavily regulated. No direct coercion is allowed, though the culture of each corporation may put pressure on its personnel to donate to the corporation's PAC.[19]

Prior to 1971, it was illegal for corporations to contribute money directly to a candidate's election campaign. There were ways around those regulations, however. Bonuses could be given to select employees, who would then contribute some part of that bonus to candidates for office. Employees could also be given time off from work to participate in the campaign.

In the early 1970s, the issue of campaign finance reform hit the top of the political agenda as examples of corruption were made known and the costs of running a political campaign escalated. For decades, the AFL-CIO had an office, the **Committee on Political Education (COPE)**, which was allowed much wider political participation than corporations. To try to even the competition, business sought to restrict COPE's activities. Labor successfully fought the challenge, but in the process a loophole in the reform laws was written that gave corporations a way to match labor's election organization. This is where the PACs began.[20]

In a very short time, corporations saw the virtue of PACs, and by the end of the 1970s, corporate and business PACs proliferated. Table 4.1 lists the number of different types of PACs from the mid-1970s through 1996. Four types of PACs are identified. First are the corporate PACs, directly tied to specific corporations. For instance, there is the AT&T PAC, the IBM PAC, and so on. Labor PACs are associated with individual labor unions. Also identified are trade association PACs. Trade associations represent specific industries, like the chemical, automobile, telecommunications, and real estate industries. Often trade associations represent private-sector interests and thus may be politically aligned with corporate PACs. Last, unconnected PACs are not tied to any segment of the private sector. Often public interest groups and groups mobilized around specific issues are found under this heading. Thus, we find pro-life and abortion groups, environmental groups,

TABLE 4.1 The Distribution of PACs, 1974–1996

Type of PAC	1974	1976	1980	1990	1996
Corporate	89	433	1204	1795	1642
Trade Association	318	489	574	779	838
Labor	201	224	297	346	332
Nonconnected	—	—	378	1062	1103
Total	608	1146	2551	4172	4079
Corporate as a Percentage of All	15%	38%	47%	43%	40%

Source: Data adapted from Harold W. Stanley and Richard G. Niemi, *Vital Statistics on American Politics, 1997–1998* (Washington, DC: CQ Press, 1998), 94.

and so on. Many such groups have mass memberships, unlike trade association PACs, whose members are often organizations.

Corporate PACs outnumber all other types of PACs; by 1980, they accounted for about 40 percent of all PACs. The combination of corporate and trade association PACs provides the business sector with the vast majority of all PACs. In 1996, they accounted for 61 percent of all PACs.

Perhaps more important than the sheer number of PACs is the resources that they command. Through their campaign contributions, PACs can have an important say in elections and potentially affect outcomes. Although it is not the case that one can buy an election victory, it *is* the case that well-funded campaigns have an easier time winning than poorly funded ones. Thus, the important questions to ask are: (1) How important is PAC money to campaigns? and (2) What percentage of PAC contributions comes from the business sector?

Table 4.2 presents information on PAC contributions to House and Senate campaigns. As is readily apparent, PACs provide a considerable proportion of the money that candidates have to spend, though in no year do PAC contributions account for more than half of all money available to candidates. Still, there are probably individual campaigns in which PAC money is the dominant financial source. The table also shows that PAC money is more important in House than in Senate contests.

The table also indicates that corporate PACs are a major funding source for House and Senate candidates, but rarely account for much more than 10

TABLE 4.2 PAC Contributions to House and Senate Campaigns

Chamber and Year	Total Money That Candidates Spend	Percentage from all PACs	Percentage from Corporate PACs	Percentage from Labor PACs
House, 1982	$190 million	30%	10%	8%
Senate, 1982	127 million	17	6	4
House, 1988	249 million	40	12	10
Senate, 1988	199 million	22	9	4
House, 1990	255 million	41	14	10
Senate, 1990	191 million	21	9	3
House, 1992	332 million	36	13	9
Senate, 1992	214 million	21	10	3
House, 1994	371 million	34	12	9
Senate, 1994	292 million	15	7	2
House, 1996	461 million	25	11	9
Senate, 1996	242 million	16	8	3

Source: Data adapted from Thomas Mann and Norman J. Ornstein, *Vital Statistics in Congress, 1997–1998* (Washington, DC: CQ Press, 1998), 97–104, 109–112.

percent of the money available to congressional candidacies. Still, these sums can mount quite high. In 1996, corporate PACs donated about $51 million to House candidates and $19 million to Senate candidates. Moreover, corporate PACs are able collectively to contribute more money than labor PACs.

Do corporate PACs take advantage of their resources and their strategic role in election campaigns? Do they target their money? If so, who are their targets, and what does this tell us about business political strategies more generally?

There are several strategies that corporate PACs can employ. First, it must be remembered that no matter how large the sums available to PACs, each PAC budget is finite. Thus, giving money to one candidate necessarily means either not giving or reducing its contribution to other candidates. Second, PACs must decide how much they want to affect the makeup of Congress through the election process versus how willing they are to work with those already in Congress. For business PACs this (until 1994) came down to trying to produce a Republican majority or working with the Democrats, who had controlled Congress almost uninterruptedly for sixty years and who appeared unbeatable. In other words, could corporate PACs use their money to make the Democrats in Congress more favorable to business's position on issues? If they tried to unseat the Democrats and failed, would this lead to more antibusiness policy from Congress as retribution?

For the most part, corporate PACs have been willing to work with entrenched Democrats, but when opportunities to put Republicans in office arose, corporate PAC money went in that direction. This strategy was not immediately apparent to corporate PACs, but evolved by the early 1980s.

In 1980, corporate PACs showed a decided preference for Republicans over Democrats. In the House, 62 percent of corporate PAC money went to Republican candidates. In the Senate, the figure was even higher, 72 percent. And given the large Democratic majorities in the House, it is notable that contributions to Republican incumbents were almost as high as those to Democrats.

Later in the decade this pattern changed, as more money was steered to Democratic incumbents running for reelection. In the House, about one-half of all corporate PAC money went to those candidates. Plus, the amount of money spent on incumbents overall dramatically increased. In the House, by decade's end, almost 90 percent went to incumbents, where it still remains. In the Senate, less PAC money is steered to incumbents, but still from one-half to two-thirds goes to incumbents; most of the remainder goes to open seat contests. Again, little money is spent on challengers trying to unseat incumbents in either chamber. Corporate PACs have shown a decided preference for working with the existing power structure in Congress; they use fewer resources to try to alter the composition of the legislature.

However, when we look at open seats, contests in which no incumbent is running, we see corporate partisan preferences reasserting themselves. By wide margins, corporate PACs in those contests give to Republicans. Thus, when opportunities present themselves to redraw partisan ratios without directly challenging the Democratic majority, corporate PAC money flows to the party that it feels more comfortable with, the Republicans.

BUSINESS INTERESTS, IDEOLOGY, AND ECONOMIC POLICYMAKING

There are basically two ways business people can think about economic policy. First, business people can view policy as it affects the operation, profitability, and viability of their business. This is the **business interest perspective.** It is based on self-interest and monetary calculations. Or, business leaders may view policy more broadly and abstractly, asking how policy affects the business climate, not just how it influences particular businesses. This is the **business ideology perspective.** The business ideology perspective emphasizes the superiority of market solutions over government solutions, seeks reductions in government burdens on business, and favors smaller government—the standard conservative, antigovernment stance.[21]

At times business interest and ideology may converge, but often they do not. It may be in the interest of a business to secure government contracts, thereby promoting big government, while business ideology, with its roots in conservative capitalist and market views of the world, would advocate smaller government. Generally, when a policy directly affects a particular business, the business interest perspective takes over, pushing business ideology to the side. Sometimes this leads a business leader to support a policy at variance with his or her business ideology. Many airline and trucking companies opposed deregulation in the 1970s because they financially benefited from regulation, though they often opposed other types of government regulations on them, such as those dealing with safety and pollution emission issues. When policy does not directly touch a particular business or when the policy is so broadly construed that it affects the entirety of the business community, business ideology becomes the dominant way for business people to think about the policy debate.

A business's competitive and market position determines its interest. As you will see, the structure of the market and the comparative place of businesses in that market often create divisions among businesses in the policymaking process because each is pursuing its own interest, which may conflict with the interest of other businesses. Thus, it is difficult to argue that there is one all-encompassing business interest.

Business ideology emerges from other factors. These forces, however, are often socially or culturally based, not politically or economically. Business ideology and the forces that help create such an ideology bring businesses together; they are cohesive factors. But they are often weak in comparison to the self-interest that motivates the business interest perspective. One consequence of this is that businesses rarely act together, and there is much competition and policy disagreement within the business sector. The challenge for the business sector has been to organize to overcome the natural inclination of each business to pursue its narrow self-interest rather than its collective ideological goals. At this, business has not been too successful. Several conditions, which we discuss next, may help businesses act in concert, but they tend to be situationally specific and are not long lasting.

THE STRUCTURE OF THE BUSINESS SECTOR

The business sector in the United States is neither very cohesive nor centrally organized. There exists no overarching organizational structure that can speak for all of business. Specific business firms, like IBM and AT&T, usually have more political impact than the general organizations that try to represent business interests in the policymaking process. In the United States, there are basically three major types of business organizations that may become involved in economic policymaking: economywide associations, industry-specific associations, and business-specific lobbies.

Economywide associations that represent business interests are venerable, dating to the last century. Two of these are very visible, the National Association of Manufacturers (NAM) and the Chamber of Commerce. Membership in NAM is restricted to manufacturing firms, like automakers, computer manufacturers, and the like. NAM was created in 1895 under the leadership of small midwestern manufacturers, who sought federal promotion of foreign trade. It began to grow rapidly in the decade just prior to World War I when its director, David M. Parry, commenced NAM activities against unions. NAM's antiunion position and activities made it very popular among business leaders during the first part of the twentieth century. By 1914, NAM counted over 3,500 members.[22] Since then, NAM has moderated its political positions.

The Chamber of Commerce developed from concerted federal sponsorship. The Department of Commerce and Labor[23] sought to contact the many small- and medium-sized businesses that dotted the nation as a way of building a constituency for its programs and services. Contacting large firms was no problem; they were easily identified. But the myriad of other firms presented a massive logistics problem. No national organization existed that could bring together these local groups, but many of these smaller firms belonged to local business associations. Under federal guidance, the national Chamber of Commerce was created formally in 1912, after President William Howard Taft called for a national conference.[24]

Although the economywide associations are well known, they are often not as politically influential as the second type of business organization, the **industrywide association**. In fact, NAM refused for many years to register a lobbyist with Congress, as required by law, because it did not view influencing legislation to be its major activity.[25]

Practically every industrial sector in the United States is organized into an association. For instance, in the telecommunications industry there are several associations, including the National Association of Broadcasters (NAB) and the National Cable Television Association (NCTA). Though members of both offer television programming and services, they often take different sides in policy debates affecting telecommunications.

For example, in 1992 Congress passed legislation to increase federal regulation of cable television companies, which had been free of most federal regulation since 1984. The NCTA opposed the new regulations, but the NAB supported them. The NCTA opposed the new regulations because cable companies would be required to pay rebroadcasting fees to local television stations. Previously, local television programming was aired for free by cable companies, with the argument that cable helped increase the size of the audience for the local station. Naturally, the NAB, whose membership is heavily composed of local television broadcasters, liked the idea of this new revenue.

Individual firms are also important actors in the economic policymaking process through the **business-specific lobby,** and, in general, they may have more political influence than either the economywide or industrywide associations. Most major firms in the United States hire lobbyists and/or have offices in the Washington, DC, area (as well as state capitals). Moreover, many major firms have PACs.

The major reason the general business organizations do not possess as much political influence as one might expect is that there are several sources of conflict within the business sector, and these conflicts get expressed in these associations. Inasmuch as these large associations represent conflicting parties, they cannot take strong or united stands in policy debates. As a result, the large associations often do not enter the policy debate, because they are unable to find a position that is amenable to all of their members and fear alienating any set of members. When they do take political or policy positions, these positions may be heavily diluted or compromised to appease their members. Such compromised positions send weak signals to policymakers, who calculate that the association will not be very active on the issue.

Moreover, these associations rely on voluntary membership. Thus, they cannot force the membership to follow the association's line in a particular debate. Without the ability to rally the troops behind a position, these associations are often considered politically ineffectual.

Inability of the Business Sector to Act as a United Interest

The political weakness of the general business associations stems from the many sources of conflict and competition within the U.S. economy. Many firms see government policy as a factor that affects their market position.

Firms thus are more likely to pursue their own economic self-interest than to engage in cooperative political activity with other firms through the economy-wide and industrywide associations. Moreover, the structure of the political system interferes with the development of a business-sector political organization that can effectively represent and speak for business interests. There is no political mechanism to foster business-sector cohesion. In economic policy-making, business more often speaks in many voices than in one united voice.[26]

The most important source of conflict within the business sector is the competition among businesses and industries. This competition means that the financial interests of different firms may come into conflict; what helps one firm or industry may hurt another. Part of the reason for the degree of economic competition among U.S. businesses stems from the great diversity of U.S. enterprises and the lack of any one firm or industry dominating the economy, as is more likely in smaller countries. The U.S. economy is very large and heterogeneous. This is one of its great strengths, but it presents a barrier to effective business coordination in the policymaking process.

It is easy to identify a multiplicity of sources of economic competition. For instance, industries and firms that rely heavily on importing and exporting are often at odds with industries or firms that are more domestically focused. Similarly, new and old industries may be at cross-purposes; new industries try to break into or create markets for their goods, while old industries want to restrict entry of new industries, lest they take away customers. Big and small businesses often hold different interests, as do industries that are capital intensive and industries that are labor intensive. Capital-intensive industries often want access to plentiful money and investments, while labor-intensive ones may be more concerned with the supply and quality of labor. Also, the relationship to government may affect business interests. Some industries and firms are highly entangled with government, either through regulation or government contracts. Others may be more independent of government. Arguably, those firms that receive more in the way of government contracts may be less opposed to big government than those that receive no such direct benefit from government programs. The tremendous diversity of the economy and the firms that comprise it is one major reason for the lack of cohesion within the business sector.

Time after time these competitive pressures get played out in the political arena. Competing firms view government policies as a way to create advantages for themselves or foist disadvantages on their competitors. As a hypothetical example, a firm with a better than average industry record on the environment may support more stringent regulations because the burden will fall more heavily on its competitors. Historically, regulated firms have used regulation to inhibit competitors from entering their markets. Prior to the deregulation of telecommunications, AT&T used its regulated status to keep other firms from developing products that could integrate into the AT&T telephone network, arguing that such products would harm the integrity of the system that AT&T had so painstakingly built.

A second reason for the degree of business conflict and lack of cohesion is the fact that no overarching political mechanism exists to impel unity among businesses. Government in the United States is highly decentralized. At the federal level, there of course exist the several branches of government, but decentralization runs even deeper. For instance, Congress does most of its policymaking work in committees, and the bureaucracy is structured along sectoral economic interests. In neither is there a unit that is given exclusive jurisdiction over economic policy.

Another decentralizing factor of the U.S. system of government is the different levels of government, those of the states and localities as well as the federal government. No level has total authority over making economic policy. When a business finds that one level of government is making policies that it does not like, it can take its concerns to another level in hopes of getting policies more to its liking. The existence of multiple policymaking venues, both across levels of government and across the branches of government, provides businesses with many places to go to seek the kind of policies they feel are in their best interests. Similarly, political units find themselves in competition to attract the most appealing businesses. Delaware, a very small state, has more than its share of corporate headquarters because its laws on incorporation are among the most liberal.

Beyond this constitutional structure that decentralizes economic policymaking, there exists a long-standing cultural norm and ideological bias against government coordination of the economy. During the New Deal, for instance, the **National Recovery Administration (NRA)** was set up. The task of the NRA was to bring together business and labor to set prices, production schedules, and the like in an attempt to stabilize the macroeconomy. Businesses that opposed NRA restrictions placed on them took the NRA to court. The Supreme Court declared the NRA to be unconstitutional, viewing it as an attempt to governmentally manage the economy, which the justices reasoned was constitutionally prohibited. The demise of the NRA impeded any further attempt at centralized economic planning during the New Deal.[27]

Without the existence of a centralized place where economic policy is made, there is little incentive for business to organize centrally either. All organization has costs. At minimum, there are the costs of running the organization, of monitoring members to ensure faithfulness to the organization's positions, and of communicating with members to learn of their desires and to explain what the organization is doing. Without a centralized policymaking body, there is no one for such a centralized organization to try to influence. Thus, there would be costs associated with creating the organization but little benefit.

There is another perspective on the lack of business organization that uses the free-rider concept described in Chapter 1. Essentially, this perspective argues that a public policy, which businesses may seek from government, is a **collective good**. A collective good is basically a public good. That is, it cannot be restricted or privately consumed. However, trying to get government to produce a favorable public policy entails costs, such as hiring a lobbyist, contributing money to candidates running for office through a PAC, and so on. If a company can share in the public policy, because of its collective nature, without having to pay the costs of lobbying government, then the company has no incentive to join a collective effort to secure the policy. Instead, companies are more likely to seek special policies earmarked for them.[28]

For example, suppose that a steel mill prefers pollution legislation that would allow more air-polluting emissions than existing policy allows. If other steel mills desire such a policy, then it is not in the interest of our steel mill to actively seek such a policy if another mill will do it for our mill. Our mill, however, might seek a policy that is directly aimed at it and not at other mills.

Further, as most policymaking that comes from this decentralized government usually speaks to only a small part of the business sector, it would be hard to mobilize overall business interest on those relatively narrow issues. And many of those policies may adversely affect members of any such overarching business organization. This may lead to discord within the organization and its inability to act, much as is the case for NAM and the Chamber of Commerce on many issues.

Thus, the extreme diversity and competitiveness of the firms and industries that make up the U.S. economy, plus the fact that there is no mechanism or institution to unite business as an interest, means that business in the United States rarely takes a concerted stand on policy issues. Instead, industries and firms form coalitions of support and opposition depending on the issue at hand. On most issues only a small part of the business sector is mobilized for political action because only that part is directly affected by the issue.

Sources of Business-Sector Cohesion

Although there is no formal unifying structure for the business sector, it is not correct to assume that business cannot ever unite. For example, there was widespread business opposition to President Clinton's health-care proposals in 1993. This opposition included almost all segments of the business sector, from small to big business, from manufacturing to commercial and trading interests. In this section we identify some of the factors that may promote policy cohesion within the business sector, noting that such cohesion is often situational and not to be taken for granted or to be expected under all circumstances.

First, there is a relatively strong belief among business people in the virtues of the market and capitalism and agreement that government involvement in the economy should be minimized. However, this commitment to free market principals may erode when particular issues are raised.[29] When the opportunity presents itself to reap a benefit from government, many business people quickly discard their free market ideology.

For example, the Chrysler corporation actively sought government help when it was in financial trouble in the late 1970s. When the corporation looked as if it were headed for bankruptcy, it was able to secure a low-interest government loan to keep it afloat. Again in the 1980s, when U.S. automakers were losing market shares to Japanese imports, Chrysler executives, like Lee Iacocca, lobbied Congress for import restrictions. Many more examples of companies using government for their needs, in fact asking for government protection from market circumstances, can be found. Such activity is very common.

Second, redistributive assaults against the business sector may also promote cohesion. Often proponents of redistribution view the business sector as a place from which to extract resources to pay for their redistributive plans, reasoning that the business sector commands considerable wealth, that it has "deep pockets" that can be dug into.

For instance, almost every time minimum wage legislation has come before Congress, the business sector has spoken with a single, loud voice against increases. When redistributive sentiment is aired in the political arena, the business sector feels threatened. Under such collective threats, those who make up the business sector will lay down their disagreements to fend off the redistributors. Once the redistributive threat is over, however, the conflicts within the business sector reemerge.

Third, **interlocking directorates** may also help promote cohesion within the business sector. Interlocking directorates occur when people from one corporation serve on the governing board of another one. For instance, banks often supply representatives to the boards of directors of corporations to which they have lent money. Also, companies that engage in considerable business with each other will trade board members. The impact of interlocking directorates is that the concerns of other firms are brought into the decision-making process of specific businesses. However, interlocking directorates are common only among the nation's largest firms.[30]

Fourth, informal means of association among corporate executives may also help instill a sense of cohesion. For instance, most business leaders share the same background. Overwhelmingly, they grew up in upper- or upper-middle-class families. They attended the same types of schools, including prep schools and, later, elite colleges. Also, business executives are almost all white males. These similarities in background help to foster a similarity of experience and perspective.[31]

Once in the work force, corporate executives belong to the same social clubs, from local country clubs to charitable associations. These clubs provide forums for interaction outside of the boardrooms, where corporate executives can learn how much they have in common with others who hold similar positions in competitor firms. They also help create and maintain networks within the corporate community among people who might not otherwise come into contact because they work in different industries.

These sources of business cohesion all have one thing in common. Their primary purpose is not to promote a business line over public policy issues. The business sector is not organized for concerted political action, but its beliefs, networks, and common orientations may help it coalesce under some conditions and situations. In this way, there is a latent, or deep, structure within the business sector that will allow it to mobilize politically when such activism is called for. Still, it is more common to see elements within the business sector opposing each other on policy issues.

In the early 1970s, in reaction to the worsening economy and attacks on business, along with public policies that increased regulatory and other burdens on business, top corporate leaders formed the **Business Roundtable.** The roundtable was explicitly created to enter policy debate on behalf of business, to be a player in the policymaking process on behalf of business interests, and to build consensus on policy among important business leaders. The roundtable, unlike NAM or the Chamber of Commerce, is limited to corporate executives from the top two hundred firms. Moreover, only the top corporate executive, the CEO, can attend a roundtable meeting. The aim here is to create a united front of top executives and to impress the political system with the importance of a roundtable policy position once it is announced.[32]

WHY DOES BUSINESS SOMETIMES LOSE?

The preceding discussion indicates that business possesses a considerable range of resources it can apply to the political system. The ideology of the political culture creates a foundation of support for business positions on many political issues. Business has an organizational base it can easily mobilize. Most important, business has substantial cash resources that it can use. Still, given this rich resource base, business does not always prevail on policy issues on which it takes a stand.

For instance, during the late 1970s and early 1980s, a number of industries were deregulated. Strong entrenched interests, like the airlines, railroads, and trucking companies, plus AT&T, opposed deregulation, but lost and were deregulated. On a broader scale, the 1960s and early 1970s saw a wave of legislation and policy that much of the business community opposed. For example, environmental and consumer protection, workplace safety, and health legislation were enacted, often imposing severe costs on business. Why does business sometimes lose?

First, business may lose because it is divided. On many of the deregulatory issues, businesses that stood to gain from deregulation were pressing politicians for the policy change.[33] When business is divided, it is hard to talk about winning or losing. Some businesses lose, while others emerge victorious. For instance, in the deregulatory example just mentioned, AT&T was on the losing side, while MCI, a new entrant into telecommunications, was a winner. Similarly, in the cable television example mentioned earlier in this chapter, the cable companies lost to local free television broadcasting companies.

Second, despite business's abundant resources, it may lose because it employs them ineptly, using them inappropriately or not maximizing their strategic impact. For example, money can easily be used inappropriately. The clearest case would be bribery of a public official, but even more ambiguous situations may raise suspicions, undercutting the value of the resource. In an embarrassing example, Speaker of the House Newt Gingrich was offered an advance of $4.5 million by publishing giant Rupert Murdoch for two proposed books. It also happened that Murdoch was planning to start a new television network, the rules of formation for which come under federal regulation. Although it is likely that no irregularities were involved in the incident, it caused political embarrassment to Gingrich and raised suspicions of Murdoch's intent. Money in this case may have harmed a business interest rather than helped it.

In another example, thirty years ago consumer advocate Ralph Nader wrote a book charging that the Corvair, a highly popular GM car, was unsafe. GM went on the offensive, but instead of rebutting Nader's claims, the auto manufacturer attacked Nader's character. Using the full power of the largest auto company against a lone crusader caused a strong negative reaction in the general public, and Nader was able to build public sympathy, air his message to a larger audience, and raise suspicions that GM was hiding something. The GM charges against Nader proved false, completely undermining the GM case, and Senate hearings on auto safety shortly followed.[34]

The category of inept use of political resources includes a large array of mistakes. Thus, it is hard to say anything complete or definitive about it. However, we can suggest that the business sector has generally improved its use of its resources. Through the early 1960s, business put few resources into lobbying efforts. Only 130 corporations had registered lobbyists on their payrolls, and merely 50 had Washington offices. The primary activity of corporate representatives in Washington was to increase "the sale of company products or services to government."[35] There was little need for business lobbying efforts at this time because there were no effective challenges to business interests until the mid-1960s.[36] When business began to be more effectively challenged by reformers like Ralph Nader, its response was often clumsy and/or inappropriate, or out of proportion to the attack. Business was out of practice in the rough and tumble of politics.

In time business learned the more subtle use of resources. Instead of direct counterthreat or character assassination, business began to cultivate public opinion with slick and sophisticated campaigns, to marshal scientific and other types of analysis to buttress its position, to work quietly behind the scenes with critical politicians, and to funnel campaign contributions through the PACs.[37] The more politically active business has become, the more skillful its action and the use of its resources. Rarely are there such embarrassing cases as happened in the past, but on occasion the scandal of a business's trying to influence a politician still occurs.

The third reason business may lose is because the public opposes the business position.[38] Business is most likely to get its way on an issue when there is little public opposition or concern. When public opinion is mobilized against business's position, business may sometimes lose. For instance, in 1990 Congress passed the Americans with Disabilities Act (ADA). Compliance with the act would increase the cost of doing business, requiring access ramps and other special accommodations for employees and customers. There was strong public support for the act, in part deriving from the large number of Americans who had disabled family members or who knew people with disabilities. In fact, public support was so strong that business, despite its opposition to the bill, did not vocalize this opposition very loudly, lest it be tagged as cruel and heartless.[39] Thus, the stronger the public voice, the more likely that public opposition will turn into voting behavior, the higher the likelihood that business will lose. Politicians are very unlikely to stand with business if it might result in being defeating in the next election.

Given such a condition, the business response is to hide the issue from the public or attempt to sway public opinion to its side. In the 1980s, when there was much economic insecurity, especially due to the loss of jobs to foreign competitors, business has found the public often highly receptive to its position. Regulations and other policies that may harm business may initially find public support but often lose that support once business makes its case that the proposals will result in job loss. The current opinion climate toward business differs dramatically from that of the late 1960s and early 1970s, when business was looked on more darkly. The result is that currently, public opinion is rarely opposed to business. Thus, business has had its chief opponent neutralized on most issues.

Another perspective on the question of why business sometimes loses looks at two types of issues with relevance for business, core issues and secondary issues, and argues that business does not lose on core issues, though it may at times lose on secondary ones.[40] **Core issues** are those that strike at the fundamental role of business in society and the economy. These include the right of private ownership and the consequent right of corporate managers to make decisions, and the importance of a free market for freedom and economic development. Core issues are rarely raised, and when they are, they are seldom considered seriously. Business has never lost this fight. During the New Deal, when Roosevelt tried to implement the National Recovery Administration, the Supreme Court struck down the program, as we discussed. In part, core issues are protected by the Constitution, but the public also agrees with those basics.

On secondary issues, business is more apt to lose, though not frequently. Secondary issues do not attack the basic way that business operates but instead affect the profit potential or costs of an activity. Thus, business is highly regulated in the United States, but even in a regulated environment, private enterprise has much freedom from government, is relatively autonomous, and can amass substantial profits. Business has even prospered under regulation.

Hence, it may be argued—though there is no evidence on this point—that business will allow losses on secondary issues to keep core issues from getting onto the agenda. Business looks less omnipotent when it occasionally loses, and critics of business do not have to attack the core if they can win sometimes on secondary issues, which may be vitally important to them.

CONCLUSION

Business is a key player in building economic policy. The business sector commands considerable resources that it can apply to the economic policy-making process. Business, however, is not a unified sector, except under special situations, the most critical being when business as a whole is under attack.

Still, business does not stand alone as a nongovernmental influence over economic policy. As discussed in the previous chapter, public opinion is also an important influence. Business influence differs from the influence of public opinion in that business is more likely to affect directly the details of policy than the public, which is more concerned about its general direction. But business faces well-organized and resourceful challengers who also try to affect the details of economic policymaking. These are labor unions and post-materialism, the topics of the next chapter.

Key Terms

business ideology perspective
business interest perspective
Business Roundtable
business-specific lobby
collective good

Committee on Political Education (COPE)
core issues
economywide associations
industrywide associations
interlocking directorates

National Recovery Administration (NRA)
political action committees (PAC)
soft money

Explore the Web

The National Association of Manufacturers can be found at http://www
.nam.org/. The Federal Election Commission is the lead agency in regulating
campaign finances and practices. Its web page, which includes information
on campaign contributions, is found at http://www.fec.gov/. Common
Cause, the leading public watchdog group, has argued for years for
campaign finance reform and maintains a web page at http://www
.commoncause.org/.

Notes

1. See M. Margaret Conway, "PACs in the Political System," in *Interest Group Politics*, 3d ed., eds. Allan J. Cigler and Burdette A. Loomis (Washington, DC: CQ Press, 1991), 213. Bush vetoed a campaign finance reform bill in 1992, however.

2. M. Margaret Conway and Joanne Connor Green, "Political Action Committees and the Political Process in the 1990s," in *Interest Group Politics,* eds. Cigler and Loomis, 168–170. For one of Clinton's statements, see his letter to congressional leaders on the agenda for the 104th Congress, Weekly Compilation of Presidential Documents, vol. 31, no. 1, January 9, 1995, 22.

3. Helen Dewar, "House Approves a Bill for Campaign Finance, Overhaul Plans Vie to Face Senate Fight," *Washington Post,* August 4, 1998, A2.

4. See, for example, the journalistic accounts of Philip M. Stern, *Still the Best Congress Money Can Buy* (Washington, DC: Regency Gateway, 1992); and Brooks Jackson, *Honest Graft: Money and the American Political Process* (New York: Knopf, 1988).

5. Charles E. Lindblom, *Politics and Markets: The World's Political-Economic Systems* (New York: Basic Books, 1977), 175.

6. Charles E. Lindblom, "The Market as Prison," *Journal of Politics* 44 (1982): 324–336.

7. David Vogel, *Fluctuating Fortunes: The Political Power of Business in America* (New York: Basic Books, 1989), 6–8.

8. Much of this discussion is based on Jonathan R. T. Hughes, *The Government Habit Redux: Economic Controls from Colonial Times to the Present* (Princeton, NJ: Princeton University Press, 1991), 78–83. For a more detailed account, see Henry N. Butler, *The Corporation and the Constitution* (Washington, DC: American Enterprise Institute, 1995).

9. For an overview of business resources, see Lindblom, *Politics and Markets.*

10. For instance, see Louis Galambos, *The Public Image of Big Business in America, 1880–1940: A Quantitative Study of Social Change* (Baltimore, MD: Johns Hopkins University Press, 1975).

11. The term *robber barons* was applied to the big businessmen of the late 1800s. Their vast fortunes and often unscrupulous business and political practices gave rise

to the colorful term. See Thomas Brewer, ed., *The Robber Barons: Saints or Sinners?* (New York: Holt, Rinehart & Winston, 1970); and Peter D. Jones, *The Robber Barons Revisited* (Boston: Heath, 1968).

12. On the Progressive movement ideology and its ties to business, see Stephen Skowronek, *Building a New American State: The Expansion of National Administrative Capabilities, 1877–1920* (New York: Cambridge University Press, 1982).

13. Cathy J. Martin, *Shifting the Burden: The Struggle over Growth and Corporate Taxation* (Chicago: University of Chicago Press, 199), reviews this idea; see pp. 30–49.

14. Ibid.

15. These figures come from the *Fortune* magazine web site http://www.pathfinder.com/fortune/fortune500.

16. Vogel, *Fluctuating Fortunes,* 171.

17. Ibid., 205–206.

18. The literature on PACs is vast. A good review of PAC influence and behavior can be found in Richard A. Smith, "Interest Group Influence in the U.S. Congress," *Legislative Studies Quarterly* 20 (1995): 89–139, esp. 91–97; Frank R. Baumgartner and Beth L. Leech, *Basic Interests: The Importance of Groups in Politics and Political Science* (Princeton, NJ: Princeton University Press, 1998), chap. 7; and John R. Wright, *Interest Groups and Congress: Lobbying, Contributions, and Influence* (Boston: Allyn & Bacon, 1996), chap. 5.

19. See Ann B. Matasar, *Corporate PACs and Federal Campaign Financing Laws* (Westport, CT: Greenwood, 1986), for details on this point.

20. Vogel, *Fluctuating Fortunes,* relates this story.

21. This distinction between business interests and ideology parallels a distinction that political scientists make between interests and ideas. See Marc Allen Eisner, *Regulatory Politics in Transition* (Baltimore, MD: Johns Hopkins University Press, 1991), 10–26, for a good discussion as it relates to regulatory policy. As Eisner states, "It is difficult to separate the influence of ideas from that of interests" (p. 20).

22. Mansel G. Blackford and K. Austin Kerr, *Business Enterprise in American History,* 3d ed. (Boston: Houghton Mifflin, 1994), 205.

23. The Department of Commerce and Labor was created in 1903. In 1914, labor was separated from commerce and became a separate cabinet department.

24. Blackford and Kerr, *Business Enterprise in American History,* 205–206.

25. John R. Wright, *Interest Groups and Congress: Lobbying, Contributions, and Influence* (Boston: Allyn & Bacon, 1996), 35.

26. Jeffrey M. Berry, *The Interest Group Society,* 2d ed. (Glenview, IL: Scott, Foresman/Little, Brown, 1989), 216–220, also makes the point that business is often divided over issues of public policy.

27. A good account of the NRA can be found in James A. Morone, *The Democratic Wish: Popular Participation and the Limits of American Government* (New York: Basic Books, 1990), 156–184.

28. On this general idea, see Mancur Olson, *The Logic of Collective Action: Public Goods and the Theory of Groups* (New York: Schocken, 1965). A business, according to this theory, will join in the effort to secure a collective good only if it is forced

to or if joining the group provides it with other incentives and services, that is, private goods.

29. On the basic free market ideology of business people and their distrust of government, see David Vogel, "Why Businessmen Distrust Their State: The Political Consciousness of American Corporate Executives," *British Journal of Political Science* 17 (1978): 45–78. For a general treatment of the political and egalitarian beliefs of top U.S. leaders, including those from business, see Sidney Verba and Gary R. Orren, *Equality in America: The View from the Top* (Cambridge, MA: Harvard University Press, 1985).

30. On interlocking directorates, see Thomas R. Dye, *Who's Running America? The Clinton Years,* 6th ed. (Englewood Cliffs, NJ: Prentice-Hall, 1995), 150–167. A detailed study of the United States and the United Kingdom is given by Michael Useem, *The Inner Circle: Large Corporations and the Rise of Political Activity in the U.S. and U.K.* (New York: Oxford University Press, 1984).

31. On the backgrounds of corporate executives, see Dye, *Who's Running America?,* 168–194.

32. On the Business Roundtable, see Dye, *Who's Running America?,* 227–230.

33. On this point as it relates to deregulation, see Martha Derthick and Paul J. Quirk, *The Politics of Deregulation* (Washington, DC: Brookings, 1985).

34. See Vogel, *Fluctuating Fortunes,* for more on this case.

35. Ibid., 33. On the state of business lobbying in this period, see Raymond Bauer, Ithiel de Sola Pool, and Lewis Anthony Dexter, *American Business and Public Policy,* 2d ed. (Chicago: Aldine-Atherton, 1972). For a more general treatment, see Edwin M. Epstein, *The Corporation in American Politics* (Englewood Cliffs, NJ: Prentice-Hall, 1969). For a study of lobbyists during this era, see Lester W. Milbrath, *The Washington Lobbyists* (Chicago: Rand McNally, 1963).

36. Vogel, *Fluctuating Fortunes,* 33.

37. One study indicates that once businesses were able to use PAC contributions in political campaigns, public policy turned in a decidedly less antibusiness direction. Dennis P. Quinn and Robert Y. Shapiro, "Business Political Power: The Case of Taxation," *American Political Science Review* 85 (1991): 851–874.

38. Richard Lehne, *Industry and Politics: The United States in Comparative Perspective* (Englewood Cliffs, NJ: Prentice-Hall, 1993), 189–191.

39. Joseph P. Shapiro, *No Pity: People with Disabilities Forging a New Civil Rights Movement* (New York: Time Books, 1993).

40. See John Manley, "Neopluralism: A Class Analysis of Pluralism I and Pluralism II," *American Political Science Review* 77 (1983): 368–383. This position is critiqued by Charles E. Lindblom and Robert Dahl in the same journal, pp. 384–385, 386–389. See Lindblom, *Politics and Markets,* for another review of this issue.

5

Extragovernmental Actors and Economic Policy II: Labor and the Postmaterial Challenge

N OCTOBER 1993, barely one year into his administration, President Clinton addressed the national meeting of the **American Federation of Labor–Congress of Industrial Organizations (AFL-CIO)** in San Francisco. It is not unusual for a president, Democrat or Republican, to speak to such a gathering. But it was unusual for a Democratic president to raise an issue that was important to him but opposed by labor. In a far-ranging speech that touched on many subjects, from health care to the budget to foreign policy, the president found time to lobby labor directly about the **North American Free Trade Agreement (NAFTA)**. Labor opposed the treaty, fearing that as it lowered trade barriers with Mexico, U.S. businesses would head south in search of cheaper labor, and Americans would lose jobs.[1]

The president was unsuccessful in convincing labor to support this policy. Neither did the president change his position, though he was under pressure from labor, a mainstay in the Democratic coalition, to do so. Rather, he pressed for NAFTA, and in a photo opportunity at the White House, he assembled business leaders who supported the policy. The business sector widely supported NAFTA, with much support coming from those in the new high-technology and telecommunications sectors of the economy.

As a result, relations between labor and the president soured, an unusual state of affairs for a Democratic president in this century. Labor even threatened to oppose Democratic members of Congress who voted for the agreement. In September 1995, two years later and almost one full year into Republican control of both houses of Congress, the president delivered a speech by satellite to the United Mine Workers, one of the nation's largest unions.[2] In that speech he touched again on many themes of the earlier AFL-CIO speech, but instead of raising divisive issues, he emphasized common purposes and unity. The president, doing poorly in the polls, began to go back to the core elements of the Democratic coalition for support. Labor has historically been one of those elements.

This story illustrates several themes that we will discuss in the chapter. Labor is an important actor in economic policymaking and has historically been associated with the Democrats. However, its influence in the political system is declining. It is being eclipsed by a new set of economic forces that has supporters and opponents in both parties. This new force we will call the postmaterial challenge. In the first half of this chapter we will discuss the role of labor in economic policymaking, and in the second half the role of **postmaterialism.**

LABOR

Labor, like business, has major interests in U.S. economic policy. For most of the past century in the United States, labor and business have been major competitors and rivals.

Labor often supports redistributive efforts, with business as the target. Moreover, political conflict between business and labor has erupted, as labor has aimed to acquire political rights and influence. Business often views this goal as a threat. In recent years, however, labor's place and role as a potent competitor to business have declined.

The Structure of the Labor Movement in the United States

When we speak of labor, we refer to the organization of workers into labor unions. Labor in the United States, again like business, is not centrally organized, though overarching associations exist. Furthermore, much of the work force is not organized in unions.

In the United States there exists a national association of unions, the AFL-CIO. The AFL-CIO tells us much about the organization of labor in this country. First, not all unions in the United States belong to the AFL-CIO. Some unions have retained their independence, the Teamsters being the largest and most important example.

Two reasons may account for lack of union membership in the AFL-CIO. First, unions may decide not to belong because of disagreements with the national union. Second, unions may be expelled from the national because of irregularities in operation and organization. For instance, the Teamsters and other unions have been suspected of being involved with organized crime. Some unions have not implemented internal democracy, thereby violating AFL-CIO policies.

Within the AFL-CIO there is also a division between the craft and the industrial unions. Craft unions represent workers with specific skills, such as printers, bakers, and so on. Industrial unions are composed mostly of workers who are employed on mass production assembly lines or jobs that require less special training. Many factory workers, miners, and longshoremen fit this second category. Industrial workers are often employed in large numbers by national firms, unlike craft workers, who may be employed by small, locally owned and operated companies. However, as technology has replaced both types of workers and as labor in general has fallen on hard times, the long-standing divisions between these two segments of the labor movement have softened; both segments now are looking more to their common interests in revitalizing labor rather than continuing to fight with each other in intraunion squabbles.

Another division among unionized workers that may be more critical for the future is that between blue- and white-collar workers. Until recent decades, most unionized workers were blue or pink collar.[3] However, white-collar workers have made gains in union membership in recent decades. This is especially true among government workers, where teachers, public university professors, police, and firefighters have joined unions.[4]

Local autonomy also plays a key role in the U.S. labor movement, a factor that finds parallels in the business community, as discussed in the previous chapter. Local autonomy has two meanings for labor. One, the labor movement is divided into industry- or firm-specific organizations, like the United Auto Workers. Two, within those industry organizations, the operating unit is the **local,** which is organized at the workplace level. The nationals cannot dictate policy to the locals, though the nationals do try to set national policies. However, inasmuch as local working, employment, and political conditions vary, national policies and standards may not be widely applicable. Moreover, like the Chamber of Commerce, the AFL-CIO is a voluntary organization, with limited ability to force its member unions to comply with it.

The local autonomy and employment divisions among labor union members inhibit labor's ability to mobilize as a unified political actor at times. Thus, not all unions will endorse the same candidates for office, and many union members vote for Republicans, a growing tendency in recent decades. In part, Republican voting on the part of union members is a result of the lack of identity of some union members with the labor movement. Thus, there are parallels in the experiences of business and labor in the United States, but labor's divisions do not seem as pronounced as business's.

The Development of Organized Labor in the United States

Labor has had a very difficult time organizing in the United States, unlike labor in Europe. At no time in the United States has labor been as well or as extensively organized as in western European nations. For example, most western European nations have a labor party. No such party exists in this country.

There are several reasons for the difficulty that labor has encountered in organizing workers. One is the culture of individualism in the United States. The ethic of individualism works at cross-purposes to organizations and movements like labor, which ask people to organize for collective action and benefit. Second, early unions were filled with large numbers of immigrants, especially from southern and eastern Europe, who happened to be Catholic or Jewish. The early union movement in the United States was, thus, viewed as a foreign element. But perhaps most important were government policies toward labor, which were antagonistic and sought to restrict union organization.

Early Government Policies Toward Unions

The foundation for government antiunion policy was the belief that unions interfered with private ownership. The objective of government during this antiunion period, which lasted from about the late 1860s until the 1930s, was to protect private property. Furthermore, collective bargaining, an objective of labor, was viewed as interfering with the freedom of laborers to move from job to job and with the idea of open, competitive markets, both of which were felt to be vitally important to sustaining capitalism. The support that government gave to business and its opposition to labor led to high levels of business-labor violence.[5]

Prior to the 1930s, government at all levels tended to be antagonistic toward unions. It made little difference which party ran the government, for both parties were antiunion. Antiunionism in the Republican party came naturally from that party's association with big business. This is still true today, though the depth of the antiunionism is not as strong as it was a hundred years ago. The Democrats of the pre–New Deal era were also antiunion. The roots of this antiunionism lay in the small-town and southern roots of the party. While the Republicans of the pre–New Deal era aimed to develop the industrial components of the economy, the Democrats often saw industrialization as a threat. Rather than counter that threat through unions, Democrats sided with the small business person and the small farmer—basically the nonurban elements of the United States. Moreover, the nativism of many Democrats, especially those residing in the South and parts of the Midwest, led them to oppose unions, which, as noted earlier, were thought to be filled with non-Protestants and immigrants from eastern and southern Europe. These ethnic divisions plagued the Democrats' relationship with unions for many years.

Both Republican and Democratic governments allowed business to employ violent tactics against unions in an attempt to break them or keep them from forming. Violence associated with the labor movement was endemic. As Mansel G. Blackford and K. Austin Kerr report, "[B]etween 1876 and 1896, there were more strikes and more persons injured or killed in labor protests than in any other nation."[6] Thus, employers might hire strikebreakers, like the Pinkerton Security Company, with little fear of government reprisal. Similarly, businesses would try to break union efforts through the use of scab labor, workers who would allow themselves to be hired to replace striking workers. Rarely would businesses be prosecuted for using violence against unions, and often government would come to the aid of business when business-union violence erupted.

Governments also used the antitrust laws to interfere with union organization attempts. The first antitrust law, the Sherman Act, enacted in 1890, was invoked against unions with the argument that union activity restrained trade. Not until the Clayton Act was passed in 1914 was labor organization and unionization exempted from antitrust regulation.[7]

Labor's Political Maturation

Partially in response to the hostile business and political environment it faced during the period from 1880 to 1920, labor began to increase its political activity and moderate some of its positions. For example, labor abandoned any radical notions about worker control of business. Instead, the aim of U.S. labor became advancing the material benefits and working conditions of workers. Labor retreated from challenging management's right to run business or the fundamentals of private property in the United States. This strategy was first espoused by **Samuel Gompers,** who was the president of the AFL from 1886 to 1924 (except for 1895).[8]

Gompers's strategy was pragmatic rather than ideological. Pragmatism, as it relates to the labor movement in the United States, refers to working with the system and attempting to become part of it, in contrast to an ideological union movement, which saw unionization as a way to transform society. This pragmatic moderation of the U.S. labor movement seemed to reduce the threat that labor posed to business. Business could work with a labor movement that would not challenge its right to manage but wanted only better wages and working conditions.

Gompers's strategy also had a political component. If labor was to integrate into the economy and extract what it sought, it needed political influence. At a minimum, labor had to neutralize the monopoly hold that business had on politicians. The chief political asset at labor's disposal was voters. Labor could follow the European path by building its own political party, but Gompers's strategy called for a different approach. Instead of establishing formal ties with either political party, labor would support candidates of either party who proved to be its friends.

This bipartisan approach had another logic. If neither party was prolabor, aligning with either would do labor little good. The party that received labor's vote would have no incentive to promote prolabor policies unless it felt that labor was willing to shift its votes toward the other party. In this way labor could create political opportunities and demonstrate to politicians the importance of the labor vote to continuing their careers.

However, as labor was to learn, the Democrats became the natural home for labor interests. This worked well for labor when the Democrats were powerful but proved costly when they were not in power. Moreover, this marriage tied the Democrats to labor, as well as labor to the Democrats, and as you will see, the decline of labor and the Democratic party occurred in tandem.

Labor and the New Deal

The earliest signs of government recognition of labor came before the New Deal with the creation of the Department of Labor in 1914. Labor had worked hard in the 1912 election for Woodrow Wilson, and this was Wilson's way of repaying its support. The Labor Department, however, had little power or duties and was mostly a symbolic gesture. Labor unions, in particular, were not granted many new rights under the new Labor Department. Instead, the major activities of the Labor Department involved the administration of the child and women's labor laws, which were important parts of Wilson's Progressive program.

During the New Deal, government recognition of the rights and power of labor grew rapidly, in part as a result of the success of Gompers's strategy. By the 1930s, the Democrats had begun to learn that labor potentially commanded a large bloc of voters. The once antiunion Democratic Party was transformed into a champion of labor under the leadership of Franklin Roosevelt. Democratic policies, thus, aimed to make it easier for labor to organize workers, who, it was hoped, would cast their ballots in increasing numbers for Democratic candidates. By helping labor, Democrats hoped to help themselves.

Labor unions specifically won government recognition and protection with the passage of the Wagner Act in 1934. This represented a marked shift in government policy toward labor. To administer this new policy, the **National Labor Relations Board** (**NLRB**) was created and charged with overseeing union elections. The board would certify elections and help establish procedures for the conduct of union elections. To unionize, all workers had to do was collect enough signatures on petitions from workers who wanted union representation. Then an election would be held among those workers to determine if majority sentiment favored unionization and, if it did, which union would represent the workers. Moreover, the activities of management were curtailed in the union election process. Management could not pressure workers in any way. Last, the Wagner Act allowed for the closed shop. **Closed shops** require all employees to belong to the union. Consequently, union representatives became important in hiring decisions.[9]

The impact of the New Deal reforms on labor was profound. Union membership increased, though it must be noted that union membership was climbing even before the New Deal reforms. Only through the accumulation of new members did labor become a big enough political asset for Democrats to push policies designed to help labor even further.

Figure 5.1 shows the trend in union membership across the twentieth century. At the turn of the century, union membership in the nonagricultural work force was below 10 percent. It increased by the end of the Wilson administration in 1920 to about 18 percent, but slipped during the 1920s. At the beginning of the Depression, union membership hovered around 12 or 13 percent. The poor job market and Republican antiunion policies account for much of that decline.

Union membership gains did not surge early in the New Deal, but between 1935 and 1940, union participation increased dramatically, from 13.5 to 22.5 percent, an increase of 9 percent. It continued to show growth into the early 1950s, when slightly over 30 percent of the nonagricultural work force was unionized. With the end of the Depression and World War II, labor entered its heyday in U.S. politics, a period that lasted until the end of the 1960s.

Labor and U.S. Politics During the Golden Age: 1940–1970

Labor was at the height of its political power from the end of the Depression until the early 1970s. During those years, the percentage of unionized workers grew, and labor exerted much political influence, especially at the presi-

FIGURE 5.1 Union Membership as a Percentage of the Nonagricultural Work Force, by Decade, 1900–1995

Source: Data adapted from Harold W. Stanley and Richard G. Niemi, *Vital Statistics on American Politics, 1997–1998* (Washington, DC: CQ Press, 1998), 399.

dential level, and oversaw the passage of many beneficial public policies. The basis of union power came from the high level of labor organization, the delivery of votes mostly to the Democrats, and the growing wealth of unions, which could contribute significant sums of money to politicians running for office.[10]

As Table 5.1 shows, union members were more likely to identify with the Democratic Party than the Republican and were more likely to identify with Democrats than nonunion employees. This fact holds to this day, though the Democratic advantage has narrowed.

More important politically than labor identification with Democrats is the voting loyalty of labor members to Democrats. As Table 5.2 shows, in all presidential elections since the 1940s, labor union members have been more likely to vote for Democrats than nonunion workers. In most of those elections, a majority of union members also voted for Democrats in House and Senate elections.[11]

This political power base served labor well, and a number of prolabor policies were enacted during this three-decade era, including minimum wage legislation and the creation of the **Occupational Safety and Health Administration (OSHA)** in the Labor Department. Still, labor was not politically omnipotent. A major defeat occurred in 1947 with the passage of the **Taft-Hartley Act,** which reformed NLRB practices concerning union certification of elections. The NLRB, which had been an advocate of labor, now began to treat labor and management more evenhandedly.

TABLE 5.1 Party Identification of Union and Nonunion Members, 1952–1996

Year	Union Member in Family			No Union Member in Family		
	Dem.	Ind.	Rep.	Dem.	Ind.	Rep.
1952	55%	23%	22%	47%	23%	30%
1956	52	27	21	43	23	34
1960	57	28	15	42	22	36
1964	64	23	13	49	23	28
1968	51	30	19	45	29	26
1972	46	39	15	39	34	27
1976	47	40	13	38	36	27
1980	46	39	14	40	34	26
1984	46	35	19	36	35	30
1988	43	37	20	34	36	30
1992	45	38	17	34	39	27
1996	47	34	19	41	27	32

Source: Survey Research Center/Center for Political Studies, University of Michigan, *National Election Study Surveys, 1952–1996.*

TABLE 5.2 Democratic Percentage of the Vote in Presidential, House, and Senate Elections of Union and Nonunion Members, 1952–1996

	President		U.S. House		U.S. Senate	
Year	Union	Nonunion	Union	Nonunion	Union	Nonunion
1952	56%	36%	61%	44%	54%	42%
1956	53	36	62	49	61	50
1960	64	44	69	51	69	50
1964	83	62	80	59	77	54
1968	56	43	58	50	60	49
1972	43	33	62	53	54	49
1976	64	47	72	52	69	56
1980	55	40	65	51	63	49
1984	57	37	62	53	64	50
1988	59	44	67	57	67	55
1992	68	57	66	58	64	54
1996	67	50	60	44	66	50

Source: Survey Research Center/Center for Political Studies; University of Michigan, *National Election Study Surveys, 1952–1996.*

The Decline of Labor

In 1993, as mentioned at the beginning of this chapter, labor lobbied heavily against NAFTA, a proposal to create a free trade zone among the United States, Canada, and Mexico. Labor's opposition was based on the idea that because Mexican workers were less well paid than U.S. workers, U.S. manufacturing and industrial jobs would move to Mexico, as business sought a way to reduce labor costs.

Labor should have had an easy time persuading Congress to reject the NAFTA treaty. Although polls indicated that the public was evenly split over NAFTA, Democrats held both houses of Congress, as well as the presidency, and Democratic opposition to it was strong.

Yet Congress passed NAFTA. Democrats split over the treaty, while Republicans lined up solidly in support of it. Most important, President Clinton vigorously supported the treaty. The passage of NAFTA illustrates the decline of the influence of labor in U.S. politics. Even with the advantage of public support and Democratic control of the institutions of government, labor lost. This is a far cry from twenty years earlier, when such a combination of political assets would have led to a relatively easy labor victory.

Over the past twenty years, labor has lost much political ground. It is still an important and powerful political and economic interest, but it does not have the political influence that it once did. Why this decline in labor's political power and consequent loss of influence over public policy?

The story of labor's decline is complex, and many factors are involved.[12] We focus·on four: (1) the decline in union membership, (2) increasing public antipathy toward labor, (3) increasingly successful business attacks on labor, and (4) government policies against labor.

Declining Membership Base

At the core of the problem is the decline in the percentage of the work force that is unionized. Figure 5.1 shows that from the 1970s on, the percentage of the nonagricultural work force belonging to unions declined dramatically. From 1950 through 1970, labor's percentage of the nonagricultural work force hovered around 30 percent. By 1995, that figure had been halved to around 15 percent.

Because of this declining worker base, labor has lost much of its political influence. It has fewer votes that it can deliver to politicians seeking office. At the same time, the loyalty of union members to Democratic candidates has dropped off. The combination of these factors results in less political influence for labor.

There are several reasons for the decline in the labor work force. Some are economic, others political. Both the economy and the political system have been working against labor, sometimes consciously, sometimes not.

First of all, the changing structure of the economy has affected labor membership. The jobs from which the bulk of union membership has come, blue-collar industrial and factory jobs, have declined as a percentage of all jobs in the United States. This is in part a function of structural economic changes: blue-collar jobs have been replaced in the economy by white-collar and middle-management jobs. That replacement comes from changes in the economy, away from industry and toward service, but also from the movement of manufacturing jobs out of the United States into developing countries, where wages are lower. This manufacturing job loss is not unique to the United States; it is occurring in most advanced industrial nations.[13]

Labor has had a hard time making inroads into the new white-collar occupations. Many such occupations require professional training, and that training acts as a bar to joining unions. Many professionally trained people view themselves, if not as part of the managerial class, at least as professionals. Individual performance and professional reputation are stronger motivations to these workers than feelings of solidarity with other workers, the kinds of feelings that labor helped instill in the industrial work force.

Labor has, however, made gains in membership among government employees, especially among teachers, public university professors, police, and firefighters. It is estimated that about one-third of government employees at all levels of government are now unionized, a figure about $2\frac{1}{2}$ times as large as that for employees in the private sector.[14] Changes in laws governing public employee unions have made it easier for them to organize.

Another factor contributing to labor's declining membership has been a geographical population shift. The Northeast and Great Lakes regions of the nation, where blue-collar industries were highly concentrated and population was most dense, have lost population to the South and Southwest. In these regions, labor's ability to organize workers is inhibited because the bulk of the states have right-to-work laws. **Right-to-work laws** permit workers to get jobs where there is union representation without joining the union, unlike closed, or union, shop settings, which require union membership when a worker is hired. In addition, the cultural norm in these regions is not as hospitable to labor as it is in the Northeast and industrial Midwest.

Public Perceptions of Labor

Public antipathy to labor has also grown, making it hard to organize new workers as well as retain old ones. For instance, approval of labor unions has declined. In the mid-1960s, about 70 percent of the public had approving attitudes toward labor. That declined to less than 60 percent by the mid-1980s. Confidence in labor has also eroded. Harris surveys found that in 1966, 22 percent of the public had a great deal of confidence in people running labor unions. In 1988, that figure dropped to 13 percent, and a survey in 1998 again found that only 13 percent had a great deal of confidence in those running labor unions.[15]

Several factors help account for the growing negativism of the public, and even of union members, toward labor. One is the belief that labor's leadership no longer represents labor. Many labor leaders now make large salaries; they often live in expensive neighborhoods; their children go to the schools that the children of corporate executives attend. An economic division between rank-and-file workers and labor leadership has opened, causing many to feel that leaders have little in common with average workers.

Moreover, since the 1960s, some labor leaders have taken positions at odds with the beliefs of ordinary labor members. This began with the civil rights movement, when some prominent labor leaders were very active in promoting civil rights, participating in civil rights marches, and the like. In time and across many issues, a vocal element of labor's leadership has come to be associated with social causes that are not very popular among labor members. Some have even felt that these labor leaders have abandoned traditional labor issues for these new social causes. All of this has caused a rift between the workers and the leaders in the labor movement.

Second, many people have come to view labor as a source of the nation's economic ills. During the 1970s, for instance, the nation suffered from high bouts of inflation. The demands of union workers for wage increases during this inflation, some believed, helped induce an inflationary spiral, in which union wage increases, rather than helping workers catch up to inflation, just fueled more inflation. In the 1970s and 1980s, the U.S. economy seemed to compete poorly against foreign nations. Some attributed part of this competitive loss to labor—not only its rigid work rules and its focus on getting better benefits but also its unwillingness to work with management to improve productivity and/or hold down unnecessary costs. Thus, since the 1970s, labor has been seen as one source of the declining performance of the economy.

Third, people associate labor with liberal economic policy positions, as well as other liberal issues, and a growing conservatism among the general public has hurt labor.[16] In the mid-1970s, for instance, public opinion polls indicated a growing support for deregulation. Labor, however, was opposed to most deregulatory measures. Thus, as public disenchantment with government grew, labor still called for government solutions to national problems. In a sense, labor was out of step with the public mood and the times. This has hurt labor, also.

Business Attacks on Unions

A third source of labor's problems is business's direct attack on unions.[17] Business found labor costs to be high, sometimes excessive, in the face of foreign competition. Among the few costs that business can control are labor costs. Thus, business and management leaders looked for a way to contain these costs. One solution was through bankruptcy reorganization. By declaring itself bankrupt, a business can nullify its existing labor contracts. The affected business can then reorganize itself under bankruptcy protection, sometimes hiring nonunion workers, sometimes entering into new contracts with labor that contain provisions more to management's liking. These provisions might include lower wage scales, greater flexibility in job descriptions, fewer job benefits, and smaller work forces. This business strategy was ultimately upheld in the courts; such legitimation of its strategy gave business a strong weapon against labor. Even the threat of bankruptcy was enough at times for management to extract concessions from labor.

Moreover, the unstable job climate, high unemployment, and movement of jobs to other nations—or management's threat to move jobs overseas—have made workers, even pro-union ones, less likely to challenge management. One survey found workers very cowed by management. One-third of all unorganized workers said that they would like union representation, indicating a demand for union representation that was not being met. But 12 percent of them would not vote for a union in a union certification election, the survey indicated, out of fear of management.[18] Management strategies and the state of the economy have eroded workers' former willingness to challenge management through unions.

Government Policies Against Unions

Last, government has grown more hostile to labor.[19] This hostility was very apparent during the Reagan administration. First of all, the Reagan administration appointed people to the NLRB who were not strong supporters of labor. Rule changes at the NLRB made it easier to decertify unions, that is, hold elections to get rid of a union or replace it with another one, often more to management's liking. At the same time, these rule changes made it harder for unions to win elections.[20]

In the most dramatic antilabor action of the decade, the Reagan administration decided to fire the **Professional Air Traffic Controllers Organization (PATCO)**, the association of federal air traffic controllers, when its members went out on strike.[21] Many issues were at stake for the strikers, the most important dealing with job stress, long hours, and not enough air traffic personnel. But to the administration the issue was the union's violation of government laws prohibiting government employees from striking.

Since the 1960s, federal workers have had the right to form unions, which could then act as bargaining agents for the unionized workers, but unlike private-sector workers, federal unionized workers were not given the right to strike because they were said to hold vital jobs in running the government and the nation. These antistrike provisions are common across all levels of government in the United States. Thus, when unionized government workers want to engage in a job action, they often call in sick en masse to get around the law. Judges often issue injunctions against such sickouts, knowing full well what is going on.

The PATCO workers did not use a sickout; instead they challenged the federal government head on. The Reagan administration gave the union members a short time to return to work, threatening to fire them if the strike persisted. A small percentage of strikers returned to work. Most stayed out beyond the deadline, and the Reagan administration fulfilled its threat.

The Reagan action had important implications. It sent a signal throughout the labor community that government would not tolerate illegal union activities. Moreover, it indicated that government would not likely side with labor in disputes. This atmosphere emboldened many private enterprises to take strong action against their unions, as mentioned earlier.

The nadir of labor in U.S. politics probably came with the NAFTA vote described at the beginning of the chapter. Even with a traditionally prolabor party in office and a president whom it helped to elect, labor could not win a vote that was highly important to it.

Is Labor on the Rebound?

After decades of decline, labor's slide appears to have halted during the late 1990s. In the summers of 1997 and 1998, two major strikes were held, and labor emerged victorious in both instances. From the early 1980s through the late 1990s, labor had lost almost every major strike and confrontation with management. Thus, these victories may indicate a less dire future for organized labor in the United States.

In summer 1997, delivery workers for **United Parcel Service (UPS)** struck. The strikers were not seeking better wages but job protections and benefits for the many part-time workers that UPS employed. UPS delivery personnel were known for their efficiency and politeness, and often built personal relations with the people whom they served on their routes. This created a groundswell of public sympathy and support for the strikers, which striking unions had been unable to amass during the preceding decade and a half. A CBS News poll in August 1997, during the height of the strike, found that public sympathies lay with labor over the company by 52 to 36. With such public backing, the company caved under public opinion pressures and settled a contract favorable to the union position.

In the wake of the UPS victory, unions' confidence around the nation grew; this led to a second major walkout in summer 1998 by **United Auto Workers (UAW)** workers at General Motors. Again, a long strike ensued, and again public sympathies rested more with the strikers than with management. A CNN/USA Today poll conducted by the Gallup organization on July 13–14, 1998, in the midst of the strike, found union support outpacing company support in the mass public 42 to 31. Again, management settled with a union that appeared to hold stronger public backing.

Two victories do not make an all-powerful labor movement, nor do they mean that labor is on the rise. The factors plaguing labor outlined in the previous section still haunt it. Both strikes took place while the economy was healthy and expanding and corporate profits were surging. Under such conditions, the public might have felt that corporations could better afford to pay labor's demands than in years past, when the economy was more precariously positioned. But it is important to note that these incidents indicate that labor can regenerate a positive image with the public, and such public support may be instrumental in labor's winning its battles with management. Labor's ability to transfer public support from these two strikes to unions in general remains to be seen, as poll results from during the strikes still show a lack of confidence in union leadership. Time will tell whether labor's prospects have really improved.

THE POSTMATERIAL CHALLENGE

A new type of challenge to business has emerged, what we will call the **postmaterial challenge**. The postmaterial challenge, in contrast to labor's, is not formally organized. Thus, we cannot identify an interest group, a social movement, a political party, or other type of organization that formally espouses a postmaterial challenge to business. Also, the lack of formal organizational structure of the postmaterial challenge means that we cannot identify particular leaders who lobby for postmaterialism and against business.

Rather, the postmaterial challenge is rooted in changing values within society. Across the population, since the end of World War II, many people have begun to adopt **postmaterial values.**[22] Postmaterial values are quality of life values, which are often pitted against material values. Another way of saying this is that many people do not judge a policy or issue merely by its economic impact but also by its quality of life impact, and many people will opt to accept some economic harm for a quality of life gain. A good example is the environment: Many people with postmaterial values desire to ensure a clean environment even at the cost of a smaller, less affluent economy. In as much as people are willing to sacrifice economics for postmaterial quality of life concerns, the rise of postmaterial values in society represents a challenge to business, which usually pushes the case for economic and material benefits and which rarely will accept the postmaterial tradeoff.

Materialism and Postmaterialism

The labor challenge to business was highly materialistic. Business-labor rivalry was rooted in economic class differences. To the postmaterialist, economic values, although important, are old issues that have been dealt with effectively. Improving one's material lot is not an important motivation, because most people feel that their economic needs are taken care of relatively well. Those who hold postmaterial values grew up in relatively affluent circumstances and feel more economically secure than their predecessors, many of whom are older and felt the deprivation and insecurity of the Depression years.[23] Economic affluence has, thus, defused economics as a driving issue.

In the place of material needs, the postmaterialists seek to satisfy nonmaterial, lifestyle needs. There is often great sensitivity to collective risks. Thus, they place a high value on the environment and the safety of goods and services and are willing to trade off economic benefit for a better environment and quality of life.

The postmaterialists also balance this collective view of the world with an emphasis on individual choice and freedom. Thus, they may be highly tolerant of diverse lifestyle choices, with strong civil libertarian sensibilities. This greater respect for individual liberties and greater tolerance for a diversity of lifestyles, even those that the postmaterialists might not agree with, undercuts traditional respect for social institutions. Thus, they view organized religion, government, business, and all traditional institutions with suspicion.

Last, the postmaterialists are not diametrically opposed to business on all issues. Their opposition to business is reserved mostly for instances where business concerns run counter to lifestyle concerns. Environmental issues are a prime example, as are consumer protection and product safety concerns. And although postmaterialists often support using government to control business, on many economic issues, they side with business, preferring deregulation and less government. Postmaterialists may be especially predisposed to the new style of regulation, which relies less on government command and more on marketlike incentives to affect business and to help reduce pollution levels. On other issues that relate to government regulation of the economy, postmaterialists are often proponents of market mechanisms and opponents of government regulation.

Who Holds Postmaterial Values, and Where Do Those Values Come From?

The rise of postmaterialism is not limited to the United States but is found in varying degrees throughout the developed world. It is not the dominant cultural position of the majority of the population but still is espoused by a significant proportion, which seems to be growing.

Table 5.3 shows the distribution of material and postmaterial values in the United States, the United Kingdom, West Germany, and France from the early 1970s to the early 1990s. The "mixed" category includes those who hold a combination of material and postmaterial values. In each case, we see that materialists outnumber postmaterialists, but the gap has narrowed considerably. For instance, in 1972 materialists in the United States outnumbered postmaterialists 3.5 to 1 (35 percent to 10 percent). By 1992, postmaterialists and materialists were roughly equal percentages of the population. And the percentage of those with mixed values increased. The percentage of materialists in the population across these two decades declined by more than half. The same basic points can be made for each of the other nations listed on the table. Materialist value holders are on the decline; postmaterial and mixed value holders are growing in number.

When we look at the demographic profile of postmaterialists, we find that they are younger, better educated, more affluent, and more likely to work as professionals than materialists. As postmaterialists grow in number and influence, postmaterial challenges to business may become more frequent and more successful. It is important to note, however, that postmaterialists are

TABLE 5.3 The Extent and Growth of Postmaterialism in Four Western Nations, 1970–1993

	U.S.		U.K.		West Germany		France	
	1972	1992	1970	1993	1970	1993	1970	1993
Materialist	35	16	36	21	46	28	38	27
Mixed	55	65	56	64	44	59	51	53
Postmaterialist	10	18	8	15	11	12	11	20

Source: Data adapted from Paul R. Abramson and Ronald Inglehart, *Value Change in Global Perspective* (Ann Arbor: University of Michigan Press, 1995), 12–13, 19.

not opposed to business on all issues. There is often a respect for markets among postmaterialists, and their civil libertarian sentiments create suspicion about government, especially big government.

The association between age and postmaterialism is important in trying to predict the future, and it also helps us understand the rise of postmaterialism and its values. Postmaterial attitudes arose in part from the affluence of the developed industrial economies of the post–World War II era. From the 1950s onward, most nations in the developed world exhibited sustained economic growth and the expansion of the middle class. More importantly, people began to feel economically secure.

Although each economy went through bouts of recession and downturns, these episodes were often shorter and less severe than those felt prior to the World War. Even the economically turbulent 1970s, when two oil shocks rocked the world economy, did not send the economies of developed nations into depression. Other than the ups and downs of the business cycle, the middle class felt secure in its economic position, there was little fear that a depression like that of the 1930s would recur, and most people felt that their children's economic lot would improve. These feelings of economic security softened the political implications of economic issues. The political question became which party was better able to manage the economy. Issues of economic redistribution and class conflict moderated.[24]

In this environment, people could turn their attentions to the fulfillment of other aspects of life, quality of life issues. When people turn in this direction, postmaterial values are often elevated. Younger members of society are more likely to hold postmaterial values more strongly than older citizens. They have no direct experience with the preaffluent world of the modern age, unlike their elders, many of whom lived through the Depression. When the business cycle sets the economy on a downward trajectory, older people may feel more economically threatened than their younger cohorts, as they remember the depth, severity, and hopelessness of the Great Depression. Younger people, without such memories, are less likely to react so strongly to business-cycle recessions and, thus, are less likely to abandon their postmaterial values in the face of business-cycle troughs. In time, as older people with memories of the Depression and life before the affluent age die and are replaced by young people without such memories, postmaterial values may become more prevalent and more immune to the rise and fall of economic cycles. All of this is, however, predicated on the continuing affluence of these economies.

There are several ironies here. First, postmaterialism grew out of affluent economic circumstances. With their support, many policies have been implemented that may undermine the ability of the economy to produce wealth, specifically, the regulatory policies of the late 1960s and 1970s. In the late 1990s, the public was feeling quite economically secure, but the policies that postmaterialists supported may, ironically, help erode the conditions that allowed postmaterialism to flower. This may undermine economic performance and lead to greater economic insecurity and a rise of materialism, along with a decline of postmaterialism. Time is required, however, to see if this speculation is borne out.

The Political Implications of Postmaterialism

A number of important political changes have occurred during the rise of postmaterialism. The rise of postmaterialism has stimulated some of these changes. Others have the same roots, while still others are changes that postmaterialists can take advantage of politically.

One of the most important changes in the political system is the decline of political parties and the rise of interest groups.[25] Closely related to the change in political structure is the revolution in participation that has occurred. Although voting rates have declined, other forms of political participation have increased.[26] A third change is that representative political institutions have been weakened, while direct democracy methods have been institutionalized and enhanced.

The political model of the industrial age before the rise of postmaterialism emphasized mass mobilization organizations, like political parties; mass political activity that focused almost exclusively on voting; and strong representative institutions, like Congress. The power of labor was based on its numbers, which it could translate into votes. Thus, labor was an important element of the political system because it controlled perhaps the most important political resource, a bloc of voters. Once elected, however, politicians were given relatively wide latitude in building public policies. If voters found the policies of incumbents acceptable, they were likely to vote for them again. Voters influenced policymaking not by direct involvement but by replacing incumbents with new political leaders.

Postmaterialists reject some of this political model, with its emphasis on voting. Instead, they seek greater direct participation in government and policymaking.[27] Institutions that mediate the relationship between the citizenry and the government, like voting, political parties, and representative bodies, have been shunted aside for those that allow more direct expressions of public concerns. For example, postmaterialists may desire to participate in bureaucratic settings, where rules and regulations are developed, and they may seek more policymaking power through referenda, rather than allowing legislatures to produce all the policies. Postmaterialists feel more capable of participating in government than people who grew up with the older mindset; they are more educated; they often hold jobs that require working with ideas and, thus, feel better prepared and able to participate in policymaking. Moreover, they are better able to pay the costs of participation, and acquiring and digesting political information is not so difficult for them.

Postmaterialists may also feel that political parties homogenize political issues too much and thus do not feel well represented by parties and their leaders. Often, they do not find parties speaking on issues important to them, or they find both parties taking the same side of the issue. In both of these senses, they may not feel adequately represented by parties and electoral-based institutions.

Finally, a cynicism toward politicians pervades postmaterialism, much as it touches on all formal societal institutions. For these reasons, postmaterialists gravitate toward direct and sometimes narrow political expression. The new political model emphasizes the role of direct participation in government and narrow intermediary bodies, like interest groups, which tend to promote a small set of political issues, not the broad band of political concerns of the political parties.

Can Business Adapt to the Postmaterial Challenge?

This new style of politics has important implications for the postmaterial challenge to business. Business finds itself challenged on more fronts than during the days when its major adversary was labor. The old political model was one of electoral competition, in which business was usually aligned with Republicans and labor with Democrats. As a consequence of the electoral base of political power, both business and labor would lobby heavily in Congress, but this was often the extent of labor rivalry with business. Once the bureaucracy took over and began the implementation of the policies that were decided on in Congress, neither labor nor business would find much interference from the other. Dissatisfaction with policy would often percolate back to the legislative setting, where elections were required to determine which side would win. Thus, business and labor battles were fought in an electoral arena with a focus on Congress.

As a result of the political changes just noted, however, business is now challenged on many fronts and in many settings. Direct demonstrations may be used to embarrass or coerce business publicly. Challengers of business may bring their criticisms to the media, seeking a public forum. Business is challenged in the panel rooms of the bureaucracy and the chambers of the courts, and it is not uncommon for business challengers to use lawsuits as one weapon in their antibusiness arsenal. Further, many states fund public interest advocates, what William Gormley calls **proxy advocates**.[28] These advocates may be located in many different types of agencies, depending on the state agencies, like the attorney general's office, or in agencies devoted exclusively to consumer interests, like the consumer affairs office. At the federal level, consumer advocates are often given standing in bureaucratic and legal venues.[29] Even within the boardrooms of corporations, business may be challenged, as small and large stockholders try to increase their leverage over corporate management. Some intense intracorporate fights have erupted during the past decade.[30] The range of places and ways of challenging business are now very wide compared with the industrial age.

This new environment is more complex than the old one. It is often difficult to find compromises now. When the debate between business and labor was about money, with labor's seeking more than business was willing to offer, a middle course that split the difference between what labor wanted and business offered could settle the issue. But when the issue is framed in more moralistic terms, like the cleanliness of the environment or the safety of products on the market, compromise is hard to arrive at. Rhetoric among adversaries is usually intense, and the debate is played out in public forums like the mass media. Those who take such hard, public stances cannot easily compromise. Doing so may look like selling out to their supporters and result in a loss of credibility.

Thus, in this new environment, these adversaries often look at each other as enemies. This is especially the case with environmental issues. "Business is often regarded in the United States as the enemy of the environment. . . . In the United States, threats to the environment are usually attributed to the profit motive of large corporations. 'We will kill ourselves and all those around us,' one environmental commentator despairs, 'for a profit.' "[31]

Enemies are not people with whom one can work; they are people whom one must defeat. The stakes are, thus, very high, perhaps higher than during the era of business-labor conflict in the industrial age. Cynicism and distrust abound, and resolving conflict in political arenas has become increasingly difficult and unsuccessful. This is a very fluid, but also fractious, political environment.

CONCLUSION

Business is one of the most important extragovernmental actors on the economic stage. But it is not the sole actor. Labor is also a key player, and the shift toward postmaterial values has implications for business's position, too.

In the days when voting and electoral institutions were most critical to the policymaking process, labor was a potent adversary, commanding many voters who were loyal to its call. However, labor's influence has declined, partially because of a decline in its ranks but also because of changes in the structure of the political world. Postmaterialism has stepped into the place that labor once held as the major adversary of business, but the postmaterial challenge is less well organized than labor's. Still, business has weathered and adapted to the changes, winning some contests, losing others, but always as a formidable presence in the economic policymaking process.

Key Terms

American Federation of Labor–Congress of Industrial Organizations (AFL-CIO)
closed shops
Gompers, Samuel
local (or union local)
National Labor Relations Board (NLRB)
North American Free Trade Agreement (NAFTA)

Office of Safety and Health Administration (OSHA)
postmaterial challenge
postmaterialism
postmaterial values
Professional Air Traffic Controllers Organization (PATCO)
proxy advocacy

right-to-work laws
Taft-Hartley Act
United Auto Workers (UAW)
United Parcel Service (UPS)

Explore the Web

The AFL-CIO has a web page at http://www.aflcio.org/. The UAW maintains its web page at http://www.uaw.org/. From these pages, one can access the web pages of many other labor unions. The major government agencies that deal with labor issues have these web locations: NLRB, http://www.nlrb.gov/; OSHA, http://www.osha.gov/; and the Department of Labor, where OSHA is located, http://www.dol.gov. One group that is postmaterially oriented is Greenpeace, which maintains a web page at www.greenpeace.org.

Notes

1. This speech, "Remarks by the President to the AFL-CIO 20th Convention," was given October 4, 1993.

2. "Remarks by the President by Satellite to the United Mine Workers," September 26, 1995.

3. *Pink collar* refers to jobs such as industrial sewing and office work that have been mostly held by women.

4. On the union movement among government employees and its growth, see Richard Stillman, *The American Bureaucracy: The Core of Modern Government,* 2d ed. (Chicago: Nelson-Hall, 1996), 186–198.

5. On early government policies and the history of labor, see Selig Perlman and Philip Taft, *History of Labor in the United States, 1896–1932* (New York: Macmillan, 1935). A more contemporary treatment is found in James W. Lindeen, *Governing America's Economy* (Englewood Cliffs, NJ: Prentice-Hall, 1994), 213–225. From the

perspective of an economist with a broad historical sweep, see Jonathan R. T. Hughes, *The Government Habit Redux: Economic Controls from Colonial Times to the Present* (Princeton, NJ: Princeton University Press, 1991).

6. Mansel G. Blackford and K. Austin Kerr, *Business Enterprise in American History,* 3d ed. (Boston: Houghton Mifflin, 1994), 179. On the clash between labor, business, and government during this period, see also pp. 179–183.

7. Ibid., 214; and Hughes, *The Government Habit Redux,* 116.

8. See Bernard Mandel, *Samuel Gompers, A Biography* (Yellow Springs, OH: Antioch Press, 1963); and Harold Livesay, *Samuel Gompers and Organized Labor in America* (Boston: Little, Brown, 1978).

9. On the politics and administration of the NLRB, see James A. Gross, *The Making of the National Labor Relations Board: A Study in Economics, Politics, and Law* (Albany: SUNY Press, 1974); Frank McCulloch and Tim Bornstein, *The National Labor Relations Board* (New York: Praeger, 1974); and Terry Moe, "Control and Feedback in Economic Regulation," *American Political Science Review* 79 (1985): 1094–1116. On the New Deal and labor, see Michael Goldfield, "Worker Insurgency, Radical Organization, and New Deal Labor Legislation," *American Political Science Review* 83 (1989): 1257–1282.

10. On the politics of labor during this period, see J. David Greenstone, *Labor in American Politics* (New York: Vintage, 1969); Charles M. Remus and Doris B. McLaughlin, *Labor in American Politics: A Book of Readings* (Ann Arbor: University of Michigan Press, 1967); and Graham K. Wilson, *Unions in American National Politics* (New York: Macmillan, 1979).

11. On the voting of labor union members, see Jong Oh Ra, *Labor at the Polls: Union Voting in Presidential Elections, 1952–1976* (Amherst: University of Massachusetts Press, 1978); and John T. Delaney, Marick F. Masters, and Susan Schwochau, "Union Membership and Voting for COPE-Endorsed Candidates," *Industrial and Labor Relations Review* 43 (1990): 621–635.

12. I have profited much by reading Paul Edward Johnson, "Organized Labor in an Era of Blue-Collar Decline," in *Interest Group Politics,* 3d ed., eds. Allan J. Cigler and Burdette A. Loomis (Washington, DC: CQ Press, 1991), 33–61. Also see Michael Goldfield, *The Decline of Organized Labor in the United States* (Chicago: University of Chicago Press, 1989).

13. Union decline seems to be occurring in many advanced industrialized nations. See Johnson, "Organized Labor in an Era of Blue-Collar Decline," 44.

14. For these figures, see Stillman, *The American Bureaucracy,* 188.

15. William G. Mayer, *The Changing American Mind: How and Why American Public Opinion Changed Between 1960 and 1988* (Ann Arbor: University of Michigan Press, 1993), 470, 472; and Harris Poll, January 1998.

16. On the public mood, see James A. Stimson, *Public Opinion in America: Moods, Cycles, and Swings* (Boulder, CO: Westview, 1991). In the early 1980s, Stimson says, there was a rebound in the public mood toward greater liberalism, but labor does not seem to have benefited from this more liberal climate. In the 1990s, there is indication of a waning of the somewhat liberal mood of the 1980s.

17. Johnson, "Organized Labor in an Era of Blue-Collar Decline," 45–48, details this well.

18. Louis Uchitelle, "Survey Points to a Cause of Union Decline," *New York Times,* June 2, 1995.

19. See Johnson, "Organized Labor in an Era of Blue-Collar Decline."

20. On some of these changes at the NLRB, see Terry Moe, "Interests, Institutions, and Positive Theory: The Politics of the NLRB," *Studies in American Political Development* 2 (1987): 236–299.

21. For a review of the PATCO incident, see Arthur B. Shostack and David Skocik, *The Air Controller's Controversy: Lessons from the PATCO Strike* (New York: Human Sciences, 1986).

22. The seminal works on postmaterialism are Ronald Inglehart, *The Silent Revolution: Changing Values and Political Styles Among Western Publics* (Princeton, NJ: Princeton University Press, 1977) and *Cultural Shift in Advanced Industrial Society* (Princeton, NJ: Princeton University Press, 1990); and Paul R. Abramson and Ronald Inglehart, *Value Change in Global Perspective* (Ann Arbor: University of Michigan Press, 1995).

23. Inglehart, *Cultural Shift in Advanced Industrial Society,* makes a strong case for the generational nature of the material-postmaterial division. Still, economic downturns, like those witnessed across the Western industrial world during the 1970s, weakened the postmaterial orientation.

24. However, as we discussed in Chapter 3, growing economic inequality across classes may have marked implications for the future. This inequality may raise economic redistribution as a political issue.

25. On the rise of interest groups, see Burdette Loomis and Allan J. Cigler, "Introduction: The Changing Nature of Interest Group Politics," in *Interest Group Politics,* 1–31. Party decline is also well documented. For a thoughtful discussion of parties in the modern age, see John H. Aldrich, *Why Parties? The Origin and Transformation of Political Parties in America* (Chicago: University of Chicago Press, 1994).

26. The classic treatment of changes in participation is Richard A. Brody, "The Puzzle of Political Participation in America," in *The New American Political System,* ed. Anthony King (Washington, DC: American Enterprise Institute, 1978), 287–324.

27. For an interesting discussion of some of these trends, see Samuel P. Huntington, *The Third Wave: Democratization in the Late Twentieth Century* (Norman: University of Oklahoma Press, 1991) and *American Politics: The Promise of Disharmony* (Cambridge, MA: Belknap, 1981).

28. William T. Gormley, Jr., *Taming the Bureaucracy: Muscles, Prayers, and Other Struggles* (Princeton, NJ: Princeton University Press, 1989), 62–88.

29. On standing in administrative and bureaucratic settings, see Cornelius M. Kerwin, *Rulemaking: How Government Agencies Write Law and Make Policy* (Washington, DC: CQ Press, 1994), 254–256. See pp. 164–212 on public participation in rule making more generally.

30. On these internal challenges, see James C. Worthy, *Emerging Issues in Corporate Governance* (Evanston, IL: Northwestern University, J. L. Kellogg Graduate School of Management, 1984); and Richard Lehne, *Industry and Politics: The United States in Comparative Perspective* (Englewood Cliffs, NJ: Prentice-Hall, 1993), 101–105.

31. Lehne, *Industry and Politics,* 255.

6

Government Institutions Responsible for Economic Policy

I N THE 1992 presidential election campaign, Bill Clinton defeated incumbent president George Bush on a wave of economic discontent. Under Bush's tenure the economy had slipped into a recession, and although the recession was not steep, it persisted longer than most, and many white-collar and middle-management workers lost their jobs in corporate downsizing. Moreover, the economy suffered other maladies, including the trade deficit, the continuing federal budget deficit, the stagnation of wages for all but the highest-paid workers, the continuing loss of manufacturing jobs, and the related loss of jobs to other nations. Clinton was faced with a hefty economic policy agenda, and economic policy was the centerpiece of his campaign for the presidency.

Clinton had strong political reasons to highlight the economy. Since Lyndon Johnson's landslide election victory in 1964, only one other Democrat had been elected president, Jimmy Carter in 1976. Then, with the disintegration of the Soviet Union, the old East-West cold war no longer loomed. Only the economy remained a pressing issue, and Reaganomics seemed spent as a solution because of the deficit and the Bush recession. Clinton's electoral success gave him a chance to reclaim the presidency for the Democratic Party well into the future *if* he could tame the economy.

Thus, one of Clinton's first actions as president was to form a new economic policymaking agency, the **National Economic Council (NEC)**, which was created by executive order on January 25, 1993.[1] The NEC was modeled after the National Security Council, which oversees security, defense, and foreign policy. It is one in a long line of presidential actions taken since the 1940s to coordinate and centralize economic policymaking at the White House. Those actions, and the role of Congress in developing economic policy, are the subjects of this chapter.

A DIVISION OF LABOR IN MAKING ECONOMIC POLICY?

No one part of the national government is solely responsible for making economic policy. The branches of government—the president, Congress, and the bureaucracy—have a role to play, but each tends to emphasize a different kind of economic policy.

Thus, we find that the president is primarily interested in the macroeconomy—the overall state of the national economy—though in recent years presidents have shown a growing concern with regulatory and distributive issues as well. Congress places much of its energies on distributive economic policies, though it plays a major role in both macroeconomic and regulatory policy. **Distributive economic policy** basically occurs when government dispenses a benefit. Regulatory policy occurs when government restricts or controls an economic activity. The bureaucracy has its greatest influence in shaping regulatory policy, though it is critical in the day-to-day implementation of distributive policies, and several bureaucracies are important as advisers to the president in macroeconomic policy formation.

THE PRESIDENT

During the twentieth century, U.S. presidents have become increasingly involved in making economic policy, especially macroeconomic policy. Since the mid-1970s, regulatory policy has also risen as a presidential priority, but this is in part due to the macroeconomic implications of regulation. Similarly, macroeconomic implications are important in understanding presidential involvement in distributive economic policy.

Two factors are important in explaining the high degree of presidential concern with the macroeconomy. First, the public expects the president to be involved and holds him responsible for the state of the nation's economy. Also, over the years, presidential responsibility has become institutionalized, with statutory requirements and the accumulation of staff resources to aid him in directing macroeconomic policy.

Public Expectations

Public expectations about the president and macroeconomics began in earnest with the Great Depression.[2] That economic cataclysm undermined the public's faith in the market's ability to correct problems. The severity of the Depression was unprecedented in U.S. life. Although the nation had undergone economic panics and distress before, none could match the depth and duration of the Depression of the 1930s. When Franklin Roosevelt was elected president in 1932, the Depression was already three years old and showed few signs of abating, despite President Herbert Hoover's prediction that "prosperity was just around the corner." In 1933, unemployment stood at 24.9 percent, and between 1929 and 1932, the gross national product declined (in constant 1987 dollars) from $827 billion to $603 billion, a decrease of 27 percent.[3] Typically, economic downturns are short lived, usually less than a year in duration. The Great Depression lasted until the end of the decade, however, and many economists believe that it was not until the United States entered World War II in 1941 that the economy finally pulled out of it.

Within this context, the public began to look elsewhere than the capitalist economy for relief. Most eyes focused on the new president. Franklin Roosevelt offered little in the way of concrete policies to deal with the Depression, but he directed attention to himself, instilling confidence that he, working with the public, could end the Depression and restore prosperity. Ironically, confidence in Roosevelt remained high despite the uneven performance of his administration. Although the economy improved somewhat, a recession occurred in 1938 on top of the already existing Depression. Roosevelt's key achievement was to alter the political culture.[4] No longer did laissez faire rule. Since his presidency, the government has been heavily involved in managing the economy and is held responsible for its performance.

Presidents respond to this public expectation because they fear the electoral and popular reactions of not doing so. For example, George Bush was roundly criticized for his seeming insensitivity to public concerns about the recession while he was in office.[5] His popularity levels declined precipitously during the recession period (1991), which probably contributed to his defeat for reelection in 1992.

The consequences of a poorly performing economy are readily apparent on presidential popularity and electoral prospects. Studies indicate that presidential popularity moves with the macroeconomic cycle. As the economy declines, popularity dips.[6] Similarly, economic distress is often cited as one reason for presidential reelection defeats, as was the case for Van Buren in 1836, Carter in 1980, and Bush in 1992.

Thus, presidents become concerned about the economy as it sours. Figure 6.1 shows the average misery index, the sum of the unemployment rate and the inflation rate, and the percentage of references to the economy in presidential State of the Union addresses. This figure shows that the two hang together. As the economy sours, presidential attention to it increases.

The Institutionalization of the President's Macroeconomic Responsibilities

As a consequence of these public expectations, presidents gradually took on important institutional responsibilities for the macroeconomy. The development

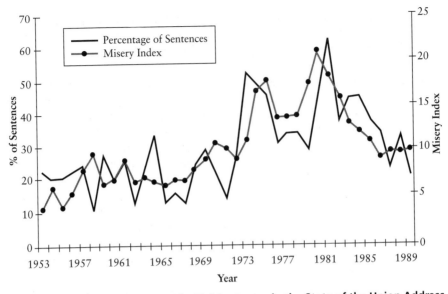

FIGURE 6.1 Comparison of Presidential Sentences in the State of the Union Address That Refer to Economic Policy and the Misery Index, 1953–1989

Sources: State of the Union Addresses; and Figure 3.3.

of institutional resources for the president to use when dealing with the economy actually began long before the Depression, although the original intention was not directly tied to macroeconomic concerns. This first step was the passage of the **Budget and Accounting Act of 1921**.[7]

The Budget and Accounting Act provided for an **executive budget**. This meant the president was responsible for submitting a budget to Congress each year. Congress would then take the president's budget proposal and amend it, with much of the detail work done by the appropriations committees of both houses. (The congressional budget process was amended in 1974.) The Budget and Accounting Act also created a staff agency to help in the preparation of the budget, the **Bureau of the Budget (BOB)**, which became the **Office of Management and Budget (OMB)** in 1970. Although this agency was not originally intended as a macroeconomic policy agency, as the budget became an instrument of macroeconomic policy, both the BOB and the budget-building process became important in formulating macroeconomic policy. Still, even before this macroeconomic role, the early Bureau of the Budget was, according to Allen Schick, successful in helping the federal government control finance and expenditures.[8]

The creation of the **Executive Office of the President (EOP)** in 1939 is also an important marker, but like the Bureau of the Budget, the EOP was not directly designed to help the president with economic policymaking. Its creation was a result of the recognition that the president needed formal staff assistance to manage the bureaucracy and the office of the presidency. Later, however, economic policy advisers came to play an important role in this office.

Formal recognition of governmental and presidential responsibility for the economy came in 1946 with the passage of the **Full Employment Act.**[9] This act specified that it was the policy and responsibility of the federal government "to use all practical means to . . . promote maximum employment, production, and purchasing power" and economic growth with stable prices, that is, without inflation. For the first time the government went on record as being responsible for the state of the economy and pledged the use of its agencies and powers to ensure economic health. Thus, the government could now *intervene* in the economy. Laissez faire was legally dead. Ensuing policy debate centered not over the legitimacy of government intervention in the economy but over the degree of such intervention and whether it was the wisest policy course. The act also helped to fuel public expectations about government's role in the economy.[10]

The Full Employment Act placed specific economic responsibilities on the president. Sixty days after the beginning of each new Congress, he was required to submit a report on the state of the economy, now known as the annual **Economic Report of the President.** The act also gave the president advisers to help him in this task by creating the **Council of Economic Advisers (CEA)**, which became part of the EOP. The act also created the Joint Economic Committee of Congress.

Last, in 1978 Congress passed the **Humphrey-Hawkins Act,** which further increased the government's responsibility for the economy.[11] Sponsors of that act intended to use the federal government as employer of last resort to attain an unemployment rate of 3 percent by 1983. Since the passage of the act, presidents have ignored the full employment timetable, as other economic problems became more pressing and as economists began to argue that a rate closer to 6 or 7 percent is a more reasonable target, because employment at a higher rate would risk fueling inflation.[12]

The Economic Subpresidency

With the institutionalization of presidential macroeconomic responsibilities came the accretion of economic advisers. The several agencies that advise the president on economic matters have come to be called the **economic subpresidency.**[13] Four agencies make up the economic subpresidency: the Office of Management and Budget, the Council of Economic Advisers, the Department of the Treasury, and the **Federal Reserve Board (Fed)**. Three of these agencies are under the direct control of the president, because they are located in the executive branch, but the fourth, the Fed, is an independent regulatory commission, over which the president has only limited control.

Scholars have included the Fed as part of the economic subpresidency because of its role in economic policymaking, but it does sit one step removed from the president when compared to the other three agencies.

OMB

The Office of Management and Budget was created in 1921, when it was called the Bureau of the Budget. It was originally housed in the Department of the Treasury, but with the creation of the Executive Office of the President in 1939, it was moved to the EOP. In 1970, Richard Nixon reorganized the Bureau of the Budget into the Office of Management and Budget, and the director assumed cabinet-level status.[14]

The principal task of the OMB is to help the president in the preparation of the annual budget. The OMB surveys each agency of the federal government each year about its budgetary needs. On compilation of agency budget requests, the OMB makes recommendations to the president about whether agency budgets should be increased or cut.

Early in its history, the Bureau of the Budget played a passive role, focusing on accounting issues, such as whether money was being properly spent. In the 1940s and early 1950s under President Harry Truman, it began to acquire policy-advising responsibilities. For instance, it began the task of **legislative clearance,** where it would require each agency to submit its legislative proposals for review. The bureau would then determine whether each proposal was consistent with the president's program and recommend action on the proposal to the president.[15] Similarly, the bureau began to review bills that Congress passed to recommend to the president whether he should veto or sign the legislation. Again, it used the standard of whether the legislation was consistent with the president's program in making its recommendation.

In the 1980s, the OMB began the task of **regulatory clearance.** (Ronald Reagan added this task to its other chores.) Regulatory clearance is similar to legislative clearance in that it requires each proposed regulation be sent by its sponsoring agency to the Office of Information and Regulatory Affairs (OIRA) of the OMB. Using cost-benefit analysis, this office determines whether the proposed regulation's benefits outweigh its costs. If so, the agency can proceed with issuing the regulation. If not, the agency is instructed to revise or drop the proposed regulation.[16]

Thus, over time, the Office of Management and Budget has acquired duties beyond budgeting and has become in a sense a central staff agency for the presidency. But the agency's primary and most time-consuming task is still budgeting. As a consequence, the OMB is most concerned with the budgetary implications of macroeconomic and budgetary policy. Due to its budgetary task, it is often antagonistic toward increasing federal spending, and over the years the agency has developed a reputation for taking the knife to federal spending and trying to find ways of reducing federal expenditures. At the same time, however, it has looked kindly on programs important to the president, thus mixing political concerns with its budgetary caution.[17]

With the acquisition of a policy-advising role, plus legislative and regulatory clearance roles, the OMB has become politicized. Politicization means that the OMB is thought to speak for the president and thus is not considered as politically neutral as it was during the first half of its existence.[18] As a consequence, the OMB's budget estimates are not considered to be reliable. Instead, they are thought to reflect the president's political needs. The OMB's estimates of revenue and spending projections are thus not held in as high regard as they once were. Rather, they are thought to be either too rosy or too pessimistic, depending on the president's needs.[19] As we will discuss later, Congress created the Congressional Budget Office to provide it with more politically neutral budget estimates and projections.

There is no standard career pattern or training for OMB directors other than the fact that most have had some previous government experience. The directors of the OMB have become important advisers to the president, especially over the past decade and a half. Many OMB directors have been among the most visible spokespersons for the administration, public personalities in their own right and highly influential within administration policymaking circles.

CEA

The Council of Economic Advisers was created in 1946 by the Full Employment Act. The duties of the CEA are to study the condition of the economy, to use that analysis to advise the president on economic policy matters, and to help the president in the preparation of his annual economic report. The intention in creating the CEA was to provide the president with a broad picture and understanding of the economy from advisers not captured by bureaucratic or special interests.[20]

The major focus of the CEA is the macroeconomic performance of the economy, in contrast to the OMB's emphasis on government budgets. Thus, the CEA is most concerned with unemployment, inflation, economic growth, and productivity. Moreover, its macroeconomic emphasis leads it away from concern with particular economic sectors and the government programs aimed at those sectors, and it may take stands against some programs and policies that it feels will adversely affect the macroeconomy. In this regard, the CEA also advises presidents on the macroeconomic implications of policies, especially in the area of regulation. For instance, the CEA under Carter argued against some environmental regulations because of the expected effect on the economy.[21] The CEA has been an advocate of applying cost-benefit analysis to regulatory policy as a way of incorporating macroeconomic concerns into regulatory policymaking.[22]

The CEA is a unique organization within the federal government. Almost all members of the CEA have been academic economists, and the staff is relatively small, ranging about from thirty-five to sixty-five. Currently the staff of the CEA numbers in the midthirties.[23] It represents no constituency and holds no statutory powers, nor does it administer any programs or laws. Thus, the CEA is in a precarious position. Its role is purely advisory, and there is nothing to make presidents listen to its advice.

What is remarkable is that a body composed of academics, often lacking in political experience, has at times become highly important and influential within presidential administrations. In part, this is a function of the type of people whom presidents have appointed to the CEA. It is not surprising that they often reflect the political and policy leanings of the president. Thus, the CEA members under Republican presidents are often economically conservative, while Democrats usually appoint more liberal people as members. But presidents have also found their advice useful.

The height of the CEA's influence came with the Kennedy administration. Kennedy's CEA adviser was Walter Heller, an economist from the University of Minnesota. Heller was trained in graduate school when Keynesian economics was becoming the intellectual standard. Among the many innovations of Keynesian thinking was the need for government intervention to regulate the macroeconomy. One task that Heller and the other members of the CEA, Keynesians all, set for themselves was to educate the new president on Keynesian modes of thinking about economic policy.

They were successful in that task. Kennedy came to the presidency with little training in economics but with a keen sensitivity to the importance of the economy to his reelection hopes in 1964. Heller convinced him to push for a tax cut in 1963 because the economy seemed to be underperforming and there was fear that it would slip into recession. Even though a tax cut would mean increasing the budget deficit, Kennedy accepted Heller's recommendation. Congress passed the tax cut, and the economy did well.[24] (Ronald Reagan used the Kennedy tax cut as a model for his own tax package in 1981.)

The prestige of the CEA climbed because of the success of the tax cut, and its influence continued during the Johnson and Nixon administrations. However, with the stagflation of the 1970s, the budget deficits of the 1980s and 1990s, and the massive trade imbalance of the past two decades, the CEA has receded in influence as other agencies, notably the OMB, the Treasury, and the Federal Reserve, have begun to eclipse it.

Still, in recent decades presidents have found that they can use the advice of the CEA to counter the demands of interest groups for more programs, more government regulation, and the like. The CEA has given the president reasons to resist them, and the reasons appear "above politics," rooted in economic analysis and what is best for the economy and the nation.

Treasury

The third member of the economic subpresidency is the Treasury Department, one of the original cabinet posts created during the Washington administration. The tasks of the Treasury Department are to collect government revenues, pay government bills, secure government credit, borrow money, and administer the nation's balance of payment with other nations.[25]

Treasury secretaries usually present a conservative and fiscally responsible position to the president. Thus, they often oppose expansion of the government and prefer a stable and sound dollar. In recent years, as the trade gap has widened, Treasury secretaries have become very concerned about the balance of payments problem—the fact that more money is leaving the country in trade than is coming in.

The business community in the United States, especially big business, often views the Treasury as its emissary to the administration. Thus, the secretary of the Treasury often has a business, banking, or finance background, as presidents accede to this expectation. Presidents most often appoint people to the Treasury Department to send signals to the business sector that business interests will be represented in the administration at the highest levels.[26]

This is most critical for Democratic presidents, whom the business sector often regards with trepidation. Democrats are not thought to be the natural allies of business, and business feels that Democratic administrations are more likely than Republican ones to increase government spending, allow inflation, and impose high taxes on business and the wealthy. To allay these fears, Democratic presidents have sought Treasury secretaries who are conservative, who hold business values, and who are acceptable to business.

Thus, John Kennedy appointed Douglas Dillon to be his Treasury secretary. Dillon was a Republican, served in the Eisenhower administration in the State Department, and worked on Wall Street. Carter had two business executives serving in that capacity for him, W. Michael Blumenthal, CEO of the Bendix Corporation, and G. William Miller. Bill Clinton has taken the same tack, first appointing Lloyd Bentsen and then Robert Rubin. Bentsen, a former Democratic senator from Texas, was chair of the Senate Finance Committee and, before his Senate career, was a business executive. Rubin, also a Democrat, was a Wall Street financier and, before becoming secretary of the Treasury, was head of Clinton's National Economic Council.

Federal Reserve Board

The Federal Reserve Board is an independent regulatory commission that was created in 1913. The Fed, as it is commonly called, is concerned with monetary policy, that is, the nation's money supply. The independent status of the Fed makes it unique among the bodies in the economic subpresidency. The president nominates the members of the seven-person board, subject to senatorial confirmation, as is the case with cabinet-level departments, but Fed members cannot be removed from office by the president. Moreover, they serve long terms—fourteen years—to further their independence from the president and from politics more generally.[27] The structure of the Fed is complex, comprising the Board of Governors, the Federal Open Market Committee, and the Federal Reserve banks.

Typically, members of the Fed's Board of Governors are bankers or have business experience; there are also many academic economists in the Fed. This is the case for all but one of the seven men who have served as the Fed chair since 1946. Due to the combination of their experience and the Fed's responsibility to regulate the money supply, the Fed usually takes a conservative position toward economic policy.[28] Thus, the Fed tends to oppose budget deficits, and its top priority is combating inflation and promoting price stability.

To fight inflation, the Fed often resorts to tight money and countercyclical policies. **Tight money** means restricting the supply of money in the economy, as well as higher interest rates. **Countercyclical policies** aim to slow the economy when inflation is running high, for example, by increasing interest rates. Such policies often run afoul of the interests of politicians, both in the White House and Congress, who feel pressures from the electorate for easier money, lower interest rates, and a growing economy. Sometimes the Fed has used tight money to squeeze inflation out of the economy, with recession a consequence.[29]

When this happens, elected politicians try to avoid blame for the recession by citing Fed action, and on occasion members of Congress have called for stronger political controls on the Fed to make it more responsive to "political realities."[30] Reform efforts have not been successful, however, because many in Washington value the independence of the Fed. It is able to make hard economic policy choices because of this independence, policies that elected politicians would not be able to make.

Coordinating Macroeconomic Policymaking

The four major economic policy advisers in the president's economic subpresidency have different institutional locations, with differing perspectives and backgrounds, each of which may lead to different advice for the president. Thus, the CEA is most concerned with economic growth and the business cycle, often supporting fiscal and budgetary means to those ends. The OMB is most concerned with containing the federal deficit and promoting the president's program. CEA and OMB officials will be liberal or conservative depending on the president in office. Generally, they will be more liberal under Democratic presidents. The Treasury Department is most concerned about government revenues, the soundness of the dollar, and government credit. The deficit has important implications for government credit and the dollar. Similarly, the Fed is concerned about the dollar but is also concerned about inflation. Most often, Treasury and Fed officials are conservative. This usually holds even when Democrats occupy the White House.

With such a cacophony of disparate advice and with economic performance's taking on such huge implications for the success of presidential administrations, presidents have sought to coordinate and make sense of these many voices. These coordination efforts have not been firmly institutionalized into government, and presidents possess considerable latitude in how they use these coordinating mechanisms. Yet institutionalization patterns and processes have developed and begun to take hold in government economic policymaking.

Since President Kennedy in 1961, presidents have tried to find a way to coordinate their economic policy advisers and advice. Each president from Kennedy through Reagan used some council where several of the advisers would come together, but no forum stuck. Each was replaced with a new body by the next president.[31] Clinton announced the creation of a National Economic Council on his election. The importance of the state of the economy to his presidency, plus the long-term trend of economic problems, including stagnant wages, lost jobs, and foreign competition, led to this move. The NEC, which is modeled on the National Security Council, is a high-level, interagency body with staff assistance. The president serves as the chair of the NEC, and the vice president and eight cabinet secretaries also hold seats (State, Treasury, Agriculture, Commerce, Labor, Housing and Urban Development, Transportation, and Energy). Moreover, the administrator of the Environmental Protection Agency (EPA), chair of the CEA, director of the OMB, and the U.S. trade representative are formally included, as well as others not normally thought of as economic policy advisers, the national security adviser and the assistant to the president for science and technology. Last, two presidential assistants, one each for economic and domestic policy, are members, as are "any other officials of the executive departments and agencies as the president may from time to time designate." Other than the president, there are seventeen formal representatives on the NEC.

The NEC has four principal functions: "1) to coordinate the economic policymaking process with regard to domestic and international economic issues, 2) to coordinate economic advice to the president, 3) to ensure that economic policymaking decisions and programs are consistent with the president's stated goals and to ensure that those goals are being effectively pursued, and 4) to monitor implementation of the president's economic policy agenda."[32] Also, the presidential assistant for economic policy, who coordinates the NEC, is given status comparable to that of the national security adviser and the presidential assistant for domestic policy, though the executive order states that the Treasury secretary retains the rank as senior economic official in the administration. Finally, the NEC is given formal staff support.

In effect the NEC is an attempt to centralize economic policymaking in the White House by the president, to limit the independent action of other government actors with control over policy areas that have economic implications. Yet, due to its independent status, the Fed is not a member of the NEC.

Early accounts suggest that the presidential assistant for economic policy has turned into an important presidential adviser. This is partially a function of the first incumbent, Robert Rubin, a strong and forceful personality with a generally conservative orientation toward economic policy. Rubin proved so important to the Clinton administration that he was named to replace the outgoing secretary of the Treasury, Lloyd Bentsen. Under Rubin's leadership, the NEC was actively involved in technology policy as it related to the economy, sought to cut subsidies to the commercial shipping industry even though they had the support of Secretary of Transportation Federico Peña and Congress, and moderated the administration's position on the massive health-care reform proposal of 1994. The NEC seemed to be so successful and useful to Clinton that it began to eclipse other economic policy advisers, especially those who headed cabinet departments.[33]

The NEC is an important institutional marker in the development of economic policy advice for the president. Under Clinton, it has been given staff, strong leadership, and presidential backing. However, it may not persist as an important policymaking locus for future presidents.

This is because different presidents have different approaches to policymaking. Moreover, institutionalizing economic policy through such a coordinating mechanism as the NEC may result in tying the president to a specific policy course. The president then may have less room to alter course because of the negotiation process among the various advisers that is a part of any attempt at coordination. As economic problems change, presidents have felt a need to be able to respond to changing conditions. Thus, coordinating bodies are more symbolic in importance. Last, presidents are held responsible for economic policy, a responsibility that they cannot share with anyone. This degree of responsibility limits how much advice presidents will take from such bodies and how important someone like the head of the NEC will become to the president.

Although the NEC head may provide the president with good economic advice, presidential economic policy decision making is a function of politics as well as economics. Presidents prefer to take advice from those to whom they choose to listen, not from an institutionalized and often rigid body. In the end, presidents will make their own economic policies.

THE CONGRESS

The president pays more attention to macroeconomic policy than other economic issues because public expectations and institutional responsibilities provide incentives for such attention. Similarly, Congress's institutional makeup and the career patterns of its members structure the way that it deals with economic policy.

Unlike the president, who has a national constituency, congressional constituencies are rooted in the districts and the states. The members of Congress focus their attention locally. No member of Congress, except perhaps one with eyes on the presidency, looks to the whole nation as his or her constituency. Rather, members of Congress are most concerned with the people in their district. To retain their seats, to get reelected, members aim to serve the voters in their districts. This leads them to emphasize the types of economic problems that most greatly affect their districts and over which they can have the most impact. Thus, members of Congress are most attuned to *sectoral* economic problems and policies, instead of macroeconomics.

To deliver appropriate policies to the districts, Congress has built an elaborate committee system that mostly revolves around the sectors of the economy. We find, for instance, committees on agriculture, banking, and transportation, among others, and it is in the committees and subcommittees that most of the work of Congress is done.

Congress, however, has not abdicated its macroeconomic policymaking responsibility completely to the president. Through the lawmaking process, Congress becomes involved in all types of economic policymaking. Moreover, as a constitutional competitor to the president, Congress has an incentive to address macroeconomic issues. Last, because Congress is an arena of party debate, macroeconomic issues will inevitably be raised. This is in part because the two parties often take opposing positions on macroeconomic policy and in part because opposition party challengers to the president find Congress an important forum for expressing their policies in hopes of building a national constituency in support of their presidential aspirations. For all of these reasons, Congress has developed several institutional resources to deal with macroeconomic policymaking. Still, the bulk of Congress's interest in economic policy focuses on sectoral economic issues.

In the following section, we discuss the congressional role in economic policymaking, spending most of our time on macroeconomic policy. In later chapters we will spend more time on Congress's role in sectoral economic policy, especially with regard to regulatory and distributive forms of economic policies.

Congress and Macroeconomic Policy

The committee and subcommittee system is the locus of most of the work of Congress. Congress has developed several committees with macroeconomic responsibilities, but, as you will see, several of these committees treat macroeconomic considerations from a sectoral perspective. The critical committees are the Joint Economic Committee, the Budget Committee, the Ways and Means Committee of the House, the Finance Committee of the Senate, and the Appropriations committees of both the House and Senate. Although all committees possess expert staff to help them in their work, a staff agency, the Congressional Budget Office, has been developed to help one of these committees, the Budget Committee, in its work.

Joint Economic Committee

The **Joint Economic Committee** was created in 1946 by the Full Employment Act. The committee contains seven members from both the House and the Senate, hence, the word *joint* in its title.

The Joint Economic Committee has several duties. First, it studies the president's annual economic report and presents by May 1 to the standing committees of Congress the results of its investigation and analysis. Supposedly, this report is to guide the standing committees in their legislative tasks. The committee is also charged with studying means of coordinating government programs to further the policy goals set out by the act, which include high employment, stable prices, increased economic productivity, and the like.[34]

The committee has not had much influence on macroeconomic policymaking, primarily because it was not given the power to introduce legislation. It operates only in investigatory and advisory roles for Congress. Without the power to introduce legislation, it is severely limited in helping to set the congressional agenda or in finding ways to produce legislation or policy that its members deem warranted.

At most, the committee has been a forum where members who are interested in macroeconomic concerns can express their views. It also serves a symbolic role, a demonstration of Congress's involvement in macroeconomic policymaking, as well as a check on the president.

Budget Committee

The **Budget Committee** has eclipsed the Joint Economic Committee. The Budget Committee and the Congressional Budget Office (CBO) were created in 1974 under the **Budget and Impoundment Act,** which implemented a major reform of the budget-building process, as well as imposed restrictions and guidelines on presidential authority to impound funds. **Impoundments** are monies that Congress has appropriated but the president refuses to spend. Congress decided to restrict impoundments because many members felt that President Nixon overstepped their proper use.[35]

The budget-building process reforms were an attempt by Congress to regain a substantial role in budget making. Congressional members felt that the president had come to dominate the process, a trend that had been building since the 1940s. Also, members felt that reform of the process would enable Congress to more tightly control federal spending, which had shown rapid growth in the 1960s and early 1970s and increased the size of the federal deficit.[36]

Traditionally, budget making in Congress had been decentralized in the appropriations committees. The 1974 reforms centralized the process in the Budget Committee. This committee is not given jurisdiction over spending decisions as they relate to specific programs or government agencies. Rather, its task is to set overall spending targets based on revenue projections and needs, as well as on macroeconomic considerations. Decisions concerning individual programs and departments remain with the two appropriations committees.

The Budget Committee is unique in several respects. First, members cannot earn seniority on the committee. Rather, they can serve for up to six years, after which they return to the committees on which they originally served. The aim of rotating members on and off the committee was to break any hold that special interests might have on the budget process. No interest group could count on having a sympathetic representative on the committee, and, thus, the committee would be less likely to become a target of interest group pressure and activity. This, it was hoped, would keep the committee focused on the national picture.

A second aim of member rotation and limited tenure was to increase participation in budget making. In this way, Congress would develop a large number of members with some budgeting experience, instead of vesting that experience in a select group of members. Moreover, those members would bring the budgeting perspective back to the other committees of Congress after their tour on the Budget Committee was over.

One limitation of the rotation and limited tenure system, however, was that no member would develop deep expertise in budgeting. At best each member would gather modest experience and knowledge of budgeting. Congress would still be at a disadvantage in comparison to the executive branch's budgeting expertise and knowledge. To help offset this problem, Congress created the Congressional Budget Office.

Congressional Budget Office

The **Congressional Budget Office (CBO)** is a nonpartisan agency of Congress designed to assist Congress in the process of budget making. The task of the CBO is to study the president's budget, make economic and budgetary projections, and provide Congress with the results of that analysis. In a sense, the CBO is to provide Congress with the kind of staff assistance that the Office of Management and Budget provided the president before that agency became so politicized.

CBO personnel are primarily economists and budget experts. They are a professional service and do not owe their jobs to any member of Congress. Moreover, the charge of the agency is to serve the institutional needs of Congress. Thus, the CBO has developed a reputation for not being in the service of either party or any congressional faction but for being a highly professional, nonpartisan agency.[37]

The CBO has grown in size and stature over the years, as Congress has found its reports highly reliable. Still, the CBO is less than half the size of the OMB and, thus, cannot offer Congress the detailed analysis that the OMB offers the president. As a consequence, the CBO, like the Budget Committee, to which it directly reports, focuses on the big picture: overall revenue and spending projections and their economic implications.

The CBO's economic projections are often more accurate than the OMB's.[38] There are several reasons for this. First of all, the CBO does its analysis after the OMB. This means that CBO has more recent economic data to work with. Predictions about the future course of the economy usually are more accurate if the prediction is made soon before the period that one is interested in rather than long before that period. The CBO's economic information is nearer that target time, the next budget year, than the OMB's.

Moreover, the OMB's economic predictions are now made with presidential policy goals in mind. In the most extreme case, David Stockman, Reagan's budget director in the early 1980s, admitted that he devised economic assumptions after deciding what he and the administration wanted the budget to look like. Thus, economic projections were made to fit budgetary assumptions, rather than the budget made to fit economic performance projections.[39]

Although this is admittedly an extreme case, presidents and their budget directors do tend to be overly pessimistic or optimistic about the future state of the economy. Their own psychologies and past experiences, plus their ideologies, may lead them in these directions. In contrast, the CBO, without a political agenda but sensitive to both parties in Congress, usually makes more cautious economic projections. Those projections tend to fall in between the rosy and the bleak scenarios of the administration and its critics. This does not mean that the CBO will *always* be more accurate than the OMB, but over time the CBO's economic projections will be closer to what actually occurs.

As a consequence, the CBO has developed a reputation for reliable, nonpartisan, and relatively accurate economic analysis. President Clinton recognized the utility of the CBO's economic projections in his first budget battle with Congress. He abandoned the OMB's economic estimates for the CBO's, hoping that that move would limit debate on the projected future condition of the economy. Such debate did lessen, but the budget-making battle between President Clinton and Congress remained intense, as it was for earlier presidents.

Ways and Means and Finance Committees

Although Congress gave the president the responsibility for submitting a budget, the Constitution places authority for raising government revenues with Congress, specifically, the House of Representatives. It is in the House that all measures to raise government revenues must originate. The House has given to the Ways and Means Committee the task of writing tax and revenue legislation.[40]

The **House Ways and Means Committee** is one of the most influential and prestigious committees. This is a function of the importance of the substantive policy over which it has jurisdiction. Not only does the Ways and Means Committee have jurisdiction over tax legislation, but it also oversees many of the largest entitlement programs, such as social security and Medicare.

The prestige and influence of Ways and Means are attractive to many members of Congress. A post on the committee is highly prized, and there is considerable competition among members for such a seat. The committee and the House leadership can pick and choose who will serve on it. Members usually have to demonstrate that they are capable legislators, are willing to work hard, and are not too far afield ideologically from their party. Members with little congressional experience tend not to get a Ways and Means assignment; the committee's posts are filled with more senior members.

The jurisdiction of the **Senate Finance Committee** parallels that of the Ways and Means Committee.[41] The Finance Committee is similarly influential, but the combination of the size of the committee and the smaller number of members of the Senate means that a higher proportion of senators can serve on the committee, so there is less competition among senators for a Finance Committee berth.

Both committees deal with tax and revenue similarly. Unlike the Budget Committee, however, which tends to be insulated from interest group pressures, these money committees are often the direct object of interest pressures.[42] When building tax and revenue policy, neither committee focuses on the aggregate needs of government. Instead, tax policy is used to serve special interests, which may be critical for the reelection of members. Thus, we find many loopholes and special preferments being given to interests. Homeowners are given mortgage interest deductions, oil companies are given special depreciation allowances, and the list goes on. As a consequence, tax policy is rarely made with fiscal issues in mind, and tax policy is not well integrated into overall budget making. Instead of treating taxes as a macroeconomic policy instrument, committee members use them to serve sectoral economic interests.

Appropriations Committees

The **appropriations committees** of the House and Senate were once the most important spending committees of Congress.[43] With the creation of the Budget Committee, however, the appropriations committees have receded in importance, though they still rank as highly influential congressional committees. The 1974 budget reforms took away from appropriations any control over overall spending limits. The Budget Committee, in cooperation with the floors of both chambers, now controls that decision. But the appropriations committees still have jurisdiction over the spending decisions of programs and governmental agencies. Within the guidelines set by the budget targets, the appropriations committees still have considerable influence over which programs and agencies will feel the budget axe, how deeply they will feel cuts, and which ones will grow.

The work of the appropriations committees is decentralized into thirteen subcommittees. These subcommittees are organized around economic sectors and parallel the organization of the substantive committees of Congress, as well as the organization of the governmental bureaucracy. Table 6.1 lists the subcommittees of the two appropriations committees.

With the 1974 budget process reforms, the ethic of the appropriations committees changed. Before 1974, the aim of the committees was to hold down federal spending, to protect the taxpayer and the tax dollar. Thus, appropriations were often lower than the totals allowed by authorizations. **Authorization** bills come from the substantive committees of Congress, like Agriculture. They authorize the specified bureaucracy to administer a program or policy. The amount of money that the bureaucracy can spend—in effect, a spending ceiling—is specified. An appropriation bill is required to tell the bureaucracy how much of that money it can spend in any given year. Before 1974, the appropriation usually fell below the allowable authorization.

With the 1974 reforms, overall spending limits were determined by the Budget Committee and the whole Congress. The appropriations committees

TABLE 6.1 The Subcommittees of the House and Senate Appropriations Committees

House	Senate
1. Agriculture, Rural Development, Food and Drug Administration, and Related Agencies	1. Agriculture, Rural Development, and Related Agencies
2. Commerce, Justice, State, and Judiciary	2. Commerce, Justice, State, and Judiciary
3. Defense	3. Defense
4. District of Columbia	4. District of Columbia
5. Energy and Water Development	5. Energy and Water Development
6. Foreign Operations, Export Financing, and Related Programs	6. Foreign Operations
7. Interior	7. Interior and Related Agencies
8. Labor, Health and Human Services, and Education	8. Labor, Health and Human Services, and Education
9. Legislative	9. Legislative Branch
10. Military Construction	10. Military Construction
11. Transportation	11. Transportation
12. Treasury, Postal Service, and General Government	12. Treasury, Postal Service, and General Government
13. Veterans Administration, Housing and Urban Development, and Independent Agencies	13. Veterans Administration, Housing and Urban Development, and Independent Agencies

no longer held such power. As a result, the appropriations committees have become targets of interest groups and others, who seek the highest funding level possible as they compete with other interests and other demands on federal revenues. Within Congress, spending advocates have gravitated to the appropriations committees, whereas before 1974, appointments to these committees were made with fiscal restraint in mind. Thus, the appropriations committees have become less committed to holding down federal spending and more open to serving important interests.

Congress and Sectoral Economic Policies

The money and appropriations committees of Congress illustrate the permeability of that institution to interest group and sectoral pressures. This permeability limits the ability of Congress to address macroeconomic concerns, though the Budget Committee and the CBO provide Congress with some institutional mechanisms for macroeconomic policymaking. It is generally through the budget process that macroeconomic concerns are addressed in Congress. Congress, however, is better suited for making sectoral economic policy.

Sectoral economic interests, especially when they are organized, may become important for congressional reelection. These organized interests may contribute money and personnel to work in reelection campaigns, endorse candidates, and, more important, represent not only large economic concerns and firms but also the major occupations of district residents. Thus, members of Congress interested in reelection are often highly sensitive to sectoral interests. To help members of Congress secure reelection and also to serve those interests, the committee system has been structured around sectoral interests.[44]

Table 6.2 lists the substantive committees of Congress. This list shows not only the representation of economic sectors in the committee structure of Congress but the overall importance of economic policy to Congress. Of the twenty-two House committees, at least fourteen have some economic policy responsibilities. Even those that seemingly do not deal with an economic sector, like Armed Services and Foreign Affairs, have economic policy implications. Armed Services has jurisdiction over many military contracts and grants. Foreign Affairs has subcommittees on international trade. The same pattern is observable for the Senate, where twelve of sixteen committees can be identified as having an economic policy responsibility or component.

Many of the committees that do not deal with economic policy are concerned with the internal rules and organization of Congress, like the Administration, Rules, and Standards of Official Conduct committees of the House and the Rules and Administration Committee of the Senate. Excluding these from the total number of committees further emphasizes the importance of economic policymaking to Congress.

TABLE 6.2 The Congressional Committee System

Standing Committees of the House	Standing Committees of the Senate
Agriculture	**Agriculture, Nutrition, and Forestry**
Appropriations	**Appropriations**
Armed Services	**Armed Services**
Banking, Finance, and Urban Affairs	**Banking, Housing, and Urban Affairs**
Budget	**Budget**
District of Columbia	**Commerce, Science, and Technology**
Education and Labor	
Energy and Commerce	**Energy and Natural Resources**
	Environment and Public Works
	Finance
Foreign Affairs	**Foreign Relations**
Government Operations	Governmental Affairs
House Administration	
Interior and Insular Affairs	
Judiciary	Judiciary
Merchant Marine and Fisheries	**Labor and Human Resources**
Post Office and Civil Service	
Public Works and Transportation	
Rules	Rules and Administration
Science and Technology	
Small Business	**Small Business**
Standards of Official Conduct	
Veterans Affairs	Veterans Affairs
Ways and Means	

Note: Committees in boldface type have economic policy responsibilities or components.

THE BUREAUCRACY

The bureaucracy, like Congress, is structured around economic sectors. There are cabinet departments for agriculture, energy, and transportation and independent regulatory commissions for communications, futures trading, and labor relations, to cite several examples. This structure means that the bureaucracy is better suited for dealing with sectoral policy than with macroeconomic policy, except for the Treasury Department and the Federal Reserve, which are parts of the economic subpresidency. Of the two major types of sectoral economic policies, distribution and regulation, the bureaucracy has more policymaking influence on the latter. This is because Congress has often given the bureaucracy more discretion and responsibility over economic regulation while retaining tighter control over distributive economic policy. There are four major types of bureaucratic agencies with implications for economic policymaking: the cabinet departments, the independent regulatory commissions, the independent agencies, and government corporations (see Table 6.3).[45]

The Cabinet Departments

There is no constitutional provision for either a cabinet or a bureaucracy. The Constitution grants the president the power to hire people to advise him, while Congress creates all bureaucratic agencies through its lawmaking power. There is often considerable tension between the president and Congress over the organization and structure of the cabinet. A compromise has been struck, wherein the president appoints the top-level cabinet officials, the secretaries and the undersecretaries. The Senate holds the power to confirm these appointments, but it rarely denies the president the cabinet secre-

TABLE 6.3 The Bureaucracy and Economic Policy

Cabinet	Independent Regulatory Commissions
Agriculture	**Commodities Futures Trading**
Commerce	**Commission**
Defense	**Consumer Product Safety Commission**
Education	**Equal Employment Opportunity**
Energy	**Commission**
Health and Human Services	**Federal Communications Commission**
Housing and Urban Development	**Federal Reserve Board**
Interior	**Federal Trade Commission**
Justice	**Interstate Commerce Commission**
Labor	**National Labor Relations Board**
State	**National Transportation Safety Board**
Transportation	**Nuclear Regulatory Commission**
Treasury	**Securities and Exchange Commission**
Veterans Affairs	

Independent Agencies	Government Corporations
Environmental Protection Agency	**National Railroad Passenger**
Small Business Administration	**Corporation**
	U. S. Postal Service
	Resolution Trust Corporation
	Tennessee Valley Authority

Note: Agencies in boldface type have economic policy responsibilities or components.

tary whom he wants. The secretaries serve under the president who appointed them; their terms expire with the president's.

Although the president has control over top-level personnel, the organization of **cabinet departments** roughly parallels the organization of the congressional committees. The parallel organization of the cabinet and the committee system provides the Congress with easy access to the departments, and congressional-bureaucratic interaction often takes place in the lower levels of the departments. At this lower level are the career bureaucrats, who are protected under civil service. Both the career civil service bureaucrats and the members of Congress may serve long tenures. This helps build stable relationships between the two, who often become allies, sometimes in opposition to the president.[46]

For the most part, the cabinet departments are engaged in distributive economic policy, though each department houses some regulatory bureaus. For instance, in the Agriculture Department we find the Marketing and Inspection Service, which inspects meat and poultry. The Occupational Safety and Health Administration (OSHA), which regulates workplace safety, is found in the Labor Department. And in the Justice Department is located the Antitrust Division, which has major responsibility for the enforcement of antitrust laws and regulations.

Still, the bulk of the work done in the cabinet departments and their subunits involves distributing benefits, not regulating. Distributive benefits may include subsidies, tax credits, technological assistance, and the like. Examples are farmers, who get low-cost crop insurance, price supports, and technological assistance in crop development and farming techniques, and mining companies, which may be allowed to extract ores and minerals from federal lands without paying any fees to the federal government for that right. Distributive programs tend not to engender much conflict, as those who receive benefits have little cause to complain about such government help, though in recent years many critics have complained about the special interests receiving such benefits and the implications of government giveaways for the federal deficit.

Members of Congress like dispensing such benefits, especially to interests that may help them get reelected. Thus, Congress often holds tight reins over distributive programs, determining who is eligible and often writing formulas to determine the size of such awards. Through these devices, members of Congress try to target the benefits to their electoral allies. Such tight controls limit the bureaucracy to awarding benefits to these congressional targets. Bureaucrats retain little discretion over these policies, though they often decide who is to receive a grant or award when there are more applicants than awards. Still, bureaucrats cannot award a benefit to someone who is not eligible.

The Independent Regulatory Commissions

The **independent regulatory commissions (IRCs)** are a unique form of government bureaucracy. Their organizational structure differs from that of the cabinet departments, and they hold more policymaking responsibility than agencies that implement distributive programs.

Economic regulation differs from distribution in that it is an attempt by government to constrain behavior. Thus, it imposes costs on those who are regulated. This makes regulation highly conflictual. In an attempt to distance itself from the direct conflict involved in imposing regulations, Congress has traditionally given the independent regulatory commissions tremendous discretion over writing and applying regulations. Thus, many of the statutes that created the independent regulatory commissions are general and vague.

Independent Agencies

Independent agencies are not regulatory commissions, though they may be engaged in regulatory activities. The independent agencies tend to be structured like cabinet departments, with a single person, a director or administrator, running the agency, though the agency does not hold cabinet status. Sometimes an independent agency is not given cabinet status because Congress and/or the president does not want to elevate the agency to that level. This is the case for the Small Business Administration, which administers grants and loans to small businesses. Other independent agencies hold special status, with direct access to the president, indicating that they are not mere agencies. This is the position of the Environmental Protection Agency, whose administrator reports directly to the president. Usually only cabinet secretaries have such presidential access.

Government Corporations

The major difference between **government corporations** (Amtrak and the Post Office are government corporations) and other government bureaucracies is that government corporations are allowed to earn a profit and are structured to resemble businesses, rather than bureaucracies. In some cases, the government sells its services for a fee in hopes that it will recoup its operating expenses. In other cases, the government has no hope of recouping costs but offers a service that it feels is vital to the nation but which the private sector is either unwilling or unable to provide because the service is not profitable. Government corporations also exist when the government does not want to allow the private sector to provide the service but feels that a corporate-style organization will run more efficiently than the traditional bureaucracy. Finally, the government corporation form is used when it is felt that organizing operations to resemble a business will result in greater efficiency.

CONCLUSION

No one part of the federal government commands the authority to make all of the nation's economic policy. The different branches share these duties, and there is some division of labor across the parts of government. Thus, the president pays greatest attention to macroeconomic policy, while paying less but still considerable attention to regulatory policy. Congress is most suited to dealing with sectoral economic policies but through the budget process has a major role to play in macroeconomic policy. And other than a few bureaucracies that are important in macroeconomic policy, most of the bureaucracy is structured to deal with sectoral economic policies, with the greatest input from bureaucracies into policymaking in economic regulation. This division and multitude of decision points reflects the often inconsistent economic policy of the federal government, as discussed in earlier chapters. In fact, to maintain such a variety of economic policies and regimes at the same time probably requires some sort of decentralization of economic policymaking.

Key Terms

appropriations
   committees
authorization
Budget and
   Accounting Act of
   1921
Budget and
   Impoundment Act
Budget Committee
Bureau of the
   Budget (BOB)
cabinet department
Congressional
   Budget Office
   (CBO)
Council of
   Economic
   Advisers (CEA)
countercyclical
   policies
distributive
   economic policy

Economic Report
   of the President
economic
   subpresidency
executive budget
Executive Office
   of the President
   (EOP)
Federal Reserve
   Board (Fed)
Full Employment
   Act
government
   corporations
House Ways
   and Means
   Committee
Humphrey-Hawkins
   Act
impoundments
independent
   agencies

independent
   regulatory
   commissions
   (IRCs)
Joint Economic
   Committee
legislative clearance
National Economic
   Council (NEC)
Office of
   Management and
   Budget (OMB)
regulatory clearance
Senate Finance
   Committee 3
tight money

Explore the Web

The federal government and its agencies maintain a number of web pages. A useful resource is the federal web locator at http://www.law.vill.edu/ Fed-Agency/fedwebloc.html. The White House web page address is http://www.whitehouse.gov. The agencies of the economic subpresidency web pages can be found at these sites: CEA, http://www2.whitehouse.gov/ WH/EOP/CEA/html/CEA.html; OMB, http://www.whitehouse.gov/WH/EOP/ omb; Department of the Treasury, http://www.ustreas.gov/; and the Fed, http://www.bog.frb.fed.us/. The House of Representatives web page is http://www.house.gov/, while the Senate maintains its page at http://www .senate.gov/. The legislative branch maintains a very informative page called THOMAS, http://thomas.loc.gov/, which links one to additional kinds of legislative and governmental materials. The Congressional Budget Office's home page is http://www.cbo.gov/.

Notes

1. The executive order is numbered 12835.

2. See, for instance, Samuel H. Beer, "In Search of a New Public Philosophy," in *The New American Political System,* ed. Anthony King (Washington, DC: American Enterprise Institute, 1978), 5–43; and Fred I. Greenstein, "Change and Continuity in the Modern Presidency," *The New American Political System,* 45–86, esp. 47–53.

3. These figures are from Harold W. Stanley and Richard G. Niemi, *Vital Statistics on American Politics,* 4th ed. (Washington, DC: CQ Press, 1994), 416, 431.

4. Scholarship on Roosevelt and the New Deal is extensive. See, for instance, James MacGregor Burns, *Roosevelt: The Lion and the Fox* (New York: Harcourt, Brace, 1956); Mario Einaudi, *The Roosevelt Revolution* (Westport, CT: Greenwood, 1977); Frank Freidel, *Franklin D. Roosevelt: A Rendezvous with Destiny* (Boston: Little, Brown, 1990); Albert U. Romasco, *The Politics of Recovery: Roosevelt's New Deal* (New York: Oxford University Press, 1983); and Arthur M. Schlesinger, *The Politics of Upheaval* (Boston: Houghton Mifflin, 1960). On the New Deal, see Anthony J. Badger, *The New Deal: The Depression Years* (New York: Noonday, 1989); and Carl N. Degler, ed., *The New Deal* (Chicago: Quadrangle Books, 1970).

5. Michael Duffy and Dan Goodgame, *Marching in Place* (New York: Simon & Schuster, 1992).

6. For a good review and analysis of the impact of the economy on presidential popularity, see Michael B. MacKuen, Robert S. Erikson, and James A. Stimson, "Peasants or Bankers? The American Electorate and the U.S. Economy," *American Political Science Review* 86 (1992): 597–611.

7. On that act, see Larry Berman, *The Office of Management and Budget and the Presidency, 1921–1979* (Princeton, NJ: Princeton University Press, 1979), 3–6; Allen Schick, *The Federal Budget: Politics, Policy, Process* (Washington, DC: Brookings,

1995), 35–37; and Aaron Wildavsky, *The New Politics of the Budgetary Process,* 2d ed. (New York: HarperCollins, 1992), 64–66.

8. Schick, *The Federal Budget,* 35. In particular, taxes, spending, and the public debt all declined in the 1920s.

9. The politics and debates of the passage are detailed in Stephen Kemp Bailey, *Congress Makes a Law: The Story Behind the Employment Act of 1946* (New York: Vintage Books, 1950). A more concise and contemporary account is found in John P. Frendreis and Raymond Tatalovich, *The Modern Presidency and Economic Policy* (Itasca, IL: Peacock, 1994), 32–37.

10. Howard E. Shuman, *Politics and the Budget: The Struggle Between the President and the Congress,* 3d ed. (Englewood Cliffs, NJ: Prentice-Hall, 1992), 161–163.

11. On Humphrey-Hawkins, see Frendreis and Tatalovich, *The Modern Presidency and Economic Policy,* 37–38.

12. See Charles L. Schultze, *Memos to the President: A Guide Through Macroeconomics for the Busy Policymaker* (Washington, DC: Brookings, 1992), 126–127, 155–162.

13. The concept of the economic subpresidency was first offered in James E. Anderson and Jared E. Hazelton, *Managing Macroeconomic Policy: The Johnson Presidency* (Austin: University of Texas Press, 1986). A good discussion is found in Norman C. Thomas, Joseph A. Pika, and Richard A. Watson, *The Politics of the Presidency,* rev. 3d ed. (Washington, DC: CQ Press, 1994), 374–381; George C. Edwards III and Stephen J. Wayne, *Presidential Leadership: Politics and Policymaking,* 3d ed. (New York: St. Martin's, 1994), 411–414; and Frendreis and Tatalovich, *The Modern Presidency and Economic Policy,* 49–64.

14. On the OMB in general, see Berman, *The Office of Management and Budget and the Presidency.* For a review of the reorganization of the BOB into the OMB, see Allen Schick, "The Budget Bureau That Was: Thoughts on the Rise, Decline, and Future of a Presidential Agency," *Law and Contemporary Problems* 35 (1970): 519–539; and Hugh Heclo, "OMB and the Presidency: The Problem of Neutral Competence," *Public Interest* 38 (1975): 80–98.

15. On the development of legislative clearance, also called central clearance, in the BOB, see Richard E. Neustadt, "Presidency and Legislation: The Growth of Central Clearance," *American Political Science Review* 48 (1959): 641–671. Also see Robert S. Gilmour, "Central Legislative Clearance: A Revised Perspective," *Public Administration Review* 31 (1971): 150–158. A broad overview is found in Stephen J. Wayne, *The Legislative Presidency* (New York: Harper & Row, 1978), esp. chap. 3.

16. A very large literature on regulatory clearance in the OMB now exists. See Barry D. Friedman, *Regulation in the Reagan-Bush Era: The Eruption of Presidential Influence* (Pittsburgh, PA: University of Pittsburgh Press, 1995), for a general overview. Also useful is Howard Ball, *Controlling Regulatory Sprawl: Presidential Strategies from Nixon to Reagan* (Westport, CT: Greenwood, 1984); Edward P. Fuchs, *Presidents, Management, and Regulation* (Englewood Cliffs, NJ: Prentice-Hall, 1988); and William F. West and Joseph Cooper, "The Rise of Administrative Clearance," in *The Presidency and Public Policy Making,* eds. George C. Edwards III, Steven A. Shull, and Norman C. Thomas (Pittsburgh, PA: University of Pittsburgh Press, 1985), 192–214.

17. See Frendreis and Tatalovich, *The Modern Presidency and Economic Policy*, 57–60.

18. See Heclo, "OMB and the Presidency," on this point.

19. For a revealing portrait of this problem from an insider, see David Stockman, *The Triumph of Politics* (New York: Harper & Row, 1986).

20. Discussions of the CEA are found in Edward S. Flash, *Economic Advice and Presidential Leadership: The Council of Economic Advisers* (New York: Columbia University Press, 1965); Erwin C. Hargrove and Samuel C. Morley, eds., *The President and the Council of Economic Advisers: Interviews with CEA Chairmen* (Boulder, CO: Westview, 1984); and Herbert Stein, *Presidential Economics: The Making of Economic Policy from Roosevelt to Reagan and Beyond*, 2d ed. (Washington, DC: American Enterprise Institute, 1988).

21. Fuchs, *Presidents, Management, and Regulation*, 64–67.

22. Ibid., 23–24.

23. Frendreis and Tatalovich, *The Presidency and Public Policy Making*, 49–55, 318–319.

24. Edward S. Flash, "Conversion of Kennedy from Economic Conservative to Economic Liberal," in *J. F. Kennedy and Presidential Power*, ed. Earl Latham (Lexington, MA: Heath, 1972), 76–81.

25. Treasury's role in economic policymaking is reviewed in Colin Campbell, *Managing the Presidency: Carter, Reagan, and the Search for Executive Harmony* (Pittsburgh, PA: University of Pittsburgh Press, 1986).

26. Frendreis and Tatalovich, *The Presidency and Public Policy Making*, 55–57, 320–321.

27. A history and discussion of the Fed can be found in Carl H. Moore, *The Federal Reserve System: The First 75 Years* (Jefferson, NC: MacFarland, 1990); Richard H. Timberlake, *Monetary Policy in the United States: An Intellectual and Institutional History* (Chicago: University of Chicago Press, 1993); Donald Kettl, *Leadership at the Fed* (New Haven, CT: Yale University Press, 1986); and William C. Melton, *Inside the Fed: Making Monetary Policy* (Homewood, IL: Dow-Jones-Irwin, 1985). A good journalistic account is found in William Greider, *Secrets of the Temple: How the Federal Reserve Runs the Country* (New York: Simon & Schuster, 1987).

28. Frendreis and Tatalovich, *The Presidency and Public Policy Making*, 61–64, 324.

29. This seemed to be the case when Paul Volker was chair of the Fed during the late 1970s and early 1980s. Michael G. Hadjimichalakis, *The Federal Reserve, Money, and Interest Rates: The Volker Years and Beyond* (New York: Praeger, 1984).

30. On political control of the Fed, Kettl, *Leadership at the Fed*; John T. Woolley, *Monetary Politics: The Federal Reserve and the Politics of Monetary Policy* (Cambridge: Cambridge University Press, 1984); and Michael D. Reagan, "The Political Structure of the Federal Reserve System," *American Political Science Review 55* (1961), 64–76.

31. For a good historical review, see Frendreis and Tatalovich, *The Presidency and Public Policy Making*, 65–72.

32. This is a direct quote from the executive order.

33. I. M. Destler, *The National Economic Council: A Work in Progress* (Washington, DC: Institute for International Economics, 1996).

34. See Frendreis and Tatalovich, *The Presidency and Public Policy Making,* 36; and Lance T. LeLoup, "Congress and the Dilemma of Economic Policy," in *Making Economic Policy in Congress,* ed. Allen Schick (Washington, DC: American Enterprise Institute, 1983), 24–26.

35. Impoundments and other spending issues are dealt with in Louis Fisher, *Presidential Spending Power* (Princeton, NJ: Princeton University Press, 1975).

36. The literature on the congressional budget process is very large. See Aaron Wildavsky, *The New Politics of the Budgetary Process,* 2d ed. (New York: Harper-Collins, 1992). Another good review with special attention to the deficits of the past decade and a half is Donald F. Kettl, *Deficit Politics: Public Budgeting in Its Institutional and Historical Context* (New York: Macmillan, 1992).

37. On the repute of the CBO, see Robert D. Reischauer, "Getting, Using, and Misusing Economic Information," in *Making Economic Policy in Congress,* ed. Schick, 38–68.

38. An analysis that compares OMB and CBO economic estimates is found in Mark S. Kamlet, David C. Mowrey, and Tsai-tsu Su, "Whom Do You Trust? An Analysis of Executive and Congressional Economic Forecasts," *Journal of Policy Analysis and Management* 6 (1987): 365–384.

39. See Stockman, *The Triumph of Politics.*

40. The classic study of the Ways and Means Committee is John F. Manley, *The Politics of Finance* (Boston: Little, Brown, 1970). A more recent analysis is Randall Strahan, "Dan Rostenkowski: A Study in Congressional Power," in *Congress Reconsidered,* 5th ed., eds. Lawrence C. Dodd and Bruce I. Oppenheimer (Washington, DC: CQ Press, 1993), 189–209. Also useful are Catherine E. Rudder, "Committee Reform and the Revenue Process," *Congress Reconsidered,* 117–139; and Randall Strahan, *New Ways and Means: Reform and Change in a Congressional Committee* (Chapel Hill: University of North Carolina Press, 1990).

41. The Finance Committee has not been studied as much as Ways and Means. See Catherine E. Rudder, "Tax Policy: Choice and Structure," in *Making Economic Policy in Congress,* ed. Schick, 200–201; and Manley, *The Politics of Finance.*

42. See Jeffrey H. Birnbaum and Allan S. Murray, *Showdown at Gucci Gulch* (New York: Random House, 1987); and Rudder, "Tax Policy."

43. The classic study of the appropriations committees is Richard F. Fenno, *The Power of the Purse* (Boston: Little, Brown, 1966). More recent analyses are found in Frendreis and Tatalovich, *The Presidency and Public Policy Making,* 78–86; and Wildavsky, *The New Politics of the Budgetary Process,* 101–106.

44. See David R. Mayhew, *Congress: The Electoral Connection* (New Haven, CT: Yale University Press, 1974), and the many references in Chapter 12 of this text.

45. A more detailed discussion of these forms of bureaucracies can be found in Kenneth J. Meier, *Politics and the Bureaucracy,* 3d ed. (Pacific Groves, CA: Brooks/Cole, 1993), 17–29.

46. This seems to hold more for distributive economic policies than regulatory policy. Compare Chapters 10 and 11 with Chapter 12.

7

Generating Government Revenue: Taxes

I N 1998, the lobbying group Americans for Fair Taxation planned a major publicity campaign to alter public opinion in favor of their proposal for a national sales tax to replace the federal income tax. The Americans for Fair Taxation had amassed a large war chest, some $15 million, from a combination of large investors and smaller contributors. Over the previous several years, important leaders in the Republican Party, including Senate Majority Leader Trent Lott of Mississippi and House Majority Leader Dick Armey of Texas, as well as 1996 vice presidential candidate Jack Kemp, had endorsed a proposal suggesting the sales tax level could be set at 23 percent without cutting into federal revenue totals. Proponents of the national sales tax identified the low savings rate in the United States as a potential problem for long-term economic growth. They argued that the sales tax would help the federal government generate the revenue that it needed and that it would create incentives for people to save money. Moreover, by moving to a national sales tax, the much detested Internal Revenue Service (IRS) could be abolished. However, opponents, among them President Clinton, argued that such a tax was inherently regressive, and consequently a larger share of the tax burden would fall on those with modest financial means.[1]

This was not the only tax policy controversy of 1998. In 1998, after a decade and a half of high and seemingly uncontrollable deficits, where the federal government spent more money than it collected, the government ran a **surplus,** which was expected to continue for nearly a decade. With a surplus in hand, that is, more federal money than expenses, many ideas were floated about what to do with the extra money. Republican leaders in Congress, following party tradition, argued that taxes should be cut. President Clinton objected, arguing instead that before major tax cuts are offered, the country needed to find a way to ensure the financial state of social security, which appeared to be heading for trouble within a short period. Essentially, Clinton wanted to earmark the surplus for social security. A third coalition, which had been outspoken in opposition to the high deficits of the previous fifteen years, argued that the surplus should be used to pay off some of the debt that had mounted during those years.[2]

That tax issues should be on the public agenda in 1998 makes 1998 no different from most other years. Taxes are a perennial issue on the public agenda, dating back to the founding of the nation and the infamous Boston Tea Party, with its still voiced refrain, "No taxation without representation." In this chapter we will look at the structure of taxes in the United States, standards by which one can judge taxes, and the politics of making tax policy. Government revenue needs, the impact of taxes on the economy, public attitudes, electoral considerations, and the power of special interest groups are all part of the story.

GOVERNMENTS AND TAXES

Government requires resources to operate: to implement programs and deliver services to its citizens. And the politicians who run the government need resources to implement the policies they promised to voters. Governments, then, cannot function without resources. Perhaps the most important resource for government is money, and the chief means by which government collects money is taxes. Thus, the collection of taxes has always been a high-priority task for government.

In ancient times, the major task of government bureaucracy was tax collection. Most of the great empires of history rarely controlled the local government. Rather, their presence was felt among alien populations mostly to collect taxes.[3]

Just as in ancient times, the modern tax-collection bureaucracy has the full backing of the coercive powers of government; this makes it a feared agency. There is probably no more despised agency of the federal government than the Internal Revenue Service. In 1995, as Congress began to amend a crime bill that would allow law enforcement agencies greater latitude in collecting evidence, the IRS was unanimously excluded from the liberalizing provisions. The IRS was too unpopular and distrusted to treat it as if it were only another government bureaucracy. In the 1995 budget, the IRS was slated to be cut deeply, partly in hopes of forcing it to stop its program of randomly auditing taxpayers, one manifestation of the agency's coercive powers.

In July 1998, Congress passed and President Clinton signed a major bill reforming the IRS. The law created seventy-four citizens rights, including a hearing before the IRS could confiscate a home, bank account, or other personal assets. Most important, the law aimed to alter the culture of the IRS, making it less intrusive and heavy handed. To such ends, the law shifted the burden of proof of tax violations from the individual to the IRS, putting it in accord with other law. Furthermore, a nine member oversight board was created; its membership would include six private citizens. That reining in the agency in these ways will hamper it in its efforts to collect tax revenue owed to the government is one charge that critics offered.[4]

Modern tax policy is not insulated from politics. Just as governments need resources, people prefer lower to higher taxes. Thus, there is a constant push by government to find sources of revenue, countered by a constant push by the body politic to lower the tax bite and/or foist it onto someone else. And in the United States, there exists a deep antitax, antigovernment political culture that impedes government collection of revenue. Many people and politicians want to limit government's ability to collect taxes as part of an overall strategy aimed at limiting government more generally. Still, government needs revenues, and taxes are a major source for government revenues. By what standard can we judge taxes? Is there such a thing as a good tax? Are some taxes better than others?

CRITERIA FOR JUDGING TAXES

Taxes are inevitably controversial. Nobody likes them, but most agree that some level of taxation is necessary. Taxes are controversial because there is so much disagreement over what the tax system should look like. How much taxation is too much? What is meant by *too much?* Does it matter who is taxed? What makes for a fair tax? What is tax equity? What are the best kinds of taxes? These are the perennial questions of politics and tax policy. In this section, we describe several criteria for judging taxes.[5] People may disagree over the answers to the questions just posed, but all the answers fall into several criteria. Two sets of criteria stand out, the economic consequences of taxes and their governmental-political implications.

Economic Criteria for Judging Taxes

There are four economic criteria by which to judge taxes: (1) economic effects, (2) economic neutrality, (3) buoyancy, and (4) distributive consequences. The first standard, **economic effects,** suggests that taxes should not harm the economy. That is, taxes should not retard economic growth or induce firms to leave the taxing jurisdiction for another jurisdiction that is not imposing such onerous taxes. Moreover, business should not view the tax as being so burdensome that it interferes with business decisions. Taxes are required in an economy that asks government for services, like transportation systems or an educated work force; thus, taxes are but one cost of doing business. But they should not be so high as to harm business. The benefits that taxes provide should be in some proportion to what they take from the private sector.

Second, and closely related to the first point, taxes should be **economically neutral**.[6] That is, they should not direct business decisions in one direction or another. Taxes should not benefit some industries at the expense of others; they should not structure the market. This is a controversial point because taxes have in fact been used to structure markets and direct the economy. Some policymakers believe that this is a proper role for taxes. For example, tax breaks have been given to businesses that locate in economically distressed areas as an inducement to locating there. Homeowners are allowed tax deductions on their property, which is felt to help a major domestic industry, construction. And tax rates are often adjusted to promote savings and investments. For instance, Republicans have been clamoring for a reduction or elimination of **capital gains taxes**. These are taxes on corporate and other types of business profits. Taxes on capital, it is argued, interfere with business investment, growth, and transactions.

It is very difficult to build a tax system that is completely economically neutral because not all businesses or people are alike, and taxes represent a large enough budget item that all financial managers, whether in big business or in households, take them into consideration.

The third criteria for judging taxes is their buoyancy. **Buoyancy** refers to the ability of the tax to collect the same "real" revenue in the face of changing economic circumstances. Policymakers should not have to reset tax rates when the economy changes if the tax is buoyant. Think of an economy in which there is a rate of inflation. A buoyant tax is one that will grow in exact proportion to that inflation. A tax that does not grow with inflation is not buoyant; neither is one that grows faster than the inflation rate. A tax that grows faster than inflation is overbuoyant.

In the 1960s and 1970s, the federal income tax was overbuoyant; it grew faster than the inflation rate. The combination of inflation and a progressive income tax created this situation, called bracket creep.[7] **Progressive income taxes** mean that as income increases, each higher income is taxed at a higher rate than the rate for the income just below. In other words, each increase in income is taxed at a progressively higher rate. Inflation had the effect of boosting people into the next higher tax bracket, though their purchasing power did not also go up because their higher income was matched by higher prices. Employers began paying their workers more as the workers demanded raises to meet the increased cost of living due to inflation. Though workers' purchasing power did not increase but only kept up with inflation, government tax revenues went up at a rate greater than inflation due to bracket creep. In response to this problem, which pinched workers' incomes as a greater and greater share of their income went to taxes, income tax brackets were pegged to the consumer price index in 1982. As we will discuss later, this bracket-creep problem was one source of the tax revolt of the 1970s and 1980s.

The fourth economic criterion by which to judge taxes is their **distributional consequences**. Distributional consequences refers to the impact of a tax on the distribution of society's wealth. The most important distributional consequence is **tax equity**. Tax equity raises issues of equality, that all people be taxed equitably; that is, the tax burden should not be felt more heavily by some people than by others, especially when they are of similar economic means. Thus, tax equity seeks to treat people similarly while realizing that people have different economic circumstances.

Equity can be viewed both horizontally and vertically. **Horizontal equity** suggests that not all people with the same incomes live under the same economic circumstances. Thus, the tax code allows tax deductions for each child in the family, assuming that a family with no children has more disposable income than a family of one child, and thus the childless family can afford to pay more in the way of taxes. Similarly, tax deductions are given for the blind and other forms of disability.

Vertical equity assumes that people with greater incomes have a greater ability to pay taxes. Thus, under vertical equity schemes, the rich pay more than the poor in both absolute and relative terms. Vertical equity arguments are the basis for progressive taxes.

The vertical equity of a tax system can be described as either regressive, proportional, or progressive. **Regressive taxes** are those in which people with higher incomes pay proportionately less than those with lower incomes. Social security is regressive because the contribution (or tax) is capped; once one reaches a certain income level, no more is taken out for social security. Thus, a lower-income person may wind up paying a greater percentage of his or her income than a wealthy person. **Proportional taxes** mean that everyone pays the same tax rate. A **flat tax,** where all would pay the same percentage of their income in taxes, is one version of a proportional tax. As stated earlier, progressive taxes take a progressively greater proportion of income from each added increase of income. The flat tax can be made somewhat progressive by putting in income floors, where people who earn less than the floor would be exempted from paying income taxes. Such a provision was included in Steve Forbes's flat tax proposal in the 1996 Republican presidential primary campaign.

Proponents of progressive taxes argue that they are the fairest taxes.[8] To make this argument, one has to distinguish between income earmarked to pay for life's necessities and **discretionary income,** or income that can be spent as one wishes. Taxes, according to the progressive tax advocates, should not come out of income in the first category but should affect only discretionary income. Poor people should not have to choose between paying for life's necessities, like food or shelter, and taxes. Thus, if we tax all people at the same rate, poor people are shouldering a heavier personal burden.

Progressive taxes, in effect, reduce income disparity by redistributing income by taxing the wealthy more heavily than those less well off. In this sense, taxes are used as an instrument toward a social end. Using taxes in this fashion is controversial and presents potential conflicts between using taxes for social equity versus using them to meet the government's financial needs.

Governmental-Political Criteria for Judging Taxes

Tax systems can also be judged through a governmental-political lens. Four criteria stand out: the adequacy of the tax, its visibility, its political acceptability, and its collectability.

One important standard for judging taxes asks if the tax raises sufficient revenue to finance the government; this is called **tax adequacy.** By this standard, taxes can be either too large or too small. During the post–Civil War era, the federal government relied heavily on import duties—taxes on goods imported into the country—to collect revenue, and throughout that forty-year period, the government generally ran a surplus.[9] The surplus indicated a tax system that was collecting too much revenue, and the surplus became an important political issue in the late nineteenth century. In a similar but reverse situation, huge deficits plagued the United States during the 1980s and into the mid-1990s, indicating an insufficient tax base. Insufficient taxes mean that government is spending more than it collects in taxes and other revenue sources—that it is running a **deficit.** Like the surpluses of the late 1800s, the deficits of the 1980s and 1990s were a major political issue, calling into question the ability of government to collect revenue, as well as the government's scope. However, by the late 1990s, the era of massive deficits seemed over, as the federal government began to run surpluses. And like the deficits of the previous years and the surpluses of the 1800s, the surpluses of the late 1990s rouse political controversy, as the opening of this chapter indicated.

Saying, however, that the tax take is insufficient does not automatically mean that taxes should be increased to close the taxes-spending gap. Tax insufficiency also can result from too much spending. Government revenue and spending needs can be brought into balance through spending cuts as well as tax increases.

The second political criterion refers to the **visibility** of the tax. This standard holds that taxes should be visible; that is, people should notice their taxes. Only by knowing their true tax burden can citizens hold government accountable. Tax visibility allows people to determine their tax burden accurately, and this is vital in promoting democratic accountability. Visible taxes cause a problem for governments, however, as people are more hostile to visible than invisible taxes, even if the latter are larger or less fair. Thus, the highly visible federal income tax has been an object of public scorn almost since its beginning.[10] To reduce the visibility of the income tax, government requires withholding of the tax from each paycheck. Thus, people feel the tax bite continually but in smaller chunks than if the tax was paid in one lump sum at tax-collection time. Still, the income tax is comparatively visible, and when April 15 rolls around and people are required to submit their income tax forms to the federal government, the tax is exposed in its most glaring light. Lump-sum tax payments are also characteristic of property taxes, which are probably the most despised of all taxes. Many state and local governments rely heavily on sales taxes, which are less visible than the property tax. Ironically, governments have an easier time collecting revenue when the tax source is invisible, but such invisibility hides the nature of the tax from the citizenry and undermines the accountability of the politicians who legislate taxes.

The third political standard refers to the **acceptability** of the tax. In part, acceptability is achieved by matching the type of tax to the political culture and political sentiments of the citizenry. In the United States, there exists a strong preference for progressive taxes,[11] and politicians seeking more revenue often have to prove to the populace that the tax is fair and progressive. Similarly, for a tax to be acceptable there must exist a case that it is needed. In the current political climate, policymakers are having a hard time making this case. Many feel that much money is wasted and that government may be offering too many services.

A fourth governmental standard for judging taxes refers to their **collectability.** Ease of collection is in part an administrative matter. Some taxes, like property taxes, are easy to collect. Property is highly identifiable, and property values are relatively easy to estimate. Income taxes may be harder to collect. This is most likely the case when people work for cash and/ or can hide their true income. Many people who work for tips to supplement their base wages, like waitresses and cab drivers, can pocket some proportion of their tip earnings, effectively hiding them from government. The same can be done by small merchants whose trade is cash based; not all sales need to be rung up on the register. The IRS has imposed rules and schedules for expected income earnings of these types to cut down on tax avoidance or noncompliance.

Ease of filling out forms may also affect collectability. The complexity of the federal tax code has led to the establishment of a whole industry devoted to helping individuals fill out their tax forms, and tax law for the wealthy and for businesses is among the most lucrative specialties of the legal profession.[12]

Although it is common for taxpayers to dislike taxes, such a standard is too vague to use to judge the worth of the tax. Both economic and political factors may account for public dislike, and tax reformers must be conscious of the source of public dislike and the needs of government, society, and the economy. Also, there are many types of taxes, some of which are more tolerated than others. We now turn to a discussion of the different types of taxes.

TYPES OF TAXES AND THEIR INCIDENCE

There are several major types of taxes—income, consumption, and property. Each type can take several forms, providing a multitude of taxes government can use. Government may also collect revenue from nontax sources.[13]

Types of Taxes

Income taxes are one of the most visible and common types of taxes. Income may come from wages, often termed **earned income,** as well as from so-called unearned sources, which are often associated with asset holdings, like bank accounts, stocks, and the like. Three major types of income taxes predominate in the United States: personal income taxes, corporate income taxes, and social security taxes. Moreover, taxes must also be paid on **capital gains,** which are profits realized from the sale of assets, like one's house, stocks and bonds, businesses, and so forth.

Consumption taxes generate revenue from an economic transaction. The most common form of consumption tax is the **sales tax,** which is relied on heavily by state and local governments but is not a source of income for the federal government. Some European governments levy a type of sales tax called a **value added tax,** or **VAT.** The VATs tax the increased value of a commodity as it moves through the production and sales process. For instance, the process of converting iron ore to steel increases the value of the ore. The increase in value is taxed as the steel is sold, say, to an auto manufacturer or construction firm. As the steel is further processed into a car part, its value again increases, and another tax increment is added. This continues along the entire exchange process until the car comes into private hands. At each exchange, each increase in value is taxed; this provides a cumulative tax across the entire exchange process.[14]

Besides sales taxes and VATs, there are two other important consumption taxes, import taxes and excise taxes. Import taxes, or tariffs, are imposed on goods and services produced outside of the United States but marketed within the country. Until the early 1900s, this was the major source of revenue for the federal government. **Excise taxes** are imposed on goods produced domestically. Two domestic products are subject to relatively high excise taxes in the United States, tobacco and alcohol. Excise taxes operate like sales taxes, but the size of the excise tax is not geared to the price of the good. Rather, the amount and type of the good that is sold determine the excise tax rate.

Property taxes are the third major source of government revenue.[15] The most common property tax is imposed on real estate, both residential and commercial. Other forms of property taxes include those on vehicles, like automobiles and boats, which some states and localities rely on. Last, gifts and estates (inheritances) may be taxed.

Nontax Revenue Sources

Government does not rely exclusively on taxes for revenue. There are at least four other revenue options. The most important of these in terms of money generated is borrowing. Government borrows money from the private sector to finance its programs with the promise that it will pay back the loan. Borrowing can come from traditional lending sources, like banks, as well as from individuals, for instance, through federal savings bonds. State governments tend to have laws restricting borrowing as a way to finance budget deficits, though they have access to other forms of borrowing, such as bonds.

Government can also generate revenue through **user fees** and charges. For instance, every time you buy an airplane ticket, an airport use or landing fee is included in the purchase. Similarly, government may exact tolls on road use, and it often collects fees for licenses to drive, hunt, camp, and otherwise use public facilities that not all people use. A third nontax form of revenue comes from government imposition of fines and penalties. Many criminal laws impose not only jail sentences but also financial punishments. Also, many regulations are enforced through financial penalties for violations.

Last, government may generate revenue from **lotteries.** State lotteries have become very popular in recent years as a way of collecting revenue without taxes.[16] In the face of tax resistance and tax revolts, lotteries have provided government a way to raise money without coercion. Lotteries are not, however, a panacea for fiscal shortfalls. Lotteries do not bring in large sums of money in most cases. They have also been criticized on other grounds. Sometimes the poor play the lottery when their limited resources might better be spent on food. Also, the "get-rich-quick" mentality of the lottery may undermine incentives for work and education, which are more realistic ways of improving one's economic circumstances. And even when lottery money is earmarked for, say, education, education will not necessarily feel this windfall, as policymakers reallocate money away from education to other purposes.

Trends in U.S. Taxation

Since 1900, taxes imposed by all levels of government as a percentage of the gross domestic product (GDP) have gone up almost tenfold. In 1900, such taxes amounted to little more than 3 percent of the GDP; in 1985, tax levels topped 29 percent. Since 1985, tax levels have remained relatively steady at approximately 30 percent.

There are several reasons for this growth in taxes. One has been the need to pay for the four major wars that the United States engaged in during the twentieth century. Moreover, the continued support of a large military presence during the cold war years added to the public finance burden. The expansion of domestic government services also put pressure on the nation to raise taxes. Thus, one source of tax growth seems to be government growth.

Another source of tax growth has been the shift in the types of taxes used. Nineteenth-century taxes at the federal level were primarily import duties and tariffs. In the twentieth century, government began to rely more heavily on taxes with greater ability to generate revenue. Thus, the federal government used the income tax and social security contributions for revenue, while state governments resorted to sales and property taxes. The ability to extract resources through taxes is an important source of tax growth, and this ability may have also spurred government growth, as policymakers found a source of revenue for their programs.

Changes in Tax Structure

Since World War II, the tax structure at the federal level has changed; the burden on individuals through personal income and social security taxes has increased, while corporate tax rates have decreased. Table 7.1 presents data on the percentage of its revenue that the federal government derives from different tax sources.

In 1950, corporate profits taxes accounted for about as much federal revenue as personal income. Corporations as a tax base for the federal government began to erode soon after, however, and continued to decline as a source of federal revenue up to the present. By 1990, only about one-tenth of federal revenue came from this source. In contrast, federal revenue from individuals increased, through both the personal income and social security taxes. From parity in 1950, personal income accounted for twice the amount of federal revenue as corporate taxes by 1960. The trend continues to the present, even

TABLE 7.1 Type of Tax as a Proportion of Federal Tax Revenues, 1950–1990 (in percentages)

Year	Personal Income	Social Security	Personal Income plus Social Security	Corporate Profits
1950	36.8	6.8	43.6	36.4
1960	45.7	13.8	59.5	23.4
1970	48.6	21.9	70.5	16.8
1980	49.3	28.0	77.3	13.8
1990	46.6	35.7	82.3	10.5

Source: Data adapted from Jon Bakija and Eugene Steuerle, "Individual Income Taxation Since 1948," *National Tax Journal* 44 (1991): 470–473.

though personal income as a source of federal revenue plateaued by 1980 and then modestly declined due to the Reagan tax cuts of the early 1980s.

The steeper increases in recent years on individuals comes from social security taxes. A modest tax in 1950, social security now nearly rivals personal income as a source of federal revenue. To be sure, only half of the social security take comes from individual paychecks, with a matching amount coming from employer contributions.

Why did the tax burden on corporations fall so steeply in the postwar era? Part of the answer clearly derives from the power of business. As government grew, so did its demands for more revenue. Business applied its resources, as discussed in Chapter 5, to protect itself from these demands.[17] However, the public also commands important political resources—the most critical being the vote. Why didn't voters expel policymakers who laid these heavier taxes on them? In a way they did, as the taxpayer revolts of the 1970s illustrate. To find better answers to these two questions, however, we should consider both business's ability to use the argument that high taxes hurt investment and growth and the visibility of different tax systems.

As discussed earlier, one of the critical sources of business influence over the political system is its ability to withdraw investment, thereby leading to smaller economic growth rates.[18] Business can argue that high taxes reduce the available capital for investment. Less investment means lower growth, which means higher rates of unemployment and other signs of economic distress. Politicians dislike contracting economies because they often feel the repercussions from the public come in the next election.[19]

During the 1960s and 1970s, taxes on the general public were relatively invisible, largely due to bracket creep. The bracket-creep problem was most severe during the inflation of the 1970s. One result of that inflation was that property values skyrocketed around much of the nation, especially in California. Increased property values led to larger property taxes, inspiring the tax revolt movement, which began in California in the late 1970s. Through citizen action, a referendum called Proposition 13 was placed on the California ballot in 1978 to cap property taxes. It was accepted by a wide margin, and its success led to taxpayer movements in other states. By the 1980 presidential election, the taxpayer revolt was a national movement that candidate Ronald Reagan tried to associate himself with and gain support from. With the success of the revolt in California, in other states, and in 1981 at the federal level (with tax cuts and reforms to be discussed later in this chapter), the energy of the revolt seemed spent, but still it left its mark on politics in the 1990s, as all observers seemed to feel that the antitax mood exemplified by the revolt was still in place and potentially easily aroused.

Social security taxes also climbed steeply in the postwar era. However, these taxes did not inspire a taxpayer revolt. Public opinion polls have found that social security is one of the most popular programs that the federal government offers.[20] Moreover, people do not view the social security payroll deduction as a tax but as a contribution into a retirement insurance fund.

People claim that they are saving for themselves for their retirement—that it is their money, not the government's. In this sense, social security is also an invisible tax. But we should point out that people are not saving for themselves into an insurance or retirement program. Social security is a pay-as-you-go system, where current contributions are paid out to current recipients. In essence, current workers are supporting current retirees.

Conservative Versus Liberal Tax Policy

Compared to other nations, the United States has a relatively conservative economic policy. The United States rarely owns or directs industries, something that all major western European nations do to some degree, and, in general, the U.S. government intervenes less in the economy than is the case in other advanced industrial nations.[21] In looking at the tax structure of the United States, however, we see that it relies on progressive taxes more than most other advanced industrial nations. Percentages of revenue from various tax sources in the United States and several other major economic powers are displayed in Table 7.2.

As the table indicates, the United States relies on progressive taxes somewhat more than the other major industrial nations and also relies on regressive taxes less. The two most progressive taxes tend to be personal income and property taxes. Property taxes are considered progressive because people with more wealth tend to buy more expensive residences and other properties. Of the twenty-one advanced industrial economies, the United States ranks fifth in use of personal income and second in terms of property taxes. The tax on corporate profits is another progressive tax that the United States relies on, ranking eighth out of twenty-one industrial nations. Among the most regressive taxes are consumption taxes, made up of sales taxes and VATs.[22] Here the United States ranks last of twenty-one nations.

TABLE 7.2 Types of Taxes by Nation, 1987: Percentage of Revenue from Various Tax Sources

Nation	Personal Income	Property	Consumption	Corporate
U.S.	36.2	9.2	7.4	8.1
U.K.	25.8	11.0	16.1	10.6
Germany	29.0	1.1	15.7	5.0
France	12.7	4.7	19.5	5.2
Japan	24.0	5.6	—	22.9

Source: Data adapted from B. Guy Peters, *The Politics of Taxation: A Comparative Perspective* (Cambridge, MA: Blackwell, 1991), 24–25.

This combination of low but progressive taxes in the United States represents a compromise between conservatives and liberals.[23] Conservatives opposed expansion of the state, except in such areas as defense. They recognized that to support the defense establishment some taxes were needed, but in general they opposed too great an expansion of government. Liberals, on the other hand, wanted a large, progressive government that would redistribute income to some degree. Conservatives relented on progressivity in order to keep overall tax rates down, thus preserving their strongly held preference for low taxes. Liberals, desiring progressivity, got their progressive taxes but at the lower rate that conservatives preferred. This seemed to be the pattern of compromise whenever major tax legislation appeared. The result became a relatively small government with relatively low but progressive taxes.

In other countries, like Sweden, the compromise seems to be high taxes that are also relatively regressive. Rarely do we find completely conservative or completely liberal tax policies, that is, either low, regressive or high, progressive taxes. Still, in recent years, U.S. taxes have become both lower and more regressive. How taxes are raised and changed are the themes of the next sections of this chapter.

THE POLITICS OF TAXATION IN THE UNITED STATES

Taxes present government with one of its most important yet most difficult policy decisions. Government, as we have stated, needs revenue to implement programs, and politicians who were elected to office need a revenue source to enact and deliver the policies and programs that they promised voters in their election campaigns. Two programs stand out because of their huge costs: entitlements and military spending. In the early 1990s, the federal government spent approximately $600 billion on entitlements, like social security, veterans' benefits, Medicare, and health care, and $300 billion on defense.[24] The money to finance these programs comes from tax revenue.

Taxes may also be used for purposes other than financing government programs. First, taxes are an important instrument of macroeconomic stabilization policy. Increases in taxes may help stem inflationary pressures, whereas tax cuts may stimulate private-sector demand. Second, as mentioned earlier, taxes may be used as a social policy instrument to reduce economic inequality through progressive rate structures. Thus, taxes have purposes beyond financing government.

These factors would seem to make taxes popular among policymakers, except that the public dislikes taxes and politicians assume that voters will take out their antitax sentiments by voting against those who help raise taxes.

This public reaction creates a political barrier to the easy implementation of new or higher taxes.

In the United States, those who make tax policy constantly have to balance off these opposing forces of the need for taxes and the antipathy toward them. This tension defines tax politics in this country. We have seen that taxes in the United States are somewhat progressive, relatively low, and full of loopholes. The reasons for this can be found by examining the parameters under which policymakers are forced to operate.

First, public preferences are an important determinant of the progressivity of U.S. taxes. The retreat from liberal, progressive ideas in the 1980s and 1990s helps account for the move to the less progressive taxes implemented during these years. Second, the low U.S. tax rate reveals the public bias against taxes. Rarely do more people feel that that tax is "about right" compared to "too high." Only tiny percentages ever find the tax "too low." It is not uncommon, especially in recent decades, for 60 percent or more of the public to feel that the income tax is too high. With this kind of public assessment, it is not too hard to understand why politicians have not raised the tax often or used the income tax as a way to bail the government out of its budgetary shortfalls during the 1980s and first half of the 1990s.

Third, the tax structure is riddled with loopholes and exemptions. Loopholes have been more kindly called **tax exemptions**,[25] and they are estimated to amount to more than the size of the federal deficit. In 1993, the OMB estimated revenue loss due to tax exemptions to equal $400 billion.[26] Some loopholes and exemptions are rather broadly cast, for instance, the deductions for children. Similarly, deductions for property tax and mortgage interest payments cover all homeowners, the majority of families in the United States. Most Americans have few complaints with these "loopholes"; they think of them not as loopholes but as reasonable deductions. But employer contributions for medical insurance and coverage are not taxed, nor are many contributions to retirement plans.[27] The classic loophole is usually given to a particular industry and cannot be shared by other industrial sectors. Some of these loopholes are so narrowly conceived that they practically name the company that is to receive this benefit.[28]

Loopholes tell us much about how tax policy is made in the United States. Obviously, the process is highly responsive to special interests. However much the process of building the overall tax system may be responsive to broader aims—whether they be the revenue needs of government, economic redistribution, or macroeconomic stabilization—loopholes and other kinds of tax breaks indicate the power of special interests. It is the tax committees in Congress, especially the House Ways and Means Committee, that make tax policy decisions,[29] and thus they are the ones who respond to the special interests by writing in loopholes and exemptions. Few nations have a tax code as complex as the United States; that complexity is mostly a function of the numerous and often arcane loopholes and specifications written into it by Congress.

Interestingly, presidents are often not particularly influential in making tax policy. This is not to say that presidents lack influence over tax policy entirely, but members of the Ways and Means Committee often stymie presidential efforts. Thus, tax policy is probably best viewed as a type of sectoral economic policy, one that may touch many economic sectors at the same time, rather than a macroeconomic policy. Presidents have to work harder to secure tax policies from Congress than many other types of macroeconomic policies.

Still, there are noteworthy examples of presidents getting Congress to pass major tax bills. Three stand out. In 1963, John F. Kennedy sought a major tax cut to stimulate an economy that indicators suggested was headed toward a recession.[30] Although tax cuts are usually received warmly by members of Congress, this proposal faced an uphill battle because it would have significantly increased the deficit. Kennedy made several addresses to the nation to educate the public on the issue and lobbied Congress strongly on it. Just as Congress was ready to vote on it, he was assassinated, although all indications were that Congress would have passed the proposal had he lived.

In 1968, Lyndon Johnson asked for a temporary **tax surcharge,** which increased income tax payments by 10 percent. Inflation, in part induced by the Vietnam War, was heating up, and Johnson wanted to cool it off.[31] Congress balked but finally gave in.

In 1981, Ronald Reagan sought a massive tax cut, which Congress rather easily granted him, but not without heated rhetoric from Democrats that the tax cut would benefit only the rich and would cause a higher deficit. Reagan argued that the cut was necessary as part of his supply-side program to restore the U.S. economy, which had been plagued with high inflation, high unemployment, and low growth through much of the 1970s.[32]

One theme runs through each of these examples of presidential tax policy success. To be successful in influencing tax policy, presidents must treat taxes as a macroeconomic issue, not a typical sectoral economic issue. Kennedy stressed the growth and antirecession aspects of his tax cut, Johnson the antiinflation aspects of his surcharge, and Reagan the private-sector growth aspects of his cut. In each case, the president was successful because he was able to convince people and policymakers to look at taxes as a macroeconomic instrument. However, seeing taxes through a macroeconomic lens is not common in U.S. politics, and presidents often have to fight to steer the issue in that direction.

THE POLITICS OF TAX REFORM

The late 1970s and 1980s saw the implementation of major tax reforms. These reforms began with the taxpayer revolts in the states in the 1970s and spread to the national level with the election of Ronald Reagan in 1980. Reagan not only presided over large cuts in personal income taxes but took part in two major reforms of the tax system. The first dealt with indexing tax rates, thereby doing away with the bracket-creep problem. The second reform came later, in 1986, and substantially simplified the tax structure, closing many loopholes and reducing the number of tax brackets. Both reforms can trace their roots to the tax revolt and the public antagonism toward taxes that had been mounting for years. Two themes are apparent in these reforms: lowering tax rates but also aiming to make taxes fairer. We can also see a retreat from the progressivity in taxes that has been characteristic of taxes at the federal level for generations.

Cutting Taxes: Retreat from Progressivity

During the 1980 campaign for the presidency, Ronald Reagan promised that he would cut taxes if elected. Not only was he swept into office but the Republicans gained a majority in the Senate as well. Although the Democrats still held the House, they were in disarray, and House Republicans were able to forge a working majority with conservative Democrats to pass Reagan's tax program. Thus, the largest tax cut in U.S. history was accomplished with the passage in 1981 of the **Economic Recovery Tax Act (ERTA)**. This tax cut had several important implications. First, it represented a retreat from progressivity. Second, it led to high deficits that persisted until the late 1990s.

The progressivity of the federal income tax was undermined but not eliminated in the ERTA by reducing the **marginal tax rates.** (The marginal tax rate is the tax on each tax bracket. Typically the higher one goes up in tax brackets, the higher the tax rate. For example, suppose there are three tax brackets, $0–$10,000, $10,001–$20,000, and $20,001–$50,000, with tax rates of 10, 15, and 20 percent, respectively. A person in the first tax bracket would pay a tax of 10 percent. A person with an income of $15,000 is in the second tax bracket. That person pays the 10 percent tax on income up to $10,000 and 15 percent on the income from $10,001 to $15,000.) These reductions were most noticeable in the highest tax brackets, where marginal rates were reduced from 73 to 50 percent over a three-year period. But lower-income individuals were not forgotten in the tax reforms, as their rates were modestly adjusted too.[33]

How did Reagan manage this feat? Several factors seem to account for it. First, Reagan was able to argue that the highest rates were too high. Thus, a distinction was made between a progressive system and an "oppressive" tax system. In his famous phrase, Reagan sought to "get the federal government off of people's backs." Moreover, Reagan attacked the previous Democratic administration of Jimmy Carter for its "tax and spend" policies. At the time, the nation was undergoing high inflation, yet economic growth was paltry. Reagan attached the tax-cut reforms to the poorly performing economy, arguing that if people had more of their own money to spend, with less of it going to the federal treasury, the economy would recover.

Third, Reagan rode to office on a wave of antitax sentiment. In 1978 California passed the famous Proposition 13, which reformed and reduced property taxes in that state. After the success of the California taxpayers' revolt, the movement spread across the nation. Reagan's 1981 tax cuts can be viewed as the culmination of this movement.

Another push to reduce taxes came from foreign competition and the weakening performance of the economy. To reduce the cost of doing business and make U.S. products more competitive on world markets, some argued that taxes needed to be cut. Thus, corporate taxes were also targeted for reform.[34] Finally, the tax cuts were coupled with the indexing of taxes, which made the overall package quite popular.

Indexing Taxes

Among the most significant of the ERTA reforms was the **indexing** of tax brackets, personal exemptions, and standard deductions to the inflation rate, a process that began in 1985, after the tax cuts that were spread from 1982 to 1984 were completed.[35] Indexing ties income tax brackets to the inflation rate. Thus, if inflation rises a certain percentage, this percentage is added to the income tax bracket. In this way, people are not pushed into a higher tax bracket with a higher tax rate because of inflation. This reform, which ended the problem of bracket creep, was very popular. Now, as people's incomes go up due to inflationary pressures, they are not jumped into a higher tax bracket.

One major consequence of this reform, however, was that it increased the visibility of future tax increases. As long as bracket creep existed, the government could increase its revenues without raising taxes. In effect, bracket creep was an invisible tax increase. Ironically, it also allowed the government to pass along tax cuts to people, something that had been very common in the late 1960s and throughout the 1970s.[36] Thus, in the 1960s and 1970s, when inflation pushed people into higher tax brackets, Congress would respond by readjusting the tax bracket downward, in effect passing a law to cut taxes, though in reality, congressional actions tended only to reset taxes at levels felt before inflation had pushed the tax bite up.

Indexing made it harder for the government to raise new revenues without incurring major political costs. Politicians now had to talk about new taxes openly. Since the general public was antagonistic toward new taxes, politicians who espoused such policies would not find much public support. Thus, in the 1984 campaign for the presidency, Democratic candidate Walter Mondale openly took a position that tax increases were needed to close the government's budget deficit. He was soundly trounced in that election by Ronald Reagan.

Four years later, George Bush seemed to have learned the "Mondale lesson." His major campaign slogan was "Read my lips. No new taxes." In 1990, however, with the Bush administration and the Democratic Congress deadlocked and unable to produce a budget, Bush accepted some "revenue enhancements" in a complicated budget deal. In the public's eyes, Bush had broken his promise. In 1992 he was defeated for reelection.

Still, throughout the 1980s and into the 1990s, new taxes were raised because of pressures from the deficit. In 1982, excise taxes on airports, cigarettes, and telephones were raised, as were gasoline and fuel taxes. Social security deductions were increased in 1983, as were payroll deductions associated with the federally administered railroad retirement program. A Deficit Reduction Act was passed in 1984, which increased taxes on distilled spirits, extended the telephone excise tax, and repealed interest exclusion, a provision of the 1981 ERTA bill. Again in 1985 taxes were raised, focusing on cigarette excise taxes, coal production, and income averaging for students. The list of tax increases extends to the 1990 compromise between Bush and congressional Democrats and the first budget under Bill Clinton in 1993.[37]

These taxes tended not to be broad-based, and often euphemisms, like "revenue enhancements," were used to disguise the fact that they were tax increases. They also tended not to raise large sums of money, indicating the difficulty politicians had in finding new revenue in the 1980s.

Simplifying Taxes: Fairness Without Progressivity

Reducing the tax burden was only one demand by the public. Another complaint was that even though the system was supposedly fair because it was progressive, many loopholes existed, and wealthy people and corporations were very adept at taking advantage of them. News stories were aired in the middle 1980s, for instance, about major U.S. corporations that did not pay any taxes at all. The public felt that the tax system was unfair, that too much of the burden was placed on the middle class, and that the wealthier segments of society did not pay their fair share. At the same time, the public felt that the tax code was too complicated and that it was difficult for the average person to fill out the federal income tax forms. Most people hired tax preparers, like H & R Block, to help them file their income tax returns. Thus, another push for reform sought to simplify the tax code and close loopholes.

Reagan was a strong supporter of such tax reform. In fact, he had sought reform during his administration but had been continually stymied by interest groups that attacked the elimination of their special tax preferences. In 1986, however, Congress passed the **Tax Reform Act** over the opposition of the special interests.[38] This was a remarkable achievement, given the historic tendency of special interests to win loopholes in the tax code from Congress. Working at times in closed sessions to insulate itself from interest group pressures, members of Congress mounted a public opinion campaign to keep the reform efforts alive. Support for the president also aided the effort, and the reform effort succeeded.

The reform was sold as being "revenue neutral." That is, it was not a tax increase in disguise, though the mix of tax liability would change. Personal income tax rates were lowered, but many former deductions were denied or lowered. Also, although the corporate tax rate was cut, rules governing minimum corporate taxes were tightened in an attempt to keep corporations from avoiding tax payments. Many explicit tax preferments for specific corporations and industries were also repealed or limited. The tax code that resulted, although still very complex, was simplified significantly. New, easier tax forms for individuals were also created.

Tax Reform in the 1990s

The tax reform efforts of the 1970s and 1980s had petered out by the 1990s. Several reforms were proposed, but few were implemented. Two reforms of consequence were implemented once the Republicans became the majority party in Congress in 1995. First was the reform of the IRS mentioned earlier in this chapter. The other was the House rule, adopted in 1995, which requires a three-fifths majority of Congress to pass a tax increase. The weakness of a House rule compared with legislation is that it can be undone when the opposition party regains control or it can be waved by a majority as it sees fit.

To strengthen their efforts to raise the bar of tax increases, Republicans have proposed a constitutional amendment. That proposal would change the constitution so that a two-thirds majority of Congress would be required to raise taxes. In April 1999 that proposal was defeated in the House by a vote of 229 to 199, which was shy 57 votes of the two-thirds majority that is required to change the Constitution. A similar proposal was defeated in 1996, falling 37 votes short of the two-thirds needed.[39]

Unlike the 1980s, when tax reform efforts aimed at not only lowering tax rates but also closing loopholes and changing the structure of the tax code, most of the efforts of the 1990s focused on lowering rates, as the preceding examples illustrate. The major reason for the lesser success and more modest aims of tax reforms of the 1990s was the sweeping reform efforts and successes of the 1980s. Most people did not see much necessity to reform taxes because so much had been done in the 1980s. Moreover, the generally healthy state of the economy in the 1990s, especially the wage gains that workers were making, lowered antagonisms to existing taxes.

CONCLUSION

Probably the defining political characteristic of the 1980s was the public's antigovernment mood, which was expressed so strongly with regard to taxes.

As a consequence, taxes were lowered, loopholes closed, and the system made less progressive, all changes that upper- and middle-class people desired. Reforms in taxes in the 1980s, while they effectively lowered tax rates and thus pleased voters, had other consequences, notably their contribution to the budget deficit of the period. However, the budget surplus that emerged in the mid-1990s seemingly ended this tax-related issue, too. Thus, in the mid-1990s we entered a relatively quiet period with regard to tax issues, as witnessed by the generally unsuccessful efforts of those who have proposed tax reform and lower tax rates.

This does not mean that tax-related issues are dead. They are potent in U.S. politics but will probably shift in emphasis as we enter the new millennium. Finding new and creative ways to finance social security, perhaps as some policy advocates have suggested by investing some of what people pay into social security in the stock market, is likely to become an important policy debate that relates to the taxes that people pay.

Key Terms

acceptability
buoyancy
capital gains
capital gains taxes
collectability
consumption
  taxes
deficit
discretionary
  income
distributional
  consequences
earned income
economic effects
economically
  neutral

Economic
  Recovery Tax
  Act (ERTA)
excise taxes
flat tax
horizontal equity
income taxes
indexing
lotteries
marginal tax rates
progressive income
  taxes
property taxes
proportional taxes
regressive taxes
sales tax

surplus
tax adequacy
tax equity
tax exemptions
Tax Reform Act
tax surcharge
user fees
value added tax (VAT)
vertical equity
visibility

Explore the Web

The IRS web page address is http://www.irs.ustreas.gov/. The entire Internal Revenue code is also on that web page at http://www.tns.lcs.mit.edu/ uscode/. Several tax reform advocacy groups maintain web pages. The

Citizens for an Alternative Tax System (CATS), who want to abolish the income tax and replace it with a national sales tax, have a web page at http://www.cats.org/. The National Center for Policy Analysis has a page devoted to analysis of the flat tax at http://www.ncpa.org/pi/taxes/tax7.html.

Notes

1. Alison Mitchell, "A New Form of Lobbying Puts Public Face on Private Interest," *New York Times,* September 30, 1998, A1.

2. Richard A. Ryan, "Voters Control U.S. Surplus: The Battle: Use It to Cut Taxes or Aid Social Security," *Detroit News,* October 1, 1998, A1.

3. A good account of taxes with a very long and expansive historical view is Carolyn Webber and Aaron Wildavsky, *A History of Taxation and Expenditure in the Western World* (New York: Simon & Schuster, 1986).

4. "Clinton Signs Law Giving IRS Less Power, More Oversight; GOP Shares Credit for Overhaul," *St. Louis Post-Dispatch,* July 23, 1998, A1.

5. The criteria for judging taxes have a long history. Adam Smith set down the first set of criteria almost two hundred years ago with his five canons of taxation: adequacy, economy, certainty, ease of administration, and equity. See James W. Lindeen, *Governing America's Economy* (Englewood Cliffs, NJ: Prentice-Hall, 1994), 154–156. Modern economists have also discussed the topic. See George Break and Joseph Pechman, *Federal Tax Reform* (Washington, DC: Brookings, 1975), 4–10; David G. Davies, *United States Taxes and Tax Policy* (New York: Cambridge University Press, 1986), 17–19; and Herbert Kiesling, *Taxation and Public Goods: A Welfare-Economic Critique of Tax Policy Analysis* (Ann Arbor: University of Michigan Press, 1992). The discussion in this text relies very heavily on B. Guy Peters, *The Politics of Taxation: A Comparative Perspective* (Cambridge, MA: Blackwell, 1991), 49–58. Peters's list of evaluation criteria is more exhaustive than that of the economists.

6. Peters, *The Politics of Taxation,* uses the term *fiscally neutral* for this effect, but I have changed the term to *economically neutral* to avoid confusing this effect with government fiscal policy.

7. Bracket creep is discussed in Susan B. Hansen, *The Politics of Taxation: Revenue without Representation* (New York: Praeger, 1983), 109, 235; John F. Witte, *The Politics and Development of the Federal Income Tax* (Madison: University of Wisconsin Press, 1985), 297–298; Davies, *United States Taxes and Tax Policy,* 47–54; Thomas J. Reese, *The Politics of Taxation* (Westport, CT: Quorum Books, 1980), 200–201; and John P. Frendreis and Raymond Tatalovich, *The Modern Presidency and Economic Policy* (Itasca, IL: Peacock, 1994), 94. A technical discussion is found in Michael R. Baye and Dan R. Black, "The Microeconomic Foundations of Measuring Bracket Creep and Other Tax Changes," *Economic Inquiry* 26 (1988): 471–485; and Jukka Lassila, "Income Tax Indexation in an Open Economy," *Journal of Money, Credit and Banking* 27 (1995): 389–404. An argument against policies that utilize bracket creep is found in David Altig and Charles T. Carlstrom, "Using Bracket Creep to Raise Revenue: A Bad Idea Whose Time Has Passed," *Economic Review* 29 (1993): 2–12.

8. For an analysis of progressive taxes and their effects on income inequality from an economist's perspective, see Joel Slemrod, ed., *Tax Progressivity and Income Inequality* (New York: Cambridge University Press, 1994). A comparison of tax progressivity across the American states is found in David R. Morgan, "Tax Equity in the American States: A Multivariate Analysis," *Social Science Quarterly,* 75 (1994): 510–524.

9. See Charles H. Stewart, III, "Lessons from the Post–Civil War Era," in *The Politics of Divided Government,* eds. Gary W. Cox and Samuel Kernell (Boulder, CO: Westview, 1991), 203–238.

10. Public opinion on the income tax is discussed in Hansen, *The Politics of Taxation,* 259–264; Witte, *The Politics and Development of the Federal Income Tax,* 337–346, 362–367; Benjamin I. Page and Robert Y. Shapiro, *The Rational Public: Fifty Years of Trends in Americans' Policy Preferences* (Chicago: University of Chicago Press, 1992), 160–166; and Cassie F. Bradley, Peggy A. Hite, and Michael L. Roberts, "Understanding Attitudes Toward Progressive Taxation," *Public Opinion Quarterly* 58 (1994): 165–191.

11. This support may be eroding as flat-tax proposals gain greater acceptance.

12. Collectability and compliance are discussed at some length in Peters, *The Politics of Taxation,* 246–270.

13. Again, I found Peters, *The Politics of Taxation,* to be a very valuable source. See 28–46.

14. A good discussion of VATs is Murray L. Weidenbaum, David G. Raboy, and Ernest S. Christian, Jr., eds., *The Value-added Tax: Orthodoxy and New Thinking* (Boston: Kluwer Academic, 1989).

15. The property tax is among the most disparaged of all taxes in the United States. In the late 1970s, taxpayer revolts, beginning in California, spread around the nation. They focused heavily on the property tax. See Clarence Y. H. Lo, *Small Property Versus Big Government: Social Origins of the Property Tax Revolt* (Berkeley: University of California Press, 1990); David O. Sears and Jack Citrin, *Tax Revolt: Something for Nothing in California* (Cambridge, MA: Harvard University Press, 1982); and Arthur O'Sullivan, Terri A. Sexton, and Steven M. Sheffrin, *Property Taxes and Tax Revolts: The Legacy of Proposition 13* (New York: Cambridge University Press, 1995).

16. A good study on the politics of lotteries is Frances Stokes Berry and William D. Berry, "State Lottery Adoption as Policy Innovation: An Event History Analysis," *American Political Science Review* 84 (1990): 395–415.

17. An interesting analysis is found in Dennis P. Quinn and Robert Y. Shapiro, "Business Political Power: The Case of Taxation," *American Political Science Review,* 85 (1991): 851–874. Also see David Jacobs, "Corporate Taxation and Corporate Economic Power," *American Journal of Sociology* 93 (1988): 852–881. From the perspective of the capital needs of the state as a reason for the decline in corporate taxation, see Cathie Jo Martin, *Shifting the Burden: The Struggle over Growth and Corporate Taxation* (Chicago: University of Chicago Press, 1991); and Ronald F. King, *Money, Time, and Politics: Investment Tax Subsidies and American Democracy* (New Haven, CT: Yale University Press, 1993).

18. See Martin, *Shifting the Burden;* and King, *Money, Time, and Politics.*

19. Studies on the impact of taxes on voting behavior, however, are inconclusive. Richard G. Niemi, Harold W. Stanley, and Richard J. Vogel, "State Economies and

State Taxes: Do Voters Hold Governors Accountable?" *American Journal of Political Science* 39 (1995): 936–957, find some effects, as does Theodore J. Eisemeir, "Votes and Taxes: The Political Economy of the American Governorship," *Polity* 15 (1983): 368–379; but Susan L. Kone and Richard F. Winters, "Taxes and Voting: Electoral Retribution in the American States," *Journal of Politics* 55 (1993): 23–39, do not.

20. See Page and Shapiro, *The Rational Public*, 118–121; and Paul Light, *Artful Work: The Politics of Social Security Reform* (New York: Random House, 1985), esp. 58–73.

21. On this point see Anthony King, "Ideas, Institutions, and the Policies of Governments, I and II," *British Journal of Political Science* 3 (1973): 291–313, 409–423.

22. These figures are from Peters, *The Politics of Taxation*, 24–25.

23. This view is developed more completely by Sven Steinmo, "Political Institutions and Tax Policy in the United States, Sweden, and Britain," *World Politics* 41 (1989): 500–535, and *Taxation and Democracy: Swedish, British, and American Approaches to Financing the Modern State* (New Haven, CT: Yale University Press, 1993).

24. See Harold W. Stanley and Richard G. Niemi, *Vital Statistics on American Politics*, 4th ed. (Washington, DC: CQ Press, 1994), 421–423, for more details on budget expenditures.

25. See Donald Axelrod, *Budgeting for Modern Government*, 2d ed. (New York: St. Martin's, 1995), 154; Howard E. Shuman, *Politics and the Budget: The Struggle Between the President and the Congress*, 3d ed. (Englewood Cliffs, NJ: Prentice-Hall, 1992); and Stanley S. Surrey and Paul R. McDaniel, *Tax Expenditures* (Cambridge, MA: Harvard University Press, 1985).

26. Cited in Axelrod, *Budgeting for Modern Government*, 154.

27. See Stanley and Niemi, *Vital Statistics on American Politics*, 428–429, for a detailed breakdown of tax expenditures by category from 1980 to 1994.

28. These are described with great verve by Shuman, *Politics and the Budget*.

29. On this point see Reese, *The Politics of Taxation*, esp. 89–119.

30. The story of the Kennedy tax cut is recounted in many places. See Irving Bernstein, *Promises Kept: John F. Kennedy's New Frontier* (New York: Oxford University Press, 1991).

31. See Martin, *Shifting the Burden*, 81–106.

32. Ibid., 107–158. On the redistributive implications of the Reagan tax program, see Douglas A. Hibbs, Jr., *The American Political Economy: Macroeconomics and Electoral Politics* (Cambridge, MA: Harvard University Press, 1987).

33. For a review of the provisions of the 1981 ERTA, see C. Eugene Steuerle, *The Tax Decade: How Taxes Came to Dominate the Public Agenda* (Washington, DC: Urban Institute, 1992), 224.

34. On the impact of international pressures on taxes, see Peters, *The Politics of Taxation*, 287.

35. Indexing is common in federal programs. Social security, for instance, is indexed. Estimates are that 30 percent of federal budget expenditures are directly tied to the consumer price index, and another 20 percent are indirectly tied. See R. Kent Weaver, *Automatic Government: The Politics of Indexation* (Washington, DC: Brookings, 1988).

36. Witte, *The Politics and Development of the Federal Income Tax,* 155–219, details these cuts.

37. A list of the tax increases of the 1980s and 1990s is found in Steuerle, *The Tax Decade,* 224–228.

38. Steuerle, *The Tax Decade,* 225, lists the major provisions. Discussion of the reform and its politics is found in Jeffrey H. Birnbaum and Alan S. Murray, *Showdown at Gucci Gulch: Lawmakers, Lobbyists, and the Unlikely Triumph of Tax Reform* (New York: Random House, 1987); David F. Bradford and Kent E. Calder, eds., *Tax Reform in the United States and Japan: Comparative Political and Economic Perspectives* (Princeton, NJ: Center for International Studies, Program on U.S.-Japan Relations, Princeton University, 1991); Timothy J. Conlan, Margaret T. Wrightson, and David R. Beam, *Taxing Choices: The Politics of Tax Reform* (Washington, DC: CQ Press, 1990); Bernard P. Herber, "Federal Income Tax Reform in the United States. How Did It Happen? What Did It Do? Where Do We Go from Here?" *American Journal of Economics and Sociology* 47 (1988): 391–408; and Randall Strahan, "Members' Goals and Coalition-Building Strategies in the U.S. House: The Case of Tax Reform," *Journal of Politics* 51 (1989): 373–384.

39. Lori Nitschke, "Constitutional Amendment on Tax Increase Is Rejected," *Congressional Quarterly Weekly Report,* April 17, 1999, 888.

8

Managing the Macroeconomy I: Fiscal Policy and the Budget

O N FEBRUARY 17, 1993, the newly inaugurated president, Bill Clinton, gave a major speech on the economy before a joint session of Congress. Alan Greenspan, chairman of the Federal Reserve Board, attended. This was quite unprecedented. Usually, the head of that independent regulatory commission attempts to maintain his distance from the political branches, both to create an image of independence and to signal that political interference with the Fed is unacceptable.

Greenspan, however, thought that he could work with the new president. The economy, although slowly coming out of a recession, was still reeling from over a decade of large budget deficits. Greenspan had met with Clinton several times after the election and had found the new president responsive to his opinion that the deficit was the economy's number one problem. Thus, in a symbolic gesture, Greenspan attended the speech and sat between the First Lady, Hillary Clinton, and Tipper Gore, wife of Vice President Albert Gore.

The seating arrangement was widely noted in the media, and interpreted as a signal of the relationship that might be expected between the White House and the Fed. Although formal coordination was not to be forthcoming, an informal arrangement was likely. Thus, perhaps for the first time in history, the three major arms of government responsible for macroeconomic policy, the president, the Congress, and the Fed, came together under one roof and appeared ready to work together to solve both short- and long-term economic problems.[1]

In this chapter and the next we will look at the making of macroeconomic policy. Federal responsibility for macroeconomic policy is relatively recent, dating only from the New Deal. In the years since, macroeconomic policy has become a top governmental priority, and several policy instruments have been developed to manage it. However, the once high hopes for effective control of the macroeconomy have been tempered, and the major responsibility for macroeconomic management has shifted from fiscal instruments to monetary ones. In this chapter we will look at fiscal policy and the budget. In the next chapter we will look at monetary policy, the impact of the economy on elections, and the attempts of politicians to manipulate the economy for electoral purposes.

THE ORIGINS OF GOVERNMENT INVOLVEMENT IN THE MACROECONOMY

Prior to the Great Depression of the 1930s, the standard government approach to the macroeconomy was best characterized as laissez faire. The existing science of economics developed a view of the economy that emphasized its ability to self-adjust, or correct problems on its own, without governmental direction. The economy was seen as a system that would seek an equilibrium, or balance. In economic terms, this meant that the two key dynamic elements of the economy, supply and demand, would, over time, move toward a balance point, where there was no surplus or deficiency of either. That is, there would be neither an oversupply nor an undersupply of goods and services. However, the economy was also seen as dynamic, that is, ever changing, and it was believed that even if the economy reached a balance point, it would not sit there long. Forces of competition, new inventions, changes in taste, population transformations and movements, and the like were all factors that might upset the balance.

In this view of a dynamic, self-correcting economy, the wisest course of action for government was not to interfere. Government action could upset the course of the economy, delaying or even disrupting its natural corrective mechanisms. The only action these laissez faire economists prescribed was for government to balance its budgets. Balanced budgets, it was felt, would restore confidence in financial markets. Laissez faire economists believe that the investment decisions of financial markets are important to the economy's ability to correct its problems.[2]

As we discussed in Chapter 2, the economy cycles through growth and contraction periods. The high points of growth, you will recall, are called business peaks, and the low points are business troughs. This movement from peak to trough is called the business cycle. If mapped over time, the business cycle looks like a wave.[3] When the troughs get low enough and extend for long enough, the economy is said to be in a recession.[4] At these low points, or recessions, unemployment often rises. At other times growth may be overheated, and inflation results. In terms of supply and demand, during recessions, we tend to have greater supply than demand. Inflation presents the opposite picture: demand outpaces supply.

Laissez faire economists suggest that the natural tendency of supply and demand to converge at equilibrium will cool inflation and get the economy out of recession. Thus, during recession, where there is too much supply, supply and demand will be brought into balance through several mechanisms. One, prices for goods may fall. This may help reduce inventories, the oversupply of existing goods, as people may feel more inclined to buy a good if it costs less than previously. Also, productive capacity may decline. Some workers will be laid off, and some plants may close. Moreover, the drop in prices may force some less competitive and less productive enterprises to close. This also reduces productive capacity.

These economists often applauded the closing of less productive enterprises in a recession, feeling that the resulting economy would be more productive, more able to grow and produce wealth at a greater clip than the prerecessionary economy. Thus, downturns in the economy were often viewed as beneficial, and some economists used to make an analogy between this process and Social Darwinist theories. Only the "fittest" enterprises could survive a recession, according to these Social Darwinists.[5]

The dynamics of supply and demand will also cool off inflation, according to laissez faire economists. Inflation occurs when demand exceeds supply.[6] When that happens, consumers may bid against one another to get scarce goods. Sensing this consumer bidding war, suppliers boost prices. Prices continue to rise until they reach the point that consumers drop out of the bidding war; then prices begin to stabilize. Also, productive capacity may be increased to meet this increased demand. Workers may be given overtime; factories may increase hours of production; new plants may be built. As supply increases, consumers find themselves in less competition for formerly scarce goods, and the pressures that push prices up begin to ease.

Thus, according to laissez faire economics, without government action, the economy adjusts to recession and inflation. Further, the economy may be stronger, due to competitive pressures and the closing of less healthy economic enterprises, especially in recessionary periods.

This laissez faire approach was very popular throughout the industrial world in the period before the Great Depression. There were several reasons for this. First, many of the economies that had been industrializing in the second half of the nineteenth and first decades of the twentieth century experienced extraordinary growth. There was a belief that the unfettered forces of this new, industrial capitalism were important to this growth. Second, laissez-faire doctrine became the ideological weapon that the new industrial capitalists used to fend off the first stirring of government to regulate them.[7] Further, in the United States, the competitive elements of the laissez faire doctrine fit comfortably with the U.S. ethic of individualism and personal responsibility. Last, government was still small, and few viewed it as having the ability or resources to alter the course of the business cycle in any fundamental way.

THE RISE OF KEYNESIAN ECONOMICS

The Depression of the 1930s shook this confidence in the laissez faire approach. We documented in earlier chapters the depth and length of the Depression. Rather than recover, as classical economics predicted it would, the economy seemed to descend ever more deeply as time passed. The economy seemed stuck, unable to turn itself around.

At this time two innovations in thought occurred that paved the way for government management of the macroeconomy. The first was that people began to look to government to solve economic problems. The political culture of the United States changed during the Great Depression. Government was seen as being responsible and perhaps able to steer the economy, or, at least, to help people who were suffering. Into this new climate rode Franklin Roosevelt, who focused people's expectations not only on government but on himself and the presidency. The presidency emerged as the paramount branch of government during this period.[8]

Another intellectual innovation changed the way that economists thought about the economy, the business cycle, and the role that government should take to deal with business-cycle problems. That innovation came about through the work of the British economist **John Maynard Keynes.**

Keynes altered people's thinking by viewing government as *part* of the macroeconomy.[9] Keynes saw the macroeconomy, or national economy, as composed of four sectors: business, households, the foreign sector, and government. Government was an economic actor not only through its policies but also its behavior, such as through its purchase of goods and services from the private sector. Moreover, it taxes people and then redistributes money through programs and transfer payments, policies that may affect the economy. And it also borrows money. All of these government actions may influence the economy.

From this view comes the **Keynesian** prescription: government can alter its behavior to affect the business cycle. To smooth out the business cycle, the government should act in a countercyclical fashion. Thus, if the economy is in a recession and suffering from lack of demand compared to supply, government should stimulate demand. Or, if the economy is overheated and inflationary, government should cool these flames by acting to reduce demand. By operating against the tides of the business cycle, government can make downturns in the business cycle less deep and shorter, according to Keynes and his followers. This is called **stabilization** of the economy. The main instrument that government can use to act countercyclically is manipulation of the budget, which is the foundation of **fiscal policy,** the government's attempt to influence the economy.

Basic Mechanics of Fiscal Policy

Theoretically, fiscal policy can operate on either demand or supply, but demand is more susceptible to short-term changes and can be more easily altered in the short term than supply.[10] To increase supply usually requires increasing the productive capacity of the economy or importing more goods from other nations. The latter is not always politically popular or possible, especially if foreign nations do not produce the goods sought in great enough quantities or if trade barriers inhibit such importation. Increasing the productive capability of the economy may require building new plants and factories and training or retraining workers, all of which takes time. Thus, operating on the business cycle from the supply perspective is comparatively difficult and slow. Keynesians thus prescribe demand management instead of supply. Furthermore, Keynes felt that the problem of the Depression was not one of oversupply but of lack of demand. His policy offerings focused on ways of stimulating demand.

Two budgetary decisions have implications for fiscal policy, taxes and spending. Government can alter its taxing and spending decisions for countercyclical purposes. Although the overall level of government spending and taxation are important, more important for countercyclical impact is the manipulation of the government's budgetary surplus or deficit. A surplus means that the government is taking in more revenue than it is spending, whereas a deficit means that government is spending more than it is receiving in revenue. To finance a deficit, government must borrow money.

Increases in the deficit will stimulate demand, while increases in surpluses will restrict it. When the economy is in recession and demand is soft, according to Keynesian theory, government should deficit spend. In contrast, when the economy is suffering from inflation, government should do the opposite and generate surpluses.

Government can create deficits in two ways: by cutting taxes or by increasing spending. Tax cuts allow consumers to keep more money, which they can then spend. This helps boost the level of demand in the economy. Increasing government spending, either by creating new programs or by expanding existing programs, will also increase demand. Either or both actions in combination help to stimulate an economy that is in recession.

In contrast, government can cool demand by raising taxes or cutting spending. Increases in taxes lessen the money available to consumers to spend; this lowers demand. Similarly, decreasing government spending, by either eliminating programs or by reducing the size of existing ones, will also reduce demand. It is through these mechanisms that government can act to counter the business cycle.

Automatic Stabilizers

The budgetary actions just described require a decision by the government before they can take effect. There are some government programs, however, that have countercyclical effects but do not require that government legislate a policy with each new business cycle. These are called **automatic stabilizers.**

Unemployment compensation is perhaps the best known and most important.

Unemployment compensation is an entitlement program, whereby people who are legally defined as unemployed may apply to the government for money. As unemployment rises with a recession, claims for unemployment compensation also go up. Moreover, the claims increase in proportion to the level of unemployment. Thus, as unemployment increases, so do government outlays, just as Keynesians argue should be the case. Further, as the economy pulls out of the recession and starts to grow, claims for unemployment compensation decline with the growth in jobs, and government spending declines. Unemployment compensation, as an automatic stabilizer, is thus sensitive to the timing, duration, and depth of the business cycle.

THE ADOPTION OF THE KEYNESIAN APPROACH

Though the Depression opened the opportunity for Keynesian fiscal policies, Roosevelt's New Deal was not consciously Keynesian. Rather, as we have discussed, it was a grab bag of programs, often at odds with each other and without an underlying theoretical rationale. Roosevelt tried many different approaches for dealing with the Depression, from government spending to stimulate demand to redistribution of income to regulation of the economy and the financial markets.

Rather than being avowedly Keynesian, Roosevelt was initially quite traditional. In his campaign for the presidency, he pledged to balance the federal budget, something that the more conservative Hoover had been unable to accomplish in the early 1930s. Like Hoover and most Americans, Roosevelt held the traditional belief that government would instill confidence in the markets if it maintained a balanced budget. Other New Deal policies worked at cross-purposes with the balanced budget model, however, and in 1938, when Roosevelt proposed a budget that reduced the size of the federal deficit, a recession occurred as a consequence. Keynes, in fact, in March 1938, sent Roosevelt several letters trying to discourage the deficit reduction and encourage a large increase in the deficit. Roosevelt did not take his advice.[11] Only with the high level of federal spending and huge deficits associated with World War II did the Depression truly come to an end.

It was not until 1946, and the passage of the Full Employment Act, that the government began to institutionalize fiscal policy. With this act, government claimed responsibility for the condition of the macroeconomy, though the act does not require particular government action to deal with the business cycle. As John Frendreis and Raymond Tatalovich say, although the act "failed to create all of the policy tools necessary to achieve its ambitious goals, the nature of the political debate over management of the macroeconomy had clearly undergone a dramatic change. The question was no longer one of laissez faire versus economic management, but instead a debate over the extent and precise nature of government management of the macroeconomy."[12]

In the ensuing years, there was little conscious effort to apply Keynesian policy tools to business cycle fluctuations. Most actions that were taken were reactive until John F. Kennedy became president in 1961. Kennedy appointed several young academic economists who were staunchly Keynesian to important posts in his administration, and they schooled the new president in the Keynesian approach.

Their opportunity came in 1962, when their analysis of the economy suggested that it might dip into a recession. Kennedy was wary of a recession, fearing it would doom his reelection chances in 1964. But he was also wary of boosting the deficit to fight a recession that had not yet arrived. Kennedy did not want to acquire the reputation of being just another fiscally irresponsible Democrat, a charge that Republicans had successfully used since the 1930s.

Still, Kennedy's Keynesian advisers were persuasive, and the president asked Congress for legislation to cut taxes to head off an imminent recession. This was the first time a president had used Keynesian policy tools in anticipation of an economic event. It marks the high-water mark for Keynesianism as a governmental approach to dealing with the macroeconomy.

The glow of Keynesianism began to dim in the middle and late 1970s as the nation suffered a bout of stagflation, something that could not be explained by Keynesian theory. Stagflation, as we discussed in an earlier chapter, takes place when both unemployment and inflation increase at the same time. Thus, the occurrence of stagflation and the government's seeming inability to deal with it effectively undermined the once rosy optimism about Keynesian fiscal policy approaches to dealing with the business cycle. As we will discuss later in more detail, other factors also undermined that faith.

Partisan Preferences for Fiscal Policy

Democrats and Republicans have different preferences for fiscal policy. Democrats seem to be more willing to use it. They, more than Republicans, have faith in government intervention in the economy. Republicans are more hesitant to use government to solve economic problems. There are several reasons for these partisan differences over intervention in the economy. One is a matter of ideology: the Republicans tend to hold an ideology that leans in a laissez faire direction, whereas Democratic ideology pulls in the opposite direction. A second related reason has to do with the origins and history of the parties. The modern Democratic Party owed its success and shape to the policies of Franklin Roosevelt in the 1930s. It was under Roosevelt that the Democratic Party adopted economic intervention policies. In contrast, Republicans in the 1920s and later under Eisenhower in the 1950s and Reagan in the 1980s were successful by promoting policies that lessened government intervention in the economy. A third reason has to do with the supporters of each party. The Republicans tend to draw from the upper and business ranks in society, people who benefit in a capitalist economy, often with minimal government interference. In contrast, the Democrats draw much of their support from people lower down in economic status. Such people tend to benefit from government programs and intervention in the economy. Thus, the two parties try to create policy packages that resemble the preferences of those who make up the core of their support.

Beyond this, Republicans and Democrats differ in their fiscal policy preferences. With their resistance to allowing government to grow, Republicans prefer to cut taxes rather than to increase spending to deal with recession. And to curb inflation, Republicans tend to resist tax increases and instead to seek cutback in government spending. Democrats show a greater likelihood for fiscal approaches that increase the size of government. In 1962, President Kennedy faced fierce resistance from liberals in his party when he offered his tax-cut scheme. Those who opposed him wanted to increase spending. They feared that tax cuts would harm social programs, which they wanted to increase. The success of the Kennedy tax cut, however, changed many Democrats' minds about tax cuts as a fiscal solution.[13]

Limitations and Criticisms of Keynesianism

Fiscal policy has fallen on hard times. It is criticized from many quarters and has not been actively used to smooth the business cycle for, perhaps, the past twenty-five years. One important critique comes from monetary policy advocates. We will deal with those criticisms in the next chapter, after presenting the monetary policy approach. The other criticisms we will deal with here.

First, fiscal policy can be used but once a year, except for the automatic stabilizers, which kick in by themselves whenever needed. Spending decisions are now tied to the annual budget process. A policy instrument that can be used but once a year lacks flexibility and cannot be fine-tuned throughout the year as conditions may require.

Second, because of the budget cycle, there is a long lead time before fiscal policies may take effect. The budget is supposed to be passed by the end of September, with October 1 marking the beginning of the new fiscal year, which stretches until the next September 30. As a result of this timing, fiscal decisions have to be made far ahead of time, and policies may go into effect long after they are needed. Increased spending may begin to take effect once the economy is already beginning to show signs of improvement. When this happens, the increased spending may be inflationary, creating a new problem rather than stimulating flagging demand.[14] Also, government spending is spread throughout the fiscal year. Some items may be spent all at once, as Congress may dictate, but the bulk of government spending comes in the form of entitlements, like social security, which are disbursed monthly. This dilutes the effect of a fiscal measure by spreading it out over time, instead of focusing its impact at one specific moment in time. This effect also reduces the timing precision of a fiscal policy decision. This budgetary constraint also reduces the flexibility of fiscal policy in creating countercyclical pressures.

Third, political pressures make it difficult for government to run surpluses or reduce the deficit in good times. When the economy is in good shape, people often feel that the government can afford new and/or expanded programs. And it may be hard to cut programs once they are in place and have created a political constituency and built some popularity, or attained some socially desirable objective.[15] Moreover, there is intense competition for government dollars, and when a new pot of money appears, prospective claimants begin their campaigns for that money.

A good example is the 1999 budget. After three decades of persistent and huge budget deficits, the federal government ran a surplus. In his 1997 State of the Union Address, President Clinton informed the nation that a surplus was likely by fiscal year 1999 and that the government would be in the black through the early part of the next decade. He also promised that he would use the surplus to ensure the financial health of social security before he would support cutting taxes, expanding existing programs, or creating new government programs. Social security, he claimed, was heading toward problems if its financial foundation was not secured. In response, Republicans argued that first the government should provide tax relief by using the surplus to allow large tax cuts. A third position, especially that of the Concord Coalition, a public interest group that had been saying for years that the deficit was too high and that the nation had been piling up too much debt, argued that the surplus should be applied to the national debt to pay it down. However, the 1999 budget found Democrats and Republicans alike supporting increases in spending for pet programs that amount to $20 billion of the projected $70 billion surplus. For instance, spending was increased for education programs that Democrats favored, while Republicans got more money for the Defense Department, and many districts saw money for special projects, which are often labeled "pork barrel" projects to denote their suspect status as true national needs. In that "pork" category include $250,000 to study caffeinated chewing gum, $2 million for a storm shelter in Florida, $750,000 for grasshopper research in Alaska, and $1 million for "peanut quality" research in Georgia. Thus, despite many strong arguments not to spend the deficit on "politics as usual" but use it instead for social security or to pay down the national debt or to provide tax relief, politicians seemed unable to resist spending some of the surplus funds.[16]

Fourth, fiscal policy may be economically inefficient. Generally, spending and taxing decisions must target specific parts of the economy. These targets, which may be favored constituents of politicians making the fiscal decisions, may not be in the sectors of the economy that will have the most impact on the macroeconomy. For instance, Democrats usually want to put money into the hands of consumers to stimulate demand. It might make more sense to stimulate demand in the business sector first, allowing businesses access to less costly money that they can borrow to expand operations and thus hire more workers. The important point is not whether consumers or businesses should be targeted but that politicians make decisions about targets of fiscal policy with political considerations in mind.

Fifth, fiscal policy may disrupt programs that were designed to deal with other problems.[17] This may be very harmful to government programs with other important social objectives. Sixth, it may be hard to build a fiscal policy that is precise enough to deal with the problem. Fiscal policy tends to be blunt, and usually large changes in government spending or taxing are required to have much of an effect on aggregate national demand, that is, the demand function for the entire economy. Fiscal policy may be better suited to major recessions and depressions, where long-term sagging demand is the problem.[18] Seventh, fiscal policy is relatively insensitive to inflation.[19] Keynesian fiscal policy had its roots in the Great Depression, when inflation was not the problem, but since then inflation has become a persistent worry.

Finally, the budget deficits of the 1980 to 1995 years underscored the limitations of fiscal policy as a corrective to recessions when budget deficits are present. Stimulating the economy, a classic way to treat recessions, may not be possible to the extent required when the country holds a large deficit, like that during the recession of 1990–1991 under George Bush. Economic stimulus usually requires increasing federal spending, and thus, the deficit will expand. However, when financial centers around the nation are concerned about deficits, the last thing they want to see is additions to the deficit, which would absorb even more money out of the private sector as the government sought loans to pay for the deficit. This action might lead to higher interest rates, which would slow the economy at the same time that increased government spending is aiming to speed up the economy. Thus, the economy may realize no net benefit, with all of the expected growth canceled because of higher interest rates.

Supply-Side Economics and Fiscal Policy

There are two major competitors to Keynesian fiscal policy. One is monetary policy, the subject of the next chapter. Rather than working on government taxing and spending decisions, monetary policy tries to regulate the supply of money in the economy. The other competitor is **supply-side economics,** the linchpin of the Reagan economic program.

Supply-side economists criticized Keynesian economists for being more concerned with smoothing the business cycle than with economic growth.[20] Moreover, the inability of fiscal policy to deal with the stagflation of the 1970s gave supply-siders another weapon against fiscal policy; it did not even work very well at modulating business cycle problems.

Supply-siders argued that large government, which imposed high taxes and absorbed much of the nation's economic resources, acted as a drag on the economy. By reducing government, they believed, the economy would expand. Specifically, supply-siders argued in favor of a tax cut that would lower marginal tax rates. The tax cut would stimulate the economy by infusing more money into the private sector, allowing for more investment and expansion. This growth in the economy would offset any loss of government revenue due to the tax cut. Thus, they argued, lower tax rates in a larger economy would produce as much government revenue as high rates in a smaller economy. Supply-siders pointed to the stimulative effects of the Kennedy tax cut of 1963, noting that Kennedy made a similar argument that economic growth would counterbalance government revenues lost due to the tax cut. However, the supply-siders differed from the Keynesians in arguing for permanently low tax rates, which, they suggested, would lead to higher growth rates over the long term. To counter fears that inflation might result from pouring the tax-cut money into the economy, supply-siders wanted the Federal Reserve to restrict the money supply, thereby keeping interest rates up, which would cool inflationary pressures.

Ronald Reagan's economic program was rooted in supply-side logic. Not only were taxes cut under Reagan's brand of supply-side economics, called Reaganomics, but government programs, at least discretionary domestic ones, were also scaled back. And the program seemed to have its intended effect. After the 1982–1983 recession ended, the economy rebounded strongly and continued to grow for the next six years, one of the longest periods of sustained economic growth in modern U.S. history. (Some have attributed this growth to the supply-side program, but others believe the growth of the economy was due to the Keynesian-like deficit spending that accompanied the Reagan package of policies. There is no clear consensus on the source of the economic expansion of the 1980s.)

Supply-side economics, however, was not without negative consequences. Supply-siders seemed little concerned with government spending and had few prescriptions to deal with the deficit problem that grew to such major proportions in the 1980s. Several forces, which we will consider in more detail, exerted great pressures on federal spending, and the deficit grew to unprecedented proportions from 1982 onward. The supply-side maxim that the economy would grow out of the deficit was clearly wrong. Other critics charged that supply-side policies were insensitive to issues of economic distribution. Although the economy grew during the 1980s, not all sectors of society shared in that newfound wealth, with most of it concentrating in the hands at the top of the economic ladder.

BUILDING BUDGETS: THE POLITICS OF DEFICITS AND SURPLUSES

The federal government was plagued with large deficits from the early 1980s through the late 1990s. Then, in 1999, the government had surpluses that were projected to last until the middle of the next decade, when deficits would likely reappear. Across the nearly two decades of deficits, debate over how to contain the deficit was high on the political agenda, although at times it seemed that politicians and the public were unconcerned because of the generally strong economy during this period. As discussed, manipulating the size of the deficit (surplus) is the major instrument through which counter-cyclical fiscal policy operates. The persistence and size of the deficits across the 1980s and 1990s undermined using fiscal policy to stabilize the economy. Whereas short-run deficits to boost the economy out of depression and recession has its benefits, long-term and large deficits, as seen in the 1980s and 1990s, has its downside. Moreover, constantly running surplus is not necessarily good economic policy or good politics. In this section, we discuss the downside of deficits, the sources of the deficit, why government had such a hard time containing the deficit, and why the surplus emerged as it did in the late 1990s.

Why Should We Worry About Deficits?

Keynesians told us that deficits are not something to worry about, that they may have positive uses in the economy. Manipulation of the size of the deficit may help a nation out of depression and recession, for instance. Yet deficits are not as benign as the Keynesians once suggested; they have both political and economic consequences.

One political consequence relates to the historic U.S. tendency to support the idea of balanced budgets, a preference that predates Keynesian economics. This public preference pressures politicians to strive for a balanced budget, though some politicians have also stoked the flames in support of a balanced budget. For example, in 1994, Republicans made a balanced budget a cornerstone of their election campaign. Doing so added pressure to create a balanced budget once the Republicans took control of both houses after the 1994 elections.

Americans have a notion that the government budget is analogous to their household budget. The household budget requires balance, therefore so should the federal government's.[21] Moreover, forty-one states have requirements for a balanced budget.[22] Table 8.1 traces support for an amendment to the Constitution requiring that the government balance its budget. Although support flagged in the 1980s, it rebounded in the 1990s.

Aside from these political reasons, there are several important economic reasons to be concerned about the budget deficit.[23] First, deficits undermine financial market confidence in the government. When financial markets lose confidence in the government's ability to control its spending, investors are less likely to put money into new ventures. Instead they seek safer and more inflation-resistant places for their money. Sometimes they will even take their money out of the country and invest it elsewhere.

TABLE 8.1 Public Support for a Constitutional Amendment to Balance the Federal Government Budget (percentages)

Date	Support	Oppose	Don't Know or No Opinion	Net Support (Support − Oppose)
1976	78	12	9	66
1981 (April)	70	22	8	48
1981 (Sept.)	73	19	8	54
1982	74	17	9	57
1983	71	21	8	50
1985	49	27	24	22
1987	53	23	24	30
1989	59	24	17	35
1994	80	12	8	68
1995	76	18	6	58

Source: Harold W. Stanley and Richard G. Niemi, *Vital Statistics on American Politics, 1997–1998* (Washington, DC: Congressional Quarterly Inc., 1999), 143. Reprinted by permission.

Second, government borrowing to finance the deficit crowds out private borrowing. Government often has advantages over the private sector in security financing. For one thing, there is no real risk as long as government pays its debts, and the U.S. government has never defaulted on a loan. When government appears riskier than the private sector, government competes to secure financing by offering to repay loans at higher rates of interest. Thus, a large deficit has two effects on capital available for lending. One, it diverts money that could be used in the private sector for investment and other economic activity, and, two, it increases the demand for capital, which pushes interest rates up. As interest rates rise, economic activity declines. Over a long time, the standard of living of citizens may decline because of this effect.

In a related vein, a large deficit means that current consumption increases at the expense of investment. This point is open to much debate among economists. Some contend that what matters is what the government is financing with deficit spending. For instance, deficit spending on government activities that may have an economic payoff in the future is supported by some advocates. Thus, they argue, government spending on the infrastructure may lead to lower costs of doing business and may stimulate future economic activity. Others argue that spending on education will improve the productivity of the work force, while still others insist that spending on research and development (R&D) will lead to new products and enhanced productivity.[24] Very little of the current federal deficit is used to finance these types of activities, however. Rather, more is spent on social consumption, like social security, medical services, and other entitlements, as well as on military needs, little of which seems to have direct productivity benefits.

A deficit also means that we are consuming more than our economy is able to produce. As a consequence, imports from other nations flood into the United States to meet our demands for goods and services, while dollars leave the economy for other nations to pay for these goods and services. In effect, jobs get exported in this process; this further pressures government to spend, as the economy is smaller than it could be. One compensation is that prices for goods are lower due to foreign competition, so consumers pay less for goods, but low prices tend to stimulate more consumption.

Last, as mentioned earlier, large and persistent deficits close off the option of using Keynesian fiscal policy to manage the business cycle. Recessions may run longer and deeper and inflation may soar higher for longer when government's ability to manage the business cycle is diminished.

What Causes Deficits?

The main problem with the deficit of 1980 to 1995 was not that it was large but that it had remained so large for such a long time. In effect, in the 1980s and 1990s we seemed to have little ability to control the deficit—what is called a **structural deficit.** There were four major contributors to the deficit problem: tax policy, entitlement growth, military spending increases, and increases in payments on the public debt.

Two major tax decisions of the early 1980s contributed to the deficit of the 1980s and 1990s. First, tax rates were cut dramatically in 1981 as a part of Ronald Reagan's economic package, as described in the previous chapter. Similarly, tax brackets were indexed to the consumer price index (CPI) in the early 1980s. The combined effect of these two moves was to reduce government revenues *and* make it difficult for policymakers to raise taxes to close the deficit.

Entitlement growth had also put pressure on the government's budget. Entitlements, such as social security, Medicare, Medicaid, and veterans' benefits, are one of the largest budget items, and they have grown enormously. Entitlement programs are designed so that any person who qualifies will receive government assistance. Thus, rather than the government's deciding how much it can afford to spend on entitlement programs beforehand, spending on entitlements is determined by the size and demands of the eligible pool of recipients.

Increases in military spending, which began in the late 1970s and continued through most of the 1980s, also contributed to the deficit problem. Figure 8.1 graphs military spending in constant 1987 dollars from 1976 through 1995. As the graph indicates, a rapid rise in military spending began at the end of the 1970s, continued until about 1986, when spending began to level off, and then declined starting in 1989.

Several factors led to this increase in military spending. First, after the cessation of the Vietnam War, military spending decreased as antimilitary senti-

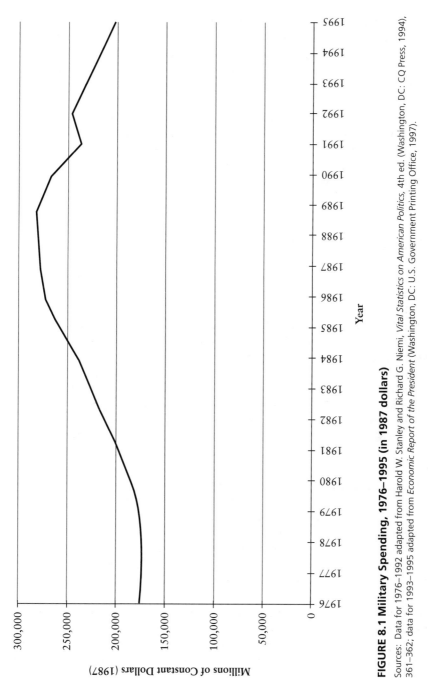

FIGURE 8.1 Military Spending, 1976–1995 (in 1987 dollars)

Sources: Data for 1976–1992 adapted from Harold W. Stanley and Richard G. Niemi, *Vital Statistics on American Politics*, 4th ed. (Washington, DC: CQ Press, 1994), 361–362; data for 1993–1995 adapted from *Economic Report of the President* (Washington, DC: U.S. Government Printing Office, 1997).

ment swept the nation. This, some critics observed, led to U.S. vulnerability in international politics. In the late 1970s, the Soviets invaded Afghanistan and Iranian students occupied the U.S. embassy in Teheran, holding many hostages for over a year. These events caused leaders in both parties to feel that the military had been undermined by cuts and neglect and that a stronger military was required.

Finally, interest on the national debt accounts for a growing proportion of federal spending. Interest on the debt is what government pays to those from whom it borrows money. As the deficit increased each year and money was borrowed to finance the deficit, the debt mounted. Adding to the interest payment pressure was the rise in interest rates in the late 1970s and early 1980s. These high interest rates were in part a function of the massive inflation of the 1970s, but they stayed high into the 1980s as the federal government's need for money to finance the deficit absorbed huge amounts of capital, leaving less money for others to borrow. While net interest accounted for about 7 percent of federal spending in 1970 and 9 percent in 1980, it reached nearly 15 percent in 1990.[25] One effect of interest payments is that they leave less money to spend on government programs.

Earlier we noted that the deficit seemed uncontrollable. Structural factors, such as tax policy, entitlement growth, and interest on the debt, contributed to its growth, but federal spending may be uncontrollable in another sense; many federal spending categories are mandatory, as opposed to discretionary. **Discretionary spending** refers to the ability of government to decide how much to spend on a particular program. **Mandatory spending** programs remove that decision-making power from government. Instead, government is forced to pay a certain level for some programs or items, with those levels' being determined by other factors, for instance, previous policy decisions.

The percentage of the budget that is composed of mandatory spending items has increased. The main mandatory spending items include the major entitlement programs for health, like Medicare and Medicaid, social security, veterans' benefits, and some income security programs, like unemployment insurance payments. Interest payments on the national debt constitute the other major mandatory spending item. In 1970, 36.4 percent of federal spending was for these mandatory programs and items. By 1980, the percentage had risen to 53.3, and in 1990 it reached 60 percent.[26] By the 1990s, the deficit was approximately equal to one-half of all discretionary federal spending, including defense. Trying to cut those programs that deeply led to the impasse in dealing with the deficit; such huge cuts seemed politically impossible.

The term *mandatory,* may, however, be inaccurate. The 1995 budget agreement, which we will discuss later in this chapter, made major progress toward controlling the growth of several major entitlement programs, such as Medicare and Medicaid. The Republicans, who offered this budget deal, drew much political heat from the president, from groups that stood to lose benefits, and from the public. Yet the case illustrates the importance of political will in determining spending patterns, even on items that are called "mandatory" and on popular entitlement programs.

Dealing with the Deficit

The deficit in 1979 was about $40 billion, rising to $74 billion in 1980 and $79 billion the next year. Reagan's economic and defense program was passed by Congress in 1981; the first year to show the effects of his policies was 1982. The deficit that year stood at $127 billion. Until the mid-1990s, the deficit hovered between $150 and $290 billion. Throughout the 1980s and 1990s, policymakers tried to stem the tide of massive deficits; most of their attempts resulted in failure.

It was not until the mid-1980s that politicians began to be seriously concerned about the deficit, because of how long it had been around and how large it had grown. In 1985, three U.S. senators, Republicans Phil Gramm (Texas) and Warren Rudman (New Hampshire) and Democrat Ernest Hollings (South Carolina) offered what was to be called the Gramm-Rudman-Hollings (GRH I) bill. The bill, which was eventually passed—although not without much legislative rancor and maneuvering—had several major provisions.[27]

First, deficit ceilings were created for the years 1986 through to 1991, until a zero deficit was reached in 1991. If the deficit target was surpassed, discretionary spending categories, both defense and nondefense, had to be cut across the board by predetermined but essentially similar percentages. The Government Accounting Office (GAO), an arm of Congress, was to implement the cuts.

Congressional opponents to GRH sued, and the Supreme Court ruled that GRH was unconstitutional in giving the GAO an executive function. A second GRH bill was passed subsequent to the Supreme Court ruling (GRH II) in 1987, which gave the OMB the power to make the cuts. New deficit targets were also created, for which the zero deficit date was pushed back to 1993.

"No New Taxes" and the 1990 Budget Summit

The GRH process fell apart in 1990. It had not worked as anticipated during the previous years, but in 1990 Congress and the president, now George Bush, were at a stalemate in passing the budget. Government came to a halt for a few days; this led to a summit between the administration and Congress, which was now controlled by the Democrats.[28] Bush had campaigned for the presidency in 1988 on a pledge not to raise taxes, but the 1990 budget summit led to new taxes, which he justified as merely one element of a more complex package to control the deficit. Many members of the public and the Republican Party felt that Bush had sold them out with this action.

Six major provisions were accepted at the 1990 budget summit. First, spending ceilings were applied to discretionary programs. Three major sets of discretionary programs were identified: defense, international programs like foreign aid, and domestic programs. Defense spending was held at a constant level from 1991 to 1993, as were international programs. Domestic programs were allowed small growth.

Second, mandatory spending programs had to implement a "pay-as-you-go" system. Any changes in these programs that would increase benefits had to be offset with savings in other programs or new revenues. Changes in mandatory programs thus had to be deficit neutral. The only exception was social security, where a "fire wall" was erected so that no program could attach itself to the social security trust fund. Thus, social security finances were separated from the rest of the budget.

Third, the summit targeted a deficit of $83 billion by 1995, a far cry from the zero deficit targets of GRH I and II. Fourth, credit programs, that is, government loan programs, were brought into the federal budget and placed under the "pay-as-you-go" directive. Fifth, if the three discretionary budget categories appeared ready to break through their spending ceilings, they would go through automatic across-the-board cuts to bring them in line with their ceilings. Each of the categories, however, would be dealt with separately. Last, the OMB was given responsibility for making sure that programs stayed within their spending ceilings.[29]

The Gulf War, plus the recession of 1990–1991, undermined much of the 1990 budget summit agreement. The deficit ballooned because of the recession, as government revenues decreased, while spending on automatic stabilizers increased. The war also led many in Washington to feel that the military was being cut into too deeply and that in the post–cold war era there would be major demands on U.S. military capability. Other hot spots around the world began to flare up, including Haiti, Somalia, and the former Yugoslavia, to all of which the United States sent troops.

Clinton came into office in 1993 facing these military, budgetary, and economic pressures. Although his campaign for the presidency focused on getting the economy out of recession, on assuming office, he came to adopt the position that deficit reduction must be given higher priority.[30] Clinton's first budget package included some program cuts but also some tax increases, such as on the wealthy and gasoline, to help meet the deficit challenge. Those moves, along with the economic recovery, narrowed the deficit, but the 1994 elections brought the Republicans to the majority in both houses of Congress for the first time in forty years. They spearheaded a new drive to balance the budget.

Republicans in Control of Congress

An ambitious effort to contain the deficit began in 1995. As part of their Contract with America, Republicans sought in early 1995 to pass a constitutional amendment requiring a balanced budget. Though passed by the House, the balanced budget amendment was narrowly defeated in the Senate. Undaunted, Republicans shifted strategy, focusing on the budget itself, and aimed at previously sacrosanct entitlements to bring it under control.

The Republican agenda was larger than just reducing the deficit and balancing the budget. It also aimed at making government smaller. Thus, Republicans sought a tax cut, which would not only help pour some money into the economy but also increase the pressure to cut existing programs by reducing funds to government that it could then spend on programs. They sought to eliminate whole government agencies, including the Commerce Department, but expected that the most significant savings would come from reform of welfare, Medicaid, and, especially, Medicare, the first middle-class entitlement program to be targeted. Although much debate centered over whether Medicare benefits would actually be cut, Republicans saying no and Democrats yes, the Republican proposal did slow the growth in Medicare, one of the fastest-growing budget categories, by, for instance, increasing deductibles and limiting government payment levels and increases to Medicare providers.

Republicans were unable to pass their budget and all thirteen appropriations bills that must accompany the budget process by the start of the fiscal year, October 1. Thus, the government operated under a **continuing resolution** until mid-November. Continuing resolutions enable government to operate, even though a budget does not exist. Basically, government operates under the previous year's fiscal model during the continuing period.

With both the continuing resolution and the debt limit expiring, Congress sent bills to the president that would further continue government and raise the debt ceiling, but each bill had attachments that Clinton objected to. Congress and the president faced another budget impasse, and in the week before Thanksgiving 1995, the government was again shut down. After four days, Congress and the president worked out an agreement to reopen the government. That agreement committed both to seek a balanced budget in seven years, a key target sought by congressional Republicans.

Finally, in late April 1996, seven months after the target deadline to pass the budget and after the president submitted his next (1997) budget to Congress, Congress and the president agreed on the 1996 budget. The president was able to preserve some programs that he lobbied for heavily, such as Americorps (the volunteer service program for young Americans), educational funding, the advanced technology support program, and the federal funding program for local police programs. The Republicans also won on several issues important to them: cutting over $23 billion in discretionary spending and eliminating approximately two hundred programs, with about half of these coming out of the departments of Labor and Health and Human Services.

Two political factors account for the final agreement between Clinton and the Republican-controlled Congress. First, Bob Dole, the Senate majority leader, had effectively secured the Republican presidential nomination. Dole, who ran his campaign for the nomination in part on his experience in getting things done during his long congressional career, had a strong incentive to wrap up the budget impasse. Moreover, congressional Republicans, especially the freshmen in the House, felt election pressures too. The agreement that emerged allowed this class of legislators to claim that they had emerged victorious in the budget process, fulfilling what they had promised to voters in the previous election campaign.[31]

THE RISE OF THE SURPLUS

After over a decade and a half of struggling with budget deficits, in 1999 seemingly overnight the federal government was running a surplus. Furthermore, the surplus was projected to continue for a handful of years, into the middle years of the first decade of the new millennium. How did the state of government finances turn about so quickly and sharply?

A complex of factors, as we have discussed, caused the deficit, and similarly a complex of factors accounts for the surplus. First, a careful study of government finances from 1948 to 1990 found that only the state of the economy seemed to affect the size of the deficit: As the economy improved, especially as unemployment abated and the economy grew, the deficit shrank.[32] True, the economy was strong from the mid- through the late 1990s, but economic growth alone cannot account for the transition from deficit to surplus.

The actions of government policymakers, coupled with a strong economy, better account for the new state of government finances. Although each attempt that policymakers made from the 1980s through the 1990s failed in containing the deficit, each attempt did chip away at sources of the deficit by containing government spending here and there. These actions, such as Gramm-Rudman-Hollings, the budget summit of 1990, and the first Clinton budget, helped slow government spending in discretionary and mandatory categories. When the economy took off in the 1990s, with unemployment the lowest recorded in several decades, economic growth at high rates, and productivity on the rebound, the economy was able to grow faster than government spending, fast enough that in time it would overtake the growth of government and result in a surplus.

However, economists predict that the surplus will come to an end around 2005 and deficits will return. They base this prediction on growth in entitlement programs, such as social security and Medicare, growth which will be fueled by an aging population. Such a scenario underscores the fragility of government finances in the face of population pressures and the fact that despite a surplus, government policymakers have not fully dealt with all the major threats to the government budget. And as we saw with the 1999 budget, given surpluses, policymakers are quite likely to spend for short-term political gain; this may exacerbate deficit problems around the year 2005.

CONCLUSION

In this chapter we have discussed the rise and fall of fiscal policy as a tool of macroeconomic management. The depth and severity of the Depression laid the foundation for a new government role in the macroeconomy, replacing the laissez faire approach that had dominated policymaking up till then. However, stagflation and the deficit, especially the latter, ended fiscal policy's effectiveness in smoothing out the business cycle.

In the 1980s the deficit became the primary fiscal policy problem. Several approaches to controlling the deficit were tried. Setting limits, as GRH did, or constitutionally requiring balanced budgets are institutional solutions and will not work unless the political will to contain the deficit also exists. That political will seemed not to be evident throughout most of the 1980s and early 1990s, as deficit targets were routinely surpassed and pushed back. More draconian institutional solutions, like the balanced budget amendment, were not passed into law and thus appeared more symbolic than substantive. Not until the Republicans took control of Congress in the 1994 midterm elections did the political will seem strong enough to counter the very strong political pressures to maintain government spending. Only time will tell how successful the effort in 1995 to control the deficit through political means was.

Key Terms

automatic stabilizers
continuing
   resolution
discretionary
   spending
fiscal policy

Keynes, John
   Maynard
Keynesian
mandatory spending
stabilization

structural deficit
supply-side
   economics

Explore the Web

The 1999 federal government budget can be found at http://www.access .gpo.gov/su_docs/budget99/index.html. The OMB, which prepares the president's budget, has a web page that links to older budgets, as well as other useful information about the budget and budget process, at http://www.access.gpo.gov/usbudget/. The national budget simulation game, which allows one to play with the budget categories and see their impacts on budget totals is located at http://garnet.berkeley.edu:3333/budget/budget.html. The Concord Coalition, which has argued for years that the deficit is too big, maintains a web page at http:///www.concordcoalition.org.

Notes

1. This story is told in Bob Woodward, *The Agenda: Inside the Clinton White House* (New York: Pocket Books, 1994), 65–69, 111–112, 148–153. On Alan Greenspan as chair of the Fed, see David M. Jones, *The Politics of Money: The Fed Under Alan Greenspan* (New York: New York Institute of Finance, 1991).

2. A good overview of the development of economic thought and policy practice as it relates to the economy is found in Herbert Stein, *The Fiscal Revolution in America,* rev. ed. (Washington, DC: American Enterprise Institute, 1990). An overview of presidential decision making with regard to macroeconomics is found in Herbert Stein, *Presidential Economics: The Making of Economic Policy from Roosevelt to Clinton,* 3d rev. ed. (Washington, DC: American Enterprise Institute, 1994). Stein served as an economic adviser in the Nixon administration, when he headed the Council of Economic Advisers.

3. I credit the wave analogy to John P. Frendreis and Raymond Tatalovich, *The Modern Presidency and Economic Policy* (Itasca, IL: Peacock, 1994), 170.

4. Specifically, the government defines a recession as two successive quarters of decline in total output, measured in terms of real GNP.

5. The most famous Social Darwinist is Herbert Spencer, the philosopher. On Spencer, see Michael W. Taylor, *Men Versus the State: Herbert Spencer and Late Victorian Individualism* (New York: Oxford University Press, 1992). On the political and social implications of Social Darwinism, see Carl N. Degler, *In Search of Human Nature: The Decline and Revival of Darwinism in American Social Thought* (New York: Oxford University Press, 1991); and Richard Hofstadter, *Social Darwinism in American Thought,* reissue (Boston: Beacon, 1992).

6. This is the classic example of *demand-pull inflation.* Inflation may also rise as the costs of production increase, which is termed *cost-push inflation.* The oil embargoes of the 1970s led not only to short supplies but higher oil prices once the embargoes ended. These higher prices diffused throughout the economy and were a major cause of the high inflation of the 1970s.

7. On this point, see Seymour Martin Lipset, *First New Nation: The United States in Historical and Comparative Perspective* (New York: Doubleday Anchor, 1963), 55.

8. On these public opinion changes, see Samuel H. Beer, "In Search of a New Public Philosophy," in *The New American Political System,* ed. Anthony King (Washington, DC: American Enterprise Institute, 1978), 5–43. On the evolution of the presidency, see Fred I. Greenstein, "Change and Continuity in the Modern Presidency," in *The New American Political System,* ed. King, 45–85. Stein, *The Fiscal Revolution in America,* Chaps. 1 and 2, is also good on these points.

9. Keynes's theory was published in 1936 in *The General Theory of Employment, Interest, and Money* (New York: Harcourt, Brace). The impact of Keynes's thinking on economists is detailed in Lawrence Klein, *The Keynesian Revolution* (New York: Macmillan, 1979). A very good, accessible introduction is found in William R. Keech, *Economic Politics: The Costs of Democracy* (New York: Cambridge University Press, 1995), 26–32.

10. A good, nontechnical discussion of these policies and others is found in Charles L. Schultze, *Memos to the President: A Guide Through Macroeconomics for the Busy Policymaker* (Washington, DC: Brookings, 1992).

11. On this see Stein, *The Fiscal Revolution in America*, 108–109.

12. Frendreis and Tatalovich, *The Modern Presidency and Economic Policy*, 37.

13. On liberal opposition to the Kennedy tax scheme, see Richard Reeves, *President Kennedy* (New York: Touchstone, 1993).

14. Schultze, *Memos to the President*, 212–213.

15. Ibid.

16. Edwin Chen, "Raid on Budget Surplus Ups Social Security Fears," *Los Angeles Times*, October 16, 1998, A1.

17. Schultze, *Memos to the President*, 212–213.

18. Ibid.

19. Keech, *Economic Politics*, 28–30.

20. Much of this discussion relies on Frendreis and Tatalovich, *The Modern Presidency and Economic Policy*, 273–276.

21. On the public and balanced budgets, see James D. Savage, *Balanced Budgets and American Politics* (Ithaca, NY: Cornell University Press, 1988).

22. Harold W. Stanley and Richard G. Niemi, *Vital Statistics on American Politics*, 4th ed. (Washington, DC: CQ Press, 1994), 327–329.

23. I owe some of this discussion to Donald F. Kettl, *Deficit Politics: Public Budgeting in Its Institutional and Historical Context* (New York: Macmillan, 1992), 29–35.

24. This last point about federal R&D spending and economic benefits is controversial. One major study finds that such spending on technology is far from universally successful. See Linda R. Cohen and Roger G. Noll, eds., *The Technology Pork Barrel* (Washington, DC: Brookings, 1991). A good, concise statement on the sources of economic productivity and the impact of government policies can be found in Schultze, *Memos to the President*, 219–235.

25. These figures are calculated from Stanley and Niemi, *Vital Statistics on American Politics*, 423.

26. Ibid., 425.

27. Details of GRH I and II are found in Howard E. Shuman, *Politics and the Budget: The Struggle Between the President and the Congress*, 3d ed. (Englewood Cliffs, NJ: Prentice-Hall, 1992), 281–298. Other good accounts are found in John R. Gilmour, *Reconcilable Differences? Congress, the Budget Process, and the Deficit* (Berkeley: University of California Press, 1990), 185–222; and Aaron Wildavsky, *The New Politics of the Budgetary Process*, 2d ed. (New York: HarperCollins, 1992), 241–265.

28. This incident is detailed in Shuman, *Politics and the Budget,* 303–341; and Kettl, *Deficit Politics,* 101–105.

29. These points rely on Kettl, *Deficit Politics,* 101–104.

30. On this struggle in the early Clinton administration, see Woodward, *The Agenda.*

31. For more details, see Jerry Gray, "Congress and the White House Finally Agree on Budget, Seven Months into Fiscal Year," *New York Times,* April 25, 1996, A1, A13; Michael Wines, "House and Senate Vote to Approve '96 Spending Bill," *New York Times,* April 26, 1996, A1, A12; and David E. Rosenbaum, "Ammunition for the Fall," *New York Times,* April 26, 1996, A1, A12.

32. Sung Deuk Hahm, Mark S. Kamlet, and David C. Lowery, "Postwar Deficit Spending in the United States," *American Politics Quarterly* 25 (1997): 139–167.

9

Managing the Macroeconomy II: Monetary Policy, Elections, and Political Business Cycles

I N JULY 1991, Secretary of the Treasury Nicholas Brady met with Federal Reserve Chairman Alan Greenspan. The topic under discussion was economic growth. The economy was in the midst of a mild recession, and the presidential election was only little more than a year away. President Bush's polls had begun sliding, and he was concerned about his reelection prospects. Further, Greenspan was up for renomination as the chairman of the Federal Reserve Board. It appeared as if the administration was trying to force Greenspan to lower interest rates in order to spur the economy. If he would not take such action, perhaps Bush would not renominate him.[1]

A year later, after being reappointed, Greenspan gave an unprecedented news conference, at which he said that he would cut interest rates if necessary for the economy but would not let political pressures influence his decisions at the Fed. (Several weeks earlier, stories had appeared in the news about the "pressure" that the Bush administration had apparently tried to put on Greenspan in 1991.) Greenspan was sending a signal to the country and to the president that the independence of the Fed would not be challenged and that any attempt to influence him during the previous year had not worked.[2]

This incident highlights several important themes that we will deal with in this chapter. One, monetary policy, as overseen by the Fed, is now the most important macroeconomic policy instrument available to government. Two, macroeconomic policy has important political implications. Although presidents and members of Congress are subject to electoral pressures, the Fed, as an independent body, is not. Yet its potential for impact on the economy through monetary policy makes the Fed an important object of concern to elected politicians. Our third theme, then, is the political business cycle. We will explore whether politicians try to use macroeconomic policy instruments to affect the economy for electoral advantage rather than for economic health.

MONETARY POLICY

Monetary policy is an alternative to fiscal policy for dealing with the business cycle. In part because of the stagflation of the 1970s and the budget deficits of the 1980s and 1990s, monetary policy has become the major instrument of business cycle control. **Monetary policy** basically involves regulating the amount of money in the economy. Its roots date back to the first national bank of the early 1800s (see Chapter 2). The first bank, you will recall, was an important element of the economic policy devised by Alexander Hamilton, the secretary of the Treasury under George Washington. Modern monetary policy differs from that early variety, however. Economists understand monetary policy now much better than during Hamilton's time, and a more well developed set of instruments for implementing monetary policy now exist.

Modern monetary policy owes much to the work of Milton Friedman, the Nobel Prize–winning economist. Friedman, and other **monetarists,** advanced the idea that the money supply was critical to the growth of the economy, as well as to the prices of goods. The main tenet of the monetarists was that the money supply should be allowed to grow at a slow but steady pace. Slow growth would quell inflation, and steadiness would help ensure growth.[3] However, political pressures to deal with the business cycle and debate among economists have led to the use of monetary policy as a way to stabilize the economy, that is, to adjust the business cycle.

Early History of the Monetary System

It is through banks that monetary policy operates, in part because banks serve as money depositories but also because banks put money into the economy and take it out through their lending activities. In the United States, a central bank, the Federal Reserve, is the critical bank in this regard. A whole banking system, called the Federal Reserve System, has been created to implement monetary policy decisions. The United States, like all Western nations, uses a central bank for monetary, as well as other, reasons. This was not always so.

The first national bank of the United States was federally owned. It could issue securities and help pay off the national debt incurred during the Revolutionary War. Through the buying and selling of government securities, the government could regulate the money supply, gain access to necessary money to finance programs, and, through payment of the debt, gain a reputation for fiscal soundness.[4]

The bank was controversial, however; many felt it was biased toward the interests of traders on the nation's East Coast and did little to help develop the interior. Thus, when the bank's charter expired in 1811, it ceased to exist. However, the federal government needed money for the War of 1812, so a second national bank was created. After the war, political controversy again swirled around the bank as opponents once again charged that it favored eastern commercial interests over western development. The second bank went out of existence when its charter expired in 1836.[5]

The next quarter-century was marked by monetary instability, as state banks replaced the central banking system. The number of banks increased rapidly, and because no uniform currency existed, each bank issued its own bank notes. This hodgepodge system proved unsatisfactory when financing was needed for the Civil War. The Currency Act of 1863 and the National Banking Act of 1864 were passed, creating national charter banks. These banks could issue government bonds to help pay the costs of the war. They also issued national bank notes, which became the national currency. (Because of their color, they were called *greenbacks*, a term that is still in use.) The two new laws also taxed state bank notes, which effectively eliminated them as a form of currency, though state banks found a way around the tax with the invention of the check.[6]

The post–Civil War era was also characterized by monetary instability. Many banks were created because federal banking charters were liberally granted. In 1907, a banking panic exposed the weakness of a system that lacked a central bank.[7] The panic of 1907 began when British citizens who had deposits in U.S. banks began to withdraw their assets, asking for them in gold. To cover these withdrawals, banks had to call in their loans and other assets. This led other depositors to worry about the security of *their* deposits, and they began to withdraw their funds also. Many banks collapsed. To stem the panic, the banker J. P. Morgan, with support from President Theodore Roosevelt, organized the nation's banking resources.

As a result of the panic, Congress appointed a national commission, which concluded that a central bank was needed. Thus, in 1913, the Federal Reserve System was created.

The Federal Reserve System

The **Federal Reserve System** is composed of private and Federal Reserve banks. The private banks represent the base of the system. About one-third of the nation's private, or commercial, banks are members of the Federal Reserve System. They, however, are among the most important and largest banks, holding about 70 percent of the nation's banking reserves and 40 percent of all deposits. In 1980, the reach of the Federal Reserve System was expanded to include all banks. Under the Depository Institutions Deregulation and Monetary Control Act, the Fed was given regulatory power over bank reserve requirements. **Reserve requirements** set the amount of money that banks must keep on hand. This is usually specified as a percentage of loans and other assets.

There are twelve federal banks in the system, dispersed throughout the nation. The Federal Reserve banks furnish currency, collect and clear checks from the private banks, make loan reserves to private banks, and hold reserves for them. The reserve accounts provide security for bank reserves, while also allowing the Fed to monitor the reserve accounts of the private banks.

The **Board of Governors** and the **Federal Open Market Committee** (**FOMC**) are the most important parts of the Federal Reserve System in terms of making monetary decisions. The Board of Governors is composed of seven members, appointed by the president with Senate confirmation to fourteen-year terms of office. The chair and vice chair are selected from the board's membership and serve in that capacity for four-year terms, again under presidential appointment and senatorial confirmation. The board sets reserve requirements and discount rates for banks. We will discuss these functions in the next section.

The Federal Open Market Committee, which directs the buying and selling of government securities, includes the seven members of the Board of Governors plus five more members, chosen from the presidents of the twelve Federal Reserve banks. The president of the New York branch is always among the five. These five serve one-year terms that rotate among the Federal Reserve bank presidents. The chair of the Board of Governors serves as the FOMC chair and the New York president as its vice chair. The chair of the Federal Reserve tends to be the most important leader, by dint of personality sometimes but also because of the chair's institutional position on the Board of Governors and the FOMC.[8]

The Operation of Monetary Policy

Although monetarists like Milton Friedman argued against using monetary instruments for countercyclical management, they can and have been used that way. There are three major monetary instruments that can be used to modulate the business cycle: open market operations, reserve requirements, and discount rates. **Open market operations,** the purchase or sale of government securities, are the most important instrument available to the Fed to regulate the money supply. Open market operations are directed by the FOMC, which meets eight or more times a year to decide on monetary policy targets. At these meetings, the FOMC analyzes current and prospective economic and financial conditions and then gives a policy directive to the domestic manager of the Systems Open Market Account at the Federal Reserve Bank of New York, who implements it.

The overall aim of open market monetary operations is to affect the supply of money in the economy. By reducing the supply of money, the Fed may contract the economy, a favored way of wringing inflation out of the economy or keeping it from developing. In contrast to this **tight money policy** is an **easy money policy,** which increases the supply of money.

One way for the Fed to affect the money supply through open market operations involves buying and selling government securities, such as bonds, to and from member banks. Through these securities, the Fed can affect the reserve levels of banks. The Fed may, for example, reduce bank reserves by selling securities to banks, for which the banks must pay in dollars. Or, the Fed may increase bank reserves when it purchases securities from banks. By doing this, the Fed pumps money into the economy.

The Fed can also affect the money supply by targeting the **federal funds rate (FFR).** The FFR is the interest rate that the Fed charges on overnight loans on deposits at the Federal Reserve. The loans are made from one Federal Reserve bank to another and, thus, are not loans made to the private sector directly by government. The FFR affects the interest rate and has been a prime target of the Fed in recent decades because credit markets seem very sensitive to it. This makes manipulation of the FFR a useful tool for the Fed.

Overall, open market operations are critical to the management of the money supply because of the large sums of money involved. Thus, the Fed has come to rely more on this policy instrument than reserve requirements or discount rates.

Reserve requirements are assets that a bank must hold and not lend out. They are usually specified as a percentage of bank assets. If the Fed increases the reserve requirement, the amount of money that a bank has available for lending is reduced. Thus, the money supply declines. In contrast, if the Fed lowers the reserve requirement, more money is available for lending, and the money supply increases. When the economy is overheating, inflation may be curbed by increasing the reserve requirement. With less money available for lending, there will be less economic activity and the economy will slow, cooling inflation pressures.

Discount rates are the prices, or interest rates, that the Fed charges commercial banks and other thrifts, like savings and loans, when it loans them money. At times, banks may face shortfalls in funds to meet deposit withdrawals and funds transfers. When a bank does not have enough money in reserve to cover the transaction and still maintain itself within Fed reserve requirements, it can borrow money to cover the transaction from the Fed. By raising or lowering the discount rate, the Fed will affect the demand of banks for this money. When the discount rate is low, the Fed may encourage banks to seek such money, rather than drawing on their reserves. This increases the funds available to banks to loan out. Raising the discount rate to levels that make it unprofitable for banks to borrow from the Fed inhibits demand for Fed funds and results in a decrease in the money supply. If banks are forced into securing Fed money at higher discount rates, interest rates to customers who want to borrow money from commercial banks are also likely to go up. As interest rates rise, demand for money decreases, cooling an economy that appears to be overheating.

The Fed and Policymaking

The Fed did not become a significant macroeconomic manager until 1951, after it signed an accord with the Department of the Treasury.[9] Prior to 1951, the Fed was required to keep interest rates stable and low to help the nation finance the debt that had accumulated from World War II. This restricted the ability of the Fed to manage monetary policy. In the 1951 accord, the Fed was able to uncouple its activities from Treasury dictates. Although Congress supported this move, both the president and the Treasury Department resisted the efforts of the Fed to become so independent. Thus, in the period shortly after the accord, the Fed moved tentatively, but as time went on, it became bolder and by the late 1970s had emerged as perhaps the most powerful and important macroeconomic policymaker.[10]

The Fed's independence allows it to make policy decisions that may be politically unpopular. One of the most unpopular decisions a policymaker can make is to slow the economy to combat inflation. Slowing the economy results in higher unemployment rates and smaller wage increases among those lucky enough to keep their jobs. Affected workers and businesses put pressure on politicians to stimulate the economy and avoid economic slowdowns. Because the Fed is insulated from these public pressures because its membership is not elected and serves long terms of office, it may be better able to make such hard decisions as combating inflation with economic slowdowns. Likewise, the Fed may be able to resist pressures to loosen the money supply, which might fuel inflation.

For instance, Paul Volker, chair of the Fed in the late 1970s and early 1980s, resisted pressures to open the money supply during the deep recession of the early 1980s. He was roundly criticized by some for this action, but he persisted in this policy because his goal was to wring inflation out of the economy. Similarly, in the mid-1990s, Alan Greenspan and the Fed resisted calls to lower interest rates to help the economy grow at a faster pace than it was doing. Greenspan felt that dormant inflationary pressures existed, and he continued the policy of relatively high interest rates to stem any inflationary tendency.

However, although the Fed is formally independent of the political branches, it can be responsive at times to the needs of politicians in office, especially the president. Presidents, and even some members of Congress, may be keenly sensitive to the operation and policies of the Fed because of the impact of Fed policies on the economy. The economy, in turn, affects how the public views the president.

Presidents, consequently, try to influence Fed policies. They have two major avenues of influence at their disposal. One is the power of appointment. Over time, through appointments, presidents may be able to stack the Board of Governors with people who are sensitive to presidential economic policies and political needs. But given the long terms of Fed officials and the position of the Federal Reserve bank presidents on the FOMC, it may take several years before the president can make enough appointments to affect Fed policies.

Presidents may also indicate their policy preferences to the Fed through meetings and public statements. The Fed may be somewhat responsive to these attempts at presidential persuasion because of the position and prestige of the president, but also because Fed members may fear that if they resist the president too much for too long, the independence and authority of the Fed may be challenged. There is some indication in the research literature that the Fed is indeed responsive to these presidential calls, but it is more the case that the Fed takes into account the president's policy wishes when deciding on a policy course, rather than simply doing whatever the president desires.[11]

The Fed may also be responsive to congressional wishes, though research suggests that congressional influence on the Fed is less than that of the president. There are several reasons for this. First, though the Fed is among the most closely watched of government agencies, with the chair of the Fed reporting to the congressional banking committees twice a year, intense congressional scrutiny is intermittent, usually visible only when the economy is in trouble or when interest rates are high. Second, few members of Congress have strong incentives to watch the Fed carefully; they are more concerned about district concerns than macroeconomic conditions. Third, there is a built-in coalition in Congress that supports the Fed. This coalition comes largely from districts that represent big banks, which are usually major supporters of Fed actions.[12]

Thus, although the Fed is responsive to the needs and preferences of the political branches and is not as fully independent as its formal status suggests, it is still able to manage these political pressures by making marginal accommodations to them. Over the long course, however, the Fed seems to pursue a policy of tighter money than elected political leaders usually prefer, using its formal independent status and political allies, such as big banks, as buffers against undue pressure from the president and Congress. Also, by being marginally accommodating to these politicians, the Fed has been able to keep extreme political pressures from the president and Congress at bay.

Evaluating Monetary Policy

Like fiscal policy, monetary policy has its supporters and its critics. Supporters point to several benefits of monetary over fiscal policy. First, unlike fiscal policy, which usually can only be implemented once a year because of its dependence on the budget process, monetary policy decisions can be made numerous times throughout the year. As a consequence, Fed policy may begin to take effect immediately. For example, during the summer months of 1998, the stock market took a deep tumble, in part because of economic crises that began in East Asia and spread to parts of Latin America, as well as continuing economic problems in Russia. To help restore confidence in the U.S. stock market, and also to dampen the volatile swings in stock prices, the Fed cut interest rates in October 1998. In the months that followed not only did the markets calm down, but they recovered much of the value lost during the previous summer.

Further, monetary policy can be fine tuned because adjustments in the money supply can be made in small increments rather than in one large dose. These small increments of change lessen the possibility that the Fed will overshoot or undershoot its targets. Still, with an economy as large as the one in the United States, it may take several months, if not longer, before the Fed sees evidence of its policy's effectiveness.

One advantage of monetary policy over fiscal policy, according to its adherents, is that monetary policymakers interfere less with the economy and market operations than fiscal policymakers do. For instance, when fiscal policy decisions, such as cutting taxes, are made, decision makers have to decide whose taxes to cut. Or if spending is increased, policymakers must decide which programs will see increases. Implementing monetary policy does not require such decisions. All that monetary policy does is act on aggregate money totals. It lets the markets decide how to distribute the money supply. Thus, distributional decisions are made on economic grounds and are not intermixed with political imperatives. Hence, supporters of monetary policy claim that it is more economically efficient than fiscal policy.

Another characteristic that monetary policy advocates point to is the fact that monetary policy can operate even when the government is small. Fiscal policy requires large government and large expenditure totals to have an effect. Changes in taxing and spending have to account for a significant portion of the economy for them to have a major effect. Monetary policy is not so restricted. Even under the small federal government of the early nineteenth century, Alexander Hamilton influenced the economy with the first national bank, as did Nicholas Biddle with the second national bank. Those who charge that large government is a drag on the economy view this aspect of monetary policy as an advantage over fiscal policy.

Still, there are major criticisms of monetary policy. Perhaps the most pronounced criticism is that policymaking at the Fed is biased in terms of being more sensitive to inflation than to recession. Thus, the Fed is more likely to take swift action to fight inflation than it is to help the economy that is in recession. In part, one can explain this bias by looking at who makes decisions. Fed decision makers are almost always bankers or have ties to the financial community, and like bankers and other financiers, they see the specter of inflation lurking almost everywhere and at all times. We may call this the **banker's bias.** Bankers fear inflation because it erodes the value of the money that they have loaned to others, whereas debtors often benefit from inflation, which reduces the value of the money that they have borrowed, making their debt burden lighter as time goes on. We see this bias in the actions of the Fed under Greenspan in the mid-1990s. Interests rates were raised to quell inflation, although economic indicators suggested only a very weak inflation present in the economy. Still, Greenspan refused to lower the rates.

This banker's bias in the Fed seems to emanate from several sources. As already noted, bankers have a strong presence on the Fed. For instance, the presidents of the Federal Reserve banks are bankers, for the most part, and on the FOMC, the Federal Reserve bank presidents occupy five of the twelve seats. Moreover, the close association between the Fed and the financial services industry, especially the nation's big banks, increases the sensitivity of the Fed to banking needs. These big banks are also important political allies for the Fed, supporting it in most of its policy decisions, as well as supporting it in its goal to maintain its autonomy from the president and Congress.

Another problem with monetary policy concerns coordination between fiscal and monetary policy. No coordinating mechanism exists. Thus, it is possible that fiscal policy will try to stimulate the economy and monetary policy will try to cool it, essentially canceling out each other's effects. Without policy coordination, neither policy instrument may work as intended.

Last, deficits may interfere with monetary policy effectiveness, just as they may impact fiscal policy. The fact that the federal government borrows much money to finance deficit may limit the effectiveness of Fed policy on interest rates. Rates may remain high because of federal competition with private markets for money. This may be especially critical when the Fed begins to loosen money, as such policies may not have as much impact as they might without a federal need for capital to finance the deficit.

THE ECONOMY AND THE VOTERS

The public holds policymakers accountable for the state of the economy. When the economy is doing well, voters tend to keep them in office. When the economy is doing poorly, voters are likely to turn them out of office and replace them with their opposition.[13] This accountability provides the incentive for policymakers to develop macroeconomic policy instruments and to implement macroeconomic policies through those instruments.

The public, however, is likely to respond not to macroeconomic policies themselves but rather to their economic outcomes. Thus, the public cares little if the government follows a Keynesian or a monetarist approach to smoothing the business cycle. But the public does care if unemployment or inflation goes up or if income declines.

It is difficult for the average person to judge the merits of various economic policies. As we have discussed in this and the previous chapter, macroeconomic policymaking is technical, complex, and controversial. Most voters are not economists and probably have only limited awareness of the issues surrounding macroeconomic policy. But all voters live in the economy and feel its effects. Thus, it is likely that voters select leaders not on the basis of their macroeconomic policies but rather by the state of the economy, which is presumably influenced by the policy choices of decision makers.[14]

There are numerous contemporary examples of elections that appear to have turned on the state of the economy. For example, Bill Clinton defeated George Bush in 1992 and Ronald Reagan defeated Jimmy Carter in 1980 because of the poor economies under the incumbent administrations. Bush presided over a recession in 1991, and the economy had not recovered sufficiently in time for his reelection. Carter governed while the economy suffered bouts of high inflation and high unemployment.[15]

The economy also affected earlier elections. Thus, Franklin Roosevelt trounced Herbert Hoover in 1932 because of the Depression. The effects of the Depression were so pronounced on electoral politics that the Republicans, once the majority party, shrank to minority status, unable to win the presidency for the next twenty years as Democrats ran against Hoover's ill-fated presidency.

Thus, although economics may not determine each election, a case can be made that the economy affects elections, and the worse the economy, the more the incumbent party and president will suffer.[16] Research indicates that each 1 percent increase in per capita income during the previous term translates into nearly a 3 percent vote gain for the incumbent party.[17]

Knowing this helps us understand why presidents since the end of World War II have either been defeated or reelected to office. For instance, Carter took barely 45 percent of the vote in 1980 when income growth was the worst during the period 1948 to 1984. Had income growth been an unspectacular +1.0 under Carter,[18] he would likely have received 5 to 6 percent more votes and presumably could have won the election.

The major landslides of 1964, 1972, and 1984 all make sense, too. During each previous administration the economy grew at a heady clip, from 3.5 to nearly 5 percent, and in each case the incumbent party was reelected handily. Change in party is associated with subpar economic performance. Thus, 1952, 1960, 1976, and 1980 all show marginal economic performance during the preceding administration, and in each case a challenger party took the presidency away from the incumbent party.

The interaction between presidential elections and the economy is more complex, however. In this section we address the following questions: (1) Which economic problems have greatest impact? Do voters respond more to inflation or to unemployment, or do they care more about their disposable income? (2) Are voters concerned only about the state of their personal finances, or do they also blame politicians for the overall state of the economy even if they are not directly affected? (3) Do voters worry more about current economic conditions or what they expect the future to bring? (4) Does the public hold different parties more responsible for some problems over others? Does the public more harshly deal with Democrats who cannot alleviate unemployment or Republicans who cannot quell inflation? (5) Who is held most responsible, the president, Congress, or state or local governments?

Which Economic Problem Matters Most?

There are many economic problems to choose from, but studies have concentrated on three with direct implications for voters: inflation, unemployment, and real income growth. The guiding idea is that increases in inflation and unemployment and decreases in real income will hurt incumbents. (We should note that unemployment and real income growth are related: when unemployment surges, income growth declines.)

We can make a case that inflation and income growth matter more to voters than unemployment. First, as noted previously, Americans seem more averse to inflation than to unemployment. Thus, unemployment might have to reach higher levels to trigger a political reaction. Moreover, unemployment is concentrated and unevenly distributed, while inflation spreads across the entire economy. Inflation, conceivably, touches more people and, thus, may stimulate a bigger political reaction. Last, unemployment seems to reduce turnout among those most affected, which again should serve to mute its effects on the political system.[19]

The bulk of the evidence suggests that inflation and income growth affect election results and popularity, but the evidence is mixed for unemployment, with some studies that suggest unemployment has an impact but several that do not.[20] One scholar, noting that different economic conditions seem to be important in some elections but not others, suggests that as the economic context changes, voters shift their perspective, focusing on the most important economic condition at the time.[21] Thus, in some elections, inflation takes center stage; in others it might be unemployment, while growth or trade might be most critical at other times.

This shifting of perspective across elections has led others to suggest that actual economic outcomes are not as important in explaining the impact of the economy on elections as voters' *perceptions* of the economy.[22] Voters learn of the economy not only from its direct impact on their lives but also from the media, from interactions with others, from all the information sources in their environment. Thus, they may construct an image of the economy that varies over time, as these information sources emphasize different aspects and characteristics of the economy. Voters' perceptions may change, even though their own experience and economic well-being do not. Thus, the perceived economy may be more politically relevant than the real economy.

Social or Personal Economic Impacts?

Some studies have asked whether voters are concerned only with their own personal economic well-being or with the state of the national economy as well in their decision about how to vote. The best way to get data on this question is to look at survey research—to ask voters themselves—rather than look at economic conditions and statistics. Thus, in a survey setting, we can ask voters how well off they feel financially, as well as their assessment of the national economy, and relate those responses to their votes.

One startling fact emerged from the early studies that did just this: personal economic circumstances did not seem to affect voting behavior. This finding, repeated in many studies across many election contexts, echoed the finding that unemployment does not result in political mobilization or action against incumbents.[23] Rather than stimulating turnout, unemployment depresses it, and rather than looking outward for blame and help, the unemployed turn inward. Similarly, when faced with a worsening economic situation in their personal lives, voters do not seem to turn against politicians. How can we square the finding that economic conditions affect aggregate election results with the survey research that reports no relationship between personal economic circumstances and voting behavior?

The answer seems to be that voters respond not to their personal finances but to the overall state of the economy. Voters make a collective economic judgment—termed **sociotropic voting**—in contrast to personal, or pocketbook, voting.[24] One should not regard sociotropic assessments as necessarily altruistic, that voters feel empathy for those who have lost their jobs or those on fixed incomes who are unable to adjust to inflation. Rather, a weak economy may instill feelings of economic insecurity in people, even if they are prospering at the time. Thus, voters may reckon that if the economy continues to weaken, if unemployment continues to rise or inflation is not checked, these ills will soon touch their lives. They may lose their jobs sometime in the future, or inflation may seriously erode their income. Thus, voters may still be acting from selfish motives, even if the sociotropic judgment is based on assessments of the overall state of the economy.

Prospective or Retrospective Judgments?

The shift from looking at actual economic performance to voters' perceptions of the economy raises the question of whether voters' expectations of the economic future color these perceptions—or do they look only at the past performance of the economy? Looking at past economic performance is called a **retrospective orientation**. A **prospective orientation** means that voters are trying to judge what will happen in the future; it is their expectation of future economic performance.

The retrospective judgment should be easier for voters to make since they possess evidence of the performance of the economy under the incumbent party. A simple rule for voters would be to vote for the incumbents if the economy performed well but vote against them if the economy did poorly.[25] Voters may also extrapolate the incumbent party's economic record into the future, believing that past indications are a good predictor of future behavior under the incumbent regime.[26] In this way, retrospective and prospective evaluations merge.

Voters can also use election campaigns as sources of information about how both the incumbent and the challenger will perform in the future. Limiting this as a reliable information source, however, is the fact that candidates tend to be ambiguous and unclear about what they will do in office and how they will do it. Candidates make promises, but these tend to be vague, lacking specificity.[27]

Oddly, considering all of these barriers to making prospective judgments, and the comparative ease of making retrospective judgments, recent research has found that most voters make prospective judgements in voting and that the popularity of presidents is tied to prospective evaluations or expectations of the economy. Most significantly, studies suggest that prospective evaluations are stronger than retrospective ones for both voting and assessments of the president's job performance.[28]

Ironically, however, voter predictions about the future of the economy are notoriously inaccurate.[29] Voters use the past state of the economy to predict its near-term future, but they are slow to update their predictions to take into account the current state of the economy. Thus, there is a lag in updating their understanding of the course of the economy. Voters' perceptions of the economy, then, are always somewhat out of sync with what is going on. They tend to remain pessimistic about the economy's future even as the economy is pulling out of recession and showing signs of growth, and they remain optimistic even though the economy may be sliding into recession or other troubles.

What are the sources of these misperceptions? Media reports are important in structuring voters' perceptions of the economy, but so are people's actual experiences and the experiences of those around them. Many people may complain that although the media are reporting improvements in the economy, they are not seeing or feeling those benefits. It may take time, however, before the effects of a growing economy diffuse enough throughout the economy that most voters become aware of them. Moreover, most media reporting on the economy comes from government studies, and voter skepticism of government may limit voters' willingness to believe news stories based on such "tainted" sources.

The difference between actual economic performance and voters' economic expectations may cause problems for politicians up for reelection. For example, although the recession appeared over by the onset of the 1992 presidential election, voters were still pessimistic about the economy.

Consequently, Bush was unable to mobilize public support in his contest with Bill Clinton, who rode to office on a tide of economic discontent. Not only did voters feel that the economy might not improve if Bush were kept in office, but they seemed to ignore the fact that the economy was already improving.

Retrospective and prospective evaluations are thus intertwined, but the latter seem more important. The combination of retrospective-prospective and personal-sociotropic orientations toward the economy leads to four possible kinds of voter assessments:

Retrospective-personal
Retrospective-sociotropic
Prospective-personal
Prospective-sociotropic

The evidence seems to suggest that prospective-sociotropic evaluations of the economy have the strongest effect on voters' decisions.

Incumbent Voting or Policy Voting?

The two parties have different economic priorities. Generally, the public can expect unemployment to rise and inflation to cool while Republicans are in office, and higher employment rates, as well as prices, under Democrats.

Party members have good reason to continue the past policies of their parties on gaining office. First, it is hard to repudiate old policies. Among other things, parties would have to explain why their past policies were failures. It is easier to charge the opposition with failed policies than to convince voters that new policies will make up for past failures. Second, parties develop a type of brand-name loyalty among voters by maintaining consistent policies over time. Voters know what to expect; this makes the job of mobilizing them against the opposition easier. It may not make sense for voters to come out on election day and support a party if they have little idea about what to expect once that party comes to power.

Because each political party is identified with different economic policies, then, the type of economic problem troubling the public may affect their voting decisions. If voters are more concerned about inflation than unemployment, they may decide to opt for a Republican administration, knowing that Republicans will more vigorously combat inflation than Democrats. Even if Republicans are in office and the economy is not in good shape, voters may decide to keep the Republican incumbents when worried about inflation, because they fear that matters will only worsen if they put the Democrats in office. Likewise, if the public is more concerned with unemployment than inflation and Democrats are in office, voters may decide to keep them there because Republicans cannot be expected to attack the unemployment problem as strongly as Democrats.[30]

Who Is Held Responsible?

Presidents are clearly held accountable by the public for the state of the economy, as we have seen. It is not clear how much the public holds other office-holders accountable for the state of the economy. Although economic conditions do affect the election chances of members of Congress,[31] economic effects appear stronger at the presidential than the congressional level. Economics seems to affect state-level offices, as well, especially the governor, but again, the impact is less than on presidential elections. Moreover, it appears that it is national economic conditions, and not state ones, that affect state-level elections. Those elections, thus, might be viewed more as referenda on the president's handling of the economy than voter assessments of state leaders' performance in office.[32]

Perceptions of the ability to affect the economy, federalism, and the system of separation of powers all affect whom the public holds accountable for the state of the economy. First, the president is seen as possessing more institutional control over the levers of public policy than other actors, and, thus, he is held more accountable. Although Congress is also thought to play a major role in budgeting, voters cast ballots not for Congress as a whole but for their individual representatives. Compared to the president, a senator or representative pales in influence over macroeconomic policymaking. Thus, it is reasonable to hold the president more strongly accountable for the economy than any one member of Congress.[33]

Similarly, even though our political system is federal, composed of many different governments at many levels, it is the national government that is perceived as having the most impact on the economy. Moreover, the national economy may have profound local economic effects, and many may feel that their localities and their political leaders are trapped by federal policies. This may be part of the reason that Republican politicians in the 1990s want to reduce the size of the federal government and transfer more responsibility and power to the states and the localities.

Third, the separation of powers may undermine the ability of voters to hold anyone accountable. It takes both Congress and a president to pass laws and make policy. When different parties control the two branches of government, gridlock, or policy stalemate, may result. No policy may be forthcoming. Whom should the public blame under such circumstances?

When different parties control Congress and the executive branch, it may be in the interest of the opposition in Congress to interfere with the president's ability to implement his policies. Compromised policies or ones that are put into effect later than desired may be less effective than those that the president had hoped to implement. Because the president is held more accountable than Congress, Congress may decide that by undermining the president's policies through compromise and/or delay, it can foist public wrath on him or her and thereby increase the chance that he or she will be ousted in the next election. The main point is that separation of powers

makes for a complex policymaking process in government, with many participants, and it may be hard for the public to hold politicians accountable under such conditions, especially compared to parliamentary systems.[34]

THE POLITICAL BUSINESS CYCLE

Politicians feel that elections turn, in part, on their handling of the economy.
The evidence that we have reviewed in the previous section suggests that this
is the case, even if economic conditions do not completely account for election outcomes. Because politicians have at their disposal policy instruments,
like fiscal and monetary policy, that may affect the economy, it seems reasonable to expect them to try to use these policy instruments to affect the economy as election time nears. This idea is called the **political business cycle,**
whereby politicians in control of government use their policy instruments to
influence the economy for the sake of electoral gain. Thus, taxing, spending,
and monetary decisions are timed for maximum electoral benefit.[35]

The political business cycle suggests that politicians who control economic policymaking instruments will stimulate the economy prior to the
election. Thus, they will promote policies that lower unemployment and increase voters' incomes. However, the economy pays a price for this type of
stimulant with greater inflation levels, which will be borne after the election.
To combat this induced inflation, policymakers will employ economic contraction policies soon after the election. Such policies may lead the economy
toward recession, causing popular support for the incumbent regime to fall
as the economy falls. To regain its popularity as the next election nears, stimulative policies are offered, and the cycle begins anew.

The concept of a political business cycle makes several important assumptions. One, voters are assumed to have short memories and to be more concerned with the state of the economy near election time, having forgotten or
discounted the midterm slowdown or recession. Two, the political business
cycle theory suggests that the policymaking instruments available to politicians and government are effective in directing the economy and are precise
enough to take effect when they will do the most electoral good. Both of
these assumptions are highly debatable, as we saw earlier in this chapter and
in the last chapter.

Still, examples of politicians succumbing to the political business cycle
logic and potential are easy to come by. The prime example is Richard
Nixon, who blamed Dwight Eisenhower, the president under whom he
served as vice president, for his election defeat in 1960.[36] The economy was
weak that year, Eisenhower refused to do anything to rev it up, and Nixon
was narrowly defeated by John F. Kennedy in the presidential race.[37] Nixon
vowed never to be a captive of economic conditions again. Once he became
president in 1968, he readied himself for his reelection campaign in 1972

with policies to ensure that the economy would be in good shape come November.

For instance, social security benefits were increased in September 1972. Social security, as noted earlier, was not indexed to the cost of living until 1974. Prior to that, Congress would routinely pass legislation increasing the benefit to make up for losses due to inflation. The 1972 increase was the largest of any during the Nixon administration.[38] The political business cycle theory would suggest that the timing and size of the increase were not accidental. Other benefit increases were given to veterans, and many types of cash transfers by the federal government were increased or speeded up to meet Nixon's electoral demands.[39]

Other presidents have engaged in similar behavior. Jimmy Carter announced major spending programs for cities during the 1980 primary campaign against Ted Kennedy in his quest for renomination and reelection. George Bush, seeking reelection in 1992, supported increases in unemployment benefits, which he had resisted for several years, and instructed the IRS to reduce withholdings from workers' paychecks.

Despite these examples, the evidence for a political business cycle is weak. Systematic and statistical analyses have not been able to detect any such cycle.[40] Why, given the examples just offered, plus the seemingly compelling logic of the political business cycle, does it not seem to exist? Many reasons have been offered, and we review four here: voters, policy instruments, party programs, and international economics.

First, the political business cycle model assumes that voters have short memories and that they look to the past; that is, they are retrospective in their evaluations and voting behavior. As we discussed earlier, however, there is a strong prospective—not retrospective—element in voters' behavior. More important, the political business cycle assumes that voters have short memories. But voters' memories may not be so short.

For instance, the Democrats ran against Hoover's Depression policies for decades. And well into his first term in office, Ronald Reagan continually reminded voters of the poor economic performance of Jimmy Carter's administration, using that memory to rally voters behind his policies. Thus, voters may have long memories. But they may also quickly forget the past. The economy was sunk in a severe, if short, recession in 1982, which was easily attributable to Reagan's economic policies. Yet in 1984, after two years of recovery and growth, Reagan was reelected by a landslide.

Voters' memories may be long or short, then, depending on the severity of past problems and how effectively the incumbent administration dealt with them, even those problems that it might have caused. Reagan warned people that the economy would slow down, which he cautioned was necessary to wring inflation out of the economy, and then it would grow. His preparing the public for what would happen and the success of his policies may have helped voters forget the 1982 recession. Moreover, as voters get more optimistic about the future, they may discount the past. That is, as they get more optimistic, they may replace their retrospective evaluations of the economy with prospective ones. Reagan's policies clearly increased voter confidence about the future of the economy.[41] The key point is that voters' decision making may be more complex than the political business cycle idea assumes. If voters do not behave as the political business cycle model assumes that they do, then there may be less incentive for politicians to operate on the economy the way that the political business cycle model predicts.

The political business cycle idea also assumes that the policy instruments under the control of policymakers are effective. This is not necessarily the case. In the last chapter and earlier in this one, we discussed the limited effectiveness of fiscal and monetary policy. The political business cycle theory puts great demands on these macroeconomic policy instruments. In particular, it requires relatively precise timing, but, as we discussed, these macroeconomic instruments might not be as precise as the political business cycle theory requires.

Moreover, presidents do not unilaterally control these macroeconomic policy instruments. Taxing and spending decisions are shared with Congress. Although Congress may be amenable to presidential policy directives when the president's party is in control, for much of the last twenty years, Congress and the presidency have been controlled by different parties. In the case of monetary policy, political control is even more limited. Though presidents have the power of appointment, members of the Fed serve long terms, and the Fed is formally independent of the elected branches. If the Fed is going to create a "political monetary cycle"—that is, use monetary policy to affect election outcomes—it will do so because it wants to cooperate with the administration, not because it is forced into such action.[42] We should not expect the Fed always to have good relations with the sitting administration, as the example of Bush and the Fed, mentioned in the opening of the chapter, demonstrates.

The political business cycle assumes that all administrations, whether Democrat or Republican, act similarly in trying to direct the economy. But, as we have discussed, the parties have different policy priorities. In particular, Republicans seem more concerned with fighting inflation, in contrast to Democrats, who place lower unemployment in higher priority. Inasmuch as parties in government follow their partisan inclinations, they might not be interested in engineering a political business cycle.

This partisan model suggests that parties are more concerned with offering policies to voters whom they have historically represented. The Phillips curve tradeoff (see Chapter 3), which suggests that fighting unemployment will increase inflation under some conditions, and vice versa, would impede the creation of a political business cycle. Republicans, for instance, would not be very willing to stimulate the economy if doing so might increase inflation. And Democrats would be relatively reluctant to slowing the economy down to fight inflation. Considerable research suggests that economic policies are more a function of partisan inclinations than political business cycle motivations.[43]

Last, the political business cycle seems to assume that the economy is generally under the control of political authorities. However, random shocks may affect the economy. These random shocks may distort any ability of political decision makers to use macroeconomic instruments to create a political business cycle. Some random shocks may emanate from the domestic economy—natural disasters, new technologies, and so on. But perhaps the most important might come from outside the domestic U.S. economy, from international competitors and trading partners.[44] For example, the oil embargoes of the 1970s severely affected the U.S. economy, helping to foster a stagflation that government policies seemed incapable of dealing with. Thus, we may say that the more open the economy is to international economic conditions, the less capable domestic macroeconomic policy instruments are of directing the economy. Not only does this limit the ability to create a political business cycle, but it also affects overall macroeconomic policymaking.

CONCLUSION

Whether or not there is a political business cycle does not mean that politicians do not try to alter the economy with an eye toward elections. Some do. Nixon is a clear example, as we discussed earlier. But others may not be as willing to manipulate the economy for electoral gain. Eisenhower serves as a good example, with his refusal to stimulate the economy in 1960. Sometimes a president's ideology might inhibit him from using policy instruments for purely electoral purposes—or from using them for any purpose. Eisenhower's market orientation and belief in smaller government surely made it harder for him to use macroeconomic policy instruments, than, say, Kennedy, who held more positive views about the role of government in the economy. As we have discussed in the past two chapters, the economy is heavily politicized in the United States, even though there is no proof that the political business cycle exists. Trying to produce a sound and growing economy is still the surest bet for incumbents intent on staying in office.

Key Terms

banker's bias
Board of Governors
discount rates
easy money policy
federal funds rate
   (FFR)

Federal Open
   Market Committee
   (FOMC)
Federal Reserve
   System
monetarists

monetary
   policy
open market
   operations
political business
   cycle

prospective orientation
reserve requirements

retrospective
orientation

sociotropic voting
tight money policy

Explore the Web

The key monetary policymaking agency of government is the Fed, which maintains a web page at http:///www.bog.frb.fed.us/. From that page you can find links to all of the Federal Reserve banks. The major stock markets also maintain web pages. Find the New York Stock Exchange at http://www .nyse.com/, the American Stock Exchange (AMEX) at http://www.amex.com/, the Chicago Board of Trade at http://www.cbot.com/, and NASDAQ at http://www.nasdaq.com/welcome.htm. The addresses http://library.uww .edu/SUBJECT/exchange.htm and http://www.supralink.net/english/link/ stock/index.html also provide links to many other stock exchanges in the United States and around the world. The major regulator of the stock exchange, the Securities and Exchanges Commission, has a web page at http://www.sec.gov/.

Notes

1. This story is recounted in Steven Greenhouse, "Administration Admits Pressuring Greenspan," *New York Times,* September 24, 1992, C2.

2. On the news conference, see "Fed to Cut Rates if Necessary, Chief Says," *Kansas City Star,* October 11, 1992, A4. This is a story from the Associated Press wire service.

3. A nontechnical discussion is found in John P. Frendreis and Raymond Tatalovich, *The Modern Presidency and Economic Policy* (Itasca, IL: Peacock, 1994), 113–114; and Charles L. Schultze, *Memos to the President: A Guide Through Macroeconomics for the Busy Policymaker* (Washington, DC: Brookings, 1992), 172–195.

4. On the first national bank and Hamilton's policies, see Forrest McDonald, *The Presidency of George Washington* (New York: Norton, 1974), 76–109.

5. On the controversy surrounding the second national bank and Andrew Jackson's opposition to it, see Donald B. Cole, *The Presidency of Andrew Jackson* (Lawrence: University Press of Kansas, 1993); Richard B. Latner, *The Presidency of Andrew Jackson: White House Politics, 1829–1837* (Athens: University of Georgia Press, 1979); Robert V. Remini, *Andrew Jackson and the Bank War: A Study in the Growth of Presidential Power* (New York: Norton, 1967); and Stephen Skowronek, *The Politics Presidents Make: Leadership from John Adams to George Bush* (Cambridge, MA: Belknap, 1993).

6. The history of the monetary system in the United States is covered well in Kenneth J. Meier, *Regulation: Politics, Bureaucracy, Economics* (New York: St. Martin's, 1985), 48–52.

7. The panic of 1907 is discussed in Meier, *Regulation,* 49–50.

8. On the importance of the chair, see Donald F. Kettl, *Leadership at the Fed* (New Haven, CT: Yale University Press, 1986).

9. The accord is discussed in William R. Keech, *Economic Politics: The Costs of Democracy* (New York: Cambridge University Press, 1995), 200–202.

10. On policymaking at the Fed, see John T. Woolley, *Monetary Politics: The Federal Reserve and the Politics of Monetary Policy* (New York: Cambridge University Press, 1984); and William Greider, *Secrets of the Temple: How the Federal Reserve Runs the Country* (New York: Simon & Schuster, 1987).

11. See Thomas Havrilesky, *The Pressures on American Monetary Policy,* 2d ed. (Boston: Kluwer Academic, 1995).

12. Ibid. For a good overview of the political influences on the Fed, see John T. Woolley, "The Politics of Monetary Policy: A Critical Review," *Journal of Public Policy* 14 (1994): 57–85.

13. The literature on the link between the state of the economy and the outcome of elections is very large. For good overviews, see Michael S. Lewis-Beck, *Economics and Elections: The Major Western European Democracies* (Ann Arbor: University of Michigan Press, 1988); Keech, *Economic Politics;* and Harold D. Clarke, Evel W. Elliott, and William Mishler, *Controversies in Political Economy: Canada, Great Britain, and the United States* (Boulder, CO: Westview, 1992), esp. 1–29. A subliterature looks at the impact of the economy on the popularity of leaders. In the United States that literature has focused very much on the president, arguing that presidential popularity may be considered an interelection referendum on the president. Inasmuch as presidents value popularity, they may be said to be engaged in a perpetual election, with the objective of boosting their popularity whenever possible. Several studies have found that popularity is a good predictor of the incumbent president's reelection chances. See Richard Brody and Lee Sigelman, "Presidential Popularity and Presidential Elections: An Update and Extension," *Public Opinion Quarterly* 47 (1983): 325–328. On the impact of the economy on presidential popularity, see Michael MacKuen, Robert Erikson, and James Stimson, "Peasants or Bankers? The American Electorate and the U.S. Economy," *American Political Science Review* 86 (1992): 597–611.

14. On this argument, see Lewis-Beck, *Economics and Elections,* 7–8.

15. A review of these elections and the impact of the economy on them is found in Paul R. Abramson, John H. Aldrich, and David W. Rohde, *Change and Continuity and the 1992 Elections,* rev. ed. (Washington, DC: CQ Press, 1995), esp. 203–207.

16. Robert S. Erikson, "Economic Conditions and the Presidential Vote," *American Political Science Review* 83 (1989): 567–573.

17. Ibid.

18. Ibid. Erikson's estimates suggest that, on average, income grew at a rate of 2.26 percent across these elections.

19. On the impact of unemployment on turnout, see Kay Lehman Schlozman and Sidney Verba, *Insult to Injury: Unemployment, Class, and Political Response* (Cambridge, MA: Harvard University Press, 1979).

20. See the studies reviewed in Friedrich Schneider and Bruno Frey, "Politico-Economic Models of Macroeconomic Policy: A Review of the Empirical Evidence,"

in *The Political Economy of Money, Inflation, and Unemployment,* ed. T. Willet (Durham, NC: Duke University Press, 1988), 243–255, for the case that unemployment affects election outcomes.

21. Lewis-Beck, *Economics and Elections,* 92–93. Also see Henry Chapell and William Keech, "A New View of Political Accountability for Economic Performance," *American Political Science Review* 79 (1985): 10–27, for a similar view.

22. Clarke et al., *Controversies in Political Economy,* 11–17, make this point.

23. Schlozman and Verba, *Insult to Injury.*

24. The sociotropic voting argument is presented in D. Roderick Kiewiet, *Macroeconomics and Micropolitics: The Electoral Effects of Economic Issues* (Chicago: University of Chicago Press, 1983); Donald R. Kinder and D. Roderick Kiewiet, "Economic Discontent and Political Behavior: The Role of Personal Grievances and Collective Economic Judgments in Congressional Voting," *American Journal of Political Science* 23 (1979): 495–527; Donald R. Kinder and D. Roderick Kiewiet, "Sociotropic Politics: The American Case," *British Journal of Political Science* 11 (1981): 129–161; and Lewis-Beck, *Economics and Elections.*

25. Perhaps the first statement of this idea is V. O. Key, Jr., *The Responsible Electorate: Rationality in Presidential Voting, 1936–1960* (New York: Vintage Books, 1968). A major and sophisticated analysis of voting behavior using the retrospective idea is Morris Fiorina, *Retrospective Voting in American National Elections* (New Haven, CT: Yale University Press, 1981).

26. See, for instance, Anthony Downs, *An Economic Theory of Democracy* (New York: Harper & Row, 1957), who makes this case.

27. On candidate ambiguity in election campaigns, see Benjamin I. Page, *Choice and Echoes in Presidential Elections: Rational Man and Electoral Democracy* (Chicago: University of Chicago Press, 1978).

28. Prospective voting is discussed in Lewis-Beck, *Economics and Elections.* Prospective economic evaluations and presidential popularity is the subject of MacKuen et al., "Peasants or Bankers?" and Harold D. Clarke, Jonathan Rapkin, and Marianne C. Stewart, "A President out of Work: A Note on the Political Economy of Presidential Approval in the Bush Years," *British Journal of Political Science* 24 (1994): 535–548. One study found that prospective economic judgments were significant vote predictors in thirteen of fourteen Senate elections from 1956 through 1988. In contrast, retrospective judgments were significant in only six of those contests. See Brad Lockerbie, "The Temporal Pattern of Economic Evaluations and Vote Choice in Senate Elections," *Public Choice* 69 (1991): 279–294; also James H. Kuklinski and Darryl M. West, "Economic Expectations and Voting Behavior in United States House and Senate Elections," *American Political Science Review* 75 (1981): 436–447.

29. Pamela Johnston Conover, Stanley Feldman, and Kathleen Knight, "Judging Inflation and Unemployment: The Origins of Retrospective Evaluations," *Journal of Politics* 48 (1986): 565–588, and "The Personal and Political Underpinnings of Economic Forecasts," *American Journal of Political Science* 31 (1987): 559–583.

30. The evidence is modest on this point. See Kiewiet, *Macroeconomics and Micropolitics.* Priscilla L. Southwell, "The Mobilization Hypothesis and Voter Turnout in

Congressional Elections, 1974–1982," *Western Political Quarterly* 41 (1988): 273–288, shows that this pattern seems to affect turnout.

31. This is a hotly debated topic. One of the first studies of the relationship between the economy and elections focused on the House and found a correlation. See Gerald H. Kramer, "Short-Term Fluctuations in U.S. Voting Behavior, 1986–1964," *American Political Science Review* 65 (1971): 131–143; also Edward R. Tufte, "Determinants of Outcomes of Midterm Congressional Elections," *American Political Science Review* 69 (1975): 812–826. The Kramer study had been heavily criticized. See Keech, *Economic Politics,* 135; and Robert Erikson, "Economic Conditions and the Congressional Vote: A Review of the Macrolevel Evidence," *American Journal of Political Science* 34 (1990): 373–399. Still, there are defenders of the proposition that economic conditions affect congressional elections. See Gary C. Jacobson, "Does the Economy Matter in Midterm Elections?" *American Journal of Political Science* 34 (1990): 400–404.

32. The effect of the economy on state and local elections is much less studied than on the national level. Two good studies are John E. Chubb, "Institutions, the Economy, and the Dynamics of State Elections," *American Political Science Review* 82 (1985): 133–152; and Robert M. Stein, "Economic Voting for Governor and U.S. Senator: The Electoral Consequences of Federalism," *Journal of Politics* 52 (1990): 29–53.

33. Mark Peffley and John T. Williams, "Attributing Presidential Responsibility for National Economic Problems," *American Politics Quarterly* 4 (1985): 393–425.

34. Clarke et al., *Controversies in Political Economy,* 12, 23.

35. The political business cycle idea has been well studied by political scientists and economists. Its first expression is found in M. Kalecki, "Political Aspects of Full Employment," *Political Quarterly* 14 (1943): 322–331. After being forgotten for almost three decades, it was rediscovered in the 1970s. Two pioneering statements are William D. Nordhaus, "The Political Business Cycle," *Review of Economic Studies* 42 (1975): 169–190; and Edward R. Tufte, *Political Control of the Economy* (Princeton, NJ: Princeton University Press, 1978). Literally hundreds of studies have now looked at this theory. Reviews are found in James Alt and Alec Chrystal, *Political Economics* (Berkeley: University of California Press, 1983); Lewis-Beck, *Economics and Elections;* and Keech, *Economic Politics.* A major study is Douglas A. Hibbs, Jr., *The American Political Economy* (Cambridge, MA: Harvard University Press, 1987).

36. Tufte, *Political Control of the Economy,* rests his case for a political business cycle very heavily on the Nixon example.

37. Ibid., 6.

38. Ibid., 30–31.

39. Ibid., 36–54.

40. See Lewis-Beck, *Economics and Elections,* 137–152; and Clarke et al., *Controversies in Political Economy,* 189–204.

41. The Consumer Confidence Surveys of the University of Michigan show a decided upsurge in expectations about the future beginning in 1983. See Harold W. Stanley

and Richard G. Niemi, *Vital Statistics on American Politics*, 4th ed. (Washington, DC: CQ Press, 1994), 434, for a time-series graph presenting these data.

42. There is also considerable debate over the existence of a "political monetary cycle." See Nathaniel Beck, "Elections and the Fed: Is There a Political Monetary Cycle?" *American Journal of Political Science* 31 (1987): 194–216.

43. The most persuasive exponent of this view is Hibbs, *The American Political Economy*.

44. Clarke et al., *Controversies in Political Economy*, 189–204, make this case.

10

Regulatory Policy I: Regulation in Theory and Practice

I N THE early 1990s, news reports began to appear about medical side effects from breast implants. Although most of the medical information was anecdotal, lawyers, acting in the name of women with these side effects, filed a class action suit against breast implant manufacturers. The charge was that the silicone used in the implants leaked into women's bodies, causing such problems as pain and swelling of joints, unusual fatigue, and swollen glands. These news stories led to much public pressure, and the Food and Drug Administration (FDA), the federal body that regulates medicines and medical procedures, put a moratorium on the cosmetic use of breast implants until better medical and scientific evidence was available to assess the safety of breast implants. Breast implants were allowed during the moratorium only for reconstructive purposes, for instance, because of a mastectomy to treat breast cancer.[1] After further study, the scientific panel at the FDA found no adverse effects of silicon implants.

The U.S. Justice Department initiated an antitrust proceeding against the computer software giant Microsoft in September 1996. Netscape Corporation precipitated this move by submitting a complaint to the Justice Department in August 1996, claiming that Microsoft was offering its Explorer Internet browser, the major competitor to Netscape's browser, free, as a part of Microsoft's Windows operating platform. As Windows was loaded on approximately 90 percent of the personal computers in the United States, Microsoft, according to Netscape and the Justice Department, was able to use its Windows monopoly position to drive Netscape out of business. In effect, Microsoft was using "unfair competitive practices," a common standard in antitrust proceedings. In 1999, the case had been brought to court but not yet resolved.[2]

These are examples of government regulation of the economy. This action limited and restricted economic activity. In this chapter and the next, we will look at government regulation, asking what regulation is and why governments regulate. In this chapter, we will look at the types of regulation and the government agencies responsible for implementing regulation. In the next chapter, our topics will be the growth of regulation, the backlash against regulation—known as deregulation—and the increasing role of presidents in regulatory policymaking.

WHAT IS REGULATION?

On the most basic level, regulation is the replacement of a private decision with a government one. Thus, almost every government policy is in some respects regulatory. But this definition does not help us distinguish among the many types of government policies. When most people use the word *regulation,* they not only mean that government is making a decision, but that government is forcing them to act in a certain way, and government is willing to use coercive means to compel them to act that way. An important aspect of regulation, then, is its coercive nature.[3]

Coercion is the use of penalties, like jail sentences, monetary fines, and withdrawal of licenses or certificates to operate. Coercion imposes a cost on the offender, whether the cost is monetary or in terms of freedom to act. Not all government policies are coercive, but coercion seems to underlie most government efforts to regulate.[4] Since regulation is aimed at stopping behaviors or impelling people to behave in specified ways, that is, changing people from behaving as they normally tend to, coercion may be necessary to gain compliance with government objectives.

There are many ways that government can implement regulations. We may call these **regulatory policy instruments,** similar to the fiscal and monetary policy instruments discussed in the previous two chapters.[5] The policies are the objectives of government regulations, like clean air. The policy instruments are the mechanisms through which government tries to attain those objectives. There are five basic instruments of regulation: price controls, exit and entry controls, standard setting, allocation of scarce resources, and incentives.

Price controls limit the freedom of service and product providers to set the price of their services and goods. Prices have been set at one time or another in the United States for railroad and airplane tickets, natural gas, local and long-distance telephone calls, cable television subscriptions, taxicab fares, insurance premiums, and a host of other goods and services. The aim of price controls is to ensure that consumers are not gouged and that producers earn a fair profit.

Exit and entry controls limit the ability of businesses to leave and enter markets.[6] Transportation regulation relied heavily on market exit and entry controls until deregulation in the 1970s and 1980s. Thus, a railroad could not discontinue service to a locality until the Interstate Commerce Commission (ICC) gave it permission to do so.[7] The same applied to natural gas pipelines under the Federal Power Commission (FPC) and later the Federal Energy Regulatory Commission (FERC). The ICC also limited the number of companies that could offer interstate trucking. During the regulatory regime of the Civil Aeronautics Board (CAB), from the late 1930s through 1980, airlines were told which cities they could fly into, the number of flights they could make per day, and the required size of airplanes for each route. Similarly, the Federal Communications Commission (FCC) grants licenses to local broadcasters to air television and radio programming. In each of these examples, the government decides who may enter a market to provide a service.

Standard setting sets minimum and/or maximum requirements on products and services.[8] The Food and Drug Administration sets standards for drug effectiveness and food safety. The FCC sets broadcasting standards, like the now-defunct equal time provision, which required broadcasters to grant candidates for political office equal access to the airwaves. The Consumer Product Safety Commission (CPSC) sets safety standards for common consumer products, like paints, children's clothing, and toys, while the Occupational Safety and Health Administration (OSHA) sets safety requirements for the workplace. The Nuclear Regulatory Commission (NRC) sets standards for the safe operation of nuclear power plants, and the Environmental Protection Agency (EPA) defines allowable pollution levels for many products and industrial operations. States heavily regulate many occupations by requiring licenses or educational certification to practice or operate. Myriad other types of standards also exist.

Another regulatory instrument is the **allocation of scarce resources.** Sometimes entry into the market is what the government is allocating, as just discussed. Government entry regulations may make such entry itself a scarce commodity. On other occasions government allocates who may use public assets, like land, for private economic purposes. Mining companies and cattle firms can secure rights to use government land for their economic operations, but government may decide which company is allowed such access. Similarly, telecommunications regulation in part began to keep broadcasters from interfering with each other's broadcasts. Thus, the FCC allocates different frequencies on the spectrum to different types of broadcasting (for example, television, radio, wireless telephone), and within frequency bands, it allocates particular frequencies to rival broadcasters in the same industry (for example, local television broadcasters).[9]

Last, government can use **incentives** to guide and regulate behavior.[10] Some incentives are regulated through the tax code. Thus, businesses may depreciate capital improvements. This provides them with incentives to invest in new capital goods, like equipment and factories. Other provisions limit the taxes that must be paid on earnings. Deductions for interest on home mortgages provide incentives for home ownership. Tax breaks for energy savings were used in the 1970s to spur people to insulate and weatherize their homes. Subsidies, another type of incentive, are also used to regulate behavior. Agriculture price supports help to increase or decrease production, depending on the structure of the pricing system.[11]

To curb environmental pollution, the government is now experimenting with **pollution credits,** a form of incentive system mixed with coercive controls.[12] Companies may buy these credits, which allow a certain level of pollution. However, the government limits overall pollution by restricting the number of credits. This is the coercive element. Thus, ownership of these credits becomes valuable, but because they are a cost of doing business, they may stimulate companies to lower their pollution output. If a company can reduce its pollution output below the level of the pollution credits that it owns, it may sell those credits to other companies less able to lower their polluting activities and in need of more pollution credits. This is where incentives come into the equation. Overall, pollution never rises above a certain level under this system. Still, some government coercion is also present because of the maximum pollution levels that are set. No companies can pollute beyond the credit level that they own without triggering coercive action against them by the government.

MARKET FAILURE AS A JUSTIFICATION FOR REGULATION

What justification is there for government to regulate economic behavior? The major reason for regulation is to correct market failure.[13]

Market failure occurs when the market cannot correct problems of over- or undersupply. Markets, as you learned in Chapter 2, are dynamic and self-correcting. They are never in equilibrium but are always headed toward equilibrium. A market is in equilibrium, you will recall, when supply and demand are in balance: when just enough, not too much or too little, of a good is being produced. It is not a market failure if an over- or undersupply exists, but it is one if the market is unable to do anything about the problem. Competition problems, information problems, and externalities are the major causes of market failure and the traditional justifications for regulation.

Competition Problems

Lack of competition, unequal bargaining power of the participants in a transaction, and lack of demand are the major competition problems that can cause market failure. The lack of competition is usually associated with monopolies and other restrictions on competition, such as cartels and oligopolies. Monopolies come in two varieties, unnatural and natural. **Unnatural monopolies** are created by the uncompetitive behavior of would-be monopolists. **Natural monopolies** arise from conditions present in the market. Government regulation has aimed to inhibit the creation of unnatural monopolies, mostly through antitrust policies. Natural monopolies, in contrast, have been regulated in an attempt to simulate market results, to create conditions that would be present if a market were possible.

Unnatural Monopolies

Unnatural monopolies exist when there is not enough competition among producers. In the extreme case, one company may be the only supplier of a good or service. In less extreme cases, one producer may command so much of the market that it effectively has control over the supply and price of the good in the market. In the early twentieth century, the Standard Oil Companies and Trust held just such power over the oil market in the United States by controlling a very large percentage of that market. During that era, other industries, from meatpacking to telephones to tobacco, also exhibited monopolistic tendencies. In the current era, some argue that Microsoft's ownership of the Windows platform has made that company a monopolist in the computer industry. Cartels, or agreements among firms within a market, may also create monopolistic problems.

Classically, cartels exist when the companies involved together control production and distribution. Cartels are most effective when demand is **inelastic**. Inelastic consumer demand means that even if the price of a good or service goes up, consumers are still willing to pay for it. Inelasticity of demand may be a function of the inability to substitute one good for another, either because of the cost of acquiring the substitute good or because the substitute good does not exist. For instance, once a home is outfitted to accept gas heating, it may be prohibitively expensive to refit for electric heating. Inelasticity also derives from the vital need for the good. No one can do without heat during cold winter months. Many modern conveniences, like the telephone, have taken on this "necessity of life" quality, making demand for them relatively inelastic. Working together, companies in a cartel may *collude,* or set industrywide supply and price levels. The most famous cartel, the Organization of Petroleum Exporting Countries (OPEC), effectively set the world's crude oil supply and price during most of the 1970s.

Monopolies and cartels interfere with economic efficiency. A monopolistic producer may restrict the supply of a good in the market. By doing this, consumer demand may not be met, and, because the good is in short supply compared with demand, the price of the good will go up. Monopolists are thus able to extract a higher price from consumers than if competition existed.

Predatory pricing exists when monopolists use the high prices in their monopolized market to subsidize entry into another market. Thus, they may undercut the prices that competing firms are offering, forcing prices to levels below cost, and sometimes forcing competitors into bankruptcy or into merging with the monopolist. The Standard Oil monopoly was built this way, and the Microsoft antitrust case is based on alleged predatory pricing behavior by the Microsoft Corporation.

John D. Rockefeller, the head of Standard Oil, began with a geographically small monopoly in the western Pennsylvania–northeastern Ohio area.[14] Once the monopoly was in place, the prices he charged his customers shot up. Then he used these "excess" profits to subsidize losses in another region—for example, Indiana—where Standard Oil might force prices below cost.[15] In time, the Indiana competitors were either driven out of business, being unable to sustain or match the prices that Standard Oil was offering, or they merged with Standard Oil. Thus, the Standard Oil monopoly spread from one area to another until it covered nearly the entire country by the early 1900s.

Monopoly, according to the theory of the market, is inefficient. It is allocatively inefficient in that prices for goods are higher than they would be under competitive conditions. It is also inefficient because the monopoly firm does not feel competitive pressures to keep production costs down; this is called **productive inefficiency.**[16] In the United States, antitrust policies have been implemented to correct this kind of market failure. The aim of antitrust policy is to restore competition to a market where monopolies and/or cartels have uncompetitive market power.

Natural Monopolies

Monopolies may result not only from business practices but also from the economics of the market. Under some circumstances, it is more efficient to allow one company to offer a service than to allow competition. When this circumstance holds, natural monopolies are said to exist.

Natural monopolies come into being, in part, because the initial costs of creating the production and delivery system are so expensive in some industries. Usually, there are high capital expenditure costs before any service can be offered. Utilities are often afflicted with this problem. For example, electric power companies must build generating plants and lay transmission wires. Adding more customers to the system is usually less expensive than starting the construction of the system. Most utilities, such as telephone, cable television, electric and natural gas power, water, and local rail systems, are common examples of situations with high upfront costs. Duplication in such cases may be economically inefficient.

A second factor that determines the existence of a natural monopoly is inelastic consumer demand, which we have already discussed. Natural monopolies present a policy problem because without some form of effective price regulation (either from the market or government), the natural monopolist is likely to act like the unnatural monopolist, increasing prices to economically inefficient levels. Because markets do not function well under natural monopoly situations, government often steps in as regulator. The major form of regulation of natural monopolies is price regulation.[17]

Under price regulation, government tries to set prices such that an efficient level of supply at a socially desirable price is reached. Thus, the price must be high enough to create an incentive for producers to continue production, but not so high that consumers cannot afford it. In effect, government aims to mimic the decision that the market would make if the market could operate effectively.[18] Another government alternative is public ownership. Earlier in U.S. history, especially in the nineteenth century, public ownership was more common. Public ownership means that the government owns a service or industry and provides the service or product to the consumer directly. In Western Europe, public ownership has been more common than in the United States. For example, the telephone and railroad systems have often been under government ownership there. However, with the current public mood to limit government intervention into the economy, there is little support for that option.

Unequal Bargaining Power

A third rationale for regulation occurs when unequal bargaining power undermines the market transaction. For instance, one party to the transaction may have coercive power over the other. When the potential for coercion exists, the transaction cannot be voluntary or free, a significant characteristic of a well-operating market. An important example concerns labor-management relations. (The market transaction here is the employee "selling" his or her labor to an employer.) One coercive power that employers hold over their employees is the power to fire them. Workers may be reluctant to voice complaints about working conditions, pay, benefits, and so on, for fear of losing their jobs. In the United States, relations between workers and employers are regulated by the National Labor Relations Board (NLRB) and the Occupational Safety and Health Administration (OSHA), among other agencies. The right to unionize is protected by the NLRB, and working conditions are regulated by OSHA.

Not Enough Demand

Last, there are situations in which not enough demand for a product exists, not because there is no potential demand but because prices are too high. Often the industry has not developed to the point of reaching economies of scale, which would expand the market, or too many firms are competing for the size of the current market.

When demand is small and government decides that it wants an industry to develop, government may use regulation to help the industry grow. The development of the airline industry in the United States is a classic example.[19]

First, the federal government supplied the airlines with business: they were allowed to transport mail long distances through an airmail classification, a service that began in the 1920s. Next, the government restricted the entry of airlines into the market and determined airline routes, schedules, and prices, beginning in the 1930s. The combination of subsidy through airmail delivery and competition restriction helped build a large, viable airline industry.

Information Problems

Efficient markets also require perfect information, especially for the consumer. Perfect information is when all parties to an economic transaction know precisely everything that they need to know, such as price, supply, quality, and competitive goods, to make the most efficient and desirable transaction. All transactions fall short of this lofty ideal. However, problems like the cost of information, incomplete information, and inability of consumers to use information may lead to market failure.

Costly Information

Some information may be too costly or difficult for consumers to acquire. A classic example is the inability of the average consumer to determine the safety of drugs. Drug testing takes a long time and is expensive and technically difficult. Thus, the government, under the jurisdiction granted to the Food and Drug Administration (FDA), tests drugs and allows only safe and effective ones onto the market.

Incomplete Information

Sometimes relevant information is hidden from consumers, and at other times information may be misleading. Misleading information is more likely when repeat sales are not expected. Thus, itinerant home repair services may misrepresent the quality, cost, and other performance conditions of their work. The used-automobile industry is widely thought by the general public to hide relevant information about its cars. Regulations exist that prohibit tampering with odometers, but the industry fought successfully in the late 1970s to keep from having to report fully on a vehicle's repair history.

Other information may be incomplete. A good example concerns food labeling. The food industry has complained about having to reveal all of the information about the contents of packaged food, arguing that it is too technical for the average person, that it is too expensive to present, and that it may reveal trade secrets. Still, the FDA rewrote the rules governing food labeling in 1994, creating uniform standards that were easier to read and understand. The new rules also included more types of foods than previously.[20]

Inability to Use Information

Last, the public may be unable to use all the presented information. The information may be too technical, and circumstances may exist in which consumers will not want to comparison shop. For instance, under many medical situations, consumers are less concerned about cost than about preserving life and limb and ridding themselves of pain.

Externalities

The third major category of market breakdown involves externalities and spillovers. Externalities are the costs or benefits of an economic transaction that affect someone not involved directly in the transaction. These effects are called externalities because someone "external" to the transaction is affected. Another term often used is **spillover effect:** costs or benefits of a transaction "spill over," affecting third parties.[21]

Externalities can be either positive or negative, and they can affect either producers or consumers. **Positive externalities** usually mean that producers are not able to capture all of the economic benefits of their product. For instance, computer manufacturers may increase the productivity of the whole economy, making adopters more efficient, but the computer manufacturers cannot share in the profits gained that a user of a computer reaps. Negative externalities mean that the parties of the transaction have not paid the full cost of the product and transaction, that someone not involved in the transaction has also paid part of the cost of the transaction. Negative externalities are more commonly the focus of public policies than positive externalities.

Pollution is one negative externality that has been the target of much government regulatory policy. Air pollution, for example, is believed to cause health problems. Thus, government has enacted a number of policies that aim to reduce air pollution levels. For example, producers are instructed to install air scrubbers or other antipollution technologies. Thus, the producer—a steel manufacturer, say—has to pay some of the cost of production formerly placed on neighbors. These increases in the cost of production may be passed on to the consumer—a building manufacturer, perhaps, who uses steel beams. In this way, the externality is internalized by the producer and consumer of the transaction, not the neighbor who has to breathe the polluted air that the steel production process created.

In recent years, negative externalities of the consumer to consumer variety have also become the focus of government policy. The most notable example involves secondhand smoke from cigarettes.[22] Again, poor health caused by the smoke is the externality. Smoking has now been banned in many public buildings and all domestic airline flights in the United States. Smokers internalize the cost by having their freedom to smoke curtailed when it might affect others.

POLITICAL RATIONALES FOR REGULATION

Market failure is an *economic* justification for government regulatory activity. The market failure model is built on the concept of efficiency. Thus, market failure is defined as the inability of the market to produce and/or supply a good at an efficient quantity and/or price. According to the market failure model, only when this inefficient condition holds should government try to correct the market.

Government policies, however, exist for a wide variety of circumstances, not all involving market failure and inefficiency. Thus, even when markets are working efficiently, we may see government regulation. In these instances, regulation is used to promote some value that the market is unable to provide.

Equity Justifications for Regulation

The most important critique of efficient markets is that they do not distribute goods, benefits, and burdens in an equitable manner.[23] The market is considered to be a good production system, but it is not always a good distribution system.

Telephone service is a good example.[24] Once telephones came to be regarded as a necessity of modern life, sometime around the beginning of the twentieth century, policymakers decided that it was important to ensure that everyone could get access to telephone service at an affordable price. For those who lived in geographic isolation, like farmers, telephones could cut the time that it took to receive emergency medical assistance; sometimes the time savings proved to be lifesaving. Similarly, people who lacked physical mobility could stay in contact with others, helping not only with medical needs but also with loneliness and social isolation. These are just two examples of the argument that telephones are a modern necessity, not just for business but for everyone.

The problem with pricing telephones at market rates is that many people might be priced out of the market.[25] A major cost of telephone service is laying the wires. The longer the wires, the greater the cost. The rural United States is further burdened because of population sparsity. Small populations spread across great distances cost huge sums to connect but provide little traffic, or telephone use, which is necessary to pay back the costs of construction, connection, and upkeep. If people had to pay the market cost of telephone service, many might be forced to stop their service, or telephone companies might refuse to provide service.

When regulation came to the telephone industry in the first quarter of the twentieth century, policymakers in the telephone policy subsystem, such as those on the Commerce Committees in Congress, the FCC, and the state public utility commissions, fashioned a goal of universal telephone service. Universal service was a policy designed to ensure that everyone who wanted service could get it but to still give the telephone companies enough revenue to operate effectively, attract investment, and expand service to all. This was done through a complex pricing policy with many subsidies to some types of users, like consumers, and higher prices to other types of users, like businesses.

Thus, government created a regulatory pricing structure to ensure universal access, though such a policy might not be construed as being narrowly economically efficient. The rationale behind the regulatory structure was equity—everyone should have affordable access to the telephone system—and a redistributive pricing system was used to ensure that the universal service goal was met. By the 1960s, government data indicate that upward of 90 percent of households had easy access to a telephone.

Airlines under the regime of the Civil Aeronautics Board (CAB) had a similar policy of ensuring service to small cities, not just to those large enough to provide profits. Like rural residents and the telephone, small cities could not always justify an airport on economic grounds.[26] Their population might be too small to create enough traffic for the airlines to make a profit. To deal with this, the CAB instituted a redistributive, equity-based pricing scheme. Thus, people who traveled on short, heavily trafficked routes, those that cost the least to operate and those that generated the greatest profits, often paid airline ticket prices considerably higher than a market-based pricing scheme would charge. These higher than market prices were used to offset the losses that airlines incurred by servicing smaller cities, those that could not generate enough traffic to be profitable. The principle behind this policy was that residents of *small* cities should have airline service. Large cities should not be comparatively advantaged in attracting business and jobs because they had superior airline service.

In both the telephone and airline cases, it was felt socially desirable to give everyone access to these goods and services. Equal access to the modern economy, as well as to other modern institutions, has been a fundamental principle behind much regulation, even though that regulation may not be economically efficient. In such cases, social equity and economic efficiency are traded off against each other, with social equity sometimes winning. In other cases, economic efficiency may be a more important value than social equity, and regulation is not imposed.[27]

TYPES OF REGULATIONS

There are two major varieties of regulation, **competitive** and **protective**.[28] Sometimes competitive regulation is called the old regulation, while protective regulation is called the new regulation. There are a number of important characteristics that differentiate competitive from protective regulation. Table 10.1 presents a list of the major differences between the two. In

TABLE 10.1 Differences Between Competitive and Protective Regulation

Competitive	Protective
Old	New
Regulates one industry	Regulates the entire economy
Market failure impetus	Externality problem
Focuses on basic business practices	Aims to protect consumers from risk
Independent regulatory commissions	Departmental agencies
Vague statutes	Specific statutes
Economic and legal analysis	Scientific and technical analysis
Interest group capture	Little interest group capture
Nonideological debate	Intense ideological debate
Federal/state separation	Strong intergovernmental component

general, competitive regulation focuses on the market activities of producers, like their pricing policies. Protective regulation aims more to safeguard consumers in their purchasing and other decisions, for instance, from unsafe products or environmental pollution.

First, compared to competitive regulation, protective regulation came relatively late, appearing on the scene in full force only in the late 1960s.[29] Competitive regulation, in contrast, appeared much earlier. The state governments began the experiment in regulation earnestly after the Civil War with their attempts to regulate the railroads. The federal government entered the regulatory arena in 1887 with the passage of the Interstate Commerce Act and the creation of the Interstate Commerce Commission (ICC). After the creation of the ICC, other competitive regulations were implemented at the federal level throughout the late 1800s and into the 1900s. Protective regulation did not come into its own until the advent of Lyndon Johnson's Great Society in the 1960s.

There was, however, some early protective regulation even before the Great Society. For example, the Meat Inspection Service of the Department of Agriculture, the agency that inspects meat for purity and safety, was established in the early 1900s. Similarly, the Food and Drug Administration, which grew out of an agency in the Agriculture Department, dates to the 1930s. Also, some competitive regulations arrive quite late. The Commodity Futures Trading Commission (CFTC) was created in the 1970s, though part of the agency originated in the Agriculture Commodities Bureau, which was established in the 1920s.

A second difference between competitive and protective regulations is their scope. Competitive regulation traditionally regulates one industry at a time, like railroads, trucks, airlines, oil, natural gas, television, telephones, or banks. In contrast, protective regulations span industries. Thus, the EPA regulates pollution no matter what the industry or the pollution source. The OSHA regulates all workplaces of a certain size regardless of industry, and the CPSC regulates all consumer products without being restricted to any one industry.

There are some exceptions to this, the most important being antitrust regulations. The Antitrust Division of the Justice Department, which oversees implementation of the Sherman Act, and the Federal Trade Commission, which is responsible for the Clayton and Federal Trade Acts, can break up monopolies, prohibit mergers, and pursue other antitrust policies in any industry. However, like traditional competitive regulation, antitrust regulation usually focuses on one industry at a time. Thus, in the early part of the century, the Standard Oil trust was broken up, as was AT&T in the 1980s.

Third, the impetus behind competitive and protective regulation differs. They focus on different kinds of market failures. Competitive regulation is used to correct market breakdowns that result from either too much or not enough competition. In contrast, protective regulation is used most often for externality problems.

A fourth difference between competitive and protective regulations follows from their names and the discussion of economic rationales for regulation. Competitive regulation focuses on basic business practices, while protective regulation aims to protect consumers from risk, whether financial, safety, or health. Sometimes protective regulation is called **social regulation** and competitive regulation is called **economic regulation** to help clarify the differences between them.

The implementation of competitive and protective regulations also differs. Generally, independent regulatory commissions administer competitive regulations, while agencies housed in the cabinet departments administer most of the protective regulations. There are, however, exceptions to the rule that competitive regulation is administered by independent commissions and protective regulation is not. For example, the Consumer Product Safety Commission is an independent regulatory commission, but it administers a protective regulation.

A sixth difference relates to the statutes authorizing bureaucrats to regulate. Generally, competitive regulatory statutes are vague. Much discretion is given to bureaucrats to write rules specifying the policy in greater detail than that found in the statute. For instance, the ICC was given responsibility to regulate the railroads to serve the public interest. Among the powers that were granted to the ICC was setting the rates that the railroads could charge to shippers of goods and riders. Legislation required that the ICC set "just and reasonable" rates, but legislators did not specify what they meant by the term *just and reasonable* in the legislative grant to the ICC. Thus, it was up to the ICC to determine if the rates that it set met the standard.

In contrast, laws creating protective regulations are often more specific. For example, the Clean Air Act and its amendments require the EPA to meet certain goals, including that certain air-quality standards should be met by a specific point in time. Further, the kind of technology that the EPA can force polluters to acquire is also specified in the statutes. Economic regulatory bureaucrats have much discretion in their work, but protective regulatory bureaucrats are often required by law to do certain things in certain ways. They have much less discretion.

The type of decision making and analysis that bureaucrats use is another difference between competitive and protective regulation. Generally, competitive regulation employs legal and economic analysis. In contrast, protective regulation relies more heavily on scientific and technological analysis, risk assessment, and some forms of economic analysis, in particular, cost-benefit analysis.

Competitive regulation has depended on two types of specialized analysis techniques, legal analysis and economic analysis. Legal analysis derived from the basic process of competitive regulation in the independent commissions, which follows an adversarial, case-based, legal style. Thus, competitive regulatory proceedings are often courtlike. One reason for this development, which began at the ICC in its early days, was to create a framework and mode of decision making that the ICC could defend in court, since the federal courts were granted the power to review ICC decisions. Making ICC regulatory decisions legally defensible under statutory and constitutional provisions became one strategy to secure the place and role of the ICC and its decisions.

Economic analysis has also been important to competitive regulation. The style of economic analysis that competitive regulators use derives from classical market theories. The major difference, however, is that markets exist only partially under regulation. Competitive regulatory economics, thus, has to estimate marketlike behavior in the absence of complete market competition. The kinds of questions that are often raised include: What are reasonable profit levels? What profit levels are necessary to attract investment capital? What kinds of rates and rate structures will promote efficient use of the regulated enterprise?

Protective regulation relies more heavily on other kinds of analysis. Among the most important is scientific analysis. Scientific analysis is important, for instance, in the case of environmental regulation, where it is used to determine the harmful effects of pollutants. It makes little sense to regulate emissions and discharges that pose no danger to life, health, and/or the environment. Along with scientific analysis, risk assessment is often employed. Again, using the case of environmental regulation, risk assessment determines how much harm may be incurred at different levels of pollution. A pollutant with a known harmful effect may be relatively harmless at low levels but cause greater harm at higher levels. Determining how much exposure to the pollutant is acceptable is one important element of risk analysis.

Public and interest group participation, as well as the consequences of that participation, is different for competitive and protective regulation. There is often little public participation in competitive regulation at either the legislative or bureaucratic stages, though exceptions to this rule exist. Public participation tends to be greater in protective regulation. This is in part because groups that represent the interests of the public or consumers—public interest groups—have been more active in protective than in competitive regulation. That increased activity is in part a function of how important the general public thinks the regulatory problem is and how much impact the regulatory problem has on large numbers of people. In general, the public is more likely to be concerned about protective regulatory problems, like the environment, than about competitive regulatory problems, like the price of airline tickets. Further, the impact of regulatory problems on masses of ordinary people may be greater for many protective regulatory problems than for competitive regulatory ones.

In contrast, narrow organized interests, often called interest groups or special interests, participate in all manner of considerations of regulatory problems. The potential impact of regulation on special interests stimulates this participation. Although it may not matter to many airline customers if airline tickets rise a nominal amount per ticket, the aggregation of these nominal increases over large numbers of tickets may represent huge sums of money to airlines. Similarly, protective regulations can impose great costs on an industry, stimulating participation in protective regulatory proceedings.

The imbalance in participation between public and special interests can affect regulatory policies. Where public participation is low, regulatory policies may tend to benefit special interests more. Thus, many studies observe that competitive regulation often serves the interests of the entities being regulated, in spite of statutory language stating that the regulation should be in the public interest. The phenomenon of special interests being served by regulation is called **interest group capture.** The relative involvement of public interest groups in protective regulation has limited the potential for capture.[30]

The style of debate between competitive and protective regulations also differs. Protective regulation is often debated in ideological terms. This means that the believers in protective regulation often view the policy in moralistic terms and are unwilling to find suitable compromise positions. Protective regulatory issues become matters of principle. Thus, many want to protect the environment no matter the cost.

Competitive regulation, with its emphasis on financial cost, lends itself more easily to compromise. It is easier to split the difference over financial concerns than it is to compromise on matters of principle. Competitive regulatory debates are, thus, less ideological. This difference may be narrowing in recent years, as deregulators have attacked competitive and protective regulations alike for their ill effects on the economy. Deregulators may have converted both types of regulatory issues into economic issues, changing the terms of debate and people's reactions to the policies.

Finally, the relationship between the states and localities and the federal government differs between the two types of regulation. Generally, subnational governments have more freedom to regulate as they wish in competitive than in protective regulation. In protective regulation, the federal government often creates national standards, allowing state implementation of protective regulatory laws only if the states can match or exceed federal standards. Still, at times, federal policies affect state and local implementation of competitive regulations, too. For example, under the recent 1992 law reregulating cable television, localities may regulate subscription rates for local cable service, but they have to do it under the review and guidance of the FCC.

THE ADMINISTRATION OF REGULATORY POLICY

Regulatory policy is administered by bureaucrats. As we mentioned earlier, two types of regulatory agencies are most common, the independent regulatory commissions (IRCs) and offices within the cabinet departments. The ICC, FTC, CPSC, and FCC are examples of the former, whereas OSHA, which is located in the Department of Labor, is an example of the latter. Sometimes an independent agency is located within a cabinet department, such as FERC, a component of the Department of Energy. Also, agencies with nonindependent status that are comparable to cabinet departments may also have regulation as their primary goal. The best known of these is the EPA. In this section, we review what regulatory bureaucrats do and discuss the structure of IRCs.[31]

Independent Regulatory Commissions

The first federal IRC was the Interstate Commerce Commission, which was created in 1887. The ICC was modeled on state commissions then in existence whose job it was to regulate the railroads. The independent commission was designed to limit political control of regulation, as well as to create a foundation for bureaucratic expertise in regulatory matters. However, when Congress set out to design the ICC for political independence, the legislature did not aim to limit *congressional* influence over the ICC but partially to insulate the ICC from both partisan and presidential politics and influence.

Independent commissions have always been considered by Congress to be arms of the legislature, unlike the cabinet bureaucracy, which is formally part of the executive. Congress has always felt protective about the IRCs because their main function is to regulate industries that are often important economic elements of members' districts. Legislators want to ensure that the regulatory commissions do not interfere with their ability to get election support from these important local interests. Thus, unlike traditional cabinet bureaucracies, the IRCs are designed to limit presidential and partisan influence while ensuring congressional influence.[32]

We can see this in the structure of the IRC. First, unlike traditional bureaucracies, in which one person sits on top and is given the job of administrator, director, or cabinet secretary, a multimember collegial body, known as a board or commission, runs the IRC. Commissions usually have an odd number of seats, most commonly three, five, or seven. The commission is formally bipartisan, with party ratios set so that the president's party can have no more than a majority of one. Thus, on a five-member commission, the president's party can claim three seats. Table 10.2 lists the major structural characteristics of IRCs.

Commissioners also serve staggered terms, with term lengths longer than the president's four-year term. Thus, each president will inherit commissioners appointed by the previous incumbent, and it may take several years before the president is able to appoint a majority of commissioners. Typically, each year one seat opens up.

As he does with other important government posts, the president nominates candidates to the commissions, and the Senate holds confirmation power. The president, however, is allowed to name the chair of the commission. The chair can come from the ranks of those already serving or from a new appointment. This is an important appointment because the chair manages the entire IRC and is responsible for budgetary and other administrative decisions. The chair is very often "first among equals."

But presidential influence is curtailed in that the president cannot remove a commissioner from office as he can appointees in his administration and cabinet. Removal must come from Congress through an impeachment process. Presidential control over IRC personnel at the commission level, thus, is modest compared to the power that the president holds over other high-level administrators and bureaucrats.

Last, presidential budgetary control over IRCs is limited because the IRC submits its budget request to the Office of Management and Budget and to Congress simultaneously. Other agencies submit their requests to the OMB, which can then modify the request as it sees fit. Congress learns of the agency

TABLE 10.2 Major Structural Characteristics of Independent Regulatory Commissions

1. Bipartisan, with party seat ratios defined.
2. President's party can have a majority of one.
3. Commissioners serve staggered terms that are longer than the president's four-year term.
4. President nominates and Senate confirms.
5. President can name the chair of the commission.
6. President cannot remove commissioners from office; removal is by Congress.
7. IRC sends budget request to the OMB and Congress simultaneously.

request through the president's budget, but it learns about the IRC budget request directly from the commission. Thus, Congress has unfiltered information from the IRC concerning its budgetary needs.

Structure of Regulatory Agencies

Regulatory agencies of any stripe, be they independent commissions or units of cabinet departments, essentially carry out the same three major functions: **rulemaking, enforcement,** and **adjudication.** It is common, then, to find within each regulatory body a rulemaking bureau, an enforcement bureau, and an adjudication bureau. Figure 10.1 diagrams the formal internal structure of regulatory agencies.

The rulemaking bureaus design the basic rules and regulations for the regulatory agency.[33] Often the agency depends on its experts, whether they are lawyers, economists, or scientists, to write its rules and regulations. The rulemaking bureaus will, for example, design rates that interstate pipeline companies can charge to oil and gas companies that want to transport their energy sources through the pipelines. Sometimes the rulemaking bureaus are called ratemaking bureaus when their major task is so assigned. Also, the rulemaking bureaus do not possess the authority to implement the rules and regulations; that power is granted to the commission or administrator.

The process of making rules and regulations is governed under the **Administrative Procedure Act (APA),** which was passed in 1946. That piece of legislation tells agencies what they must do to make rules and regulations. The aim of the legislation was to systematize rulemaking procedures across agencies and specify a set of expectations and rights associated with rulemaking. Furthermore, the rulemaking process was designed to mimic the judicial process. This was done to ensure citizen procedural and civil rights and to limit challenges to agency rulemaking on procedural grounds.

The broad outlines of the APA require each agency to publicize beforehand its intention to write a rule or regulation. This public notification is accomplished through publication in the **Federal Register,** a publication on the activities of government, including government regulation. On such notification, interested parties are allowed to comment on the proposed regulation. Comments may be submitted in writing or in some circumstances by testifying before a hearing on the proposal. This process of publication and comment is called the "notice and comment" period. After the specified time period, and following the procedures outlined, the agency can issue its rule or regulation.

Once regulations are in place, they must be enforced. This is done through the enforcement bureau, which is sometimes called the investigations bureau. Much enforcement activity takes place through government inspection of financial documents that regulated firms must provide. Other inspection may take place in the field. For instance, the EPA may visit manufacturing sites to test for pollution emissions and runoff from production processes. The OSHA regularly visits workplaces to inspect for compliance with workplace safety standards. Health inspectors visit restaurants to check for cleanliness and compliance with health guidelines.

Violators may be sanctioned or punished. Many punishments for noncompliance or regulatory avoidance exist, and there is no uniform standard across agencies. Some agencies, like the Securities and Exchange Commission, may begin criminal prosecutions for some violations, like insider trading. More commonly, monetary fines are imposed on violators, while in other circumstances licenses to operate may be suspended or revoked.

A person or firm that has been sanctioned by the enforcement-inspection bureau may appeal the sanction to the agency's adjudication bureau, which is often called the administrative law court. The first stage in the appeal process usually requires both the appellant and a member of the enforcement staff to appear before a hearing examiner to present their cases. The hearing examiner is an agency employee. If the appellant does not like the hearing examiner's decision, the case may be appealed before an administrative law judge of the agency's administrative law court. Again, the administrative law judge is an agency employee. Finally, within the agency, the case may be appealed to the commission or administrator.

As a last resort, the appellant may take his or her or its case into the federal court system, which is normally given jurisdiction over agency decisions.

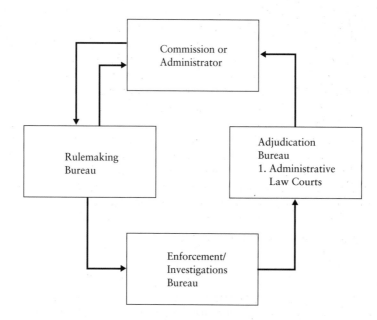

FIGURE 10.1 The Structure of Regulatory Agencies

That process usually begins in the District of Columbia Court of Appeals, located in Washington, D.C. Courts traditionally defer to agencies, except when agencies violate processes, overstep their legislative mandates, or do not take actions required by law. Environmentalists have taken the EPA to court on many occasions to force the agency to implement regulations.[34]

Regulatory agencies, especially IRCs, are sometimes called "quasi" agencies, because their rulemaking, enforcement, and adjudicating responsibilities parallel the responsibilities of the three branches of government. Regulatory agencies are thus quasi-legislative, quasi-executive, and quasi-judicial.

CONCLUSION

Regulation is a common activity of modern governments. Governments regulate economic behavior when markets fail or for equity reasons. Although all regulation is an imposition on behavior, some regulation aims at narrow economic behaviors, which we call economic regulation, whereas other regulation focuses on risks that derive from modern industrial practices, which we call social regulation. However, not all cases of market failure result in economic regulation, nor are all social risks regulated. Moreover, sometimes government decides to abandon regulations, to deregulate. Politics is a major factor in determining what is regulated and why regulations change, why they are enforced more or less strictly over time, and why we replace regulation with deregulation. These are the topics of the next chapter.

Key Terms

adjudication
Administrative
    Procedure Act
    (APA)
allocation of scarce
    resources
competitive
economic regulation
enforcement
exit and entry
    controls

Federal Register
incentives
inelastic demand
interest group
    capture
natural monopolies
pollution credits
positive
    externalities
predatory pricing
price controls

productive
    inefficiency
protective
regulatory policy
    instruments
rulemaking
social regulation
spillover effects
standard setting
unnatural
    monopolies

Explore the Web

The federal web locator can be used to find a federal agency's web page merely by typing in its name (http://www.law.vill.edu/Fed-Agency/ Fedwebloc.html). Of the major independent regulatory commissions, the Securities and Exchange Commission is located at http://www.sec.gov/, the Federal Communications Commission at http://www.ftc.gov/, the Federal Trade Commission at http://www.ftc.gov/, the National Labor Relations Board at http://www.nlrb.gov/, the Nuclear Regulatory Commission at http://www.nrc.gov/, and the consumer Product Safety Commission at http://www.cpsc.gov/. Two other important regulatory agencies that are not independent regulatory commission are the Environmental Protection Agency (http://www.epa.gov/) and the Antitrust Division of the Department of Justice (http://www.usdoj.gov/atr).

Notes

1. On the breast implant case, see B. D. Daniel and Michael Weiss, "Implanting Fear: Commissioner David A. Kessler's Food and Drug Administration and Silicone Breast Implant Bans," *National Review,* October 9, 1995, 47–50.

2. Steve Lohr, "Justice Department in New Inquiry into Microsoft," *New York Times,* September 20, 1996, D1.

3. Coercion is a common element in definitions of regulation. See Theodore J. Lowi, "American Business, Public Policy, Case Studies, and Political Theory," *World Politics* 16 (1964): 677–715, and "Four Systems of Policy, Politics, and Choice," *Public Administration Review* 32 (1972): 298–310; Barry M. Mitnick, *The Political Economy of Regulation: Creating, Designing, and Removing Regulatory Forms* (New York: Columbia University Press, 1980); Randall B. Ripley and Grace A. Franklin, *Policy Implementation and Bureaucracy,* 2d ed. (Chicago: Dorsey, 1986); and Alan Stone, *Regulation and Its Alternatives* (Washington, DC: CQ Press, 1982).

4. In recent years, regulators have been trying to lessen the coercive aspects of regulation in some policy areas. Thus, incentive and market-style decision making has been incorporated in regulation, especially environmental regulation. We have more to say about this later.

5. For a general discussion of policy instruments, see B. Guy Peters, *American Public Policy: Promise and Performance,* 3d ed. (Chatham, NJ: Chatham House, 1993), 5–10.

6. A good discussion is found in Mitnick, *The Political Economy of Regulation,* 396–415.

7. The abandonment policy of the ICC is discussed in Richard P. Barke, "Economic Regulation and the Body Politic: Congress and the Interstate Commerce Commission," in *The Political Economy of Public Policy,* eds. Alan Stone and Edward J. Harpham (Beverly Hills, CA: Sage, 1992), 163–185.

8. Standard setting is discussed more thoroughly in Mitnick, *The Political Economy of Regulation,* 401–404.

9. For FCC allocation policies, see Erwin G. Krasnow, Lawrence D. Longley, and Herbert A. Terry, *The Politics of Broadcast Regulation,* 3d ed. (New York: St. Martin's, 1982).

10. The use of incentives for regulation is discussed in Mitnick, *The Political Economy of Regulation,* 364–395.

11. On agricultural regulation, see Kenneth J. Meier, *Regulation: Politics, Bureaucracy, and Economics* (New York: St. Martin's, 1985), 119–138.

12. For a review of this type of incentive policy as it pertains to environmental pollution, see A. Myrick Freeman, III, "Economics, Incentives, and Environmental Regulation," in *Environmental Policy in the 1920s,* 2d ed., eds. Norman J. Vig and Michael E. Kraft (Washington, DC: CQ Press, 1994), 189–208.

13. A very good discussion of market failure is found in David L. Weimer and Aidan R. Vining, *Policy Analysis: Concepts and Practice* (Englewood Cliffs, NJ: Prentice-Hall, 1989), 29–93. A less technical discussion is found in Stone, *Regulation and Its Alternatives,* 61–166.

14. The story of Standard Oil is told in Daniel Yergin, *The Prize: The Epic Quest for Oil, Money, and Power* (New York: Simon & Schuster, 1991).

15. A mathematical example may help some understand this point. In the monopolized market, the monopoly firm can charge $C + P + n$, where C is the cost of producing the good, P is the expected profit, and n is the extra profit that it charges because there is no competition. In the competitive market, the same firm now charges $C - P - n$. That is, it offers the good at less than the cost to produce it. Its competitors have two options. One, they can match the price, but they cannot do this for long. Companies that sell goods at less than cost eventually go bankrupt. Or the competitor does not have to match the price, perhaps selling at C (or $C + P$). Doing so, however, will cause the competitor to lose customers to the predatory monopolist, and eventually the competitor will go out of business.

16. Richard Lehne, *Industry and Politics: The United States in Comparative Perspective* (Englewood Cliffs, NJ: Prentice-Hall, 1993), 110–111.

17. More on natural monopolies can be found in Stone, *Regulation and Its Alternatives,* 68–74.

18. See Alan Stone, *Public Service Liberalism: Telecommunications and Transitions in Public Policy* (Princeton, NJ: Princeton University Press, 1991).

19. This is discussed in Anthony Brown, *The Politics of Airline Deregulation* (Knoxville: University of Tennessee Press, 1987).

20. On the new food labeling requirements, see Pam Black, "Dietary Info That's Easier to Digest: New Food and Drug Administration Nutrition Labeling Standards," *Business Week,* March 21, 1994, 119.

21. See Stone, *Regulation and Its Alternatives,* 91–124, for a more extended discussion of externalities.

22. On the regulation of cigarettes and tobacco, see A. Lee Fritschler, *Smoking and Politics: Policymaking and the Federal Bureaucracy,* 3d ed. (Englewood Cliffs, NJ: Prentice-Hall, 1983).

23. Weimer and Vining, *Policy Analysis*, 89–93.

24. This discussion follows from Stone, *Regulation and Its Alternatives;* Jeffrey E. Cohen, *The Politics of Telecommunications Regulation: The States and the Divestiture of AT&T* (Armonk, NY: Sharpe, 1992); Alan Stone, *Wrong Number: The Breakup of AT&T* (New York: Basic Books, 1989); and Paul Teske, *After Divestiture: The Political Economy of State Telecommunications Regulation* (Albany: State University of New York Press, 1990).

25. On the history and development of telephone regulation, see Cohen, *The Politics of Telecommunications Regulation*, 17–78.

26. This system is described in Larry N. Gerston, Cynthia Fraleigh, and Robert Schwab, *The Deregulated Society* (Pacific Grove, CA: Brooks/Cole, 1988), 85–114.

27. For more on political rationales for regulation, see Michael D. Reagan, *Regulation: The Politics of Policy* (Boston: Little, Brown, 1987), 34–43; and Kenneth J. Meier, *Regulation: Politics, Bureaucracy, and Economics*, 6–7.

28. This distinction was first proposed by Ripley and Franklin, *Policy Implementation and Bureaucracy*, 116–176. It has been used through the literature. See also Reagan, *Regulation*, 45–71, 85–11.

29. A good, brief introduction to the history of regulation in the United States is found in Gerston et al., *The Deregulated Society*, 19–39.

30. Interest group capture has been a major theme of research on regulation. Early and important statements of the theory are found in Marver H. Bernstein, *Regulating Business by Independent Commission* (Princeton, NJ: Princeton University Press, 1955); and Samuel P. Huntington, "The Marasmus of the ICC," in *Bureaucratic Power in National Politics,* ed. Francis E. Rourke (Boston: Little, Brown, 1965). A good review of the idea is found in Mitnick, *The Political Economy of Regulation*, 206–241.

31. Reagan, *Regulation*, 45–71, is very good on these points.

32. See Louis Fisher, *The Politics of Shared Power: Congress and the Executive*, 3d ed. (Washington, DC: CQ Press, 1993), 119–144.

33. Regulatory rulemaking is the topic of Cornelius M. Kerwin, *Rulemaking: How Government Agencies Write Law and Make Policy* (Washington, DC: CQ Press, 1994). A concise introduction is Stone, *Regulation and Its Alternatives*, 197–236.

34. On this, see R. Shep Melnick, *Regulation and the Courts* (Washington, DC: Brookings, 1983); and Rosemary O'Leary, *Environmental Change: Federal Courts and the EPA* (Philadelphia, PA: Temple University Press, 1993).

11

Regulatory Policy II: From Regulation to Deregulation

F OR SEVERAL years prior to 1992, consumer advocates had been trying to persuade Congress to reregulate the cable television companies. They argued that the cost of subscription to cable services had skyrocketed in the years since 1984, when Congress deregulated cable. That legislation prohibited local regulators from setting cable prices. As a consequence, cable companies, which generally held local monopolies, raised rates at a pace much faster than the inflation rate. Those who wanted to bring cable companies back under price regulation claimed that local cable providers were in effect monopolies that were gouging the public.[1]

Cable rate reregulation made little progress until 1992, when regulatory advocates decided to expand the issue. Broadcasters and other providers of cable programming were not being paid by the cable companies for their programming. In effect, cable companies could "rebroadcast" for free. Advocates of reregulation rallied broadcasting interests to their side by including a provision in their reregulation bill to force cable companies to pay rebroadcasting fees. This move broke the logjam that had stopped the progress of the cable reregulation bill, and in September, Congress passed reregulatory legislation that not only allowed local regulators to set cable prices for customers, under FCC supervision, but also required cable companies to pay rebroadcasting fees.

President Bush vetoed the legislation.[2] He claimed that reregulation would hurt consumers and limit the growth of the cable industry, that it was but another example of poorly conceived federal regulation. Bush's veto came just as the presidential campaign was gearing up for the final phase before the vote in November, and it catapulted the issue into the national spotlight, making cable reregulation a campaign issue. Democrats, who controlled both houses of

Congress, saw a chance to damage the sitting Republican president's reelection effort. Displaying strong party loyalty, and with many defections from Republicans, who worried about the political implications of opposing reregulation in an election year, Bush's veto was overridden. This was the only veto that was overridden during Bush's tenure.

This cable case illustrates several themes that we will develop in this chapter. First, political interests are important in determining whether to regulate or deregulate. These political interests also have considerable impact on the way that regulation is implemented. There are, in other words, both winners and losers when government decides to regulate. Moreover, in recent years presidents have become more involved in regulation than in the past. These themes, plus the history of regulation and the rise of the deregulatory movement, are the topics of this chapter.

REGULATORY WAVES

Although the emphasis on the benefits and costs of regulation require us to look at each individual regulation and regulatory agency to understand its origins, most new regulations have come in three waves.[3] The first wave is associated with the Progressive era at the turn of the twentieth century. The second major wave occurred with the New Deal in the 1930s. The third wave, an offshoot of Lyndon Johnson's Great Society, came in the late 1960s and early 1970s. Other new regulations have been issued outside of these waves, of course, but they are fewer in number.

The three waves are identifiable not only because of the number of regulations initiated during those years, but because each wave had an underlying theme.[4] That is, certain characteristics were common to the regulations passed during each wave. The regulations passed during each wave tend to be inspired by the same outlook concerning government regulation, sharing a common method of attacking a problem that the public and policymakers feel is in need of a regulatory solution.

The Progressive Regulations

During the end of the nineteenth century, the federal government began its experiment with regulation. The first national regulatory body was the Interstate Commerce Commission (ICC), which was created by the Interstate Commerce Act, passed by Congress in 1887.[5] The ICC was charged with regulating the railroads, the dominant industry in the last quarter of the nineteenth century.

Railroad regulation began at the state level during the years just after the Civil War. In many states, especially those in the Midwest, like Kansas and Wisconsin, members of a grassroots protest movement called the Granger movement were voted into office.[6] The Grangers were primarily farmers who felt threatened by the large, new industrial concerns of the age, especially the railroads. As a part of their policy program, they instituted independent regulatory commissions, sometimes called public utility commissions, to regulate the railroads and other industries, like grain elevator companies, where grain was stored and loaded onto the rails.[7] Also supporting the Grangers were the Populists, people who came from all backgrounds but were fearful of the power of corporations and other moneyed interests, of politicians thought to be in cahoots with the moneyed interests, of intellectuals, and of people of privilege and high position in society.

Railroad pricing policies deeply affected farmers and residents of the nation's interior, especially in the smaller towns. To get their goods to market, farmers relied on the railroads, but because the small towns that they lived near tended to be served by only one railroad, they were at the mercy of potential railroad monopolists. Shippers of goods from the East to the West often had an advantage, in part because they could contract with many different, competing railroads but also because of special arrangements that they made with the railroads. Some heavy shippers, like the oil, coal, and steel companies, were given secret rebates by the railroads who wanted to carry their goods.

Publicly, these heavy shippers were charged a rate comparable to others, but the railroads secretly returned some of the money that the shippers paid them. This gave the appearance that big shippers were being treated just like others, but they were really being given lower prices. When knowledge of these secret rebate schemes became public, antagonism toward the railroads and other large industrial concerns of the age was fueled.

States attempted to regulate the railroads until 1886, when the Supreme Court issued the *Wabash* decision, which prohibited the states from regulating interstate commerce. Immediately, the structure of state regulation of the railroads that had been built up over the previous decade was rendered useless. But many voters and legislators believed the need for regulation still existed. The federal government filled the void with the **Interstate Commerce Act** the following year. This act was a landmark, not only because it signaled the beginning of federal regulation of the economy but also because a new federal entity was created, the independent regulatory commission.

A few years later, in 1890, Congress passed another landmark piece of regulatory legislation, the **Sherman Antitrust Act.** That act created the Antitrust Division of the Department of Justice, which was given the duty of regulating monopolistic behavior across the economy. In the ensuing years, other regulatory legislation was passed, creating new regulatory bodies and giving existing regulatory agencies expanded powers. Government antitrust capability was enhanced in 1914 with the passage of the **Clayton Antitrust Act** and the **Federal Trade Act,** which created the Federal Trade Commission.

Underlying the regulation of the Progressive era was faith in the idea of a competitive market. To the Progressives, regulation was to be used to create marketlike results, to try to simulate a market. This goal was to be accomplished through administrative agencies, often in the form of IRCs, whose personnel would be experts about regulatory matters. Thus, the Progressives combined beliefs in markets, government activism, and expertise.[8]

The New Deal Regulations

The second wave of regulation came in the 1930s as part of Franklin Roosevelt's New Deal. The New Deal regulations had some similarities with the regulations of the Progressives, especially in regard to faith in government, the role of experts, and reliance on the IRCs, but the rationale and aims of these regulations differed markedly from the Progressive variety.

The New Deal regulations were more concerned with stabilizing the depressed economy and with stimulating growth in economic sectors. Although abuses associated with monopoly and unfair competitive practices were of concern to New Dealers, these problems did not hold the same high priority in creating regulatory policies that they had for the Progressives.

One important goal of the New Deal regulations was to try to restore confidence in the nation's financial institutions, which were critical in solving the problems associated with declining growth during the Depression. Thus, the Securities and Exchange Commission (SEC) was established in 1934. The task of the SEC was to regulate the buying and selling of securities and stocks, to prohibit insider information, and to provide consumers with better information about stock market transactions. **Insider information** is information that people, especially those who work for a corporation or are involved in trading corporate stock shares and securities, have access to about corporate dealings that is not open to the public. Regulations prohibit the use of this information because it provides unfair advantages to those with the information. The Federal Deposit Insurance Corporation (FDIC) was created to insure bank deposits and to regulate bank accounting and financial practices. The hope was to instill faith in the soundness of deposits and restore confidence in the nation's banks, many of which had failed during the early years of the Depression.[9]

A second goal of the New Deal regulations was to help new industries develop, providing a source of economic growth to the depressed economy. In 1934, the Federal Communications Commission (FCC) was created. The FCC was a comprehensive reform of an existing agency, the Federal Radio Commission, which was created in the late 1920s. The FCC, however, created a federal model for the regulation of all telecommunications, including telephone as well as radio. One aim of the FCC was to limit the granting of licenses to operators to ensure their profitability. Through this incentive, regulators hoped that the telecommunications sector of the economy would grow, helping the economy out of the Depression.

In a similar move, the Civil Aeronautics Board (CAB) was created in 1938 to regulate the airline industry. As with telecommunications, the airline industry was already under some federal regulation, but with the CAB, federal regulatory power was rationalized and expanded. The CAB set prices for airline travel and determined routes and schedules in an attempt to ensure profitability for the new industry, while also aiming to increase demand for airline services. Again, the goal was to help a new industry develop, one that not only would provide jobs but would also modernize the transportation system and thus make the economy more productive.

The Great Society and Social Regulation

Both the Progressive and New Deal waves of regulation were primarily economically focused, attacking one industry at a time, often in isolation from other industries. With the Great Society, a new, more radical departure in regulation commenced. A host of new regulations began to emerge in the middle and late 1960s, continuing into the mid-1970s. Lyndon Johnson and his Republican successor, Richard Nixon, sponsored many of these new regulatory efforts, and the Democratically controlled Congress often lent a sympathetic ear to them, as well as initiating many regulations on its own.

Great Society regulations were social in nature, rather than economic. Their aim was to reduce the risk of living in modern industrial society. Many of the Great Society regulations were very detailed, requiring specific kinds of bureaucratic action, unlike the Progressive and New Deal regulations, which allowed considerable discretion to regulatory bureaucrats. Moreover, the Great Society regulations usually focused on the entire economy, not on particular industrial sectors. As with the Progressive and New Deal regulations, however, strong public support existed for these regulatory efforts.

Three major substantive themes are evident in the Great Society regulations. The first is environmental. Environmental pollution became a major public issue in the mid-1960s. Several environmental disasters, like the Santa Barbara oil spill of 1969, plus scientific reports that generated media attention, were important in raising public concern about the environment. Health effects due to environmental pollutants, especially airborne particles, and degradation of waterways, the result of industrial and urban runoff, led the list of public environmental concerns. Air and water pollution legislation was passed by Congress, and a new regulatory agency, the Environmental Protection Agency (EPA), was created to implement the regulations.

A second substantive theme relates to consumer product safety. Originally, consumer protection advocates pushed for a cabinet department for consumer affairs, but heavy industry lobbying and resistance from President Nixon led to weaker legislation that created the Consumer Product Safety Commission (CPSC). The CPSC was one of the few IRCs established during this period. It was given jurisdiction over all consumer products except food and drugs, which were regulated by the Food and Drug Administration

(FDA). (The FDA dates back to the 1930s; it is one of the few social regulatory agencies created by an earlier regulatory wave.)

A third theme focuses on working conditions. In 1970, Congress established the Occupational Safety and Health Administration (OSHA) within the Department of Labor. The mandate for OSHA was to develop health and safety standards for the workplace and to inspect places of work for health and safety violations. Strongly supported by the labor movement, OSHA has been actively criticized by industry.

Each of these major social regulatory initiatives targeted the entire economy, not just one sector; this represents a major departure in the thrust of federal regulation. Moreover, they tended to focus on the risks associated with life in industrial society more than on economic behavior. Environmental protection, in particular, focused on externalities. The accumulation of these new regulations, and their increasing scope and cost, led in the late 1970s to protest, reaction, and political mobilization to reduce the regulatory burden.

THE ATTACK ON REGULATION: THE DEREGULATORY MOVEMENT

In the 1970s and 1980s, a wave of reform hit regulatory policy. During that period a number of deregulatory actions were taken, scaling back government regulation in a number of industries and economic sectors. This movement, supported by presidents and leaders of both parties, was based on the charge that regulation had led to a number of negative results or costs.[10]

One charge is that regulation is ineffective, that government cannot regulate effectively. This argument maintains that government cannot match the expertise that business has about its operations. Thus, government is less likely than business to make sound economic decisions. Examples of ineffective government regulation include efforts to help the ailing merchant marine industry. Despite government regulations, the industry had not rebounded, and its competitive position continues to erode compared to the merchant fleets of other nations.[11] Similarly, some critics claim that standard setting by the EPA and OSHA has not demonstrably reduced pollution or workplace accidents.

A second, related charge is that regulation has not worked as intended; instead, it has backfired. Here the argument is that regulated firms are intensely interested in what government does. Therefore, they mobilize their considerable resources to steer government policies to help them, rather than hurt them. Thus, the regulated take over their regulators, and regulatory policy helps the regulated. This is the interest group capture phenomenon we discussed in the previous chapter.

A classic example is the ICC. Some contend that for many years, railroad interests were able to guide ICC policy so that railroads were helped at the expense of truckers. In the end, consumers and shippers were hurt, as the railroad industry insulated itself from competitive pressures, the trucking industry was not able to develop effectively, and transportation charges were higher than they had to be.[12]

Similarly, telecommunications regulation at the FCC was criticized for being too preferential to AT&T, which then held a near monopoly in the provision of telephone service. Regulations prohibited other manufacturers from making telephone equipment, which, critics charged, kept equipment prices high and limited innovation and consumer choice. Moreover, lack of service competition, especially in long distance, artificially inflated prices.

A third critique follows from the second; regulation corrupts government. Interest group capture can be viewed as a form of corruption, since when it occurs, policy implementation does not follow from what legislators intended. On a narrower level, potential corruption and/or misuse of office may arise as regulated interests hold out the lure of a future job in the regulated industry to the regulators.[13] Regulators may then make decisions with an eye on how those decisions will be seen by potential future employers rather than on the public interest.

A fourth criticism of regulation points to its intrusiveness. Libertarians, especially, see government regulation as heavy-handed. Freedom of choice is limited under regulation; this is part of the character of regulatory policy.

The first four criticisms focus on government and its operations. Another set of criticisms looks at the impact of regulation on the economy. The first economic criticism of regulation considers its costs. Two factors are looked at, the actual increased costs of government and the costs of regulatory compliance.

Almost every time that government adds to its regulatory arsenal, it increases the size of government. New employees must be hired; sometimes new agencies are created. One way to estimate the cost of regulation is to look at these additional administrative costs of government.

A second cost of regulation is called compliance costs. **Compliance costs** are those additional costs that firms must pay to obey government regulations. One set of compliance costs involves the additional paperwork and forms that companies must submit to government and the additional employees and their work time required to fill out these forms. Other compliance costs involve new equipment necessary to meet pollution and workplace safety standards or alterations in protection techniques and processes.

Economists have tried to estimate the cost of regulations. For example, Murray L. Weidenbaum estimated the administrative costs of regulation in 1980 to be $6 billion and compliance costs to be $120 billion, for a grand total of $126 billion.[14] A more recent estimate by Thomas Hopkins suggested that compliance costs in 1992 totaled $564 billion.[15] There exists disagreement among economists about how and what to consider in making these estimates, and some contend that the figures are too high, yet there is agreement that regulation has costs.

Both administrative and compliance costs are considered to be dead weight losses. That is, businesses must pay these costs, but they do not add to the productivity of the company or to the economy; they raise the costs of producing goods without increasing their supply. This money could have been used to invest in new equipment or new products or to enhance worker training or other productivity-related ventures. If regulatory costs are large enough, they can slow economic growth and add to inflation, as some critics of regulation allege. Dead weight losses act like a tax that increases the cost of regulated goods. Consumers of regulated goods, thus, have less income to spend on other goods. Some demands will go unmet due to these costs of regulation.

Regulation may also interfere with economic efficiency through a problem known as regulatory lag. **Regulatory lag** is the time that regulation adds to the production process. All products must go through development and testing periods. Thus, there is always a gap between the idea of a new product and its market introduction. Regulation adds another stage in that process. This is especially the case with drugs and pharmaceuticals, which must meet standards of safety and effectiveness. To meet these standards, drugs must be tested, and evidence of safety and effectiveness submitted to the FDA. The testing may take years, and FDA approval may add still more years. One potential loss that may result from regulatory lag at the FDA is a person's life, when a life-saving drug is kept from the market. On the other hand, one of the aims of regulation is to keep drugs with dangerous side effects off of the market. As another example, the EPA requires environmental impact statements. Researching and writing these impact statements, the EPA review process, and the right of third parties to critique and comment on them adds time and cost to much plant construction, expansion, and even retooling.

Moreover, the regulatory review process may be used strategically by firms and their opponents. The process may be dragged out by submission of additional reports and by court suits from those who want to slow the process even further. Their aim is often to maintain the status quo for as long as possible. Thus, competing firms may use regulatory review to frustrate competitors' introduction of products, and environmentalists have often used delay tactics to inhibit construction, especially of nuclear power plants. Regulatory lag slows down the ability of firms to respond to market conditions. This lessens the efficiency of the economy.[16]

Another criticism of regulation is that its interference with competition reduces the ability and incentive for companies to innovate, to develop new products. Companies that are protected by regulation have few incentives to offer new products because regulation guarantees them a fixed profit, based on their operating expenses, and also protects their market share. Competition exposes companies to rivals who may cut into their markets and profits. Consider, for example, the customer telephone before and after federal deregulation. Now telephones can remember numbers called, can be attached to fax and answering machines, may be cordless, and so on. All of these innovations resulted from relaxing regulatory controls over telephones. During the regulatory era, AT&T had little reason to learn about customer demand and faced few rival products on the market; it had little incentive to upgrade, enhance, or make innovations in its customer telephones. Innovation and new products are also inhibited by the added costs associated with regulation, as previously mentioned. When regulatory costs are high, it may not be economical or profitable to introduce and develop new products.

The Rise of the Deregulators

Several factors favorable to those bent on deregulation converged in the 1970s.[17] First, the social disorder in the nation's urban centers and campuses in the 1960s, the Vietnam War, and Watergate all implicated government or exposed its seeming inability to deal with problems effectively. This created a situation in which the public mood turned against government. Deregulators effectively attached their program to the souring public mood, suggesting that the heavy hand of regulation was just another example of what was wrong with government.

Consumer advocates also lashed out against regulation, charging that many regulations limited consumer choice and cost consumers too much money. Thus, several political leaders often associated with the liberal end of the political spectrum, like Senator Edward Kennedy of Massachusetts, began to suggest deregulation as a solution to these problems. Kennedy's Senate committee held hearings on deregulation of the airlines, an important step in putting deregulation on the public agenda.

Economists, who had studied the effects of regulation for years, had determined that many regulations were detrimental to the regulated industries and to the economy as a whole. This economic evidence slipped into the public debate, legitimizing the position of the deregulators. Businesses with a stake in deregulation also mobilized their political resources. As you learned in Chapter 4, reform of the campaign finance laws in 1974 allowed businesses to contribute money to political action committees (PACs), which could in turn contribute to election campaigns. Thus, for the first time, businesses had an open and legal method for making campaign contributions. The number of business PACs skyrocketed in the late 1970s, contributing tens of millions of dollars to election campaigns.

Business was not, however, uniformly opposed to regulation. Many companies benefited from it and actively opposed deregulatory efforts aimed at them. Thus, AT&T resisted efforts to deregulate the telephone industry, and many airlines fought against deregulation of their industry, as did some trucking firms and railroads. Business was more united, however, against the social regulations that were implemented in the 1960s and 1970s. Then

OSHA came under heavy attack, and the CPSC nearly failed to be reauthorized and ultimately had its mandate weakened. The Reagan administration also tried to scale back the EPA's activities, though this attempt was short lived, as public and congressional support stopped the deregulatory attack on that agency.

Last, overregulation was cited as a reason for the decline in the macroeconomy, the stagflation of the mid-1970s, the drop in productivity growth, and the loss of markets, both domestic and international, to foreign competitors. The deregulators successfully attached their notions to these macroeconomic concerns, catapulting deregulation into the world of public opinion politics. Public support was critical in the success of the deregulatory movement.

What Is Deregulation?

Deregulation is a catchall term. On a basic level, it means stepping back from government regulation, but it can be done in several ways. Just as there are several types of regulation and regulatory instruments, so there are several different ways to deregulate.

The most extreme approach to deregulation is to replace government regulatory decisions and policies with market decisions and policies. The deregulatory movement resulted in one example of government regulation replaced by the free market: airline deregulation. Economic regulation of the airline industry was completely removed, and the agency that had overseen regulation of the airlines, the Civil Aeronautics Board, was dismantled by 1980. The only regulations of the airlines left in place concerned safety, regulations that the CAB did not administer. Airline safety was a concern of the Federal Aviation Administration.

A second approach to deregulation is partial replacement of government policy with market mechanisms. This is the approach often found in the deregulatory legislation of the 1970s and 1980s. For example, interest ceilings on demand deposits that banks and savings and loans could pay to depositors was lifted, but reserve requirements, though lowered, remained in place. Restrictions on the program content of television broadcasts was reduced, though broadcasters still had to secure licenses from the FCC to operate.

A third approach to deregulation is to reduce government regulatory effort. Here regulations are not removed, but enforcement rates are slowed, penalties are made less severe, fewer new rules are written, and compliance standards are made easier to meet. For instance, the Paperwork Reduction Act of 1980 made it easier and less costly for people and firms to comply with and fill out federal forms.[18]

A fourth form of deregulation is the application of new styles of economic analysis when deciding whether to regulate. The major theme here is to bring into the decision-making process information about the greater economic consequences of regulation, not merely information on the effectiveness of regulation. The most important of these analytic tools is **cost-benefit analysis.** Cost-benefit is an analysis technique. Although technical and sometimes quite complex, its underlying theory is straightforward and simple. Basically, cost-benefit analysis in regulation estimates the costs of the regulation, for instance, jobs lost, and compares the costs with the benefits of the regulation, say, illnesses avoided. Both the costs and benefits are set in monetary terms. If the cost is greater than the benefit, theory tells one not to implement the regulation. If, however, the benefits are greater than the costs, then the regulation, under this type of logic, can be implemented. Through an executive order, President Reagan forced regulators to use cost-benefit analysis when deciding on new regulatory rules.

Other types of economic analysis with potential deregulatory implications include inflation and growth impact analysis. During the Ford administration, some attempts were made to judge the impact regulation might have on inflation with the idea of halting new regulations that were excessively inflationary. Similarly, economic growth impact analysis asks whether a regulation significantly harms economic growth. If it does, the regulation might not proceed. Analysis of the impact on economic growth was also a theme of the Reagan years.

A fifth type of deregulation is the transfer of regulatory authority from the federal government to the states. The states then can decide to fill the regulatory gap or not. The transfer of authority from the national to local governments is called **devolution,** and it was another deregulatory strategy of the Reagan administration. Here the scaling back of regulatory sweep is mostly a federal phenomenon. If the states fill in where the federal government has left, it is possible that no regulatory reduction will occur.

A sixth type of deregulation is the substitution of directive and "command and control" policies with incentive modes of affecting behavior. Incentive approaches allow market mechanisms to stay in place, but private decision makers still must take into account these government incentives when deciding what to do. The advantages of incentive systems, according to their advocates, are that greater freedom of choice is allowed, less government coercion is applied, and less government bureaucracy is needed, thus lowering the cost and imposition of government on people. We illustrated incentives approaches in environmental pollution policies in the previous chapter.

A type of incentive program has been adopted by many states in the pricing of utilities, like power and telephones. Traditionally, utility pricing has been based on rate of return regulation, which allows utilities to recoup a certain percentage after costs. Public utility commissions determine costs, and since aggregate return to the utility goes up with increases in the cost of operations, though the percentage return stays the same, it is in the interest of regulated utilities under rate of return pricing to increase their costs of operations.

Price cap regulation eliminates the rate of return, replacing it with an incentive system. Prices are capped by regulators at a certain level. If utilities reduce their cost of operation, they may, under price cap systems, keep all or part of the earnings, which in effect become recovered profits. Thus, utilities have an incentive to operate more efficiently and cost-effectively.

The Scope and Limits of Deregulation

Deregulatory efforts began to be implemented in the mid-1970s. By the mid-1980s, when the deregulatory movement had effectively ended, several key economic sectors had been deregulated, including banking and finance, transportation, and telecommunications. The first set of deregulations, in the late 1970s, were mostly legislative enactments. Other deregulations were effected by administrative means, stimulated by White House edicts and presidential executive orders. The most important of these were issued early in the Reagan administration. The courts also got into the deregulatory act, especially with regard to the divestiture of AT&T and ensuing deregulation of telephone communications.

Federal regulatory effort slowed during the deregulatory decade. By 1981, regulatory rule production had been cut considerably, as shown in Figure 11.1 by the decrease in the number of pages in the Federal Register, which publishes all federal regulations. By the end of the decade, regulatory rule production began to creep back up. Even so, regulatory effort in the late 1980s and into the 1990s did not reach the peak of the late 1970s, though it remained much higher than the levels of the mid-1960s, before the wave of Great Society regulations began to be implemented.

The ability of regulatory bureaucracies to write new regulations and enforce them was further slowed by diminishing bureaucratic capacity. Many agencies saw reduced budgets and smaller work forces. As you can see in Table 11.1, the ICC was reduced in size by about two-thirds, the FTC saw about one-half of its personnel removed, and the NLRB lost about one-fourth of its staff. Only the EPA and the NRC, both concerned with safety and environmental regulation, and the SEC, which grew along with the growth in the number and size of the stock exchanges, saw staff increases. Overall, the independent agencies, excluding the Postal Service, saw staff reductions of over one-half, from about 440,000 in 1980 to just over 185,000 in 1990.[19]

Deregulation did not end federal regulation, but it clearly reduced the amount of existing regulation and the pace of new regulations. In the process of rethinking the federal commitment to regulation, not only was regulation reformed but the role of the president was altered, too. The president became a major player in regulatory policy formulation and administration, where before he had been only an intermittent player. And regulation became an

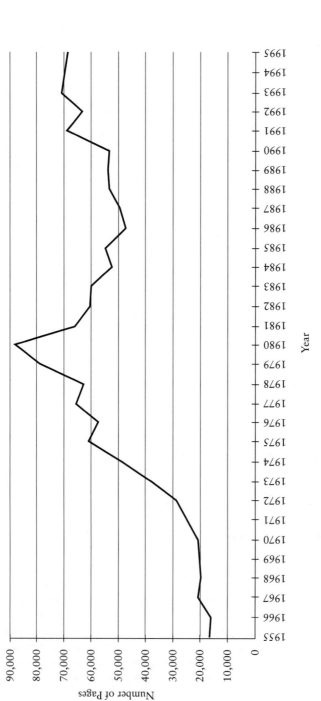

FIGURE 11.1 Number of Pages in the Federal Register, 1965–1998

Sources: Data for 1955–1992 adapted from Harold W. Stanley and Richard G. Niemi, *Vital Statistics on American Politics, 1997–1998* (Washington, DC: CQ Press, 1998), 258; and data for 1997–1998 adapted from the *Federal Register* (Washington, DC: U.S. Government Printing Office, 1997, 1998).

TABLE 11.1 Personnel Size of Major Independent Regulatory Commissions, 1980, 1986, 1990, and 1996

Agency	1980	1986	1990	1996	Percent Change, 1980–1996
Civil Aeronautics Board	734	0	0	0	−100.0
Environmental Protection Agency	14,715	14,081	18,360	17,160	+16.6
Federal Communications Commission	2,244	1,835	1,872	2,069	−7.8
Federal Trade Commission	1,846	1,129	993	941	−49.0
Interstate Commerce Commission*	1,998	809	627	0	−100.0
National Labor Relations Board	2,936	2,437	2,199	1,970	−32.9
Nuclear Regulatory Commission	3,283	3,587	3,564	3,148	−4.1
Securities and Exchange Commission	2,056	1,905	2,610	2,838	+38.0

*In 1996, the ICC was replaced by the Surface Transportation Board, an agency of the Department of Transportation.

Sources: Data for 1980 and 1986 adapted from Gary King and Lyn Ragsdale, *The Elusive Executive: Discovering Statistical Patterns in the Presidency* (Washington, DC: CQ Press, 1988); data for 1990 adapted from Lyn Ragsdale, *Vital Statistics on the Presidency: Washington to Clinton* (Washington, DC: CQ Press, 1995), 280; and data for 1996 adapted from Lyn Ragsdale, *Vital Statistics on the Presidency: Washington to Clinton,* rev. ed. (Washington, DC: CQ Press, 1998), 287.

important policy concern of presidents, where before it had only been a minor interest.

PRESIDENTS AND REGULATION

Until the mid-1970s, presidents were only sporadically interested in regulation. At times a regulatory issue would appear on the political agenda that interested a president, but in general presidents tended not to make regulation a major element of their legislative programs. Nor were they very interested in the administration of regulations.[20] In the 1970s this changed, and regulation moved up in presidential priority. To understand this change, we must look at presidential incentives and the transformation of regulation. Then we will look at attempts to bring regulatory policy under greater presidential control.

Presidential Incentives and Regulation

The modern presidency grew out of the events of the 1930s, especially the Depression and the election of Franklin Roosevelt. Among the defining characteristics of the modern president are his enhanced role as policy leader, the accumulation of staff resources to help in that policy leadership role, increasing public expectations about presidential policy leadership, and the development of public opinion as an important presidential resource.

As we have documented in other chapters, the political culture of the United States changed during the Depression years of the 1930s. The public began to look to government to solve economic problems, abandoning its long-held belief in a relatively unfettered free market. Roosevelt focused these new public expectations on the office of the presidency. The president became politically responsible for the state of the economy.

The catch was that the president was now held accountable. The public had the power to enhance or harm the administration by its ability to give or withhold support. Lack of public support could undermine the chances that Congress would go along with presidential policies. Moreover, lack of support could undermine the president or his party's reelection chances. Because the president is held accountable by a national constituency, he has to weigh the impact of national public opinion more heavily, on most occasions, than that of special interests. This means that policies or issues with national implications usually capture more presidential attention, interest, and time than issues of lesser scope.

Because of this focus on national issues, presidents had few incentives for sustained attention to regulatory matters. Until the 1970s, regulation was thought of in sectoral terms. That is, regulatory problems were isolated to particular economic sectors or industries. Regulation was not thought to have major national or macroeconomic implications. Also, regulatory policy is inherently conflictual. Being embroiled in a policy conflict, especially one in which the likelihood of losing is great, does little in the way of generating public support. In fact, conflict and losing seem to undermine public support for the president. Thus, presidents had another incentive to distance themselves from regulatory affairs.

The Transformation of Regulation

In the 1970s, regulatory policy changed in a way that increased the motivation for presidents to be concerned with it, and, accordingly, presidents increased their regulatory activity in the legislative and bureaucratic arenas. They developed new and more potent ways of controlling regulatory bureaucrats and the policy decisions that these bureaucrats made.

Two important changes in regulation and the economy heightened presidential incentives to be concerned with regulation. First, new, sweeping social regulations were legislated beginning in the 1960s. As we have discussed, these regulations differed in kind and impact from the older forms of regulation, which were more narrowly economic in focus. These new social regulations had a greater impact on the economy than the traditional economic regulations, costing affected businesses large sums and, thus, arousing intense business opposition.

Second, the economy began to suffer in the 1970s. This came after a period of twenty-five years or so in which the economy generally grew strongly and exhibited solid productivity gains, with corresponding improvements in workers' standards of living. But by the mid-1970s, the economic climate changed. The Vietnam War escalated and continued longer than expected, draining the treasury and causing mounting federal deficits. Many economic rivals, like West Germany and Japan, began to eat into both foreign and domestic markets that U.S. firms had once dominated. The United States began importing increasing numbers of foreign goods, and a once positive trade balance turned negative. The Arab oil-exporting nations (OPEC), which supplied the United States with a substantial fraction of its oil needs, restricted world oil supplies twice during the 1970s. Oil and energy prices rose dramatically in response. Energy-induced inflation rippled through the economy, raising prices on all goods. Economic growth slowed, and unemployment increased.

Regulation was identified as one source of the nation's economic ills. Rather than being concerned with excesses of specific industries or with the environment, many blamed the performance of the macroeconomy on the effects of regulation. When this connection was made, the incentive for presidential action on regulatory matters increased. Controlling regulation became a subtask in the larger presidential task of managing the economy. Regulation became a submacroeconomic policy.

From the mid-1970s onward, all presidents saw the same solution: deregulation.[21] Industries in the United States could become more competitive and efficient if economic regulation were lifted whenever possible. The entire economy could be improved if social regulations were made less costly and burdensome. Presidents of both parties supported deregulation—Democrats Carter and Clinton as well as Republicans Ford, Reagan, and Bush.

As a consequence, presidents became more active on the regulatory policy front. Regulation rose as a presidential policy priority. Reagan made regulatory reform one of the four corners of his economic program, the others being lowering taxes, reducing federal spending, and fighting inflation. Presidents became more active on regulatory legislation before Congress, while also introducing innovations to try to control regulatory bureaucrats and their decisions. Thus, OMB control over the decisions of regulatory bureaucrats was strengthened, and a regulatory review process was invented that changed the standards by which new regulations were judged and implemented.[22]

Presidents and Regulatory Legislation

As regulation became an issue with implications for the presidency, presidents became more active in the legislative design of regulation. They took more positions on roll calls before Congress after 1974 than before, as Table 11.2 shows. On average, 15 percent of presidential positions on roll calls before Congress for Presidents Eisenhower and Nixon were on regulatory issues. This nearly doubled for Presidents Ford through Reagan (up to 1984)—up to 28 percent. And presidential legislative activity on regulatory legislation increased even though regulation is the least successful policy area for the president.[23]

Arguably, regulation has become an important enough issue for presidents to take stands on and even to run for reelection on those stands, despite the legislative risks involved. Thus, Bush vetoed the cable reregulation bill in 1992, and even though the cable industry is relatively small, strong public support for the reregulation bill existed, and Democrats exploited his unpopular position in the contest for the presidency that year, as mentioned earlier.

Presidents and the Administration of Regulation

Perhaps more important than presidential legislative actions on regulatory policy were presidential attempts to reign in the regulatory bureaucracy. Here

TABLE 11.2 Regulatory Bills as a Percentage of All Presidential Bills

President	Percentage of Bills
Eisenhower	17
Kennedy	9
Johnson	16
Nixon	18
Ford	38
Carter	33
Reagan	9
All	19
Eisenhower–Nixon	15
Ford–Reagan	28

Source: Data adapted from Mark A. Peterson, *Legislating Together: The White House and Capitol Hill from Eisenhower to Reagan* (Cambridge, MA: Harvard University Press, 1990), 236.

presidents, especially Ronald Reagan, were very innovative, and the OMB was given new tools to control the decisions of regulatory bureaucrats.[24]

The first tentative steps for presidential involvement in controlling regulations began with Richard Nixon, who created a Quality of Life process, which focuses on environmental matters and aims to balance the concerns of consumers, business, and environmental groups. With the inflationary pressures of the mid-1970s, Presidents Ford and Carter expanded their efforts to look at the impact of regulation on inflation. Thus, Ford required agencies to prepare inflation impact statements when considering new regulations, and Carter created the Regulatory Analysis Review Group, with a similar task. But both efforts proved ineffective because neither mechanism had enforcement power. Teeth came to presidential control of regulations with the Reagan administration in 1981.

On his first day in office, Reagan created the Task Force on Regulatory Relief and appointed his vice president, George Bush, as its chair. The task force's job was to monitor existing regulations and to cancel those that undermined Reagan's deregulatory efforts.[25] Thus, a high-level presidential agent was active on the regulatory control front.

Perhaps more important were the two executive orders that Reagan issued. These revised regulatory standards and created a new institutional mechanism for presidential control of regulation. The first, issued in 1981, required cost-benefit analyses of regulations. An agency in the OMB, the Office of Information and Regulatory Affairs (OIRA), was to conduct the cost-benefit analyses.[26] Proposed regulations that failed to meet the cost-benefit standard could not be implemented.

Some in Congress attacked the imposition of this standard and the use of OIRA for this purpose, arguing that no regulatory legislation required cost-benefit analysis. Thus, it was felt the president had overstepped his authority with the executive order. But despite these objections and congressional hearings on the use of cost-benefit analysis and OIRA, Congress took no action to stop this development.

In 1985, Reagan issued his second major executive order on regulation. This order tightened the presidential noose around regulatory agencies even further by requiring them to disclose regulations that were being planned, not just those already under design, and to evaluate the consistency between these planned regulations and the president's program. Through these two executive orders a regulatory clearance process was developed, giving the president centralized control over regulation through his chief staff agency, the OMB. The president was now a legitimate actor in the administrative regulatory process.

President George Bush, Reagan's stalwart vice president, continued the Reagan regulatory control program. First, Bush created the Council on Competitiveness, which was to be chaired by his vice president, Dan Quayle. The council was to review regulatory proposals and was seen as a continuation of the Task Force on Regulatory Relief.

However, by the time Bush became president, the deregulatory movement had petered out, and the pace of regulatory initiation by the bureaucracy began to pick up. By 1991, Bush was being characterized as the "reregulatory president" because of the increase in regulatory activity.[27] Regulation activity increased under Bush primarily because he appointed people to office who were less antagonistic to regulation than their predecessors who served under Reagan. The number of pages in the Federal Register began to increase under Bush (see Figure 11.1), and the number of regulatory bureaucrats also increased, by some estimates as much as 20 percent.[28]

Under Clinton, presidential interest in regulation continued but not to the same degree as under previous presidents. Clinton was more occupied with budgetary issues, and the general health of the economy reduced the need to contain regulation. Still, OIRA remained in place, and Clinton considered regulation an important part of economic policy. He restricted OIRA's review to significant regulations—those costing $100 million or more—but other than this minor scaling back, the institutional features begun in earnest under Reagan remain in place.[29] Very little else in the way of regulatory reform from the perspective of presidential control efforts has come out of the Clinton administration.

CONCLUSION

Regulation has changed considerably from its roots in the nineteenth century. First used to restore the market, by the 1930s regulation became a tool to regulate and stimulate the economy. Another transformation occurred in the 1960s, as regulation began to be used to counter the risks of living in a modern, industrial society. With the advent of these social regulations, the costs of regulation to the economy soared, leading to a counterreaction, deregulation.

Adding to the fortunes of the deregulatory advocates were two other changes. First, the economy declined in the 1970s, and overregulation was seen as one cause of that decline. Second, the president became more interested in regulation, in part because of its supposed effects on the economy. Regulation is now looked on as an important element of economic policymaking affecting the whole economy, not just a sectoral issue, and gets sustained presidential attention.

Key Terms

Clayton Antitrust Act
compliance costs
cost-benefit analysis
deregulation

devolution
Federal Trade Act
insider information
Interstate Commerce Act

price cap regulation
regulatory lag
Sherman Antitrust Act

Explore the Web

The Federal Register, which publishes all federal documents, including regulations and proposals for regulations, can be found at http://www .access.gpo.gov/su_docs/aces/aces140.html. The White House office in charge of regulatory rule oversight, the Office of Information and Regulatory Affairs (OIRA), is a component of the Office of Management and Budget (OMB). Although OIRA does not maintain its own web page, its reports are documented by OMB at http://library.whitehouse.gov/ omb/OMBREGS.HTM.

Notes

1. The cable reregulation story is found in Mike Mills, "Scarred by Media War, Cable Bill Wins Solid Vote from House," *Congressional Quarterly Weekly Report,* September 19, 1992, 2796–2801; and Beth Donovan, "Big Donations from Cable, Hollywood," *Congressional Quarterly Weekly Report,* September 19, 1992, 2798–2799.

2. On Bush's veto, see Edmund L. Andrews, "Bush Considers Signing Cable TV Bill," *New York Times,* October 2, 1992, C1; and "Text of Bush's Veto Message," *Congressional Quarterly Weekly Report,* October 10, 1992, 3149.

3. Much of the following discussion relies heavily on Marc Allen Eisner, *Regulatory Politics in Transition* (Baltimore, MD: Johns Hopkins University Press, 1993).

4. For another perspective on regulatory regimes, see John Francis, *The Politics of Regulation: A Comparative Perspective* (Cambridge, MA: Blackwell, 1993); Richard A. Harris and Sidney M. Milkis, *The Politics of Regulatory Change: A Tale of Two Agencies* (New York: Oxford University Press, 1989); and Eisner, *Regulatory Politics in Transition.*

5. The ICC has been the subject of much research because it is the first regulatory body and the first IRC. For a thorough review, see Barry M. Mitnick, *The Political Economy of Regulation: Creating, Designing, and Removing Regulatory Forms* (New York: Columbia University Press, 1980), 173–199.

6. On the Grangers, see Gabriel Kolko, *Railroads and Regulation, 1877–1916* (New York: Norton, 1965).

7. On the state regulatory commissions during this period, see James W. Fesler, *The Independence of State Regulatory Agencies* (Chicago: Public Administration Service, 1942).

8. For more on the ideology of the Progressives and the importance of regulation in building national government capability, see Stephen Skowronek, *Building a New American State: The Expansion of National Administrative Capacities, 1877–1920* (New York: Cambridge University Press, 1982). Also see Eisner, *Regulatory Politics in Transition,* 33–40.

9. These regulations are discussed in Kenneth J. Meier, *Regulation: Politics, Bureaucracy, and Economics* (New York: St. Martin's, 1985), 48–55.

10. One of the most forceful and important deregulatory advocates is the economist Murray L. Weidenbaum. See his *Business, Government, and the Public,* 2d ed.

(Englewood Cliffs, NJ: Prentice-Hall, 1981), and *Rendezvous with Reality: The American Economy After Reagan* (New York: Basic Books, 1988).

11. On the maritime industry in the United States and its regulation, see Edward Mansfield, "Federal Maritime Commission," in *The Politics of Regulation*, ed. James Q. Wilson (New York: Basic Books, 1980), 75–122; and Ernst G. Frankel, *Regulation and Policies of American Shipping* (Boston: Auburn House, 1982).

12. On interest group capture, see Marver H. Bernstein, *Regulating Business by Independent Commission* (Princeton, NJ: Princeton University Press, 1955); Samuel P. Huntington, "The Marasmus of the ICC," *Yale Law Journal* 61 (1952): 467–509; and George Stigler, "The Economic Theory of Regulation," *Bell Journal of Economics and Management Sciences* 2 (1971): 3–21. A review of the literature and empirical study is found in Jeffrey E. Cohen, "The Dynamics of the 'Revolving Door' at the FCC," *American Journal of Political Science* 30 (1986): 689–708.

13. This "revolving door" theme is discussed in Cohen, "The Dynamics of the 'Revolving Door' at the FCC," and Paul Quirk, *Industry Influence in Federal Regulatory Agencies* (Princeton, NJ: Princeton University Press, 1981).

14. Weidenbaum, *Business, Government, and the Public*, 344.

15. Cited in Barry D. Friedman, *Regulation in the Reagan-Bush Era: The Eruption of Presidential Influence* (Pittsburgh, PA: University of Pittsburgh Press, 1995), 16.

16. Regulatory lag and delay is the topic of Richard P. Barke, "Regulatory Delay as a Political Strategy," in *Federal Administrative Agencies*, ed. Howard Ball (Englewood Cliffs, NJ: Prentice-Hall, 1984), 144–157; Cornelius M. Kerwin, *Rulemaking: How Government Agencies Write Law and Make Policy* (Washington, DC: CQ Press, 1994); and Bruce M. Owen and Ronald Braeutigam, *The Regulation Games: Strategic Use of the Administrative Process* (Cambridge, MA: Ballinger, 1978).

17. A good treatment of these factors is found in Martha Derthick and Paul J. Quirk, *The Politics of Deregulation* (Washington, DC: Brookings, 1985).

18. Mitnick, *The Political Economy of Regulation*, 427, calls this *nonenforcement* and distinguishes it from formal deregulation.

19. These figures are estimated from Lyn Ragsdale, *Vital Statistics on the Presidency: Washington to Clinton* (Washington, DC: CQ Press, 1995), 280.

20. There are a few exceptions here. F. D. Roosevelt tried to gain control over IRC commissioners by removing them from office but was rebuffed by the courts in the Humphrey case. On Roosevelt and the Humphrey case, see John R. Hibbing, "The Independent Regulatory Commissions: Fifty Years After Humphrey's Executor v. US," *Congress and the Presidency* 12 (1985): 57–68. And L. B. Johnson, who owned local television stations in Texas, was interested in FCC policies, but these are more the exceptions to the rule. On Johnson, see David M. Welborn, *Regulation in the White House: The Johnson Presidency* (Austin: University of Texas Press, 1993).

21. For a similar view of presidents and regulation, see Lester M. Salamon, "Federal Regulation: A New Arena for Presidential Power," in *The Illusion of Presidential Government*, eds. Hugh Heclo and Lester A. Salamon (Boulder, CO: Westview, 1981), 147–174.

22. Overviews of increased presidential activity with regard to regulatory policy can be found in Edward Paul Fuchs, *Presidents, Management, and Regulation* (Englewood Cliffs, NJ: Prentice-Hall, 1988); Marshall R. Goodman and Margaret T.

Wrightson, *Managing Regulatory Reform: The Reagan Strategy and Its Impact* (New York: Praeger, 1987); Lawrence Rothenberg, "Deregulation and Interest Group Influence," in *Interest Group Politics,* 4th ed., eds. Allan J. Cigler and Burdett A. Loomis (Washington, DC: CQ Press, 1995), 299–318; and Richard W. Waterman, *Presidential Influence and the Administrative State* (Knoxville: University of Tennessee Press, 1989).

23. Mark A. Peterson, *Legislating Together: The White House and Capitol Hill from Eisenhower to Reagan* (Cambridge, MA: Harvard University Press, 1990), 179.

24. Much of the following benefits from Friedman, *Regulation in the Reagan-Bush Era.* Also see Howard Ball, *Controlling Regulatory Sprawl: Presidential Strategies from Nixon to Reagan* (Westport, CT: Greenwood, 1984); Joseph Cooper and William F. West, "Presidential Power and Republican Government: The Theory and Practice of OMB Review of Agency Rules," *Journal of Politics* 50 (1988): 864–895; George C. Eads and Michael Fix, eds., *The Reagan Regulatory Strategy: An Assessment* (Washington, DC: Urban Institute, 1984); Fuchs, *Presidents, Management, and Regulation;* Goodman and Wrightson, *Managing Regulatory Reform;* and William F. West and Joseph Cooper, "The Rise of Administrative Clearance," in *The Presidency and Public Policy Making,* eds. George C. Edwards, III, Steven A. Shull, and Norman C. Thomas (Pittsburgh, PA: University of Pittsburgh Press, 1985), 192–214.

25. Formally, the task force had no power to cancel a regulation, but its recommendation to the OMB and OIRA weighed heavily.

26. OIRA was created by the Paperwork Reduction Act of 1978.

27. This label came from press stories; one of the most important was Jonathon Rauch, "The Regulatory President," *National Journal,* November 30, 1991, 2905.

28. Friedman, *Regulation in the Reagan–Bush Era,* 163.

29. Ibid., 176–178.

12

The Politics of Distributive Economic Policy

OVERNMENT REGULARLY subsidizes economic activities. For years the U.S. government provided subsidies to the producers of many products, including honey, angora wool, and mohair. None of these products constituted a large segment of the agricultural sector of the economy, yet until the budget battles of 1994, each was able to secure government programs that supported their production.[1]

Such programs are classic distributive economic programs. With **distributive economic programs,** government provides benefits and/or incentives for people to engage in certain economic activities. Often these programs help to minimize the economic risk of some activities, as the honey, angora wool, and mohair subsidies illustrate. The contours of the economy may be affected by such programs, because beneficiaries claim that they would not be able to engage in these activities without government support. In this sense distributive economic programs may have an effect on the economy.

Not everyone views distributive economic programs as benign. Opponents claim that the programs are classic pork barrel, motivated more by politics than economics. This view sees special interests capturing benefits from government by dint of their political power and influence and believes that the resulting programs are economically inefficient and wasteful. In this chapter we will discuss distributive economic policies and programs, looking at how they are made and at the role of Congress, the president, bureaucrats, and special interests in forging and implementing them. Then we will look in detail at one specific distributive economic problem, the military-industrial complex, with special attention to the problem of base closings.

THE NATURE OF DISTRIBUTIVE ECONOMIC POLICY

Government distributes many benefits to its citizens, firms, and industries. Some of these benefits are tangible and have economic implications. Distribution of benefits has been a major way for government to influence the economy and direct it along certain paths, and thus we can think of distributing benefits as one way that the government makes economic policy.

These benefits come in many forms. Among the most common and important are subsidies, tax breaks, tax credits, and tax exemptions. Also important are grants, which may be monetary but may also take the form of land, rights to operate, and government contracts. Further, government lends large sums of money to people and firms at interest rates that are often lower than those found in the market. And often, government guarantees lenders that it will pay the loan if the debtor defaults. Thus, government possesses a host of ways of distributing economic resources to people and economic enterprises.

One rationale for government distribution of benefits is that only with government action will an activity take place. In essence, through these programs, government absorbs some of the risk of the economic activity. Subsidies, for instance, help ensure that an enterprise will turn a profit, and low-cost loans help reduce the cost of production.

To create political support for these programs, however, their advocates must show that the nation as a whole benefits from them and that they are not just government giveaways to powerful interests. One benefit might be that these programs help stimulate an economic activity, which, in effect, increases the size of the economy. Making all congressional districts potentially eligible for such programs helps reduce competition among districts for these benefits and also undermines the charge that special interests benefit at the expense of citizens and the economy.

Critics claim, however, that very few distributive economic programs have this kind of economic growth payoff. Rather, they view distributive benefits as subsidies that politically influential groups and people extract from government or that government dispenses to the politically influential. Often detractors charge that distributive economic programs and benefits are **pork barrel,** a term of derision to suggest a wasteful program developed for political, not policy, reasons.[2] Similarly, such programs are seen as examples of special interest group influence over government.

This perspective views distributive economic programs as economically inefficient. If the activity that receives the benefit were economically efficient, the market would provide it. Instead, government dispensing of such benefits diverts economic resources into these activities, which reduces overall economic growth by keeping needed investment and resources out of more productive economic sectors. Moreover, according to this view, government is not as able as the market to make decisions about the economy. Thus, government distributive programs interfere with the smooth functioning of the market. Government subsidizes economic activity that is not as productive or profitable as others in the market and does so because of the political influence of the beneficiaries and/or the political needs of those in government. Rather than helping economic growth, critics claim, such programs actually retard it.[3]

To both its critics and its supporters, distributive policy is important not only for its economic implications but also because it is perhaps the most common form of policymaking in the United States.[4] This has given rise to an important theory of U.S. policymaking, the **theory of distributive benefits.** The ability to dispense benefits without imposing costs on interests important to the election of legislators is a driving proposition of that theory.

Characteristics of Distributive Economic Programs

Distributive programs have several characteristics in common. First, they tend to reduce the private risk of engaging in an activity. Government absorbs the risk, and it does so to stimulate the activity. For example, government provides low-interest loans to college students to increase the number of students attending college, reckoning that a better-educated populace will be more productive. In the 1800s, government often gave grants of land to railroads with the aim of helping them expand. Myriad other examples exist.

Second, the costs of distributive programs tend to be hidden. For the most part, these costs are paid out of general revenues and thus are spread across all taxpayers. The cost per taxpayer for each specific program tends to be quite small, which mutes much of the opposition to the programs. There may be little to gain by opposing a program that imposes so little cost to each.

Moreover, those who receive these benefits are rarely asked to pay for them (except in the case of loans). Thus, distributive benefits tend to be low in conflict. The costs are spread across all taxpayers and intermixed into the overall budget. Benefits are concentrated and highly specific. Beneficiaries are thus pleased to get the government distribution but do not see that distribution directly affecting their taxes. Distributive programs, consequently, are often highly popular. Cutting them may be politically difficult, if not impossible.

Last, distributive programs are usually sectoral in nature rather than macroeconomic. Different economic sectors or classes of people are identified as eligible to receive benefits. Sometimes these definitions are quite narrow and specific. Other times, large groups of people may be beneficiaries.

The Growth of Distributive Economic Programs

Distributive economic programs are among the most common government programs. Hundreds exist, yet in monetary terms, they have become increasingly squeezed because of the growth in entitlements.

One study has attempted to detail as comprehensively as possible the contours of government programs from the 1970s to the 1990s.[5] This study classifies domestic programs into three types: entitlements, discretionary, and insurance and loan. Onetime projects, like the Chrysler bailout, are not included, nor are **off-budget** items. Off-budget items are government programs that are kept off the annual budget. Financing for off-budget items tends to come not from general government revenues, like taxes, but instead from other sources, like user fees, fines, and contributions to government trust funds. The idea of off-budget items is that they will pay for themselves and thus do not add to the cost of government; hence they do not need to be included in the government budget. Many government insurance programs operate off budget, in part because they pay for themselves and thus do not need to dip into general revenues. Also, because of its high cost at the time of the huge federal deficit, aid to the savings and loan industry was kept off budget in order to make it more politically acceptable.

Entitlement programs are defined as "formula programs, block grants, revenue sharing, direct payments for a specified use (e.g., agricultural acreage set-asides) and direct payments for unspecified use (e.g., social security)." There may be some distributive economic programs in this set, especially among the direct payments for specified use. Discretionary programs are defined as "project grants and cooperative agreement programs."[6] Many of these are distributive. Last, insurance and loan programs are almost always distributive. Noting that these categories do not exactly match the distinction between distributive economic programs and all other government programs, we can combine discretionary and insurance and loan programs, considering them to be mostly distributive economic programs. By looking at them, we can gain a general idea of the nature and growth of distributive economic programs.

First, the "distributive" variety is very common, more common than entitlements. From 1971 to 1990, there were on average 197 entitlement programs per year, in contrast to 499 discretionary and 128 insurance and loan programs. In other words, these distributive economic programs accounted for, on average, 76 percent of domestic federal programs. Over time, the number of discretionary programs has increased from 447 in 1971 to 620 in 1990, while insurance and loan programs have dropped in number from 134 to 112.[7]

Still, these distributive programs are small in monetary terms compared to entitlements. Over these two decades, entitlements averaged about 70 percent of expenditures among these three groupings. Also the entitlement expenditures ate an increasingly larger portion of the budget pie over time— about 58 percent of the total in 1971 but 82 percent by 1990.[8]

THE STRUCTURE OF DISTRIBUTIVE BENEFITS POLICYMAKING

Distributive economic policy tends to be made in narrow, contained subgovernments that deal exclusively or primarily with one issue area or policy.[9] The term **subgovernment** refers to subsets of government participants. In other words, policy is not made at peak governmental levels, like the floors of the Congress, but at lower levels of government, like congressional committees and subcommittees.

Thus, we find congressional committees to be highly active in distributive policymaking, as are concerned interest groups and bureaucrats at the sub-cabinet level. System-level policymakers, like the president and the House and Senate as wholes, are less involved in distributive benefits policymaking, though sometimes these system-level actors are important. The government plays a role when legislation is passed, but this is more often than not just a ratification of a policy hammered out and developed in a congressional committee.

For many years, distributive policy subgovernments have been described as **iron triangles.** Since the 1970s, another variety of subgovernment has also been noted, **issue networks.**[10] Today we find both iron triangles and issues networks. Iron triangles and issue networks are two types of subsystems that are important in making distributive economic policy.

Iron triangles and issue networks differ in several important respects. First, participation in iron triangles is narrower and more stable than in issue networks. The classic iron triangle is composed of the relevant congressional committees, concerned interest groups, and the bureaucratic agency with implementation jurisdiction over the program. Issue networks have a broader group of participants and may add to the traditional iron triangle participants such actors as journalists, policy experts and academics, competing interest groups, and even participants from other subgovernments. Moreover, although participation in iron triangles is stable, issue network participation is unstable; new participants may appear and old ones drop out depending on the particular issue being dealt with (see Figure 12.1).

Another crucial difference between iron triangles and issue networks concerns the degree of conflict within these policymaking communities. Iron triangles exhibit low levels of conflict; their participants may be thought of as a coalition, each providing support for other members. Once the iron triangle

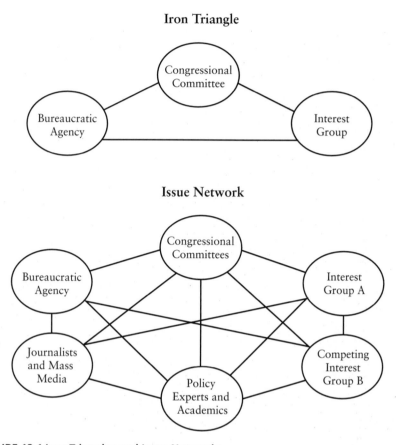

FIGURE 12.1 Iron Triangles and Issue Networks

has forged a policy response to a problem, each participant behaves to continue that alignment. In a sense, the resolution of a policy within an iron triangle is much like the act of signing a treaty. The aim of the iron triangle is to maintain that agreement. In contrast, conflict and competition among participants is much higher in issue networks. This conflict arises from the nature of the issues, the large number of participants, the instability of participation over time, and the intersection of competing subgovernments.

However, there is one similarity between iron triangles and issue networks in distributive economic policymaking. The objective of both is to stay out of the eye of the public and system-level policymakers like the president. Each seeks some degree of autonomy from the outer political environment in shaping policy, though the more fluid nature of issue networks makes them more permeable to system-level influence.

Congress and the Politics of Distribution

Congress is especially well suited to produce distributive economic policies. Some even contend that Congress is organized with this objective in mind.[11] To understand how this works, we begin with a basic assumption about members of Congress: that they are primarily interested in getting reelected. No doubt this assumption is a simplification of reality, but one does not have to stretch to say that members are so inclined. From this motivation, several things follow.

First, members will try to target interest groups and others that may contribute to their reelection efforts. Several kinds of contributions are especially sought: financial contributions, endorsements, and votes.

Second, in the process of attracting electoral support, members of Congress will try to avoid controversy. Distributive economic policies fit this requirement very well. As mentioned earlier, they possess low conflict levels, they are popular among recipients, and they tend not to arouse the ire of taxpayers because the costs of each program are hidden and are spread across all taxpayers, thereby diluting the cost of each program to each taxpayer. The beneficiaries are more motivated to protect their benefits than opponents are to attack them because the beneficiaries receive a comparatively greater benefit than the costs that taxpayers and opponents bear.

Another way that distributive economic policies avoid controversy and conflict is that they are applied across both parties; in other words, they are bipartisan. Members of Congress from both parties may sponsor the same distributive economic program, and bipartisan coalitions of this sort are quite common. This is because members of both parties may have beneficiaries within their districts. As James Lindsay says, speaking about military bases, "[M]embers of Congress, be they Democrats or Republicans, hawks or doves, junior or veteran legislators, fight for military installations in their districts and states."[12] This description may be applied to *all* types of distributive programs.

To be most efficient in the production of distributive economic policies, Congress organizes itself around economic sectors and does the bulk of its policymaking in subunits, committees and subcommittees especially designed to deal with particular economic sectors. Efficiency here means that Congress can produce appropriate distributive economic policies, ones that target beneficiaries as intended, using a minimum of congressional resources and incurring a minimum of conflict within the legislature.

You may recall from our discussion of Congress in Chapter 6 that congressional committees are sectorally structured. That structure is mirrored in the bureaucracy. This parallel organization is intentional; Congress, through its legislative power, creates bureaucracies to match its election and committee needs. Doing so gives each committee easier access to the bureaucracy that is responsible for implementation of these programs.

Efficiency in producing distributive economic policies is enhanced by this committee-based structure. Each committee and subcommittee develops expertise around a particular policy area or economic sector. That committee then can use its expertise to lead the rest of Congress to support its proposals. Furthermore, noncommittee members have little incentive to vote against another committee's proposals, as that committee may retaliate against *its* proposals. In this way, conflict within the legislature is further dampened.

Because economic sectors fall unevenly across congressional districts, with some sectors being a larger influence in one district than another, the congressional committee system attracts members from the most greatly affected districts. Thus, some members have stronger incentives to work on one committee than another because of the presence of certain economic sectors and interests in their home district. We are likely to find, for example, most of the members on the congressional agriculture committees coming from heavily rural districts. Members thus use their committee posts strategically. By being seated on the proper committee, members can increase the likelihood of directing distributive economic benefits to critical sectors and interests within their districts.

This system leads to distributive economic policies with the following characteristics. As already noted, they are bipartisan and tend not to rouse partisan conflict. They are also universal and nonexclusive.[13] Every district with the type of interest or person designated as eligible will receive benefits, including districts not represented formally on the committee or subcommittee. This spillover helps to build support for the program. Third, over time the program tends to grow to include more congressional districts receiving such program benefits,[14] which enlarges the support coalition behind the program and reduces the likelihood of attack from other quarters. These *supercoalitions* also help insulate programs from attacks that budget-conscious system-level politicians, like the president, might make.

Thus, distributive programs have a life cycle. They start out relatively small. Because small programs have modest costs, they are not likely to meet much opposition. However, such small programs are also politically vulnerable. To strengthen the political support behind such programs, they are increased in scope to enfold more and more districts into their orbit. Over time, vast majorities of congressional districts may receive such benefits. With so many members representing districts that receive benefits, opponents have a hard time attacking the programs.

What do members of Congress get for all of this hard work? First, they receive the goodwill of constituents and interest groups. Some of this may result in a reputation for helping the district. Other forms of goodwill may be more tangible, like campaign support. Both reputation and campaign support may result in greater electoral security.

Bureaucrats and Distributive Programs

Bureaucrats are the people primarily responsible for the implementation of distributive economic programs. For the most part, implementation of these programs goes smoothly, with few breakdowns.[15] The lack of conflict over these programs is one source of their success. Also critical to their success is the fact that the bureaucrats, unlike those who implement regulatory policy, do not have to force people to do things that they do not want to do or keep people from doing things that they would like to do. Instead, accepting these benefits is voluntary, and beneficiaries usually have to apply to receive the program benefits. Moreover, bureaucrats who implement distributive economic programs mostly review grant applications and mail checks to program recipients. As long as money is sufficient and the applicant is eligible, applications will not be denied.

But not all programs are funded at levels such that all applicants will receive benefits, and not all eligible people and firms apply. Under conditions of scarce money, which characterize all but entitlement programs, bureaucrats possess the discretion to determine who will receive the program awards. It is through these types of decisions that bureaucrats have some influence in distributive economic policymaking.

When bureaucrats have to decide among applicants for limited awards, by what criteria do they select those who receive benefits? One claim is that bureaucrats target beneficiaries who reside in districts that important members of Congress represent.[16] These would be members who hold positions on committees important to the agency and its programs. Also, congressional leaders, like the Speaker of the House and the party leaders, might be so targeted.

Targeting beneficiaries in this way should theoretically build goodwill among members of Congress with some control over these bureaucracies. Under conditions of scarce resources, biasing the award system to these beneficiaries may also ward off attacks from legislators who can do damage to the agency. What the bureaucracy wants to ensure is that it maintains its budgets and control over its programs. Having important friends and no important enemies is one way to help create such a climate.

Congress, however, is not always amenable to allowing bureaucrats to make such important decisions.[17] As a consequence, Congress has often depoliticized the bureaucratic decision-making process, taking the choice of recipient out of bureaucratic hands. One way of doing this is for Congress to create a formula that the bureaucracy must apply in program awards. Formulas can be more or less specific, but in general they tend to specify how much of an award will go to certain districts based on certain characteristics. Population, employment and industry figures, poverty, and minority group makeup are some of the criteria that have been used to determine priority in granting awards.

Even with formulas, bureaucrats maintain some discretion and influence over distributive economic policymaking. They may, for example, decide the timing of award announcements. Studies find that bureaucracies speed up the announcement of awards as elections near.[18] Bureaucrats do this, presumably, to help members of Congress in their reelection bids. Members can then make the announcement of the grant or contract during their campaign, demonstrating to district voters that they can bring federal government benefits into the district, that they hold some power and influence in Washington, and that they should be returned to the legislature to continue this practice. On the other hand, bureaucrats may adversely affect the timing of awards to recipients who come from districts represented by enemies of the agency.

Interest Groups and Distributive Benefits

Interest groups are the third important leg of the subgovernment. They stand to gain much from membership in the subgovernment, and they provide it with important resources.

A primary but not exclusive motivation for interest groups is to secure public policies, such as subsidies, tax breaks, and the like, that will help them in their economic activity and that may shift some of the risks of doing business onto the public sector. But policies are not all that they stand to gain from participation in distributive economic subgovernments. They also stand to gain access to government and, through that access, political influence. For instance, interests may gain formal access to government through participation on advisory panels.[19] Many bureaucracies develop advisory groups to help develop policies and to promote the appearance, if not the reality, of public participation. Business groups tend to be well represented on such bureaucratic panels.

Also, the political influence that interests acquire through subgovernment participation might be used to block the attempts of competing interests to forge policies, or it might be used to deny rival interests resources that could be used to compete with the entrenched interest. Impeding government from making new policies can be an important result of interest group membership in a subgovernment. This is one way that interests help maintain the status quo from which they benefit. Interaction with government is not always a matter of gaining a direct benefit in the form of a supportive public policy. It may be a way of denying a harmful policy from taking effect and of keeping challengers to the status quo from getting onto the government policy agenda.

Another benefit that interests gain from subgovernment participation is influence over the implementation of policy. Usually, statutes are vague, and the bureaucracy is allowed to fill in the details, to design the operation of programs. Bureaucracies may seek interest group input at this program design stage. From such input, interests may maximize the benefits that they get from policies, ensuring that the benefits of the programs flow to group members in the most desirable fashion.

Interest groups also bring resources to help the subgovernment. Those resources may aid both members of Congress and bureaucrats. Most critically, interest groups bring members of Congress election support, which comes in two major forms, campaign contributions and endorsements. Through such support, interests help members of Congress get reelected, thereby encumbering some debt from them. Although this does not mean that the interests "own" members of Congress, such electoral support should ensure that they have access to Congress, and on some votes or issues, this might determine how a member votes.

Interest groups in a subgovernment also provide bureaucrats with political support and good publicity about the job that they do implementing the policy. Political support comes in many forms. One of the most important is supporting an agency's efforts to increase the programs under its jurisdiction. In fact, it may be easier for an interest group to lobby Congress to increase an agency's budget or mandate than for the agency to seek such an increase itself. Most important, interest groups may publicize the good job that an agency does in implementing its programs. Such positive publicity may enable the agency or its supporters in Congress to fend off attacks.

Last, for the subgovernment as a whole, interest groups bring information about the popular perceptions of the policy and its effectiveness. Such information may be hard for members of Congress and bureaucracies to gather. Moreover, much important information about the operation of programs comes from members of the interest group who receive those benefits. In a sense, the interest group has a monopoly over the information that emanates from its members, especially information about the popularity of the program. This is important given that political payoff is so crucial a motivator in subgovernments. Political popularity may be even more important than policy effectiveness.

Presidents: Ambivalence Toward Distribution

Compared to members of Congress, presidents are not highly active participants in most distributive economic policies, though as we will discuss, there are conditions under which they may be active.[20] Moreover, we will see that although we would expect presidents generally to be opponents of distributive economic policy subsystems, there are certain times and circumstances under which they become allies of those policies and programs.

Distributive economic policies, as we have already discussed, are mostly geared toward economic sectors, and rarely are individual sectors of such importance that they can garner presidential attention. Only when they raise issues affecting the whole economy are presidents likely to take notice of them and participate more actively. Still, some sectors, due to their towering impact on the economy, have built-in appeal for presidents. In the late 1800s, railroads held such prominence, as did the steel industry in the 1940s and 1950s and the automobile industry throughout most of the twentieth century. Most recently, the information industries, computers and telecommunications, seem to have attracted presidential attention. This attention tends to subside, however, once an industry recedes in macroeconomic importance.

Our discussion of Congress and distributive economic policies emphasized the support of Congress for such policies and programs. Presidents, in contrast, may be actively opposed to distributive economic programs, either as single programs or as a way of making policy. One good example comes from the Carter administration.

River and harbor projects are well liked in Congress. Each year, it initiates projects to enhance harbors, make rivers more navigable and less flood prone, and the like. On one level these programs seem commendable because they strengthen the transportation infrastructure of the nation. However, very early in his administration, President Carter criticized a bill appropriating money for these projects, saying that they were wasteful and often unnecessary, especially given the tight federal budget. In effect, he criticized Congress for playing politics with these programs, bringing home the "pork" rather than using more "rational" and cost-effective criteria to assess whether such projects were needed. Carter threatened to veto the bill and found himself embroiled in a face-off with the Speaker of the House, also a Democrat, and with Democrats from the western part of the nation, where the bulk of the projects were to be built. Finally, Carter backed down, but relations between him and Congress never healed fully.[21]

What might drive a president to attack such a popular measure in Congress?[22] First, as the Carter case illustrates, presidential concern over the impact of distributive programs on the budget may lead the president to try to do something about those projects. More often than not, single programs and projects will not incur such presidential attention because they are too small. But some projects are very costly and, thus, invite presidential attention. Other times, a president will attack special interest legislation of this sort en masse. For instance, Ronald Reagan rallied against interest groups in general and used that theme to help move his budget-cutting plan through Congress. Also, Reagan, Bush, and Clinton have argued for a line-item veto for the president so that the president could resist interest groups that were able to gain special provisions, especially in budget legislation. On April 9, 1996, President Clinton signed into law the Line Item Veto Act. That act allowed the president to veto specific items in spending bills. The president took advantage of this newfound power, employing it ten times. It is calculated that the president excised slightly over $1.9 billion, although about $1 billion was eventually restored. Two actions led to the restorations. First, on January 5, 1998, Congress overrode the president's veto of $287 million slated for military construction. The next day, the Supreme Court restored

$854 million for Treasury Department and general government spending by nullifying the act. The Court argued that the act violated the Constitution by, in effect, allowing the president to write legislation.[23]

A president may also oppose distributive economic programs because the intended beneficiaries are not members of his support coalition and may in fact be opponents. This is often the case when the president faces a Congress held by the opposition party. Then, many members of the opposition may be receiving benefits for their districts, though these beneficiaries did not support the president in the previous election. Ronald Reagan ran into this problem and attacked what he termed "liberal special interests." Thus, for budgetary, macroeconomic, or political reasons, presidents often find themselves standing in opposition to distributive economic programs.

At times, however, presidents find that support of such programs may be beneficial. Although a president may support some distributive economic programs because he agrees with them or because the programs help his supporters, he may also support them because these programs build support for him in Congress. We noted earlier how popular these programs tend to be among members of Congress. If that is the case, a president may perceive that his support for these programs may help build good relations with members of Congress, and he may be able to extract support from members of Congress on other programs important to him by supporting the distributive economic ones.

Still, such presidential support for already popular programs may not mean much because these programs would pass Congress anyway. To make his presence more credible, a president must indicate that he can harm a program or otherwise manipulate it. Only by having an impact on these programs can a president cause members of Congress to be concerned about his position on distributive economic policy.

For instance, a president may suggest that he will veto a distributive economic program to extract support from members of Congress for something that the president wants but Congress is resisting. Also, a president may instruct the bureaucracy in such a way as to affect the timing of award announcement, along the lines discussed previously in the section on the bureaucracy and distributive policy.

Last, a president may support distributive economic programs because of his own electoral needs.[24] There are several instances of presidents' announcing program awards during election campaigns. In 1980, during his primary fight against Senator Edward Kennedy of Massachusetts, who was challenging him for the Democratic nomination, Carter announced urban grants to major U.S. cities in an attempt to sway voters in these liberal urban areas from the more liberal Kennedy. Similarly, Richard Nixon boosted the spending of several programs in his reelection bid in 1972. One major study of government awards finds that their announcements bunch during October of a presidential election year, though awards per month are constant in nonelection years.[25] Clearly, presidents seem to be trying to influence election outcomes with this behavior.

THE MILITARY-INDUSTRIAL COMPLEX AS A DISTRIBUTIVE ECONOMIC SUBSYSTEM

In his farewell address to the nation in 1797, George Washington warned of the "mischiefs of faction," asserting that political factions—what we now call *parties*—were sowing division into the body politic. Washington's farewell address is among the most famous of U.S. political speeches, and it set a tradition for presidents to look above politics in directing the nation's attention to important problems. But it would be 163 years before another farewell address would be so well remembered. On leaving office in 1960, Dwight Eisenhower, like Washington, warned the nation about what he viewed as an ominous threat to democracy: the military-industrial complex.

The military-industrial complex, according to Eisenhower, was a cozy relationship between the military and defense contractors, along with key members of Congress who made defense decisions not out of policy needs alone but also out of political and corporate needs. In essence, Eisenhower felt that this "subgovernment" led the United States to purchase too much defense, as corporations pursued contracts and profits, the military bureaucracy sought political influence, and members of Congress sought to bring military contracts to their districts, with the hope of building local economies. By this definition, the military-industrial complex is an important example of a distributive economic policy subsystem, all the more important because of the huge size of the expenditures involved and the impact on the local, and even the national, economy.

The military-industrial complex, however, is not one big subsystem but many subsystems revolving around weapons development and the procurement and the location of military bases and economic enterprises.[26] Thus, there is at times competition among the various sub-subsystems that make up the military-industrial complex, yet they are linked through their ties to the Defense Department, pertinent committees in Congress, and defense policy.

Origins of the Military-Industrial Complex

The military-industrial complex had its origins in World War II. The military made a conscious decision when mobilizing the economy for the war effort to work chiefly with large industrial concerns, like GM, U.S. Steel, and Du Pont. Military procurement specialists felt that only big business could deliver on large government contracts. It alone, they believed, had the plant capacity and expertise to meet military supply needs on time. Further, they thought uniformity and reliability of products could be better assured by giving contracts to one or a few large firms, rather than spreading them across numerous small businesses.

Thus, while 100 companies accounted for 30 percent of the nation's manufacturing output in 1940, with 175,000 producing the remaining 70 percent, in 1943, 100 companies accounted for 70 percent of the national manufacturing output.[27] This dramatic change was due almost entirely to military contracts. In effect, this procurement policy had led to one of the greatest concentrations of economic power in U.S. history.

After World War II, cold war military expenditures also had great impact on the economy. A large part of the economy remained geared to weapons development and supplying the military with all manner of products, from food to cars to uniforms to high-technology weapons. Some have called this **military Keynesianism,** meaning that government demand, through military spending, buoyed the economy, ensuring that as the war ended, the nation would not sink back into depression. Thus, there was an economic rationale for the size of the military establishment.

The cold war military-industrial complex, however, was not just an extension of the one that flourished during World War II. First, many industries moved out of military construction and back into the consumer sector with the war's end, determining that greater profits could be made there. Thus, the auto industry, which produced planes and tanks, as well as trucks and jeeps for the military, greatly reduced its military contracting, replacing it with expanded consumer automobile manufacturing to meet pent-up demand.

Second, the development of new technologies of war, like the atomic bomb, the rocket, and radar, shifted the needs of the cold war military away from traditional industrial weaponry to high-technology weaponry. A new aerospace industry was created, and electronics became another industry with strong military ties. Federal research and development (R&D) accounted for over 80 percent of all aerospace R&D and 43 percent of all electronics R&D in 1989, compared to 33 percent of all manufacturing R&D. These two industries together received over 80 percent of all federal R&D monies.[28] Much military manufacturing and testing moved to sparsely settled areas in the Southwest, where security could be better maintained. The Southwest has been termed the "Gun Belt" in recognition of its economic dependence on military contracting.[29]

These evolutions in the military-industrial complex had important economic implications. First, the military became important to the technological advancement of the nation. Products that it developed—jet propulsion engines, microchips, satellites, computers, and lasers, for example—were adapted to domestic use. The military and its contractors became one of the major employers of scientists and engineers. It should be noted that some dispute this viewpoint, contending that military contracting actually drained off inventive and innovative activity from the domestic sector and may have hurt overall productivity and new product development, as scientists and others had to redirect their efforts toward the aims of government contracts.[30]

Second, some companies became almost completely dependent on the military for their existence. For instance, between 1985 and 1988, federal contracts to Grumman and General Dynamics accounted for 88 and 81 percent, respectively, of their total sales.[31] These captive companies certainly aided the military in gaining its budget shares by lobbying Congress and the executive branch, knowing that they would share in budgetary generosity to the military.[32]

Third, once sleepy communities grew as military bases and contractors moved into them. Local economies became dependent on the bases. Some communities became like the proverbial "company town," but now the company was the military. Noting the economic benefits that derived from the placement of military contractors and bases, members of Congress competed to see such enterprises located in their districts.

Dismantling a Distributive Policy Subsystem: Closing Military Bases

The military-industrial complex is arguably the most influential policy subsystem in the United States because of its size and economic impact. But its size also makes it a tempting target. Thus, in the 1980s and 1990s, as government deficits mounted, cutbacks in military spending were viewed by many, especially liberals and Democrats, as a way to control the size of the deficit. And the end of the cold war in the late 1980s opened up another threat against high levels of military spending as many began to question the need for such a large military establishment. By the late 1990s, however, the situation seemed to turn around as Congress and the president agreed on increases in military budgets, learning that even without the cold war, the international arena was a dangerous place, as most recently evidenced by the Kosovo crisis. Still, we can learn much about the entrenched power of distributive policy subsystems by looking at how policymakers tried to cut back on military budgets in the 1980s and early 1990s. One method of retrenchment included closing military bases, called **military base realignment.** Base closings illustrate how difficult it is to dismantle distributive policy subsystems.

Congress is very protective of the economic benefits that it can distribute to the districts, including military bases, which members feel encourage economic growth. Healthy local economies, members believe, increase their reelection chances, besides being good for their districts.[33] The political and district interests of Congress play a larger role in decisions about where to locate military bases than in decisions about weapons systems, which are more influenced by policy, ideological, and partisan issues.[34] The struggle between these two sides—the need for military retrenchment and the desire of congressional members to keep military bases in their districts—reveals a great deal about the strengths of the distributive economic policy system.

Before 1977, hundreds of military bases were closed, as the Vietnam War ended and military expenditures decreased. But between 1977 and 1987, however, no major U.S. military bases were closed.[35] Why did this happen? It happened because legislation passed in 1976 made it difficult for the Defense Department to close bases. The new law created a multistep process, whereby the Defense Department had first to inform Congress of impending base closures, then provide detailed justifications, and then sit through a waiting period. Moreover, an environmental impact study had to be done, which added as much as a year to the process, in addition to increasing the administrative costs. Last, Congress had to implement specific appropriations to close a base. (Each base closing has a cost attached, such as movement of personnel to other bases.) Specifying appropriations this way altered the terms of debate away from the savings accrued from a base closing to its costs. After the 1976 legislation, no base was closed until reforms in 1985. Over the years, pressures began to build to allow greater flexibility in base-closing decisions and policy. The most important source of pressure came from budget-conscious legislators and personnel in the Defense Department, who saw base closings as a way to hold down defense expenses in an era of tight budgets and huge deficits.

By 1985, momentum for reform of this law began to gather steam, after nearly a decade in which no major base had been closed. Aiding the momentum was the military buildup under the Reagan administration, which allowed additional military spending so that districts would not suffer a net loss due to a base closure. After considerable political wrangling, legislation was passed in 1988.

That legislation called for the creation of a base-closure commission. The commission would submit base closing and realignment recommendations to the secretary of defense, who would transmit them to Congress. The secretary could not choose from among the base-closing recommendations. He had either to accept or reject the entire package. The creation of the commission and the limitation on the secretary of defense were intended to prevent the Defense Department from using base closings to harm members of Congress who opposed military budgets and other policies.

The act also required that Congress vote on the package of base closings as one set, not on individual bases. And Congress had to take action to stop the closings. If it took no action, the closings would automatically be implemented. This effectively changed the terms of debate in Congress. Although it was natural for a member of Congress to come to the aid of a targeted base, the package of base closings allowed each member to point to the spreading of the costs of base closings to other parts of the nation. No district was singled out. Moreover, the package of closings allowed members of Congress to point out the budgetary savings to their voters, who were presumably as interested in the budget deficit as in local economic losses. Thus, a national debate about a national economic issue, the deficit, could be employed by members of Congress seeking to explain to voters their support for base closings.

Moreover, the bill granted Congress a comment period to debate the base closings. This period allowed members to go on record before their constituents that they opposed the closing of their district's base, while still voting for the overall package of closings. The base-closings bill also put the burden of proof that a base closing would not be efficient or would not produce savings on those intent on stopping the closing. Under the old legislation, the burden of proof of savings rested on the Defense Department and the proponents of closing a base.

The base-closing act further lowered the barriers by setting aside money in the annual Defense Department budget for base closings and realignments without naming any particular sites. Thus, it became more difficult for members of Congress to charge that base closings cost money. Now base-closing money was a normal part of Defense Department operations. This allowed members to focus more exclusively on future savings from base closings. To help make the transition easier for impacted communities, Congress also could use economic adjustment and conversion programs, many of which already existed. This, it was hoped, would soften the local economic cost of a base closing, as well as reduce potential social disruption.

Thus, in 1989, a package of 86 base closings was submitted to Congress, which it did not disapprove. In 1994 a second round was attempted, with a lack of action by Congress. However, California, whose economy was heavily dependent on military spending, was hit very hard, which almost derailed the efforts. President Clinton, aware of the importance of California to his reelection chances, hinted at his displeasure but in the end took no action against the recommendation because such efforts looked too political.

The efforts needed to close military bases highlight just how strong distributive economic policy subsystems can be. Their strength derives in part from the way their costs and benefits are distributed. As we have discussed, concentrated and significant benefits are dispensed, but the costs are spread across all taxpayers, thus making the "bite" of any one subsystem very small. Hence, there are few incentives to attack a subsystem but great incentives to promote, enhance, and safeguard it.

To attack the military base subsystem required creating barriers between key players in the subsystem and decisions about its fate. Thus, a commission was established, the secretary of defense could not tinker with its recommendation, and the floor of Congress controlled the fate of the recommendation, not committees representing subsystems. A committee could not table legislation, keeping Congress from taking action. Congress had, instead, to take action on the whole package to stop base closings.

Moreover, the debate over base closings had to be moved out of subsystem protection and into national policy debates, such as those concerning the efficient running of government, the budget deficit, and military needs in the post–cold war era. Dismantling—or even reducing—the benefits of a distributive subsystem is not easy, as this case illustrates.

CONCLUSION

Distributive economic programs are among the most common programs produced by the U.S. government. They do not, however, account for the bulk of federal spending, being easily overshadowed by large entitlement programs like social security and Medicare. In the 1980s, the rising tide of antitax sentiment and the mounting budget deficit focused an unusual amount of public and political attention on these programs. The good economic times of the late 1990s have, however, dissipated these sources of attack on distributive economic programs, which tend to be very popular among program recipients. Whether the continuing mood for smaller government that began in the late 1970s will continue into the future is unknown, but such a mood alone does not seem enough to bring distributive economic programs under intense scrutiny. Thus, for the near future at least, such programs are likely to be relatively unscathed, until another major source of system stress, like tax burdens or deficits, combines with a public mood for smaller government to rally opponents of distributive economic programs to take political action against them.

Key Terms

distributive
   economic
   programs
iron triangles
issue networks

military base
   realignment
military
   Keynesianism
off budget

pork barrel
subgovernment
theory of
   distributive
   benefits

Explore the Web

A good web site for the Department of Defense can be found at
http:///www.defenselink.mil/. Several committees oversee military spending.
All House committees can be found at http://www.house.gov/house/
CommitteeWWW.html. From there the crucial committees are
Appropriations and National Security. The comparable Senate page is
http://www.senate.gov/committee/committee.html. Again, the pertinent
committees are Appropriations and Armed Services. The Project on
Government Oversight (POGO) is a public interest watchdog group that has
extensive material on the military-industrial complex. Its page is at
http://www.pogo.org/mici/index.html. Taxpayers for Common Sense is
another watchdog group that is concerned about government spending
overall. It has a site at http://www.taxpayer.net/.

Notes

1. On the history of government supports to these programs plus the budget battles that eventually eliminated these subsidies, see Bob Benenson and Jeffrey L. Katz, "Changing Harvest," *Congressional Quarterly Weekly Report* 51 (December 11, 1993): S23; and Bob Benenson, "Cuts in Subsidy Programs Rattle Farm Coalition (Wool, Mohair and Honey Subsidies)," *Congressional Quarterly Weekly Report* 51 (October 23, 1993): 2884. For a good general discussion of agriculture programs, see Randall B. Ripley and Grace A. Franklin, *Congress, the Bureaucracy, and Public Policy,* 5th ed. (Pacific Grove, CA: Brooks/Cole, 1991), 84–87.

2. A good discussion of pork barrel is found in John Ferejohn, *Pork Barrel Politics* (Stanford, CA: Stanford University Press, 1974).

3. See Linda R. Cohen and Roger G. Noll, *The Technology Pork Barrel* (Washington, DC: Brookings, 1991).

4. The idea of distributive benefits was first given a theoretical cast in Theodore J. Lowi, "American Business, Public Policy, Case-Studies, and Political Theory," *World Politics* 16 (1964): 677–715. It was further developed in his "Four Systems of Policy, Politics, and Choice," *Public Administration Review* 32 (1972): 298–310. Another good introduction is Ripley and Franklin, *Congress, the Bureaucracy, and Public Policy,* 72–102.

5. Kenneth N. Bickers, "The Programmatic Expansion of the U.S. Government," *Western Political Quarterly* 44 (1991): 891–914.

6. Ibid., 907.

7. Figures estimated from Bickers, "The Programmatic Expansion of the U.S. Government," 907.

8. Ibid.

9. The classic statement describing policy subsystems is J. L. Freeman, *The Political Process,* rev. ed. (New York: Random House, 1965). Also see Arthur Maass, *Muddy Waters: The Army Engineers and the Nation's Rivers* (Cambridge, MA: Harvard University Press, 1951).

10. Issue networks and their contrasts to iron triangles are described in Hugh Heclo, "Issue Networks in the Executive Establishment," in *The New American Political System,* ed. Anthony King (Washington, DC: American Enterprise Institute, 1978), 87–124.

11. See David R. Mayhew, *Congress: The Electoral Connection* (New Haven, CT: Yale University Press, 1974). Another version of this idea is found in R. Douglas Arnold, *Congress and the Bureaucracy: A Theory of Influence* (New Haven, CT: Yale University Press, 1979); Allen Schick, "The Distributive Congress," in *Making Economic Policy in Congress,* ed. Allen Schick (Washington, DC: American Enterprise Institute, 1983), 257–274.

12. James M. Lindsay, "Congress and the Defense Budget: Parochialism or Policy?" in *Arms, Politics, and the Economy: Historical and Contemporary Perspectives,* ed. Robert Higgs (New York: Holmes & Meier, 1990), 180.

13. On universalism in Congress, see Barry Weingast, "A Rational Choice Perspective on Congressional Norms," *American Journal of Political Science* 23 (1979): 245–262.

14. On this dynamic, see John A. Hamman, "Universalism, Program Development, and the Distribution of Federal Assistance," *Legislative Studies Quarterly* 18 (1993): 553–568.

15. A good description is found in Arnold, *Congress and the Bureaucracy.* Also see Michael J. Rich, "Distributive Politics and the Allocation of Federal Grants," *American Political Science Review* 83 (1989): 193–213; Kenneth R. Mayer, "Electoral Cycles in Federal Government Prime Contract Awards: State-Level Evidence from the 1988 and 1992 Presidential Elections," *American Journal of Political Science* 39 (1995): 162–185; and John A. Hird, "The Political Economy of Pork: Project Selection at the U.S. Army Corps of Engineers," *American Political Science Review* 85 (1991): 429–456.

16. See Arnold, *Congress and the Bureaucracy.*

17. Theodore J. Anagnoson, "Bureaucratic Reactions to Political Pressure: Can an Agency 'Manage' Its Political Environment?" *Administration and Society* 15 (1983): 97–118.

18. For example, see Theodore J. Anagnoson, "Federal Grant Agencies and Congressional Election Campaigns," *American Journal of Political Science* 26 (1982): 547–561.

19. Mark A. Petracca, "Federal Advisory Committees, Interest Groups, and the Administrative State," *Congress and the Presidency* 13 (1986): 83–114.

20. There is very little on presidents and distributive politics. See Cohen and Noll, *The Technology Pork Barrel,* 63–65.

21. This case is detailed in Ripley and Franklin, *Congress, the Bureaucracy, and Public Policy,* 90–92.

22. On presidential antagonism to subgovernments, see Charles H. Levine and James A. Thurber, "Reagan and the Intergovernmental Lobby: Iron Triangles, Cozy Subsystems, and Political Conflict," in *Interest Group Politics,* 2d ed., eds. Allan J. Cigler and Burdett A. Loomis (Washington, DC: CQ Press, 1986), 202–220.

23. Robert J. Spitzer, "The Item Veto Dispute and the Secular Crisis of the Presidency," *Presidential Studies Quarterly* 28 (1998): 799–805.

24. See Cingranelli, "Federal Aid to the States as a Presidential Resource"; Mayer, "Electoral Cycles in Federal Government Prime Contract Awards"; and John A. Hamman, "Bureaucratic Accommodation of Congress and the President: Elections and the Distribution of Federal Assistance," *Political Research Quarterly* 46 (1993): 863–880.

25. Mayer, "Electoral Cycles in Federal Government Prime Contract Awards."

26. The military-industrial complex is widely studied, as is the impact of defense spending and policy on the economy. Recent studies include Steve Chan and Alex Mintz, eds., *Defense, Welfare and Growth* (New York: Routledge, 1992); Ethan Barnaby Kapstein, *The Political Economy of National Security* (Columbia: University of South Carolina Press, 1992); James E. Payne and Anandi P. Sahu, eds., *Defense Spending and Economic Growth* (Boulder, CO: Westview, 1993); and Andrew L. Ross, ed., *The Political Economy of Defense: Issues and Perspectives* (Westport, CT: Greenwood, 1991).

27. John M. Blum, *V Was for Victory: Politics and American Culture during World War II* (New York: Harcourt Brace Jovanovich, 1976), 123.

28. Ann Markusen and Joel Yudken, *Dismantling the Cold War Economy* (New York: Basic Books, 1992), 65.

29. Ibid., 172–199.

30. On this view and other negative economic consequences of the military-industrial complex, see Seymour Melman, *Profits Without Production* (New York: Knopf, 1983); and Lloyd J. Dumas, *The Overburdened Economy* (Berkeley and Los Angeles: University of California Press, 1986).

31. Markusen and Yudken, *Dismantling the Cold War Economy*, 78.

32. This situation, where there is one consumer but potentially numerous suppliers, is called *monopsony*. Theoretically, government could exercise great influence over firms so tied to government contracts.

33. On Congress and the military benefits that it receives from local bases, see Lindsay, "Congress and the Defense Budget," 178–180.

34. This is detailed quite well in Kenneth R. Mayer, "Patterns of Congressional Influence in Defense Contracting," in *Arms, Politics, and the Economy,* ed. Higgs, 202–235.

35. The following is based heavily on Charlotte Twight, "Department of Defense Attempts to Close Military Bases: The Political Economy of Congressional Resistance," in *Arms, Politics, and the Economy,* ed. Higgs, 236–280.

13

International Economic Policy

with Jonathon Crystal

I N JUNE 1989, the Chinese government massacred students and other
prodemocracy protesters in Tiananmen Square.[1] Universal condemnation
of the Chinese action exploded across the United States, but debate ensued
over what action the country should take. Some wanted to withdraw most
favored nation status from the Chinese. Most favored nation status means
that a country having that status does not face any extra restrictions or barriers in the exportation of its goods to the country granting the status beyond
those that the granting country might impose against any nation.

The Bush administration balked at such a sanction, fearing that China
would react hostilely to any major U.S. sanction against what the Chinese
government regarded as an internal political matter. Administration policymakers felt that "quiet diplomacy" would bear more fruit as far as helping
the Chinese reform their human rights record. Many U.S. business groups
also strongly opposed any actions that would interfere with their efforts to
gain access to the vast Chinese market.[2]

A decade later in 1999, the Clinton administration became alarmed over
the possible effects of a global financial crisis that had started in Asia and
subsequently spread throughout the world. Although the U.S. economy continued to perform well, it could not completely escape the effects of economic turmoil in other countries. Exports from the United States to the rest
of the world slowed while U.S. steel producers accused some of the countries
hit by the crisis of unfairly "dumping" their output in the U.S. market, that
is, selling their goods at a price below their production costs.[3] While administration officials were sympathetic to the steel industry's complaints, they
were also concerned about restoring economic (and in some cases political)
stability in the beleaguered nations that were the targets of the accusations.

The global financial crisis also affected U.S. macroeconomic policy; the Federal Reserve repeatedly lowered interest rates (despite the strength of the domestic economy) in order to stave off any potential ill effects from the international situation.

These examples illustrate some of the ways in which domestic and international politics have become increasingly intertwined. Policies toward other countries have major effects on domestic groups; these groups in turn seek to influence the international policies. The examples also show the interconnections between economic factors and more traditional foreign policy concerns. In some cases economic tools are used to achieve political goals. At other times, the government's purpose is to further the country's economic ends, that is, to promote prosperity, ensure growth, maintain price stability, smooth out economic fluctuations, and so forth. Over the past few decades economic relations among countries have increased and national governments find themselves less able to achieve these important economic goals without seeking the cooperation of other states. The economic relations among nations is called international economic policy. This international aspect of U.S. economic policymaking has become increasingly important over the past few decades and is the topic of this chapter.

WHAT IS INTERNATIONAL ECONOMIC POLICY?

Simply, **international economic policy** consists of government actions that affect the economic relations between nations. Examples might include policies limiting international trade, maintaining the value of the dollar at a certain level, regulating investment by multinational corporations, lending or granting money to a foreign government, or imposing trade sanctions to pressure another country to change its behavior.

International economic policy is distinguishable from foreign policy, though the two may intersect at many points. Foreign policy refers to the plan or course of action of one nation toward other nations, and as such, international economic policy is a subset of foreign policy. But foreign policy also includes other matters, such as defense and military relationships.[4] Often international economic policy is subordinated to foreign political policy and defense needs, but this may be changing as the economic relationships between nations become increasingly important to domestic economies—as trade between nations, for instance, increases.

Throughout much of its history, the U.S. economy has been relatively insulated from international economic forces. This began to change in the post–World War II era, as the percentage of the economy engaged in trade increased, and this trend has accelerated since the early 1970s. Trade now accounts for about 17 percent of the gross national product (GNP). This represents a doubling since the 1950s.

Although the U.S. economy has become increasingly exposed to the world economy through trade, it is nowhere near as exposed as the economies of Japan, the United Kingdom, or Germany. In fact, the United Kingdom and Germany have about 40 percent of their economies engaged in trade, more than twice the percent of the United States.

A second major trend can be seen from comparing the trade behaviors of these four countries in Table 13.1. The United States is the only one with a negative balance of trade, that is, a **trade deficit;** we import more goods than we export. The **balance of trade** refers to the comparative amount of foreign goods imported into the United States versus the amount of U.S. goods purchased by foreign nations. Once a net exporter, the United States has become a net importer. Figure 13.1 details the trend in U.S. **merchandise trade balance.** The merchandise trade balance measures imports and exports of (tangible) goods. The merchandise trade deficit began in 1971; there has been only one surplus since then.[5] The **current account balance,** a more general indicator, also started to hit large deficit numbers at about the same time. Current account balances make up the merchandise trade balance, as well as imports and exports of services; investment income and payments; and government exports, imports, and foreign aid.

Although the United States has become a net importer, this is not true of all economic sectors or commodities. For instance, in advanced technology, the United States has a positive trade balance. Most of that came from aerospace, which includes airplanes, while a small positive trade balance also exists in electronics. Services is another economic activity for which the United States possesses a strong positive trade balance.

TABLE 13.1 Imports and Exports as a Percentage of GNP, 1994

Country	1994
United States	
Exports	7.4
Imports	9.6
Japan	
Exports	7.9
Imports	5.5
United Kingdom	
Exports	19.5
Imports	21.6
Germany	
Exports	20.4
Imports	18.2

Source: Calculated from the *Statistical Abstract of the United States,* 1998, 835, and 1997, 857.

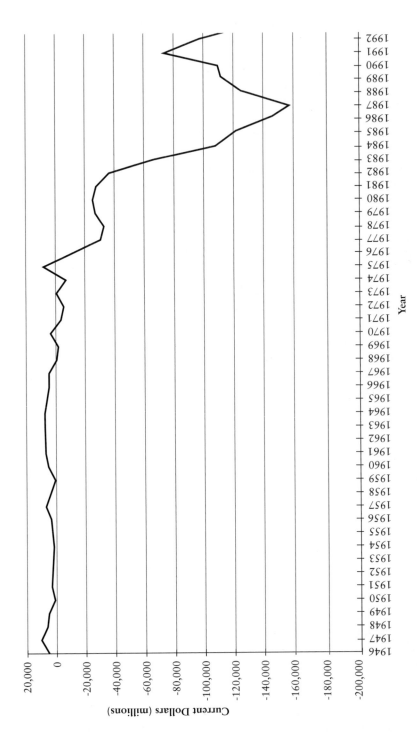

FIGURE 13.1 The U.S. Merchandise Trade Balance, 1946–1997

Sources: To 1995, *The Economic Report of the President* (Washington, D.C.: U.S. Government Printing Office, 1997), Table B-101; 1996, U.S. Department of Commerce, *News*, press release, "U.S. International Transactions: Fourth Quarter and Year 1996," March 13, 1997, 10; and 1997, *Statistical Abstract of the United States*, 1998, 786.

Still, the sources of the U.S. deficit represent important sectors of the economy. Three stand out: oil, machinery, and transportation equipment (which includes automobiles). Were it not for these three categories of imports, the U.S. trade picture would look much healthier, with a positive net trade balance. The sources and economic significance of the trade deficit remain the subject of much debate among economists.[6] Politically, however, there is little question that these imbalances matter a great deal, especially to the people who work in these affected sectors.

Although the United States trades with most nations of the world, our trade is concentrated among several major trading partners. Canada, Japan, and Mexico are the three most important. Of the United States's major trading partners, the only nation that the United States holds a trade surplus with is the United Kingdom, while Japan and China hold the largest trade advantages against the United States.

Generally, U.S. trade surpluses with other nations pale in comparison to our huge trade deficits with the likes of Japan and China. It is thus not surprising that trade conflicts often erupt between the United States and these two countries. Trade surpluses that the United States has tend to be with the smaller industrial nations of the world, especially in Western Europe and parts of Latin America. In 1997, we held trade surpluses of more than $2 billion with nine nations: the Netherlands ($12.5 billion), Belgium ($5.5 billion), Australia ($7.5 billion), the United Kingdom ($3.8 billion), Egypt ($3.2 billion), Brazil ($6.3 billion), Chile ($2.1 billion), Hong Kong ($4.8 billion), and Argentina ($3.6 billion).[7]

WHO MAKES INTERNATIONAL ECONOMIC POLICY?

As the U.S. economy has gotten more exposed to the world economy and to the economic decisions and policies of other nations because of increased trade, international economic policy has become a more important policy arena, too. Although no elaborate international economic policymaking apparatus has developed, the institutional capability for making international economic policy has been enhanced in recent decades. As with macroeconomic policy, the president and top-level administration advisers take the lead in making international economic policy, but Congress has an important role to play, too.

The rise of presidential interest in trade policy began in the 1930s. Before then, Congress was the lead player in trade policy, most of it concerned with tariffs. But in the Reciprocal Trade Agreements Act of 1934, Congress gave the president responsibility for negotiating trade agreements. With this act, the president leapt to the forefront of trade and international economic policy. The president is not alone, however, in making international economic policy. As is the case for macroeconomic policy, he has numerous advisers. We may call this the **international economic subpresidency,** much like the economic subpresidency discussed in Chapter 6. The international economic subpresidency, however, is much less developed than the economic subpresidency.

The International Economic Subpresidency

The international economic subpresidency is composed of several of the advisers from the economic subpresidency, especially the secretary of the Treasury and the Federal Reserve Board chair. These two economic advisers are important in both domestic and international economic policy because of the intersection of macroeconomic concerns and the international economy. Further, the use of economic power as a foreign policymaking lever makes the secretary of state an important actor as well. Another key international economic adviser is the U.S. trade representative (USTR).

The post of USTR was created in 1963. Originally a staff assistant to the president, the USTR is now considered to hold cabinet-level status and runs a staff of over 150.[8] The primary responsibility of the USTR is to negotiate trade agreements and to resolve trade disputes with other nations. The USTR has taken over many of the responsibilities that Congress delegated to the president in the 1934 Trade Agreements Act and has also been the primary negotiator for the United States at the General Agreement on Tariffs and Trade (GATT) and its successor, the World Trade Organization (WTO), meetings.

The secretaries of commerce and agriculture also play a role in international economic policy, but their influence is generally less than the other members of the international economic subpresidency. The Commerce Department houses the International Trade Administration, whose task is to develop trading opportunities for U.S. firms, a responsibility that has existed since the early 1900s, when the Commerce Department was created.[9] The Agriculture Department is concerned with trade because agriculture commodities, especially grains, are among the United States's most important trade goods. However, these two departments pale in importance to the others that make up the economic subpresidency and the international economic subpresidency.[10]

Congress and International Economic Policymaking

Congress plays an important role in international economic policymaking, but it is too decentralized to take the lead in making international economic policy, especially when such policymaking is concerned with general world trading arrangements, such as those that come out of the WTO, or when attention is given to the macroeconomic implications of international economic policy. Congress is highly permeable to domestic interests and thus feels the pressure of economic sectors the most. Domestic political and economic concerns, especially when they have specific local implications, provide the major incentive for congressional involvement in international economic policymaking. It is through Congress that subnational domestic concerns make an impact on U.S. international economic policy.

Policy is detailed and executive branch actions are watched and investigated in the congressional committees, and there are numerous committees with some jurisdiction over the policymaking area. The House and Senate Banking Committees, plus the Senate Finance Committee and House Ways and Means Committee, are the lead panels for Congress, but the Senate Foreign Relations Committee also has important jurisdiction over international monetary matters. The House Ways and Means Committee presides over international trade for that chamber, while agricultural trade matters are under the oversight of the House Agriculture Committee. Also in the House, the Merchant Marine and Fisheries Committee and the Energy and Commerce Committee have some jurisdiction. Moreover, the increasing interplay of domestic and international economic matters has pulled many other committees into debates over international economic policy, as industries and interests served by those committees are touched by international economic matters.

This decentralization of policymaking sites in Congress undermines the impact of Congress on international economic policy compared with that of the president. The president, as a consequence, has taken the lead; he sets most policy initiatives, and for the most part, Congress reacts to him in making international economic policy. Members of Congress themselves have recognized the value of the executive branch's ability to act quickly, decisively, and independently of the demands of particular interest groups. Thus, for example, in the 1934 Trade Agreements Act (and in subsequent legislation), Congress voluntarily ceded its constitutional prerogative to make trade policy to the president. Nevertheless, it also retained for itself ultimate authority to approve or reject the agreements that the president might make. Therefore, presidents must anticipate what Congress will accept, and in several instances, Congress has objected to treaty provisions, requiring that the president amend them before it will ratify the treaty. The constitutional role of Congress in passing laws and ratifying treaties, and its legitimacy as a popular representative institution, make it a body that the president cannot ignore.

International Economic Policy Instruments

There are three major formal international economic policy instruments: legislation, treaties, and executive agreements. Through the Constitution, Congress is important in the treaty and legislation-making processes.[11] The president is, however, generally independent of Congress in using executive agreements to make international economic policy, and bureaucrats, especially in the International Trade Commission, administer many important international trade policies.

Some international economic policy is legislated, such as most tariff and trade barrier policies. Tariffs are, essentially, taxes on imported goods. They raise the cost of the imported good, making them less price competitive. Participation by the United States in international agreements like GATT and treaties with other nations constrains the use of legislation as an international economic policy instrument more now than was the case historically.

Treaty acceptance requires ratification by two-thirds of the Senate. Treaties like NAFTA have become more important to international economic policymaking, and the Senate's constitutional duty to ratify treaties gives that legislative chamber an important role. Still, Congress rarely refuses treaties, with only two rejected and six withdrawn out of two hundred treaties considered in the period from 1981 to 1993.[12]

Trade treaties also may be presented to Congress under fast-track provisions, as was the case with NAFTA in 1993. Under the fast-track provision, Congress must reject or accept a treaty in its entirety, without amendment within ninety days. This makes it impossible for interest groups to change specific aspects of an agreement or to delay its ratification indefinitely. Rather, those who oppose the trade agreement must try to convince Congress to reject the entire treaty. Such a drastic action is a much more difficult goal for protectionist groups to obtain, especially since they would be sure to face the active opposition of other groups, such as exporters, who benefit from the agreement.[13] Thus, many who dislike free trade have opposed granting fast-track authority to the president, and in 1998 these opponents succeeded in blocking such authorization. As a result, foreign leaders were hesitant to enter into trade negotiations with the United States because they faced the prospect of having Congress attach myriad amendments to the final product.

Even under the fast-track provision, however, congressional influence over the substance of the treaty may be felt through the floor debates, and at times Congress has suggested that the president seek modifications and/or side agreements before the United States is allowed to sign the treaty. Congressionally suggested modifications often come in the form of side agreements that the United States negotiates with the other nation. The congressional threat is that if the president and/or the other nation refuses to accept these suggestions, Congress may refuse to accept the treaty or may nullify the treaty if it is already in effect. In the case of NAFTA, Clinton negotiated side agreements with Mexico, especially over environmental issues, because such concerns were raised in the congressional debates. Environmentalists objected that Mexico's efforts in that area did not meet U.S. standards.

Executive agreements, the third policymaking instrument, have become an important tool for presidents in making all types of foreign policy decisions, including international economic policy. Executive agreements between the

United States and other nations require no legislative action and are analogous to executive orders, which the president may use to affect domestic policy and government. Executive agreements have standing in law and have been justified by presidents as part of their constitutional power over foreign policy. Many executive agreements specifically derive their justification from existing treaties.[14]

Most executive agreements are routine, and many merely spell out details or elaborate on provisions of existing treaties. Still, an executive agreement may have important policy implications, and their use has grown in all areas of foreign relations since the end of World War II, as the United States has become more involved with other nations. Between 1949 and 1993, there were over ten thousand executive agreements, and although it is difficult to determine the number with international economic policy implications, about three thousand deal with foreign diplomacy and trade, foreign aid, and government and economic management.[15]

The International Trade Commission (ITC) administers four types of policies, sometimes jointly with other agencies.[16] The first are **escape clause** cases. Under these provisions an industry that is seriously harmed by imports may be exempted from U.S. trade agreements. Thus, higher tariffs, quotas, and the like may be implemented for a protected industry, but because these adjustments are understood to be temporary, ITC grants of such protections are usually limited to a specified period.

Also, the ITC administers **antidumping policy. Dumping** is the practice of one country exporting a product to another country at less than its cost of production. If the Commerce Department and the ITC find a nation engaged in dumping that harms a U.S. industry or firm, the ITC may assess the "dumped" good with a special duty to bring its price up. In recent years, there have been several well-publicized cases of U.S. industries and firms seeking relief under antidumping provisions. The steel industry, for example, has sought restrictions on imported steel coming from Brazil, India, Italy, Japan, and Spain. Bic, the manufacturer of disposable lighters, sought action against lighters from China and Thailand. And in 1995, Rockwell International sought duties ranging from 67 to 165 percent against imported printing presses from several nations.[17] One problem in implementing antidumping duties is determining if dumping is actually occurring or if domestic concerns are merely seeking protection from strong competitors.

Countervailing duties are assessed on goods that receive subsidies from their government. As with dumping, the Commerce Department is responsible for investigating whether such practices exist, and like dumping, a duty is assessed on the good equal to its subsidy.

Last, the ITC monitors unfair import practices. The main focus of unfair import practices is on patent claims. If a U.S. company holds a patent on a foreign product and the foreign product does not recognize the patent rights, the ITC may refuse importation of the product. There are other trade policy tools the government has at its disposal, aside from treaties or tariffs. Referred to as "low-track" or "administered" protection, these instruments involve decisions by bureaucratic agencies that determine whether domestic industries are eligible to receive certain types of relief from foreign competition as prescribed by U.S. law.[18]

As mentioned earlier, Congress plays a more limited role with respect to international monetary policy. In trying to affect the value of the dollar, the president (along with the secretary of the treasury and the chair of the Federal Reserve) takes the lead. The important role that financial markets play in determining currency values sets limits on the tools available to policymakers; however, government officials can try to intervene in currency markets by making public statements (sometimes called "jawboning") or by taking actions (such as raising or lowering interest rates) designed to affect the expectations of international currency speculators.

International Actors

The United States interacts with three kinds of actors in making its international economic policy: single nations, groups of nations, and international organizations.[19] Engagement with one nation at a time is called a **bilateral relationship**. Thus, the United States will sign a treaty or an executive agreement with, say, Canada. Or it may apply pressure on, say, Japan to open its domestic market to U.S. goods.

Multilateral relationships are those that involve more than two countries at the same time. These have become increasingly important in recent decades. Such groups might include a few nations or virtually every nation in the world. An example of the former to which the United States belongs is the **Group of Seven (G-7)**. The members of the G-7 are the major industrial powers in the world: the United States, the United Kingdom, Germany, France, Japan, Italy, and Canada. (When, on occasion, Russia is included in the meetings, the group is called the G-8.) Since the 1970s, the G-7 nations have met in annual summits to discuss economic matters. Among the issues that the G-7 nations discuss at these summits are dealing with global financial crises, regulating world monetary prices, coordinating fiscal policy, and, with the fall of the Soviet Union, assisting with the conversion to market economies in that region of the world.[20]

Another important category of groups are regional trading blocs such as countries of the North American Free Trade Agreement (NAFTA). Mexico and Canada are the other members who, along with the United States, agreed to eliminate tariffs among themselves. The NAFTA was signed in part as a response to the **European Community (EC)**, later renamed the **European Union (EU)**, a regional bloc composed of most of the Western European nations. The EC has not only lowered trade barriers among its members to encourage free movement of people, money, and goods across member borders, but it has also developed a central bank with a uniform currency and is establishing political institutions to promote cooperative relationships in the foreign political and defense policy areas.[21]

Other regions have also begun to develop trading blocs to varying degrees. For instance, Brazil, Argentina, Paraguay, Uruguay, and later Chile formed a common market (called Mercosur), while in Asia, a number of nations have established the Asia Pacific Economic Cooperation (APEC) forum, which has just begun reducing trade barriers among its members. The United States has involved itself in both regions. In 1990, George Bush proposed a Free Trade Area of the Americas (FTAA) covering the entire hemisphere and thus merging NAFTA and Mercosur (although momentum toward this goal slowed considerably over the course of the 1990s). In Asia, meanwhile, the United States is itself a member of the APEC group and attends its annual summit meetings. The aim of these trading blocs is to increase trade among bloc members and to enhance the competitiveness of member nations, while in some cases providing protection from nonmember nations.

International organizations are also important actors in making international economic policy. The most important with respect to trade is the **World Trade Organization (WTO)**, which was created in 1996 as the successor to the **General Agreement on Tariffs and Trade (GATT)**. The GATT was created in 1947, when twenty-two nations signed what was supposed to be a temporary agreement. However, its intended replacement—the International Trade Organization (ITO)—was rejected by Congress in 1950, and the GATT became the de facto organization regulating foreign trade. Its major aims are to settle trade disputes and to lower trade barriers. Since its creation, most of the nations of the world have joined, and there have been eight rounds of negotiations, including the Uruguay Round, which began in 1986 and produced an agreement in 1994, which the United States has signed.

The GATT was spectacularly successful in bringing down tariffs. When the GATT was founded, the average tariff for manufactured goods in developed countries was around 40 percent; by the late 1990s, that figure had plunged to less than 4 percent.[22] However, the GATT proved less adept in addressing many of the newer trade issues, such as the proliferation of more subtle nontariff barriers, the growing importance of trace in services, and measures related to foreign direct investment or to the protection of intellectual property. Growing dissatisfaction with the slow and cumbersome GATT led the negotiators at the Uruguay Round to create the WTO. Although the WTO has jurisdiction over many of the new trade issues, the most important innovation in the WTO is its new dispute resolution mechanism, which unlike under the GATT, cannot be thwarted by a single member country. This stronger enforcement power is what led many critics in the United States to worry that the WTO would threaten U.S. sovereignty. Others argued that such fears were exaggerated and that, in fact, the United States would benefit from a more effective trade organization.

Other organizations that are important in international economic policy are the **International Monetary Fund (IMF)** and the **World Bank** (formally known as the International Bank for Reconstruction and Development). The IMF and the World Bank date from the end of World War II. The IMF was created originally to regulate currency values and oversee the Bretton Woods system of fixed exchange rates (which eventually collapsed in 1971). The World Bank was intended to aid in the rebuilding of Western Europe after World War II. As these original rationales became less relevant, both institutions shifted their focus and began to concentrate on other tasks such as managing international financial crises and promoting economic reform in the developing countries.

THE POLITICS OF U.S. TRADE POLICY

International trade policies may fall anywhere along a continuum that stretches from free trade at one end to protectionism on the other. **Free trade** means no trade restrictions between nations. It is the policy model that the United States, at least in principle, has adhered to and has pushed other nations to subscribe to since the end of World War II. **Protectionism** is a policy that tries to restrict imports from other nations to help domestically produced products retain their market and competitiveness. The most famous and common trade restriction is the tariff.

Nontariff barriers may also be used as part of a protectionist policy.[23] Although the United States has generally avoided tariff-based restrictions for the past fifty years, it has at times used these other methods, as have other nations. Among the most common of these other devices are **quotas,** or limits on the amount of imported goods, **voluntary export restraints** (**VERs**), and national product standards. Voluntary export restraints are agreements between the United States and another country whereby the other country voluntarily agrees to limit its exports into the United States. The threat behind these agreements is that if the other country refuses to set a limit, the United States may counter with legislated restrictions, like import quotas or tariffs. The United States used voluntary export restraints to reduce Japanese auto imports in the early 1980s. Japan accepted such restrictions to keep access into the U.S. auto market, where it had been doing quite well competing against U.S. car manufacturers. Domestic content requirements are another way to limit foreign imports. Such legislation requires that a certain percentage of a product be manufactured and/or assembled in the United States. Environmental and safety regulations, which may impose standards beyond those found in other nations, have also been employed to restrict foreign imports.

Between the polar opposites of free trade and protectionism are the fair-trade and managed trade options. The United States has begun to back away from free trade as a policy because of its trade deficit problem and the realization that few nations practice free trade. Still, U.S. policymakers argue that their overall aim is still to lower trade barriers and that both fair trade and managed trade may help attain that goal.

Fair-trade policies refer to actions the United States takes against trading partners who are perceived as restricting the flow of U.S. goods into their markets. In essence, fair trade requires that the United States treat its trading partner the way that partner treats the United States. Generally, the aim of fair trade is not retaliation in itself. Rather, it is hoped that retaliation or merely its threat will induce the trading partner to lower its trade barriers. Still, critics claim that these policies (which some call "aggressive unilateralism"[24]) undermine the rule of law in international trade since the WTO, not any one country, is supposed to determine whether another nation is unfairly restricting trade.

Managed trade can be considered a type of fair-trade policy. This approach seeks to establish trading relationships with trade targets in mind. For example, the United States has been negotiating with Japan to increase the importation of certain goods such as auto parts. Although many free-trade advocates condemn "results-oriented" trade policy, defenders of the approach argue that it is the only solution in dealing with countries like Japan whose market is closed, as a result of informal and private-sector barriers. Such measures are not easy to negotiate away and the long history of bitter trade conflicts between the United States and Japan has led many to advocate abandoning any attempt to remove Japanese barriers and, instead, simply to demand some level of guaranteed market share.[25]

These policies also seek to promote trade strategies for specific industries.[26] For instance, concern has heightened that the United States might lose its lead in high-technology sectors such as semiconductors or aerospace, much as it has in consumer electronics. There is considerable policy debate about ways to protect these economic sectors, which many view as vital to the overall health and productivity of the economy in the future.[27]

Several factors determine whether a nation will support free trade or protectionism or something in between.[28] Obviously, the greater its competitive advantage, the more a nation will support free trade. From the end of World War II until the 1970s, the United States was the dominant economic power in the world. The war destroyed most of the world's economic productive capacity, except in the United States, which suffered no destruction to its plants and facilities. On the European continent and in Japan, in contrast, hardly a factory was left standing. The United States stood to gain amply as Europe and Japan rebuilt their economies, so it became a major free-trade advocate.

Nations at a competitive trade disadvantage tend to support protectionist policies. Thus, we can see why protectionist sentiment increased in the United States once we lost our competitive advantage. As our international trading advantage eroded, a trade deficit became the norm and continues to grow, making free trade less attractive. Similarly, when economies are in trouble, for instance, during recessions, protectionist sentiment grows, as workers, already feeling insecure in their jobs, feel even greater insecurity from foreign workers, who may not be paid as well as U.S. workers.

The relative competitive position of industries, as well as nations, also affects whether they will seek protection from foreign competition. Thus, the auto industry has sought protection from Japanese imports. In contrast, industries seeking to expand their markets have opposed protection. Many high-technology industries have taken such a stand in recent years. The domestic situation of an industry may also lead it to seek protection. When the industry is in decline, for instance, because of changing technologies, it may seek government protection.[29] Thus, while a nation may generally follow a free-trade path, it may selectively protect some industries, either because those industries are believed to be vital to the economy or because they possess enough political influence that policymakers respond with protectionist policies.

History and ideology may also affect whether a nation adopts protectionist or free-trade policies.[30] During the nineteenth century, the major source of government revenue was the tariff. Republicans, who found their support among industry, supported high tariffs to protect U.S. industry from foreign competition. Democrats, whose supporters were more agrarian, opposed high tariffs because nations to which U.S. farmers wanted to export imposed retaliatory tariffs against U.S. food products. With the ascendancy of the Republican Party in the late nineteenth and early twentieth centuries, protectionist tariffs became a fixture of U.S. trade policy. When the Depression hit in 1929, affected interest groups pushed for tariff protection, which resulted in the infamous Smoot-Hawley Act of 1930, a wide-ranging set of high tariffs. Other nations acted like the United States by imposing high tariffs against foreign imports with the mistaken hope that local industries and economic sectors would thus be protected. Instead international trade markets were choked off, and everyone's economy suffered. As a consequence, after the end of World War II, and with greater understanding of international economics, a new trade policy was fostered by the United States, which emphasized free trade and lowering trade barriers and restrictions. Presidents of both parties in the postwar era supported easing trade barriers. Effective tariff levels dropped from 36 percent in 1940 to 5 percent by 1984.[31]

However, in the 1980s and 1990s, several forces led to increasing sentiment in some sectors of the U.S. economy for trade protection. These include increasing competition from developing nations, where wages are low compared with those in the United States and other industrial nations. The relaxing of cold war tensions meant that the United States was less willing to overlook protectionist policies of its trading partners for the sake of promoting harmony within the anti-Soviet alliance. Finally, the growth of trading blocs, especially the European Union, led to fears that these regional groups would turn inward and erect barriers between nations within and without the bloc. As a consequence the United States sought its own trade bloc among North American nations by the signing of the North American Free Trade Agreement (NAFTA).

Free Trade, Politics, and NAFTA

The North American Free Trade Agreement was an attempt to create a trade bloc among the United States, Mexico, and Canada. The agreement had its origins in the development of the European Union and the decline of U.S. competitiveness in foreign markets. Moreover, breakdowns in the Uruguay

Round of the GATT negotiation, which had been going on since the early 1980s, led the United States to seek another method of lowering trade barriers while demonstrating to other trading partners that the United States had alternative options should multilateral negotiations collapse. Business groups in the United States also believed that a free-trade agreement would boost the competitive position of U.S. industry and allow them to compete more effectively with Europe and Japan. Finally, the U.S. government was eager, for foreign policy reasons, to encourage the consolidation of economic reform and political stability in Mexico.

The United States had negotiated an earlier free-trade agreement with Canada, which took effect in January 1989. Subsequently the Bush administration moved to include Mexico. Mexican membership in NAFTA was politically controversial. Labor opposed a free-trade agreement with Mexico, fearing that U.S. jobs would go to Mexico because of lower wages there. For the previous two decades, labor had been fighting the flight of U.S. jobs to other nations, where wages were much lower than those for U.S. workers. Mexico was viewed as a greater threat than other nations because it shared a border with the United States, cutting down on transportation costs to the United States as businesses opened operations along the U.S.-Mexico border.

Environmentalists also opposed a free-trade agreement with Mexico. They charged that Mexican environmental efforts were weak and not up to U.S. standards. As business and industry expanded in Mexico because of free trade, the quality of the environment would suffer. Moreover, environmentalists and others felt that businesses would relocate from the United States to Mexico to avoid the costs of U.S. environmental regulation or that regulations would be relaxed at home in order to induce firms not to move.

Naturally, the importance of labor and environmental groups to the Democratic Party led many in that party to oppose free trade with Mexico. Further widening the party split was the fact that a Republican administration was negotiating the pact with Mexico.

However, Democrats won the election in 1992, and their candidate, Bill Clinton, supported free trade and NAFTA. To deal with the criticisms of labor, environmentalists, and Democrats in the party and to avoid the appearance that he was accepting a Bush policy, Clinton initiated a series of supplemental negotiations with the Mexican government on attaining office. Those side agreements focused on environmental, labor, and import issues.[32]

Despite these efforts, labor opposition to NAFTA intensified as the vote drew near. Labor leaders threatened to cut off political support in the 1994 midterm congressional elections to those who supported the deal. With the prospect of a defeat in the House looming, the administration decided on a risky gamble—debating Ross Perot, the independent candidate for president who vocally opposed NAFTA. The debate was held on November 9, just a week before the scheduled House vote. Vice President Albert Gore was called in to debate Perot. The gamble seemed to pay off for the administration. Gore was prepared for the debate with facts, figures, and rationale. Perot, meanwhile, appeared uninformed, unable to marshal evidence to support his claims. This media event was the breakthrough that the administration needed, creating movement to its position in the public opinion polls.

Clinton won easily in the Senate, with a 61–38 split, despite defection by many Democrats. The House vote was much closer, 234–200, and Clinton needed strong Republican support to win. A majority of 156 Democrats voted against the treaty, with only 102 in support. Republicans split more decisively in favor of the treaty at 132–43. The passage of NAFTA illustrates the forces that affect international economic policymaking in the 1990s. Domestic economic and social forces, government factors, and international factors were all important. The interplay of all these elements is what makes international economic policy in the United States so complex.[33]

THE POLITICS OF INTERNATIONAL MONETARY POLICY: STABILIZING THE DOLLAR

International trade cannot take place unless nations are able to set the value of foreign goods in their own currency. For example, Indians must know the relative value of dollars and rupees if they are to be able to determine whether buying a U.S. product is a good deal. The comparison of different national currencies is known as **exchange rates.** Thus, the dollar is worth X yen, or pounds sterling, and so on.[34]

Exchange rates affect trade balances and domestic inflation. For instance, if the value of the dollar rises, then it takes more yen to purchase a dollar. When the dollar's value rises, then, the price of U.S. goods to foreign consumers increases. This makes the U.S. goods less competitive, and U.S. exports decline. Eventually, as exports decline, a trade deficit may be created. When a country has a trade deficit with another country, the country with the trade surplus may redeem the surplus for gold, it may keep the surplus "dollars" at home, or it may invest in the deficit nation. Thus, when the United States runs a deficit in trade with Japan, the Japanese have the option of keeping the U.S. dollars, converting them to gold, or investing in the United States. Investing would, of course, reduce the trade deficit.

There are three other ways a country can try to deal with its trade deficit. First, as discussed earlier, it can impose restrictions on imports (or on the outflow of capital to pay for these imports). Second, it can reduce the economy's overall demand through fiscal or monetary tightening; for obvious reasons, this is not a politically popular option. Third, the deficit nation can devalue its currency, that is, lower its currency's value. Then its goods will be priced more competitively in world markets, and trade exports should increase, reducing the size of the trade deficit. Similarly, **devaluation** may increase the cost of foreign goods that are imported. This will reduce their competitiveness in the market, which again will help to reduce the trade deficit. However, devaluation of the currency to affect the trade deficit may affect inflation because of the increased cost of foreign goods and the increase in demand for domestic goods, which will fuel the economy. Other countries may also object to the devaluation because they will be the ones whose products are less competitive internationally. If other countries retaliate, a spiral of competitive devaluations may develop in which case any benefits from the original devaluation will be canceled out. Thus, policymakers are in a quandary over trade policy and its implications for the domestic economy. As trade becomes a larger portion of economic activity, the issue of international currency values will be more important, with greater implications for the domestic economy.

International Exchange Rates Before World War II

Before World War II, international currency exchange rates were fixed to the **gold standard**.[35] This meant that each currency was fixed to a certain amount of gold. For instance, the dollar might be pegged at $35 an ounce of gold (the actual rate in the postwar era). The gold standard was taken very seriously by nations prior to World War I. Their macroeconomic policies were built on adherence to the gold standard and maintenance of that system. Thus, to stem the flow of gold reserves out of a country that was a deficit trader, the government often relied on policies that would depress demand in the domestic economy. This might mean raising interest rates, reducing the money supply, cutting government spending, or inducing a recession.

Many of the tense policy debates between Democrats and Republicans in the late nineteenth century revolved around the gold standard issue. Some Democrats, like those associated with the populist William Jennings Bryan, desired a looser money policy, not the tight money policy of the gold standard. Farmers, especially, preferred a loose money policy. Bryan promised, if elected president, to put the nation on a dual gold and silver standard. This policy would allow the money supply to grow not only with the gold supply but with the silver supply too. As Bryan thundered to the Democratic National Convention in 1896, "You shall not press down upon the brow of labor this crown of thorns, you shall not crucify mankind upon a cross of gold." Of course, such a policy was also inflationary and was opposed by those who feared inflation and supported the international gold standard.

In the 1920s, with the growth of many new democracies in Europe and the increased strength of labor movements, political pressure for a looser, inflationary policy grew stronger. The public, especially debtors, prefers a **loose money** policy, which may lead to inflation. Loose money usually means that more money is available for credit at lower interest rates. Because of the voting power of debtor classes, democratic governments are less insulated from pressures for looser money than nondemocratic regimes. And many countries, for a time at least, violated the standard way of dealing with trade deficits by reducing domestic economic demand. Many countries increased tariffs on imported goods. This policy made foreign goods more expensive, which reduced imports. In effect, with lower demand for their goods because of high tariffs, foreign exporters paid the price, while the nation into which they exported did not have to implement demand-depressing policies to deal with its trade deficit or gold outflow. However, these policies of trade restriction through tariff increases choked off international markets; this, many believed, not only contributed to the depth and longevity of the Depression but, by doing so, indirectly contributed to the outbreak of the next world war.

The Bretton Woods System

The linkage among the gold standard, tariffs, and world war led to the creation of a new international monetary system, known as the **Bretton Woods system,** named after the location in New Hampshire where in 1944 the allied powers began building the postwar economic order. A return to the stability of the gold standard of the pre–World War I era was sought, but without its rigidity. Instead of gold as the international standard, dollars became the world standard. The dollar's value was fixed at a certain amount of gold ($35 an ounce). Although other currencies were, in turn, linked to the dollar, the dollar was employed because the United States possessed the largest share of the world's gold at the time, estimated at between 60 and 75 percent.[36]

In addition, the International Monetary Fund was established, from which deficit trading nations could borrow funds on a short-term basis to deal with their balance of payment problems. The IMF's funds came from payments of gold and currency by member nations, with the United States's supplying about one-third of the contributions.[37] Often the IMF required austerity measures reminiscent of the tight money policies of the gold standard era, but IMF loans also provided nations with breathing room so that their attempts to deal with the balance of payments would not overly shock their domestic economy. However, if the IMF determined that the balance of payment deficit was the result not of short-term problems but rather reflected a "fundamental disequilibrium," then the government was permitted to devalue its currency. This type of system is called an **adjustable peg system.**

The Demise of Bretton Woods

In the early years of the Bretton Woods system, the main problem was getting enough dollars into the hands of foreign consumers. The Western European economies in particular were in worse shape than many had realized and could not generate enough foreign exchange to purchase the goods that they needed. The United States was able to alleviate this "dollar shortage" through a combination of foreign aid (funneled through the Marshall Plan), military spending, and investment in Europe.

As recovery from World War II continued, industries in the rest of the world began to catch up to (and in some cases even surpass) those in the United States. Thus, the large U.S. trade surplus began slowly to dwindle and eventually turned into a trade deficit. This posed a problem for the Bretton Woods system. When the United States was a surplus trader, there was no threat that it would have to redeem its dollars in gold, and so draw down its gold reserves and potentially upset the international monetary markets by doing so. When the trade deficit appeared and did not seem likely to abate, the dollar shortage turned into a dollar glut. As a result, those who held U.S. currency began to worry that there would not be enough gold in the United States to redeem the ever-increasing number of dollars in circulation. As long as people had confidence that everyone else would hold on to their dollars and not convert them into gold, there was no reason to worry about this situation. But as it became clear that the United States was not going to be able to eliminate its trade deficit anytime soon, the prospect arose that one day the U.S. government might no longer agree to exchange dollars for gold. As a result, confidence in the dollar fell; this rocked the foundation of the international monetary system.

Several factors led to the chronic U.S. trade deficit, including the cost of the Vietnam War, the U.S. importation of foreign oil, and the continued rise of the Western European and Japanese economies. President Johnson was, for political reasons, hesitant to raise taxes in order to pay for the increasingly unpopular Vietnam War, but he also did not want to abandon his ambitious domestic agenda to create what he called the Great Society. Thus, the budget deficit increased, fueling inflation and making U.S. goods more expensive on world markets and foreign goods cheaper.

Because other countries were obliged to exchange their currencies for dollars, the increased volume of dollars in circulation compelled them to print additional currency; this caused worldwide inflation. Many foreign leaders resented what they perceived as U.S. irresponsibility in living beyond its means. For instance, French President Charles de Gaulle complained that the Bretton Woods system gave the United States an "exorbitant privilege" by allowing it to print as many dollars as it wanted and forcing other countries to adjust. France announced that it would immediately convert any new accumulation of dollars into gold. Although other countries did not take as aggressive an approach, they too expressed concern that the United States was exploiting its position as the key currency country.

For their part, U.S. leaders responded that they were the ones who were being taken advantage of. Other countries, they argued, were deliberately maintaining low exchange rates in order to sell more exports in the U.S. market and promote their own economic welfare. Any other country in its position could simply devalue its currency, but given the special role of the dollar, such a course of action was not possible for the United States. Because every currency was pegged to the dollar, any change in its value would simply change the value of every other currency as well. Leaders in the United States urged other countries to inflate their own currencies further. They also tried to prevent dollars from leaving the country by imposing restrictions and taxes on any outflows. Neither approach had much success.

One problem was that the creators of the Bretton Woods system had not anticipated the dramatic increase in the size of international flows of speculative capital. These flows made it much more difficult for governments to maintain the value of their currency at a fixed rate once investors started to believe that a devaluation was inevitable. Indeed, spectators could create a self-fulfilling prophecy by selling a currency off in such large volumes that governments were forced to take steps such as devaluing that they might otherwise not have had to. Such pressure was put on the dollar that by the early 1970s, the system was close to collapse. The flight from the dollar came to a head in 1971 when President Nixon announced a policy that stopped the payment of dollars with gold, imposed wage and price controls to stem domestic inflation, and placed a 10 percent surcharge on imports into the United States.[38] He also called on international markets to devalue the dollar. (On world markets the dollar was being traded at greater than the fixed rate of $35 an ounce.)

Essentially, the United States was no longer willing to subordinate its own interests in being able to pursue whatever domestic and foreign policies it wanted to its other interest in preserving the existing international monetary system. The tradeoff between domestic autonomy and international stability had not been as acute when the United States was the undisputed economic superpower. But by the early 1970s, policymakers were feeling unduly constrained by the restrictions of the Bretton Woods system. Many countries objected to this unilateral abdication by President Nixon, but there was little they could do and eventually a new international agreement was reached whereby the dollar was devalued and the surcharge dropped, though the United States did not recommit to exchanging gold for dollars.

Still, the U.S. trade deficit continued, and it increased as well. Continued pressure on the dollar led to another 10 percent devaluation, but eventually, in March 1973, the system of fixed rates was abandoned and currencies were allowed to **float** against each other on the open market (a decision formalized three years later at a conference in Jamaica). In a **floating system,** governments allow international markets to determine the value of a currency, rather than pegging the currency at a fixed value. In reality, because the exchange rate has such an important effect on trade and on prices throughout the economy, governments often intervene to affect the value of their currency, and hence the current system is often called a **managed** or **"dirty" float.**

The dollar fell through much of the 1970s but then rebounded in the 1980s. The dollar strengthened mostly because of the high interest rates that were in part a consequence of the growing budget deficits of the 1980s and the Fed policy in the early 1980s to quell the inflation of the 1970s with a tight money policy.

The strong dollar made U.S. goods less competitive, both at home and abroad; this led to skyrocketing trade deficits and growing protectionist pressure from U.S. industries that were suffering from import competition. In order to avoid a breakdown in the international trading system, President Reagan abandoned his earlier policy, called **benign neglect,** in which the government did not do anything about the value of the dollar. Instead, the United States, along with the other major economic powers, agreed in 1985, in a meeting at the Plaza Hotel in New York City, to cooperate in bringing the value of the dollar down. The agreement was successful, and in fact two years later, at another meeting at Louvre Museum in Paris, governments agreed to halt the dollar's slide and try to stabilize the major world currencies.

Given the enormous size of international currency markets, governments often find that they cannot affect exchange rates. In order for their interventions in world currency markets to have a lasting effect, nations need to address the underlying domestic economic policies that are contributing to the destabilizing imbalances. Many governments are reluctant to let important economic decisions be dictated by foreign countries; therefore, macroeconomic coordination is extremely difficult to achieve and international negotiations are often driven by conflict. For instance, the United States has tried to deal with its trade deficit by getting other nations, especially Japan and Germany, to stimulate their economies, thereby increasing their demand for U.S. goods. But the Germans, especially, recalling the high inflation of the 1920s, which they felt helped pave the way for Hitler, have been resistant to stimulating demand. Instead, Germany, Japan, and other nations have tried to get the United States to bring its budget deficit under control as a means of dealing with the trade deficit problem.

The dominant role that the dollar has played in the international monetary system (even after the end of the Bretton Woods system) has given the United States significant bargaining power in these disputes; no matter what the United States does, people still consider dollars to be essential for conducting international transactions. However, with the recent introduction of a single European currency, the Euro, many wonder whether the age of dollar dominance is coming to an end.[39] Again, we see the linkage between domestic and international economic policies.

CONCLUSION

Although trade and monetary policies are the most prominent types of international economic policies, they are not the only ones. For instance, the U.S. government must formulate policies on matters such as regulating the activities of multinational corporations, responding to global financial crises, maintaining access to crucial raw materials like oil, and a whole host of other important issues. International economic policymaking has grown in importance as the volume of transactions among nations has increased. Consequently, the U.S. economy is no longer as insulated from world economic patterns as it once was. The international economic policymaking environment in the United States is very complex. Although the president holds the greatest share of authority and responsibility now, Congress and economic interests are also important. But international economic circumstances and the international political system also shape U.S. international economic policymaking.

Key Terms

adjustable peg
  system
antidumping policy
balance of trade
benign neglect
bilateral
  relationship
Bretton Woods
  system
countervailing
  duties
current account
  balance
devaluation
"dirty" float
dumping
escape clause cases
European
  Community
European Union
  (EU)

exchange rates
fair trade
float
floating system
free trade
General Agreement
  on Tariff and
  Trade (GATT)
gold standard
Group of Seven
  (G-7)
international
  economic policy
international
  economic
  subpresidency
International
  Monetary Fund
  (IMF)
loose money
managed float

managed trade
merchandise trade
  balance
multilateral
  relationship
protectionism
quotas
trade deficit
voluntary export
  restraints (VERs)
World Bank
World Trade
  Organization

Explore the Web

Two important U.S. international economic policymakers and their web pages are the U.S. Trade Representative (www.ustr.gov) and the International Trade Commission (www.usitc.gov). The World Trade Organization maintains its web page at www.wto.org and the International Monetary Fund can be located at www.imf.org. Two periodicals with extensive coverage of international economic issues are the *Financial Times* (www.ft.com) and *The Economist* (www.economist.com).

Notes

1. The Bush administration's response to this event is discussed in Larry Berman and Bruce W. Jentleson, "Bush and the Post–Cold War World: New Challenges for American Leadership," in *The Bush Presidency: First Appraisals,* eds. Colin Campbell and Bert Rockman (Chatham, NJ: Chatham House, 1991), 108–109.

2. See I. M. Destler, *American Trade Politics,* 3d ed. (Washington, DC: Institute for International Economics, 1995), 234.

3. "American Trade Policy: Throwing Sand in the Gears," *The Economist,* January 30, 1999, 63–65.

4. Some of the differences and tensions between foreign and international economic policy are discussed in Richard N. Cooper, "Trade Policy as Foreign Policy," in *U.S. Trade Policies as a Changing World Economy,* ed. Robert M. Stern (Cambridge, MA: MIT Press, 1987), 291–322.

5. Details on trends in the U.S. trade deficit are found in Thomas D. Lairson and David Skidmore, *International Political Economy: The Struggle for Power and Wealth* (Fort Worth, TX: Harcourt, Brace, 1993), 97–98.

6. For two contrasting views, see Paul Krugman, *Pop Internationalism* (Cambridge, MA: MIT Press, 1996); and Lester Thurow, *Head to Head: The Coming Economic Battle Among Japan, Europe, and America* (New York: Morrow, 1992).

7. These figures come from the *Statistical Abstract of the United States.*

8. A useful yet concise discussion of the USTR is found in John P. Frendreis and Raymond Tatalovich, *The Modern Presidency and Economic Policy* (Itasca, IL: Peacock, 1994), 152–153.

9. The responsibility for developing trading markets has been variously located in the Departments of State and Commerce. Once attached to embassies, which are a part of the State Department, this function has been moved to Commerce, supposedly because of Commerce's better ties to U.S. firms and its better economic and trade expertise.

10. They are part of the "outer" cabinet, rather than the "inner" cabinet, an informal designation that identifies the general importance and political influence of cabinet advisers to the president. On this notion of "inner" and "outer" cabinets, see Thomas Cronin, *The State of the Presidency,* 2d ed. (Boston: Little, Brown, 1980). The idea is developed and refined in Jeffrey E. Cohen, *The Politics of the U.S. Cabinet: Representation in the Executive Branch, 1789–1984* (Pittsburgh, PA: University of Pittsburgh Press, 1988), 122–145.

11. This is based in part on Robert A. Pastor, *Congress and the Politics of Foreign Economic Policy, 1929–1976* (Berkeley: University of California Press, 1980), and "The Cry-and-Sigh Syndrome: Congress and Trade Policy," in *Making Economic Policy in Congress,* ed. Allen Schick (Washington, DC: American Enterprise Institute, 1983), 158–195.

12. The figures come from Lyn Ragsdale, *Vital Statistics on the Presidency: Washington to Clinton* (Washington, DC: CQ Press, 1996), 314. Included in these totals are protocols and conventions, as well as treaties.

13. See Michael A. Bailey, Judith Goldstein, and Barry R. Weingast, "The Institutional Roots of American Trade Policy: Politics, Coalitions, and International Trade," *World Politics* 49 (April 1977): 309–338.

14. A good discussion of executive agreements and their growing importance is Forrest McDonald, *The American Presidency: An Intellectual History* (Lawrence: University Press of Kansas, 1994), esp. 388–409.

15. These figures come from Ragsdale, *Vital Statistics on the Presidency: Washington to Clinton,* 320.

16. Decision making at the ITC is discussed in Judith Goldstein, "The Political Economy of Trade: Institutions of Protection," *American Political Science Review* 80 (1986): 161–184; and Wendy L. Hansen, "The International Trade Commission and the Politics of Protectionism," *American Political Science Review* 84 (1990): 21–47.

17. On the steel issue, see "Steel Producers Urge Duties," *New York Times,* January 1, 1994, 26, 52. On cigarette lighters, see "Trade Petition Filed by Bic," *New York Times,* May 10, 1994, D7. On printing presses, see Jim Rosenberg, "Rockwell Asks for Anti-dumping Duties," *Editor & Publisher* 128 (July 29, 1995): 26–27.

18. J. M. Finger, H. Keith Hall, and Douglas R. Nelson, "The Political Economy of Administered Protection," *American Economic Review* 72 (June 1982): 452–466.

19. To this list of international actors we could add private economic agents such as multinational corporations or currency speculators. For more on the increasing importance of these market actors, see Susan Strange, *The Retreat of the State: The Diffusion of Power in the World Economy* (New York: Cambridge University Press, 1996).

20. The economic summits of the G-7 are the subject of Robert Putnam and Nicholas Bayne, *Hanging Together: Cooperation and Conflict in the Seven Power Summits* (Cambridge, MA: Harvard University Press, 1987).

21. Details on EC structure and organization can be found in Lairson and Skidmore, *International Political Economy,* 115–120.

22. "Where Next? A Survey of World Trade," *The Economist,* October 3, 1998, 6.

23. A good discussion is found in Richard Lehne, *Industry and Politics: The United States in Comparative Perspective* (Englewood Cliffs, NJ: Prentice-Hall, 1993), 217–219. Also see Lairson and Skidmore, *International Political Economy,* 147–149.

24. Jagdish Bhagwati and Hugh Patricks, eds., *Aggressive Unilateralism: America's 301 Trade Policy & the World Trading System* (Ann Arbor: University of Michigan Press, 1990).

25. For a discussion, see C. Fred Bergsten and Marcus Noland, *Reconcilable Differences: United States–Japan Economic Conflict* (Washington, DC: Institute for International Economics, 1993).

26. See Lehne, *Industry and Politics,* 224–225. For a critique, see Douglas Irwin, *Managed Trade: The Case Against Import Targets* (Washington, DC: American Enterprise Institute, 1994).

27. Laura D'Andrea Tyson, *Who's Bashing Whom? Trade Conflict in High-Technology Industries* (Washington, DC: Institute for International Economics, 1992).

28. For an overview, see John Odell, "Understanding Trade Policies: An Emerging Synthesis," *World Politics* 43 (October 1990): 139–67.

29. See Hansen, "The International Trade Commission and the Politics of Protectionism."

30. On the power of ideas in international trade policy, see Judith Goldstein, "Ideas, Institutions, and American Trade Policies," *International Organization* 42 (1988): 179–217.

31. Lairson and Skidmore, *International Political Economy,* 64. Keech and Pak, "Partisanship, Institutions, and Change in American Trade Politics," 1131, graphically illustrate trends in U.S. tariffs from the 1820s to 1990. In 1930, after passage of Smoot-Hawley, tariff levels neared 60 percent.

32. Bruce Stokes, "Mexican Roulette," *National Journal,* May 15, 1993, 1160.

33. Another study that argues that a mix of international and domestic factors affects a nation's international economic policies is Beth A. Simmons, *Who Adjusts? Domestic Sources of Foreign Economic Policy During the Interwar Years* (Princeton, NJ: Princeton University Press, 1994).

34. A good discussion of exchange rate policies and their implications is found in Lairson and Skidmore, *International Political Economy,* 24–33.

35. This system is described well in Simmons, *Who Adjusts?*

36. Lairson and Skidmore, *International Political Economy,* 65.

37. Ibid.

38. See the discussions in Lairson and Skidmore, *International Political Economy,* 88–90; and Frendreis and Tatalovich, *The Modern Presidency and Economic Policy,* 54–159.

39. See C. Fred Bergsten, "America and Europe: Clash of the Titans?" *Foreign Affairs* 78 (March–April 1999): 20–34.

14

Economic Policymaking in the United States

THE NATURE OF U.S. ECONOMIC POLICYMAKING

There is no easy way to characterize U.S. economic policies and policymaking. There are numerous types of economic policies that are decided on by many different policymakers. Thus, decision making tends to be highly decentralized, allowing for a variety of policy participants and policies. No one sector of government makes all of the nation's economic policies.

Further, no one level of government makes all of the nation's economic policies. We have treated only policies made at the federal level of government in this book, but the states and localities have their own economic policies.[1] Thus, economic policymaking in the United States is made within the structure of separation of powers, checks and balances, and federalism.

Within this decentralized system of policymaking, there is also some specialization among policymakers. That is, some policymakers give more attention to some types of economic policies than to others. For instance, presidential attention focuses first and foremost on macroeconomic policy, though presidents have been giving increasing attention to regulatory policy over the past twenty years. Distributive economic policy, in contrast, is of much less interest to presidents, who have yet to develop any institutional or organizational mechanisms to treat such policies other than on an occasional and ad hoc basis.

Congress, although certainly also interested in macroeconomic policy, has expended the bulk of its efforts in making distributive economic policy. Electoral concerns and the focus on individual congressional districts motivate such behavior, which we see institutionalized in Congress through the committee system. Still, considerable attention is given to macroeconomic policymaking, especially through the budget process, and to regulatory policy, in part because of Congress's central role in passing legislation. Thus, almost all types of economic policies must pass through Congress before they can be implemented. But even in the macroeconomic realm, Congress has the tendency to treat taxation, an aspect of fiscal policymaking, as a distributive policy more than a macroeconomic one. However, just as the presidents have increased their efforts with regard to regulatory policy, the budget process and the persistent federal deficit of the 1980s and 1990s have caused Congress to focus more attention on macroeconomic concerns, which it continues to do despite newfound budgetary surpluses.[2]

The bureaucracy is also involved in economic policymaking, and it too shows the pattern of specialization. However, the size and scope of the bureaucracy mean that different parts of the bureaucracy specialize in different policymaking areas. The Fed, for instance, is charged with making and implementing perhaps the most important macroeconomic policy, monetary policy. And bureaucratic agencies are primarily responsible for implementing regulatory and distributive economic policy. The regulatory bureaucrats, however, may have greater impact on the substance and details of such policy because of the discretion given to them. Even this, in recent years, may have eroded as regulation has shifted from economic regulation to social regulation, where statutes are much more detailed and specific, and also because of deregulation, which has hit economic regulatory agencies harder than social regulatory ones.

The tremendous decentralization of economic policymaking in the United States means that the economic policy regime at any one time tends toward policy inconsistency: many different types of policies with different aims, sometimes working at cross-purposes, may exist simultaneously. Thus, the government may increase subsidies to certain economic sectors while also trying to reduce its presence in the economy. Tobacco is a good example. On the one hand, subsidies and protections are given to tobacco farmers to increase production, tobacco quality, and income to tobacco farmers; on the other hand, the National Cancer Institute of the National Institute of Health spends millions on research and treatment of diseases caused by tobacco use, like lung cancer.

Decentralization of economic policymaking lends itself to policy inconsistency because new economic policy regimes are not able to affect all economic policymakers equally. For example, new regimes and movements that support reduction of federal involvement in the economy may greatly affect the regulatory policymaking centers without having much impact on the distributive or macroeconomic policymaking centers. Similarly, forces that affect the federal government may not be felt in the states or localities. Decentralization allows old policies to continue in spite of changes in other policymaking centers and in part may immunize some policymaking centers from new economic policy directions, while not impairing the ability of others to respond to them.

Decentralization makes it possible for a tremendous diversity of participants and forces to affect economic policy in the United States. But it also means that it is hard to mobilize the forces necessary to produce comprehensive overhauls in economic policy. Thus, government has had a hard time dealing with economic policies that touch on a wide range of economic issues, the budget deficit being the best case in point. Only rarely in U.S. history have forces come together and altered a large number of economic policies in fundamental ways. This happened in the 1930s with Roosevelt's New Deal. But the "Reagan Revolution" was hampered by Democratic control of Congress, and the "Gingrich Revolution" of 1995 was stymied by Democratic occupancy of the White House.[3]

SOURCES OF INFLUENCE ON U.S. ECONOMIC POLICY

The sources of influence on U.S. economic policy are varied and diverse. Clearly, political institutions have an impact on economic policy, as do political and economic interests, but ideas also influence economic policy. We will discuss these three influences on U.S. economic policymaking: ideas, institutions, and interests.

Ideas

At different times in U.S. history, different ideas take hold of the collective imagination, motivating and sometimes altering how people, participants, and policymakers think about public policies. When an idea provides the foundation for thinking about many economic issues and policies and affects the construction and implementation of those policies, we have one component of an economic policy regime. Policy inconsistency is in part a result of different ideas animating different economic policies.

Although many ideas are important in economic policy development, the concept of the market serves as an anchor against which all ideas are evaluated in the United States. In fact, it may not be too far off the mark to suggest that all economic policy ideas in the United States lean either toward or away from the market concept, though it is important to note that some antimarket solutions never get considered seriously in this country. These, of course, are the state ownership and operation alternatives.[4] Even regulation in the United States is based on private ownership and often its aim is to simulate marketlike conditions and results.

The market idea emphasizes economic efficiency, individual choice, private decision making, and distribution through the private market. Nonmarket or antimarket approaches in the United States, in contrast, look at equity, collective decision making, and government involvement as virtues, with boundaries on the set of acceptable antimarket policies, as just noted.

Ideas may stimulate policymakers and advocates to think about issues in new ways, from a new perspective. Thus the generation of new ideas may be an important first step in the policymaking process. The deregulation movement of the 1970s had its inspiration first as an idea—an idea whose roots lie in notions of the superiority of the market.[5] Similarly, Keynesianism became an important idea behind efforts to increase government intervention in the economy. In the 1980s Reaganomics, with its emphasis on reducing government involvement in the economy gained great currency, supplanting more interventionist policy ideas. And the idea of free trade, which is closely related to the notion of the free market, has been the foundation for much of the United States's international economic policy since the Depression.[6] What is important about ideas is that they become the intellectual justification for a whole host of economic policies.[7]

Institutions

Ideas, however, require institutions if they are to be converted into public policies and if they are to persist. The conversion of ideas into policies by authoritative policymaking institutions is what is required to create a policy regime. Thus, economic policy regimes need both ideas and institutions. Institutions are those authoritative political bodies that make and implement public policies. New bureaucratic agencies responsible for new policies are critical in this regard. Without institutions, ideas may quickly fade from view. With institutions, ideas may become embedded in the policymaking fabric. Institutions, to a degree, carry out policy ideas, putting ideas, which are often abstract, into concrete terms.

However, institutions not only transform ideas into policies, they may themselves be transformed by ideas. Thus, the idea of government intervention in the economy as a result of the crisis of the Depression may have been instrumental in transforming the presidency and the bureaucracy.

Moreover, in some instances, institutions are themselves the results of ideas. This is most apparent with the creation of bureaucratic agencies to carry out ideas. For instance, the ICC was created in the 1880s to implement the idea of market regulation. It is through the longevity of institutions that ideas persist. Institutions create a "bias of mobilization" in favor of some ideas over others.[8] Similarly, when institutions are dismantled, as they were under deregulation in the 1970s and 1980s, the ideas that were once present in the policy may fade as well. The creation and destruction of political institutions has a great impact on the staying power and policy impact of ideas.

Perhaps the most important institutions, aside from the political decision-making branches of the presidency and the legislature, are the bureaucratic ones. Bureaucracies implement policies as constructed in the halls of the legislature and the presidency, and in some cases, like economic regulation and monetary policy, actually influence the substance and details of policy. Bureaucracies as policy institutions are also important because it is here that past and present meet.

The Congress and the presidency are highly responsive to short-term changes. The turnover of personnel through elections is a major source of their responsiveness, and anticipation of what ideas and issues will play in upcoming elections also motivates legislative and presidential responsiveness.[9] Although bureaucracies are not immune to change, the past has greater impact on them and the policies they implement than on Congress or the presidency. In a sense, the bureaucracy, which is responsible to its legislative mandate, negotiates between the past and the present in the policymaking process.[10] Thus, bureaucracies are important institutions in keeping ideas alive, helping them weather political storms.

Interests

Political and economic interests are also important in making U.S. economic policy. No one political or economic interest is active across all economic policy issues, a function of the dispersion of political authority and the decentralization of policymaking just discussed. Since economic policy issues operate on two different levels, macroeconomic and sectoral, the types of political and economic interests that are influential at each level also differ. Macroeconomic issues involve system-level political forces, politicians, and economic factors. Sectoral economic issues are made mostly within policy subsystems, while different specific political and economic interests are active and influential across these subsystems.

Interests with national perspectives are most active and influential in macroeconomic policymaking. Public opinion, parties, and voters—and the politicians who seek their support—are the most important of these political interests. The "economy" and the "business sector" are important here, too, often carrying their impact as abstract notions rather than as concrete enterprises, although specific firms and business leaders may speak out and try to influence macroeconomic policymaking.

Public opinion and voters represent a "deep background" to which macroeconomic policymakers often refer when making policy. The public tends not to send clear messages to policymakers about policy options and preferences, but it holds policymakers accountable for its economic well-being. Thus, policymakers aim to build macroeconomic policies that will improve voters' economic circumstances.

Also, policymakers must interpret what the general public will tolerate in terms of policies, hoping that their interpretation is correct. Polls help to some extent, but if the right questions are not asked or if questions are not asked in the right way, polls may provide little clear guidance for policymakers. Moreover, polls do not help policymakers anticipate public reaction to their policies. There is always some uncertainty about future public reaction. This unpredictability forces politicians constantly to refer to the public, giving it an important if indirect and passive role in the macroeconomic policymaking process.

Public opinion has tended to waver between two tendencies: to support or to oppose increased government intervention in the economy; that is, the public "mood" may be more or less liberal. In the 1960s, the mood veered toward the liberal pole; currently it seems tilted more toward the conservative end. National policymakers tend to be very sensitive to the public's mood, and, thus, when the mood is more liberal, macroeconomic policies are likely to reflect that tendency.

Complicating matters for policymakers is that the public mood may not allow the best possible policies to be adopted, and policies that call for short-term economic pain are almost universally despised by the public, though such bitter medicine may be required for the longer-term health of the economy. The public mood and the ideological leanings and proclivities of policymakers may clash as well. Plus, the public mood and the preferences of other groups important to political careers, like parties and their supporters, may also be at variance. Navigating policy through such potentially rough political waters is risky and not always successful.

Political parties must also be addressed by policymakers when making macroeconomic policy. Parties are critical to political careers, especially for those at the top of the political hierarchy, like leaders of Congress and the president. Thus, macroeconomic policymakers often pay great attention to the policy preferences of their parties. But political parties are also important in macroeconomic policymaking because they tend to take opposing positions on the concept of increased or decreased government intervention in the economy and have thus helped structure the terms of political debate at the system level. During this century, Democrats have stood most firmly in the liberal, interventionist camp, with Republicans taking the opposite position.

We see the engagement of parties in macroeconomic policy through the participation of the president and the party leaders in Congress. Moreover, party nomination of candidates for office, especially for the presidency, becomes an important venue to articulate party differences in economic policy, while also trying to mobilize public support behind those positions.

The parties adopt different economic policy positions, in part because of their long-standing traditions and ideologies but also because of the groups and voters who make up the party, who have been loyal to and supportive of the party. Parties try to serve those who have been loyal to them in the past and whom they want to keep loyal in the future. Republicans find support among middle- and upper-class voters and business groups, whereas Democrats have found greater success among workers in the bottom half of the income brackets and among labor, with much less support coming from the business sector than for Republicans. These reservoirs of support motivate Republicans toward generally promarket policies, whereas Democrats are more willing to restrict and regulate the market. The self-interest of economic sectors influences macroeconomic policy through the parties. Specific economic sectors have much less direct impact on macroeconomic policymaking.

Peak-level economic interests, like national business associations and labor unions, also are important elements of macroeconomic policymaking. The privileged position of business in the United States means that business does not actively have to advocate its preferences for its concerns to be taken into account. Thus, macroeconomic policies are always judged by how they will affect growth. Similarly, the inflationary nature of government economic policies is a perennial concern of policymakers. Even when silent, business has great influence on the shape of macroeconomic policy. No politician involved in macroeconomic policy can ignore its effects on the economy, as those effects will be felt later in the ballot box.

Sectoral economic interests have greater influence over economic policies when we look at sectoral issues rather than macroeconomic ones. National political forces lose some of their influence when sectoral-level policies are being built. Sectoral-level policies, whether regulatory or distributive, tend to be constructed in policy subsystems. These subsystems make every effort to insulate themselves from national political forces. Thus, voters, the public mood, and political parties recede into the background and perhaps even vanish from the sectoral economic policymaking process. Often, especially with distributive policy, bipartisan coalitions support policies most of which may be too minor to generate voter interest. System-level politicians, like presidents and congressional party leaders, may not play an active role; congressional committees and specific economic interests may be most influential.

Finally, the greater exposure of the U.S. economy to international economic factors has catapulted the international context into the policymaking process. International economic and political conditions affect U.S. economic policymaking much more strongly now than a generation ago, and the impact of these factors is likely to increase in the future. Thus, the economic policymaking context in the United States has become even more complex with the introduction of these external actors and conditions.

Despite the booming economy of the late 1990s, economic policy is likely to remain high on the political and policymaking agenda of the nation. The quality of life of the nation's citizens is greatly affected by the state of the economy, and we have seen throughout this book that governmental policy choice affects the economy. Government policy choice may affect who will become winners and losers in the economy, how economic benefits will be distributed throughout society, the structure of the economy, and the strength of economic performance. With such a potentially great impact, it is of little surprise that many take their economic grievances and issues to the government arena for resolution, redress, and advantage. Thus, although the issues may change, the fact of political activity surrounding economic policy choice remains a constant of U.S. politics and policymaking.

Notes

1. See Paul Brace, *State Government and Economic Performance* (Baltimore, MD: Johns Hopkins University Press, 1993).

2. On the increasing attention of Congress to fiscal policy, especially with regard to the budget, see James A. Thurber, "The Impact of Budget Reform on Presidential and Congressional Governance," in *Divided Democracy: Cooperation and Conflict Between the President and Congress,* ed. James A. Thurber (Washington, DC: CQ Press, 1991), 145–197.

3. Reform is also hampered by the increasing capacity of government, which is built up over the years through laws, regulations, bureaucratic expertise, and the creation of constituencies that benefit from programs. It may actually be easier to create new economic policies and programs than alter old ones. See Paul C. Light, *Thickening Government: Federal Hierarchy and the Diffusion of Accountability* (Washington, DC: Brookings, 1995).

4. John W. Kingdon, *Agendas, Alternatives, and Public Policies,* 2d ed. (New York: HarperCollins, 1995), 140–145.

5. On the idea of deregulation, see Martha Derthick and Paul J. Quirk, *The Politics of Deregulation* (Washington, DC: Brookings, 1985), 29–57. On ideas in general, see Anthony King, "Ideas, Institutions, and the Policies of Government," *British Journal of Political Science* 3 (1973): 291–313, 409–423.

6. Judith Goldstein, "Ideas, Institutions, and American Trade Policy: The State and American Foreign Economic Policy," *International Organization* 42 (1988): 179–217.

7. This conception of ideas may be close to what Kingdon calls *solution streams* in his study of the agenda-building process. See Kingdon, *Agendas, Alternatives, and Public Policies.*

8. This is Schattschneider's famous phrase. See E. E. Schattschneider, *The Semi-Sovereign People* (New York: Holt, Rinehart & Winston, 1960).

9. James A. Stimson, Michael B. MacKuen, and Robert S. Erikson, "Dynamic Representation," *American Political Science Review* 89 (1995): 543–565.

10. See B. Dan Wood and Richard W. Waterman, *Bureaucratic Dynamics: The Role of the Bureaucracy in a Democracy* (Boulder, CO: Westview, 1994), 103–140.

Index